Beginning Programming with Java®

for dummies®
A Wiley Brand

Beginning Programming with Java®

5th Edition

by Barry Burd

Beginning Programming with Java® For Dummies®, 5th Edition

Published by: **John Wiley & Sons, Inc.**, 111 River Street, Hoboken, NJ 07030-5774, www.wiley.com

Copyright © 2017 by John Wiley & Sons, Inc., Hoboken, New Jersey

Published simultaneously in Canada

Contents at a Glance

Table of Contents

Introduction

What's your story?

>> Are you a working stiff, interested in knowing more about the way your company's computers work?

>> Are you a student who needs some extra reading in order to survive a beginning computer course?

>> Are you a typical computer user — you've done lots of word processing and you want to do something more interesting with your computer?

>> Are you a job seeker with an interest in entering the fast-paced, glamorous, high-profile world of computer programming (or, at least, the decent-paying world of computer programming)?

Well, if you want to write computer programs, this book is for you. This book avoids the snobby "of-course-you-already-know" assumptions and describes computer programming from scratch.

About This Book

The book uses Java — a powerful, general-purpose computer programming language. But Java's subtleties and eccentricities aren't the book's main focus. Instead, this book emphasizes a process — the process of creating instructions for a computer to follow. Many highfalutin books describe the mechanics of this process — the rules, the conventions, and the formalisms. But those other books aren't written for real people. Those books don't take you from where you are to where you want to be.

In this book, I assume very little about your experience with computers. As you read each section, you get to see inside my head. You see the problems that I face, the things that I think, and the solutions that I find. Some problems are the kind that I remember facing when I was a novice; other problems are the kind that I face as an expert. I help you understand, I help you visualize, and I help you create solutions on your own. I even get to tell a few funny stories.

How to Use This Book

I wish I could say, "Open to a random page of this book and start writing Java code. Just fill in the blanks and don't look back." In a sense, this is true. You can't break anything by writing Java code, so you're always free to experiment.

But I have to be honest: If you don't understand the bigger picture, writing a program is difficult. That's true with any computer programming language — not just Java. If you're typing code without knowing what it's about, and the code doesn't do exactly what you want it to do, you're just plain stuck.

In this book, I divide programming into manageable chunks. Each chunk is (more or less) a chapter. You can jump in anywhere you want — Chapter 5, Chapter 10, or wherever. You can even start by poking around in the middle of a chapter. I've tried to make the examples interesting without making one chapter depend on another. When I use an important idea from another chapter, I include a note to help you find your way around.

In general, my advice is as follows:

» If you already know something, don't bother reading about it.

» If you're curious, don't be afraid to skip ahead. You can always sneak a peek at an earlier chapter, if you really need to do so.

Conventions Used in This Book

Almost every technical book starts with a little typeface legend, and *Beginning Programming with Java For Dummies*, 5th Edition, is no exception. What follows is a brief explanation of the typefaces used in this book:

» New terms are set in *italics.*

» When I want you to type something short or perform a step, I use **bold.**

>> You'll also see this `computerese` font. I use the computerese font for Java code, filenames, web page addresses (URLs), onscreen messages, and other such things. Also, if something you need to type is really long, it appears in computerese font on its own line (or lines).

>> You need to change certain things when you type them on your own computer keyboard. For example, I may ask you to type

```
class Anyname
```

which means you should type **class** and then a name that you make up on your own. Words that you need to replace with your own words are set in *italicized computerese*.

What You Don't Have to Read

Pick the first chapter or section that has material you don't already know and start reading there. Of course, you may hate making decisions as much as I do. If so, here are some guidelines you can follow:

>> If you already know what computer programming is all about, skip the first half of Chapter 1. Believe me, I won't mind.

>> If you're required to use a development environment other than Eclipse, you can skip Chapter 2. This applies if you plan to use NetBeans, IntelliJ IDEA, or a number of other development environments.

Most of this book's examples require Java 5.0 or later, and some of the examples require Java 7 or later. So make sure that your system uses Java 7 or later. If you're not sure about your computer's Java version or if you have leeway in choosing a development environment, your safest move is to read Chapter 3.

>> If you've already done a little computer programming, be prepared to skim Chapters 6, 7, and 8. Dive fully into Chapter 9 and see whether it feels comfortable. (If so, read on. If not, skim Chapters 6, 7, and 8 again.)

>> If you feel comfortable writing programs in a language other than Java, this book isn't for you. Keep this book as a memento and buy my *Java For Dummies,* 7th Edition (also published by Wiley).

If you want to skip the sidebars and the material highlighted by a Technical Stuff icon, please do. In fact, if you want to skip anything at all, feel free.

Foolish Assumptions

In this book, I make a few assumptions about you, the reader. If one of these assumptions is incorrect, you're probably okay. If all these assumptions are incorrect . . . well, buy the book anyway.

>> **I assume that you have access to a computer.** Here's good news. You can run the code in this book on almost any computer. The only computers you can't use to run this code are ancient things that are more than eight years old (give or take a few years). You can run the latest version of Java on Windows, Macintosh, and Linux computers.

>> **I assume that you can navigate your computer's common menus and dialog boxes.** You don't have to be a Windows, Linux, or Macintosh power user, but you should be able to start a program, find a file, put a file into a certain directory — that sort of thing. Most of the time, when you practice the stuff in this book, you're typing code on your keyboard, not pointing and clicking the mouse.

On those rare occasions when you need to drag and drop, cut and paste, or plug and play, I guide you carefully through the steps. But your computer may be configured in any of several billion ways, and my instructions may not quite fit your special situation. So when you reach one of these platform-specific tasks, try following the steps in this book. If the steps don't quite fit, send me an email message or consult a book with instructions tailored to your system.

>> **I assume that you can think logically.** That's all there is to computer programming — thinking logically. If you can think logically, you've got it made. If you don't believe that you can think logically, read on. You may be pleasantly surprised.

>> **I assume that you know little or nothing about computer programming.** This isn't one of those "all things to all people" books. I don't please the novice while I tease the expert. I aim this book specifically toward the novice — the person who has never programmed a computer or has never felt comfortable programming a computer. If you're one of these people, you're reading the right book.

How This Book Is Organized

This book is divided into subsections, which are grouped into sections, which come together to make chapters, which are lumped finally into five parts. (When you write a book, you get to know your book's structure pretty well. After months of writing, you find yourself dreaming in sections and chapters when you go to bed at night.) The parts of the book are listed here.

Part 1: Getting Started with Java Programming

The chapters in Part 1 prepare you for the overall programming experience. In these chapters, you find out what programming is all about and get your computer ready for writing and testing programs.

Part 2: Writing Your Own Java Programs

This part covers the basic building blocks — the elements in any Java program and in any program written using a Java-like language. In this part, you discover how to represent data and how to get new values from existing values. The program examples are short, but cute.

Part 3: Controlling the Flow

Part 3 has some of my favorite chapters. In these chapters, you make the computer navigate from one part of your program to another. Think of your program as a big mansion, with the computer moving from room to room. Sometimes the computer chooses between two or more hallways, and sometimes the computer revisits rooms. As a programmer, your job is to plan the computer's rounds through the mansion. It's great fun.

Part 4: Using Program Units

Have you ever solved a big problem by breaking it into smaller, more manageable pieces? That's exactly what you do in Part 4 of this book. You discover the best ways to break programming problems into pieces and to create solutions for the newly found pieces. You also find out how to use other peoples' solutions. It feels like stealing, but it's not.

This part also contains a chapter about programming with windows, buttons, and other graphical items. If your mouse feels ignored by the examples in this book, read Chapter 20.

Part 5: The Part of Tens

The Part of Tens is a little beginning-programmer's candy store. In The Part of Tens, you can find lists — lists of tips, resources, and all kinds of interesting goodies.

I added an article at `www.dummies.com` to help you feel comfortable with Java's documentation (`www.dummies.com/programming/java/making-sense-of-javas-api-documentation`, to be precise). I can't write programs without my Java programming documentation. In fact, no Java programmer can write programs without those all-important docs. These docs are in web page format, so they're easy to find and easy to navigate. But if you're not used to all the terminology, the documentation can be overwhelming.

Icons Used in This Book

If you could watch me write this book, you'd see me sitting at my computer, talking to myself. I say each sentence several times in my head. When I have an extra thought, a side comment, or something that doesn't belong in the regular stream, I twist my head a little bit. That way, whoever's listening to me (usually nobody) knows that I'm off on a momentary tangent.

Of course, in print, you can't see me twisting my head. I need some other way of setting a side thought in a corner by itself. I do it with icons. When you see a Tip icon or a Remember icon, you know that I'm taking a quick detour.

Here's a list of icons that I use in this book:

A tip is an extra piece of information — something helpful that the other books may forget to tell you.

Everyone makes mistakes. Heaven knows that I've made a few in my time. Anyway, when I think of a mistake that people are especially prone to make, I write about the mistake in a Warning icon.

Sometimes I want to hire a skywriting airplane crew. "Barry," says the white smoky cloud, "if you want to compare two numbers, use the double equal sign. Please don't forget to do this." Because I can't afford skywriting, I have to settle for something more modest. I create a Remember icon.

Writing computer code is an activity, and the best way to learn an activity is to practice it. That's why I've created things for you to try in order to reinforce your knowledge. Many of these are confidence-builders, but some are a bit more challenging. When you first start putting things into practice, you'll discover all kinds of issues, quandaries, and roadblocks that didn't occur to you when you started reading about the material. But that's a good thing. Keep at it! Don't become frustrated. Or, if you do become frustrated, visit this book's website (`www.allmycode.com/BeginProg`) for hints and solutions.

TRY IT OUT

 Occasionally, I run across a technical tidbit. The tidbit may help you understand what the people behind the scenes (the people who developed Java) were thinking. You don't have to read it, but you may find it useful. You may also find the tidbit helpful if you plan to read other (more geeky) books about Java.

TECHNICAL STUFF

 This icon calls attention to useful material that you can find online. (You don't have to wait long to see one of these icons. I use one at the end of this introduction!)

 "If you don't remember what such-and-such means, see blah-blah-blah," or "For more information, read blahbity-blah-blah."

CROSS REFERENCE

Beyond the Book

In addition to what you're reading right now, this book comes with a free access-anywhere Cheat Sheet containing code that you can copy and paste into your own Java program. To get this Cheat Sheet, simply go to `www.dummies.com` and type **Beginning Programming with Java For Dummies Cheat Sheet** in the Search box.

Where to Go from Here

If you've gotten this far, you're ready to start reading about computer programming. Think of me (the author) as your guide, your host, your personal assistant. I do everything I can to keep things interesting and, most importantly, help you understand.

 If you like what you read, send me an email, post on my Facebook wall, or give me a tweet. My email address, which I created just for comments and questions about this book, is `BeginProg@allmycode.com`. My Facebook page is `/allmycode`, and my Twitter handle is `@allmycode`. And don't forget: To get the latest information, visit this book's support website — `http://allmycode.com/BeginProg`.

1

Getting Started with Java Programming

» **Understanding the software that enables you to write programs**

» **Revving up to use an integrated development environment**

Chapter **1**

Getting Started

Computer programming? What's that? Is it technical? Does it hurt? Is it politically correct? Does Google control it? Why would anyone want to do it? And what about me? Can I learn to do it?

What's It All About?

You've probably used a computer to do word processing. Type a letter, print it, and then send the printout to someone you love. If you have easy access to a computer, you've probably surfed the web. Visit a page, click a link, and see another page. It's easy, right?

Well, it's easy only because someone told the computer exactly what to do. If you take a computer directly from the factory and give no instructions to this computer, the computer can't do word processing, it can't surf the web, and it can't do anything. All a computer can do is follow the instructions that people give to it.

Now imagine that you're using Microsoft Word to write the great American novel, and you come to the end of a line. (You're not at the end of a sentence; just the end of a line.) As you type the next word, the computer's cursor jumps automatically to the next line of type. What's going on here?

Well, someone wrote a *computer program* — a set of instructions telling the computer what to do. Another name for a program (or part of a program) is *code*. Listing 1-1 shows you what some of Microsoft Word's code may look like.

LISTING 1-1: **A Few Lines in a Computer Program**

```
if (columnNumber > 60) {
    wrapToNextLine();
} else {
    continueSameLine();
}
```

If you translate Listing 1-1 into plain English, you get something like this:

```
If the column number is greater than 60,
    then go to the next line.
Otherwise (if the column number isn't greater than 60),
    then stay on the same line.
```

Somebody has to write code of the kind shown in Listing 1-1. This code, along with millions of other lines of code, makes up the program called Microsoft Word.

And what about web surfing? You click a link that's supposed to take you directly to Facebook. Behind the scenes, someone has written code of the following kind:

```
Go to <a href="http://www.facebook.com">Facebook</a>.
```

One way or another, someone has to write a program. That someone is called a *programmer*.

Telling a computer what to do

Everything you do with a computer involves gobs and gobs of code. For example, every computer game is really a big (make that "very big"!) bunch of computer code. At some point, someone had to write the game program:

```
if (person.touches(goldenRing)) {
    person.getPoints(10);
}
```

Without a doubt, the people who write programs have valuable skills. These people have two important qualities:

>> They know how to break big problems into smaller, step-by-step procedures.

>> They can express these steps in a very precise language.

A language for writing steps is called a *programming language,* and Java is just one of several thousand useful programming languages. The stuff in Listing 1-1 is written in the Java programming language.

Pick your poison

This book isn't about the differences among programming languages, but you should see code in some other languages so you understand the bigger picture. For example, there's another language, Visual Basic, whose code looks a bit different from code written in Java. An excerpt from a Visual Basic program may look like this:

```
If columnNumber > 60 Then
    Call wrapToNextLine
Else
    Call continueSameLine
End If
```

The Visual Basic code looks more like ordinary English than the Java code in Listing 1-1. But, if you think that Visual Basic is like English, then just look at some code written in COBOL:

```
IF COLUMN-NUMBER IS GREATER THAN 60 THEN
    PERFORM WRAP-TO-NEXT-LINE
ELSE
    PERFORM CONTINUE-SAME-LINE
END-IF.
```

At the other end of the spectrum, you find languages like Forth. Here's a snippet of code written in Forth:

```
: WRAP? 60 > IF WRAP_TO_NEXT_LINE? ELSE CONTINUE_SAME_LINE? THEN ;
```

Computer languages can be very different from one another, but in some ways, they're all the same. When you get used to writing IF COLUMN-NUMBER IS GREATER THAN 60, you can also become comfortable writing if (columnNumber > 60). It's just a mental substitution of one set of symbols for another. Eventually, writing things like if (columnNumber > 60) becomes second nature.

From Your Mind to the Computer's Processor

When you create a new computer program, you go through a multistep process. The process involves three important tools:

>> **Compiler:** A compiler translates your code into computer-friendly (human-unfriendly) instructions.

>> **Virtual machine:** A virtual machine steps through the computer-friendly instructions.

>> **Application programming interface:** An application programming interface contains useful prewritten code.

The next three sections describe each of the three tools.

Translating your code

You may have heard that computers deal with zeros and ones. That's certainly true, but what does it mean? Well, for starters, computer circuits don't deal directly with letters of the alphabet. When you see the word *Start* on your computer screen, the computer stores the word internally as 01010011 01110100 01100001 01110010 01110100. That feeling you get of seeing a friendly looking five-letter word is your interpretation of the computer screen's pixels, and nothing more. Computers break everything down into very low-level, unfriendly sequences of zeros and ones and then put things back together so that humans can deal with the results.

So what happens when you write a computer program? Well, the program has to get translated into zeros and ones. The official name for the translation process is *compilation*. Without compilation, the computer can't run your program.

I compiled the code in Listing 1-1. Then I did some harmless hacking to help me see the resulting zeros and ones. What I saw was the mishmash in Figure 1-1.

The compiled mumbo jumbo in Figure 1-1 goes by many different names:

>> Most Java programmers call it *bytecode*.

>> I often call it a *.class file.* That's because, in Java, the bytecode gets stored in files named *SomethingOrOther*.class.

>> To emphasize the difference, Java programmers call Listing 1-1 the *source code* and refer to the zeros and ones in Figure 1-1 as *object code*.

To visualize the relationship between source code and object code, see Figure 1-2. You can write source code and then get the computer to create object code from your source code. To create object code, the computer uses a special software tool called a *compiler*.

```
11001010 11111110 10111010 10111110 00000000 00000000
00000000 00101110 00000000 00010101 00001010 00000000
00000101 00000000 00010000 00001010 00000000 00000100
00000000 00010001 00001010 00000000 00000100 00000000
00010010 00000111 00000000 00010011 00000111 00000000
00010100 00000001 00000000 00000110 00111100 01101001
01101110 01101001 01110100 00111110 00000001 00000000
00000011 00101000 00101001 01010110 00000001 00000000
00000100 01000011 01101111 01100100 01100101 00000000
00000000 00001111 01001100 01101001 01101110 01100101
01001110 01110101 01101101 01100010 01100101 01110010
01010100 01100001 01100010 01101100 01100101 00000001
00000000 00001011 01100100 01110011 01101101 01110010
01101100 01100001 01111001 01010111 01101111 01110010
01100100 00000001 00000000 00000100 00101000 01001001
00101001 01010110 00000001 00000000 00001110 01110111
01110010 01100001 01110000 01010010 01101111 01110111
01100101 01111000 01110100 01001100 01101001 01101110
01100101 00000001 00000000 00010000 01100011 01101111
01101110 01110100 01101001 01101110 01110101 01100101
01010011 01100001 01101101 01100101 01001100 01101001
01101110 01100101 00000000 00000000 00001010 01010001
01101111 01110101 01110010 01100011 01100101 01000110
```

FIGURE 1-1:
My computer understands these zeros and ones, but I don't.

```
if (columnNumber > 60)...   Java source file (a .java file)

            │
            │  Compiler
            ▼

    11001010 11111110         Object file (a .class file) also known as bytecode
```

FIGURE 1-2:
The computer compiles source code to create object code.

TECHNICAL STUFF

Your computer's hard drive may have a file named javac or javac.exe. This file contains that special software tool — the compiler. (Hey, how about that? The word javac stands for "Java compiler!") As a Java programmer, you often tell your computer to build some new object code. Your computer fulfills this wish by going behind the scenes and running the instructions in the javac file.

Running code

Several years ago, I spent a week in Copenhagen. I hung out with a friend who spoke both Danish and English fluently. As we chatted in the public park, I vaguely noticed some kids orbiting around us. I don't speak a word of Danish, so I assumed that the kids were talking about ordinary kid stuff.

WHAT IS BYTECODE, ANYWAY?

Look at Listing 1-1 and at the listing's translation into bytecode in Figure 1-1. You may be tempted to think that a bytecode file is just a cryptogram — substituting zeros and ones for the letters in words like if and else. But it doesn't work that way at all. In fact, the most important part of a bytecode file is the encoding of a program's logic.

The zeros and ones in Figure 1-1 describe the flow of data from one part of your computer to another. I illustrate this flow in the following figure. But remember: This figure is just an illustration. Your computer doesn't look at this particular figure, or at anything like it. Instead, your computer reads a bunch of zeros and ones to decide what to do next.

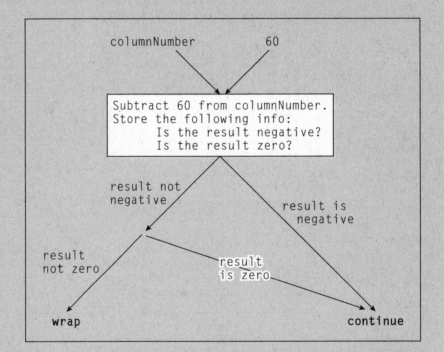

Don't bother to absorb the details in my attempt at graphical representation in the figure. It's not worth your time. The thing you should glean from my mix of text, boxes, and arrows is that bytecode (the stuff in a .class file) contains a complete description of the operations that the computer is to perform. When you write a computer program, your source code describes an overall strategy — a big picture. The compiled bytecode turns the overall strategy into hundreds of tiny, step-by-step details. When the computer "runs your program," the computer examines this bytecode and carries out each of the little step-by-step details.

Then my friend told me that the kids weren't speaking Danish. "What language are they speaking?" I asked.

"They're talking gibberish," she said. "It's just nonsense syllables. They don't understand English, so they're imitating you."

Now to return to present-day matters. I look at the stuff in Figure 1-1, and I'm tempted to make fun of the way my computer talks. But then I'd be just like the kids in Copenhagen. What's meaningless to me can make perfect sense to my computer. When the zeros and ones in Figure 1-1 percolate through my computer's circuits, the computer "thinks" the thoughts shown in Figure 1-3.

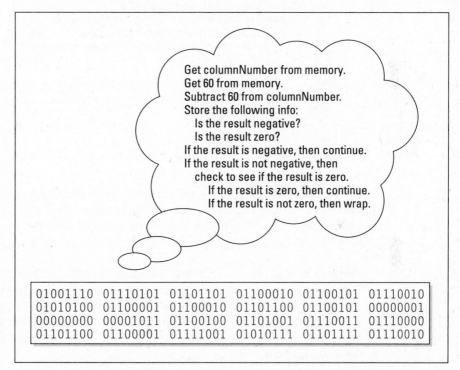

FIGURE 1-3:
What the computer gleans from a bytecode file.

Everyone knows that computers don't think, but a computer can carry out the instructions depicted in Figure 1-3. With many programming languages (languages like C++ and COBOL, for example), a computer does exactly what I'm describing. A computer gobbles up some object code and does whatever the object code says to do.

That's how it works in many programming languages, but that's not how it works in Java. With Java, the computer executes a different set of instructions. The computer executes instructions like the ones in Figure 1-4.

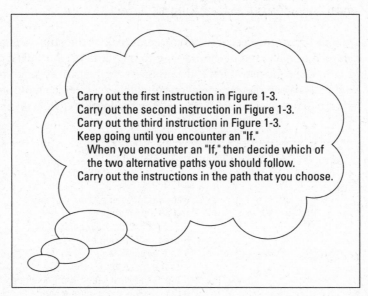

Carry out the first instruction in Figure 1-3.
Carry out the second instruction in Figure 1-3.
Carry out the third instruction in Figure 1-3.
Keep going until you encounter an "If."
    When you encounter an "If," then decide which of
    the two alternative paths you should follow.
Carry out the instructions in the path that you choose.

FIGURE 1-4:
How a computer runs a Java program.

The instructions in Figure 1-4 tell the computer how to follow other instructions. Instead of starting with Get columnNumber from memory, the computer's first instruction is, "Do what it says to do in the bytecode file." (Of course, in the byte-code file, the first instruction happens to be Get columnNumber from memory.)

There's a special piece of software that carries out the instructions in Figure 1-4. That special piece of software is called the *Java Virtual Machine* (JVM). The JVM walks your computer through the execution of some bytecode instructions. When you run a Java program, your computer is really running the JVM. That JVM examines your bytecode, zero by zero, one by one, and carries out the instructions described in the bytecode.

Many good metaphors can describe the JVM. Think of the JVM as a proxy, an errand boy, a go-between. One way or another, you have the situation shown in Figure 1-5. On the (a) side is the story you get with most programming languages — the computer runs some object code. On the (b) side is the story with Java — the computer runs the JVM, and the JVM follows the bytecode's instructions.

Your computer's hard drive may have files named `javac` and `java` (or `javac.exe` and `java.exe`). A `java` (or `java.exe`) file contains the instructions illustrated previously in Figure 1-4 — the instructions in the JVM. As a Java programmer, you often tell your computer to run a Java program. Your computer fulfills this wish by going behind the scenes and running the instructions in the `java` file.

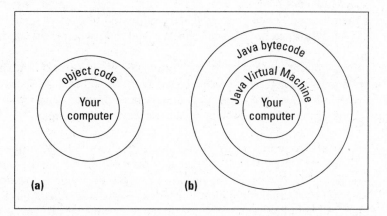

FIGURE 1-5:
Two ways to run a computer program.

WRITE ONCE, RUN ANYWHERE

When Java first hit the tech scene in 1995, the language became popular almost immediately. This happened in part because of the JVM. The JVM is like a foreign language interpreter, turning Java bytecode into whatever native language a particular computer understands. So if you hand my Windows computer a Java bytecode file, the computer's JVM interprets the file for the Windows environment. If you hand the same Java bytecode file to my colleague's Macintosh, the Macintosh JVM interprets that same bytecode for the Mac environment.

Look again at Figure 1-5. Without a virtual machine, you need a different kind of object code for each operating system. But with the JVM, just one piece of bytecode works on Windows machines, Unix boxes, Macs, or whatever. This is called *portability,* and in the computer-programming world, portability is a precious commodity. Think about all the people using computers to browse the Internet. These people don't all run Microsoft Windows, but each person's computer can have its own bytecode interpreter — its own JVM.

The marketing folks at Oracle call it the *Write Once, Run Anywhere* model of computing. I call it a great way to create software.

Code you can use

During the early 1980s, my cousin-in-law Chris worked for a computer software firm. The firm wrote code for word processing machines. (At the time, if you wanted to compose documents without a typewriter, you bought a "computer" that did nothing but word processing.) Chris complained about being asked to write the same old code over and over again. "First, I write a search-and-replace program. Then I write a spell checker. Then I write another search-and-replace program. Then, a different kind of spell checker. And then, a better search-and-replace."

How did Chris manage to stay interested in his work? And how did Chris's employer manage to stay in business? Every few months, Chris had to reinvent the wheel. Toss out the old search-and-replace program and write a new program from scratch. That's inefficient. What's worse, it's boring.

For years, computer professionals were seeking the Holy Grail — a way to write software so that it's easy to reuse. Don't write and rewrite your search-and-replace code. Just break the task into tiny pieces. One piece searches for a single character, another piece looks for blank spaces, and a third piece substitutes one letter for another. When you have all the pieces, just assemble these pieces to form a search-and-replace program. Later on, when you think of a new feature for your word-processing software, you reassemble the pieces in a slightly different way. It's sensible, it's cost efficient, and it's much more fun.

The late 1980s saw several advances in software development, and by the early 1990s, many large programming projects were being written from prefab components. Java came along in 1995, so it was natural for the language's founders to create a library of reusable code. The library included about 250 programs, including code for dealing with disk files, code for creating windows, and code for passing information over the Internet. Since 1995, this library has grown to include more than 4,000 programs. This library is called the *Application Programming Interface (API)*.

Every Java program, even the simplest one, calls on code in the Java API. This Java API is both useful and formidable. It's useful because of all the things you can do with the API's programs. It's formidable because the API is extensive. No one memorizes all the features made available by the Java API. Programmers remember the features that they use often and look up the features that they need in a pinch. They look up these features in an online document called the *API Specification* (known affectionately to most Java programmers as the *API documentation,* or the *Javadocs*).

The API documentation (see `http://docs.oracle.com/javase/8/docs/api`) describes the thousands of features in the Java API. As a Java programmer, you consult this API documentation on a daily basis. You can bookmark the documentation at the Oracle website and revisit the site whenever you need to look up something, or you can save time by downloading your own copy of the API docs using the links found at www.oracle.com/technetwork/java/javase/downloads/index.html.

Your Java Programming Toolset

To write Java programs, you need the tools described previously in this chapter:

>> **You need a Java compiler.** (Refer to the section "Translating your code.")

>> **You need a JVM.** (Refer to the section "Running code.")

>> **You need the Java API.** (Refer to the section "Code you can use.")

>> **You need access to the Java API documentation.** (Again, refer to the "Code you can use" section.)

You also need some less exotic tools:

>> **You need an editor to compose your Java programs.** Listing 1-1 contains part of a computer program. When you come right down to it, a computer program is a big bunch of text. So, to write a computer program, you need an *editor* — a tool for creating text documents.

An editor is a lot like Microsoft Word, or like any other word processing program. The big difference is that an editor adds no formatting to your text — no bold, italic, or distinctions among fonts. Computer programs have no formatting whatsoever. They have nothing except plain old letters, numbers, and other familiar keyboard characters.

REMEMBER

When you edit a program, you may see bold text, italic text, and text in several colors. But your program contains none of this formatting. If you see stuff that looks like formatting, it's because the editor that you're using does syntax highlighting. With *syntax highlighting,* an editor makes the text appear to be formatted in order to help you understand the structure of your program. Believe me, syntax highlighting is very helpful.

>> **You need a way to issue commands.** You need a way to say things like "compile this program" and "run the JVM." Every computer provides ways of issuing commands. (You can double-click icons or type verbose commands in a Run dialog box.) But when you use your computer's facilities, you jump from one window to another. You open one window to read Java documentation, another window to edit a Java program, and a third window to start up the Java compiler. The process can be *tedious.*

A tool for creating code

In the best of all possible worlds, you do all your program editing, documentation reading, and command issuing through one nice interface. This interface is called an *integrated development environment (IDE)*.

A typical IDE divides your screen's work area into several panes — one pane for editing programs, another pane for listing the names of programs, a third pane for issuing commands, and other panes to help you compose and test programs. You can arrange the panes for quick access. Better yet, if you change the information in one pane, the IDE automatically updates the information in all the other panes.

An IDE helps you move seamlessly from one part of the programming endeavor to another. With an IDE, you don't have to worry about the mechanics of editing, compiling, and running a JVM. Instead, you can worry about the logic of writing programs. (Wouldn't you know it? One way or another, you always have something to worry about!)

In the chapters that follow, I describe basic features of the Eclipse IDE. Eclipse has many bells and whistles, but you can ignore most of them and learn to repeat a few routine sequences of steps. After using Eclipse a few times, your brain automatically performs the routine steps. From then on, you can stop worrying about Eclipse and concentrate on Java programming.

As you read my paragraphs about Eclipse, remember that Java and Eclipse aren't wedded to one another. The programs in this book work with any IDE that can run Java. Instead of using Eclipse, you can use IntelliJ IDEA, NetBeans, BlueJ, or any other Java IDE. In fact, if you enjoy roughing it, you can write and run this book's programs without an IDE. You can use Notepad, TextEdit or vi, along with your operating system's command prompt or Terminal. It's all up to you.

What's already on your hard drive?

You may already have some of the tools you need for creating Java programs. But, on an older computer, your tools may be obsolete. Most of this book's examples run on all versions of Java. But some examples don't run on versions earlier than Java 5.0. Other examples run only on Java 6, Java 7, Java 8, or later.

The safest bet is to download tools afresh. To get detailed instructions on doing the downloads, see Chapter 2.

» Downloading and installing the Eclipse integrated development environment

» Checking your Eclipse configuration

» Getting the code in this book's examples

Chapter **2**

Setting Up Your Computer

This chapter goes into much more detail than you normally need. If you're like most readers, you'll follow the steps in the "If You Don't Like Reading Instructions . . ." section. Then you'll jump to the "Importing This Book's Sample Programs" section, near the end of this chapter. With about 20 percent of this chapter's contents, you'll have 100 percent of the required software.

Of course, there are always glitches. One person has an older computer. Another person has some conflicting software. Joe has a PC and Jane has a Mac. Joe's PC runs Windows 10 but Janis runs Windows 8. Joe misreads one of my instructions and, as a result, nothing on his screen matches the steps that I describe. Eighty percent of this chapter describes the things you do in those rare situations in which you must diagnose a problem.

If you find yourself in a real jam, there's always an alternative. You can send an email to me at BeginProg@allmycode.com. You can also find me on Facebook at /allmycode or on Twitter at @allmycode. I'm happy to answer questions and help you figure out what's wrong.

So, by all means, skip anything in this chapter that you don't need to read. You won't break anything by following your instincts. And if you do break anything, there's always a way to fix it.

If You Don't Like Reading Instructions . . .

To start writing Java programs, you need the software that I describe in Chapter 1: a Java compiler and a Java Virtual Machine (JVM, for short). You can also use a good integrated development environment (IDE) and some sample code to get you started.

All the software you need for writing Java programs is free. The software comes as three downloads: one from this book's website, another from Oracle, and a third from eclipse.org.

Here's how you get the software for creating Java programs:

1. **Visit** www.allmycode.com/BeginProg **and download a file containing all program examples in this book.**

2. **Visit** www.oracle.com/technetwork/java/javase/downloads **and get the latest available version of the JDK.**

   At the top of the page, you might see links and buttons for Java 8. That's okay, but to get the most from this book's content, I recommend Java 9. With Java 9, you can run JShell, a new interactive environment for testing Java features. If Oracle's web page highlights Java 8, scroll down to find an early access preview of Java 9. Follow the links and buttons to get the cutting edge technology.

   Choose a version of the software that matches your operating system (Windows, Macintosh, or whatever). If you have trouble choosing between the JRE and the JDK, pick the JDK.

   If you run Windows and you have trouble choosing between 32-bit software and 64-bit software, flip a coin and make a note of your choice. (If you make the wrong choice, you'll get an error message when you try to install Java or when you try to launch the Eclipse IDE.)

   REMEMBER

   Most people who have trouble with this chapter's instructions have installed either 32-bit Java with 64-bit Eclipse or 64-bit Java with 32-bit Eclipse. If you experience pain when you get to Step 6, download and install alternative versions of Java or Eclipse.

3. **Find the icon representing the Java software that you downloaded in Step 2. Double-click the icon to begin installing Java.**

TIP

If you're in a hurry (and who isn't?), you may benefit from a quick visit to `http://java.com`. The `http://java.com` website offers a hassle-free, 1-click Java installer. (Simply click the big Java Download button. You can't miss it.) The Java Download button doesn't work on all computers. But if it works for you, with a wave of a virtual magic wand, you're finished with this step. You can bypass the complexities of the `java.oracle.com` website and move immediately to Step 4.

4. **Visit** `http://eclipse.org/downloads` **and get the Eclipse IDE.**

   Most of the time, Eclipse's website automatically checks your computer's operating system and offers you a download that's optimized for your system. But if the website gives a choice, select Eclipse IDE for Java Developers.

   The resulting download is either an executable installer file (with the `.exe` extension) or a compressed archive file (with the `.zip` or `.tar.gz` extension).

5. **If you downloaded an** `.exe` **file in Step 4, double-click this file's icon to begin the installation of Eclipse.**

   If you downloaded a `.zip` **file or a** `.tar.gz` **file in Step 4, extract the contents of this compressed archive.**

   If you have a compressed archive, you see a folder named `eclipse` or `Eclipse.app` when you uncompress it. Copy this folder to a handy place on your computer's hard drive. For example, on my Windows computer, I end up with a `C:\eclipse` folder. On my Mac, I end up with an `Eclipse` or `Eclipse.app` icon inside my `Applications` folder.

TECHNICAL STUFF

In Windows, the blank space in the name `Program Files` confuses some Java software. I don't think any of this book's software presents such a problem, but I can't guarantee it. If you want, extract Eclipse to your `C:\Program Files` or `C:\Program Files (x86)` folder. But make a mental note about your choice (in case you run into any trouble later).

6. **Launch Eclipse and click the Welcome screen's Workbench icon.**

   Initially, the Welcome screen's icons may have no text labels. But when you hover over an icon, a tooltip appears. Select the icon whose tooltip has the title Workbench.

7. **In Eclipse, import the code that you downloaded in Step 1.**

For details about any of this stuff, see the next several sections.

THOSE PESKY FILENAME EXTENSIONS

The filenames displayed in Windows File Explorer or in a Finder window can be misleading. You may browse one of your directories and see the name Mortgage. The file's real name might be Mortgage.java, Mortgage.class, Mortgage.*somethingElse*, or plain old Mortgage. Filename endings like .zip, .java, and .class are called *filename extensions*.

The ugly truth is that, by default, Windows and Macs hide many filename extensions. This awful feature tends to confuse programmers. So, if you don't want to be confused, change your computer's system-wide settings. Here's how you do it:

- **In Windows 10:** In the taskbar's Search box, type **File Explorer Options**. On the list of choices that appears, choose File Explorer Options. Then follow the instructions in the In All Versions of Windows bullet.

- **In Windows 8:** On the Start screen, hold down the Windows key while pressing Q. In the resulting search box, type **Folder Options** and then press Enter. Then follow the instructions in the In All Versions of Windows bullet.

- **In Windows 7:** Choose Start ➪ Control Panel ➪ Appearance and Personalization ➪ Folder Options. Then follow the instructions in the In All Versions of Windows bullet.

- **In all versions of Windows (7 and newer):** Follow the instructions in one of the preceding bullets. Then, in the Folder Options (or File Explorer Options) dialog box, click the View tab. Look for the Hide File Extensions for Known File Types option. Make sure that this check box is *not* selected.

- **In Mac OS X:** On the Finder application's menu, select Preferences. In the resulting dialog box, select the Advanced tab and look for the Show All File Extensions option. Make sure that this check box *is* selected.

- **In Linux:** Linux distributions tend not to hide filename extensions. So, if you use Linux, you probably don't have to worry about this. But I haven't checked all Linux distributions. So, if your files are named Mortgage instead of Mortgage.java or Mortgage.class, check the documentation specific to your Linux distribution.

Getting This Book's Sample Programs

To get copies of this book's sample programs, visit http://allmycode.com/BeginProg and click the link to download the programs in this book. Save the download file (BeginProgJavaDummies5.zip) to your computer's hard drive.

COMPRESSED ARCHIVE FILES

When you visit www.allmycode.com/BeginProg and you download this book's Java examples, you download a file named BeginProgJavaDummies5.zip. A .zip file is a single file that encodes a bunch of smaller files and folders. For example, my BeginProgJavaDummies5.zip file encodes folders named 06-01, 06-02, and so on. The 06-02 folder contains some subfolders, which in turn contain files. (The folder named 06-02 contains the code in Listing 6-2 — the second listing in Chapter 6.)

A .zip file is an example of a *compressed archive* file. Some other examples of compressed archives include .tar.gz files, .rar files, and .cab files. *Uncompressing* a file means extracting the original files stored inside the big archive file. (For a .zip file, another word for *uncompressing* is *unzipping*.) Uncompressing normally re-creates the folder structure encoded in the archive file. So, after uncompressing my BeginProgJavaDummies5.zip file, your hard drive has folders named 06-01, 06-02, with subfolders named src and bin, which in turn contain files named SnitSoft.java, SnitSoft.class, and so on.

When you download BeginProgJavaDummies5.zip, your web browser may uncompress the file automatically for you. If not, you can see the .zip file's contents by double-clicking the file's icon. (In fact, you can copy the file's contents and perform other file operations after double-clicking the file's icon.) One way or another, don't worry about uncompressing my BeginProgJavaDummies5.zip file. When you follow this chapter's instructions, you import the contents of my BeginProgJavaDummies5.zip file into the Eclipse IDE. And behind the scenes, Eclipse's import process uncompresses the .zip file.

TIP

In some cases, you click a download link but your web browser doesn't offer you the option to save a file. If this happens to you, right-click the link (or Control-click on a Mac). On the resulting context menu, select Save Target As, Save Link As, Download Linked File As, or a similarly labeled menu item.

Most web browsers save files to a Downloads directory on your computer's hard drive. But your browser may be configured a bit differently. One way or another, make note of the folder containing the downloaded BeginProgJava Dummies5.zip file.

Setting Up Java

You can get the latest, greatest versions of Java by visiting www.oracle.com/technetwork/java/javase/downloads. Look for the newest available version of the JDK. Select a version that runs on your computer's operating system.

Figure 2-1 shows me clicking a Download JDK button (*circa* March 2014) at the Oracle website. When you visit the site, the page on your computer screen probably looks a lot like Figure 2-1, but you might see Java SE 9 instead of Java SE 8.

>> **If you see Java 9, go for it.**

>> **If you see Java 8 instead of Java 9, scroll down to find an early access Java 9 preview.**

With plain, old Java 8, you can run all the programs in this book. But if you have Java 9, you can use JShell — a tool for experimenting quickly and easily with snippets of Java's code.

FIGURE 2-1:
Getting the
Java JDK.

REMEMBER

The Oracle and Eclipse websites that I describe in this chapter are always changing. The software that you download from these sites changes, too. A specific instruction such as "click the button in the upper-right corner" becomes obsolete (and even misleading) in no time at all. So in this chapter, I provide long lists of steps, but I also describe the ideas behind the steps. Browse each of the suggested sites and look for ways to get the software that I describe. When a website offers you several options, check the instructions in this chapter for hints on choosing the best option. If your computer's Eclipse window doesn't look quite like the window in this chapter's figures, scan your computer's window for whatever options I describe. If, after all that, you can't find what you're looking for, check this book's website (www.allmycode.com/BeginProg) or send an email to me at BeginProg@allmycode.com.

If you can't identify the most appropriate Java version or if you want to know what the acronyms *JRE* and *JDK* stand for, see the later sidebar entitled "Eenie, meenie, miney mo."

Downloading and installing Java

After you accept a license agreement and click a link to a Java installation file, your computer does one of two things:

>> Downloads and installs Java on your system

>> Downloads the Java installation file and saves the file on your computer's hard drive

If the installation begins on its own, follow the instructions, answer Yes to any prompts, and (unless you have good reason to do otherwise) accept the defaults. If the installation doesn't begin on its own, start the installation by double-clicking the downloaded installation file.

TECHNICAL STUFF

If your computer runs Linux, the downloaded file might be a .tar.gz file. A .tar.gz file is a compressed archive. Extract the archive's contents to a folder of your choice and follow the installation instructions posted on the Oracle website.

For more information about filenames, file types, and archives, see the earlier sidebars entitled "Those pesky filename extensions" and "Compressed archive files" in this chapter.

While you're visiting www.oracle.com/technetwork/java/javase/downloads, you can also download a copy of the Java API documentation. Look for a download labeled Java SE Documentation (or something like that). Accept the license agreement, click the download link, and watch the file flow downward onto your computer's hard drive. The downloaded file is a compressed .zip archive, so you can uncompress it the way you uncompress all other such archives. (The uncompressed folder is a bunch of web pages. To start reading the Java API documentation, look in that folder for an index file or an index.html file. Double-click the file, and you're on your way.)

EENIE, MEENIE, MINEY MO

The Java Standard Edition download page (www.oracle.com/technetwork/java/javase/downloads) has many options. If you're not familiar with these options, the page can be intimidating. Here are some of the choices on the page:

- **Word length: 32-bit or 64-bit**

  You may have to choose between links labeled for 32-bit systems and links labeled for 64-bit systems. If you don't know which to choose, start by trying the 32-bit version. (For more information about 32-bit systems and 64-bit systems, see the later sidebar "How many bits does your computer have?")

- **Java version number**

  The Java download page may have older and newer Java versions for you to choose from. You may see links to Java SE 7, Java SE 8, Java SE 9u4, and many others. (Numbering such as *9u4* stands for the fourth update to Java 9.) If you're not sure which version number you want, choosing the highest version number is probably safe. For additional help with the decision, consider these facts:

  - If you have Java 9 or higher, you're okay.

  - If the only Java versions that you have are older than Java 7 (including Java 1.4.2, Java 5.0, and Java 6), your computer can run some but not all of the programs in this book.

  - If you have Java 7 or Java 8 but not Java 9, your computer can run all the programs in this book but you can't run Java's JShell tool. I introduce JShell in Chapter 6. You can learn all about Java without ever running JShell. But JShell is handy and it's fun to use.

  The numbering of Java's versions is really confusing. First comes Java 1.0, and then Java 1.1, and then Java 2 Standard Edition 1.2 (J2SE 1.2). Yes, the "Java 2" numbering overlaps partially with the "1.x" numbering. Next come versions 1.3 and 1.4. After version 1.4.1 comes version 1.4.2 (with intermediate stops at versions like 1.4.1_02). After 1.4.2_06, the next version is version 1.5, which is also known as version 5.0. (That's no misprint. Version 5.0 comes immediately after the 1.4 versions.)

  The formal name for version 1.5 is Java 2 Platform, Standard Edition 5.0. And to make matters even worse, the next big release is Java Platform, Standard Edition 6 with the 2 removed from *Java 2* and the .0 missing from 6.0. That's what happens when a company lets marketing people call the shots.

Mercifully, from Java 6 onward, the version numbers settle into a predictable pattern. After Java 6 comes Java Platform, Standard Edition 7 and then Java Platform, Standard Edition 8 with updates such as 8u2 (Java 8, update 2). And starting with Java 9, there's no longer such a thing as version 1.9. Now it's plain old version 9.

- **JDK versus JRE**

  The download page offers you a choice between the JDK (Java Development Kit) and the JRE (Java Runtime Environment). The JDK download contains more stuff than the JRE download. The JRE includes a Java Virtual Machine and the application programming interface. (Refer to Chapter 1.) The JDK includes everything in the JRE, and in addition, the JDK includes a Java compiler. (Again, refer to Chapter 1.)

  The Eclipse IDE contains its own Java compiler. So you can survive by downloading the smaller JRE (and avoiding the big JDK download). But I recommend downloading the entire JDK. Why? Because you never know when another compiler (separate from Eclipse) will come in handy. Besides, the installation and configuration of Eclipse on a Mac can be convoluted if you haven't installed the full JDK. So, if you want to have a smooth ride, download the JDK instead of the JRE.

  By the way, another name for the JDK is the Java SDK — the Java Software Development Kit. Some people still use the SDK acronym, even though the folks at Oracle don't use it any more. (Actually, the original name was the JDK. Later, Sun Microsystems changed it to the SDK. A few years after that, the captains of Java changed it back to the name JDK. This constant naming and renaming drives me crazy as an author.)

- **Java SE, Java EE, and Java ME**

  While you wander around, you may notice links labeled Java EE or Java ME. If you know what these are, and you know you need them, by all means, download these goodies. But if you're not sure, bypass both the Java EE and the Java ME links. Instead, follow links to the Java SE (Java Standard Edition).

  The abbreviation Java EE stands for Java Enterprise Edition, and Java ME stands for Java Micro Edition. The Enterprise Edition has software for large businesses, and the Micro Edition has software for handheld devices. (Google's Android software bears a passing resemblance to Java's Micro Edition, but in many ways, Android and Java ME are very different animals.)

  You don't need the Java EE or the Java ME to run any of the examples in this book.

- **Additional Java-related software**

  You can download Java alone, or you can download Java with Oracle's NetBeans IDE. You can download a collection of demos and samples. You can probably even download Java with fries and a soft drink. You can download plenty of extra stuff, but in truth, all you need is the Java JDK.

TIP

For an introduction to the Java API documentation, refer to Chapter 1.

Most people have no difficulties visiting the Oracle website `java.oracle.com` and installing Java using the website's menus. But if your situation is more "interesting" than most, you may have to make some decisions and perform some extra steps. The next few sections describe some of these "interesting" scenarios.

HOW MANY BITS DOES YOUR COMPUTER HAVE?

As you follow this chapter's instructions, you may be prompted to choose between two versions of a piece of software — the 32-bit version and the 64-bit version. What's the difference, and why should you care?

A *bit* is the smallest piece of information that you can store on a computer. Most people think of a bit as either a zero or a one, and that depiction of "bit" is quite useful. To represent almost any number, you pile several bits next to one another and do some fancy things with powers of two. The numbering system's details aren't showstoppers. The important thing to remember is that each piece of circuitry inside your computer stores the same number of bits. (Well, some circuits inside your computer are outliers with their own particular numbers of bits, but that's not a big deal.)

In an older computer, each piece of circuitry stores 32 bits. In a newer computer, each piece of circuitry stores 64 bits. This number of bits (either 32 or 64) is the computer's *word length*. In a newer computer, a word is 64 bits long.

"Great!" you say. "I bought my computer last week. It must be a 64-bit computer." Well, the story may not be that simple. In addition to your computer's circuitry having a word length, the operating system on your computer also has a word length. An operating system's instructions work with a particular number of bits. An operating system with 32-bit instructions can run on either a 32-bit computer or a 64-bit computer, but an operating system with 64-bit instructions can run only on a 64-bit computer. And to make things even more complicated, each program that you run (a web browser, a word processor, or one of your own Java programs) is either a 32-bit program or a 64-bit program. You may run a 32-bit web browser on a 64-bit operating system running on a 64-bit computer. Alternatively, you may run a 32-bit browser on a 32-bit operating system on a 64-bit computer. (See the figure that accompanies this sidebar.)

```
┌─ 32-bit computer ──────────────────────────────────┐
│  ┌─ 32-bit operating system ───────────────────┐   │
│  │  ┌─ 32-bit software ──────────────────────┐  │   │
│  │  │                                        │  │   │
│  │  └────────────────────────────────────────┘  │   │
│  └──────────────────────────────────────────────┘   │
└──────────────────────────────────────────────────────┘

┌─ 64-bit computer ──────────────────────────────────┐
│  ┌─ 32-bit operating system ───────────────────┐   │
│  │  ┌─ 32-bit software ──────────────────────┐  │   │
│  │  │                                        │  │   │
│  │  └────────────────────────────────────────┘  │   │
│  └──────────────────────────────────────────────┘   │
└──────────────────────────────────────────────────────┘

┌─ 64-bit computer ──────────────────────────────────┐
│  ┌─ 64-bit operating system ───────────────────────┐ │
│  │  ┌─ 32-bit software ──┐   ┌─ 64-bit software ──┐ │ │
│  │  │                    │   │                    │ │ │
│  │  └────────────────────┘   └────────────────────┘ │ │
│  └──────────────────────────────────────────────────┘ │
└──────────────────────────────────────────────────────┘
```

When a website makes you choose between 32-bit and 64-bit software versions, the main consideration is the word length of your operating system, not the word length of your computer's circuitry. You can run a 32-bit word processor on a 64-bit operating system, but you can't run a 64-bit word processor on a 32-bit operating system (no matter what word length your computer's circuitry has). Choosing 64-bit software has one big advantage — namely, that 64-bit software can access more than 3 gigabytes of a computer's fast random access memory. And in my experience, more memory means faster processing.

How does all this stuff about word lengths affect your Java and Eclipse downloads? Here's the story:

- If you run a 32-bit operating system, you run only 32-bit software.

- If you run a 64-bit operating system, you probably run some 32-bit software and some 64-bit software. Most 32-bit software runs fine on a 64-bit operating system.

- On a 64-bit operating system, you might have two versions of the same program. For example, on my Windows computer, I have two versions of Internet Explorer — a 32-bit version and a 64-bit version.

  Normally, Windows puts 32-bit programs in its `Program Files (x86)` directory and puts 64-bit programs in its `Program Files` directory.

(continued)

(continued)

- A chain of word lengths is as strong as its weakest link. For example, when I visit http://java.com and click the site's Do I Have Java? link, the answer I get depends on the match between my computer's Java version and the web browser that I'm running. With only 64-bit Java installed on my computer, the Do I Have Java? link in my 32-bit Firefox browser answers No working Java was detected on your system. But the same link in my 64-bit Internet Explorer answers You have the recommended Java installed.

  On a Mac, Safari and Firefox are 64-bit browsers, but Chrome is a 32-bit browser. So on a Mac, you're likely to see slightly different behavior when using Firefox versus Chrome.

- Here's the most important thing to remember about word lengths: When you follow this chapter's instructions, you get Java software and Eclipse software on your computer. Your Java software's word length must match your Eclipse software's word length. In other words, 32-bit Eclipse runs with 32-bit Java, and 64-bit Eclipse runs with 64-bit Java. I haven't tried all possible combinations, but when I try to run 32-bit Eclipse with 64-bit Java, I see a misleading No Java virtual machine was found error message.

- Finally, some websites use unintuitive names for their software downloads. If you see *i365* or *i586* in the name of a download, that usually means *32-bit*. If you see *x86* without the number *64* anywhere in a download's name, that also means *32-bit*s. If you see *64* in the name (with or without the *x86* designation), that indicates a *64-bit* program.

If you want to find Java on your computer . . .

Chapter 1 describes the Java ecosystem with its compiler, its virtual machine, and its other parts. Your computer may already have some of these Java gizmos. If so, you can either live with what you already have or add the newest version of Java to whatever is already on your system. If you need help deciding what to do, refer to the sidebar entitled "Eenie, meenie, miney mo."

TECHNICAL STUFF

Java's versions aren't like indoor cats — they can coexist on the same computer without fighting or hissing at one another. If you have more than one version of Java on your computer, you're okay. You can even mix 32-bit versions and 64-bit versions on the same computer (as long as you have at least one Java version whose word length matches your Eclipse version). I have three versions of Java on my Windows 10 computer, and I never run into trouble. (Occasionally, I cause my own trouble by confusing one version of Java for another. But this chapter's later section "Configuring Java in Eclipse" helps me sort things out. What would I do without this book by my side?)

To find out what you already have and possibly avoid reinstalling Java, keep reading.

On Windows 10

In the taskbar's Search box, type **Programs and Features**. In the list of choices that appears, choose Programs and Features. A list of installed programs appears. In that list, look for items labeled *Java*. (See Figure 2-2.)

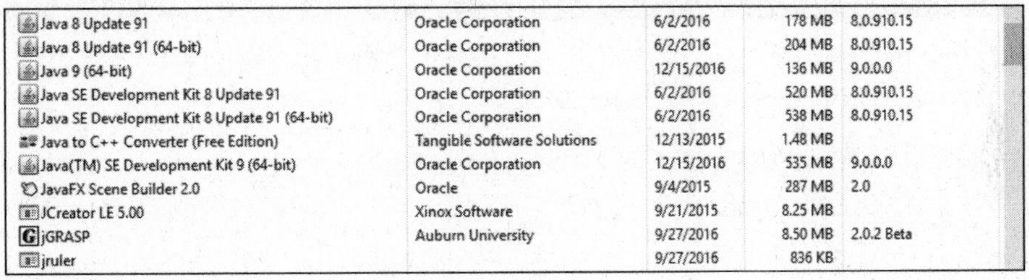

FIGURE 2-2:
The Programs and Features dialog box on Windows.

Java 8 Update 91	Oracle Corporation	6/2/2016	178 MB	8.0.910.15
Java 8 Update 91 (64-bit)	Oracle Corporation	6/2/2016	204 MB	8.0.910.15
Java 9 (64-bit)	Oracle Corporation	12/15/2016	136 MB	9.0.0.0
Java SE Development Kit 8 Update 91	Oracle Corporation	6/2/2016	520 MB	8.0.910.15
Java SE Development Kit 8 Update 91 (64-bit)	Oracle Corporation	6/2/2016	538 MB	8.0.910.15
Java to C++ Converter (Free Edition)	Tangible Software Solutions	12/13/2015	1.48 MB	
Java(TM) SE Development Kit 9 (64-bit)	Oracle Corporation	12/15/2016	535 MB	9.0.0.0
JavaFX Scene Builder 2.0	Oracle	9/4/2015	287 MB	2.0
JCreator LE 5.00	Xinox Software	9/21/2015	8.25 MB	
jGRASP	Auburn University	9/27/2016	8.50 MB	2.0.2 Beta
jruler		9/27/2016	836 KB	

On Windows 8

On the Start screen, hold down the Windows key while pressing Q. In the resulting search box, type **Programs and Features** and then press Enter. A list of installed programs appears. In that list, look for items labeled *Java*. (Refer to Figure 2-2.)

On Windows 7

Select Start ⇨ Control Panel ⇨ Programs ⇨ Programs and Features. A list of installed programs appears. In that list, look for items labeled *Java*. (Refer to Figure 2-2.)

On a Mac

A Macintosh computer can support two different flavors of Java: a flavor developed in-house at Apple, Inc., and another flavor developed under Oracle's auspices. Certain commands and procedures apply to one flavor of Java but not to the other. For example, to find Apple's version of Java, you look in the `/System/Library/Java/Java Virtual Machines` directory or the `/System/Library/Frameworks/JavaVM.framework/Versions` directory. But to find Oracle's Java, you look in the `/Library/Java/JavaVirtualMachines` directory. You might also find Oracle's Java in the `/Library/Internet Plug-Ins/JavaAppletPlugin.plugin/Contents/Home` directory.

Tiger, Leopard, and Snow Leopard (OS X 10.4, OS X 10.5, and OS X 10.6) have Java preinstalled. Java isn't preinstalled on later Mac operating systems. On these later systems, the computer prompts you to install either Apple's Java or Oracle's Java the first time you launch an application that requires Java. (For example, later in this chapter, you install Eclipse. When you first try to launch Eclipse, if you haven't already installed Java, your computer advises you to do so.)

Table 2-1 describes the correlations between Mac OS and Java versions.

TABLE 2-1   **Mac OS X Versions and Java Versions**

If You Have This Mac OS X Version . . .	Then You Have This Version of Java . . .	And You Can Install This Java Version
OS X 10.4.11 (Tiger)	Apple's Java 5.0	Apple's Java 5.0
OS X 10.5.8 (Leopard) PowerPC and/or 32-bit		
OS X 10.5.8 (Leopard) Intel-based and 64-bit	Apple's Java 6	Apple's Java 6
OS X 10.6.8 (Snow Leopard)		
OS X 10.7.5 (Lion)	(no Java)	Apple's Java 6
OS X 10.8.5 (Mountain Lion)		Oracle's Java 9
OS X 10.9 (Mavericks)		
OS X 10.10 (Yosemite)		
OS X 10.11 (El Capitan)		
macOS 10.12 (Sierra)		

To find out which version of OS X you're running, do the following:

1. **Choose Apple ⇨ About This Mac.**

2. **In the About This Mac dialog that appears, look for the word *Version*.**

   You see Version 10.12.4 (or something like that) in faint gray text.

TIP

The information in Table 2-1 applies to updated versions of Mac OS X. If you don't regularly apply software updates, you may be running OS X 10.8.1 instead of 10.8.5. If so, select Software Update in the Apple menu and follow the resulting prompts.

TIP

Here and there on the web, I see postings describing ways to install Java 5.0 on OS X 10.3 and other ways to circumvent the restrictions in Table 2-1. But if you don't like to tinker, these workarounds aren't for you. (For every hardware or software requirement, someone tries to create a workaround, or *hack*. Anyway, apply hacks at your own risk.)

If you don't trust Table 2-1 (and frankly, you shouldn't trust everything you find in print), you can perform tests on your computer to discover the presence of Java and (if your Mac has Java) the Java version number. Here are some tests:

WITH OS X 10.6 OR EARLIER

1. **In the Spotlight's search field, type** Java Preferences.

2. **When the Spotlight's top hit is Java Preferences, press Enter.**

The Java Preferences window appears. (See Figure 2-3.)

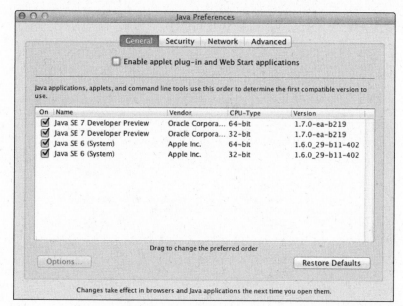

FIGURE 2-3:
The Java
Preferences
application.

3. **The Java Preferences window lists versions of Java that are installed on your computer.**

In Figure 2-3, the computer has four versions of Java: the 32-bit (i386) versions of Java 6 and Java 7 and the 64-bit (x86_64) versions of Java 6 and Java 7.

WITH OS X 10.7 OR LATER

1. **On the Apple menu, select System Preferences.**

2. **In the System Preferences application window, click the Java icon.**

The Java Control Panel appears. It looks like the panel in Figure 2-4 or the one in Figure 2-5.

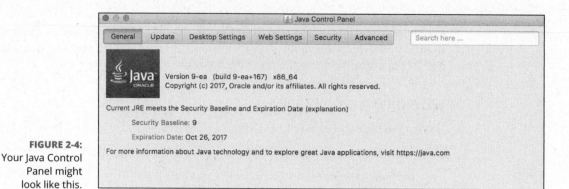

FIGURE 2-4:
Your Java Control
Panel might
look like this.

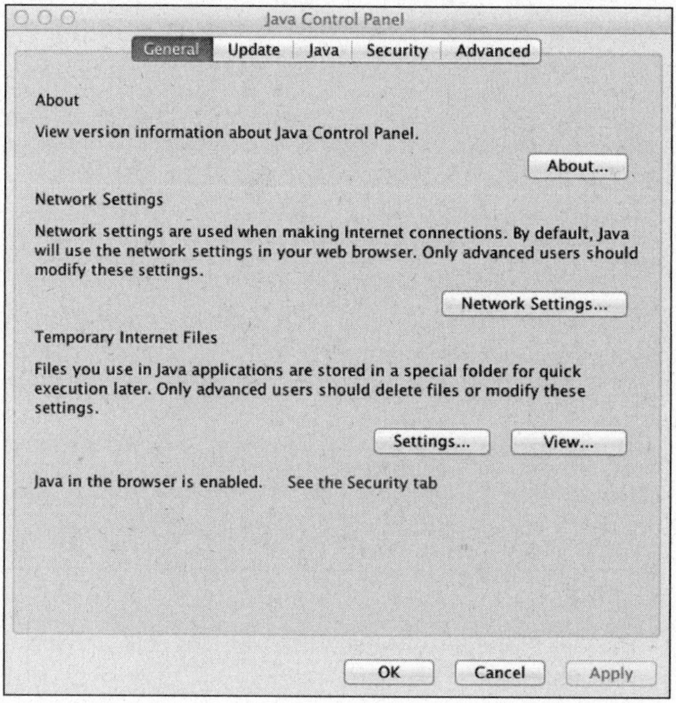

FIGURE 2-5:
Another
incarnation
of the Java
Control Panel.

3. **If your Java Control Panel looks like the panel in Figure 2-4, you see your computer's Java version on the panel's General tab.**

   According to the panel shown in Figure 2-4, my computer has an early access (ea) version of Java 9. You can skip the rest of these steps.

4. **If your Java Control Panel looks like the panel in Figure 2-5, select the panel's Java tab. (See Figure 2-6.)**

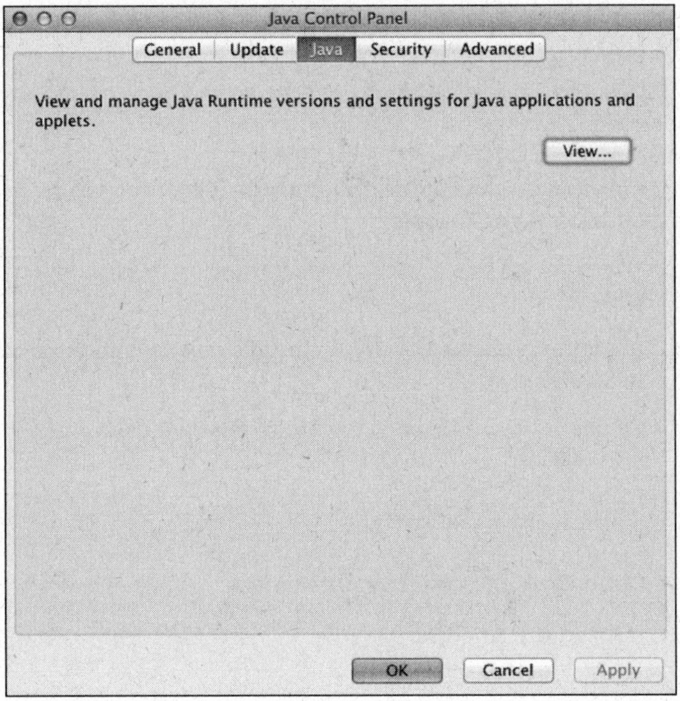

FIGURE 2-6:
The Java tab
in the Java
Control Panel.

5. **On the Java tab, click View.**

The Java Runtime Environment Settings window appears. (See Figure 2-7.)

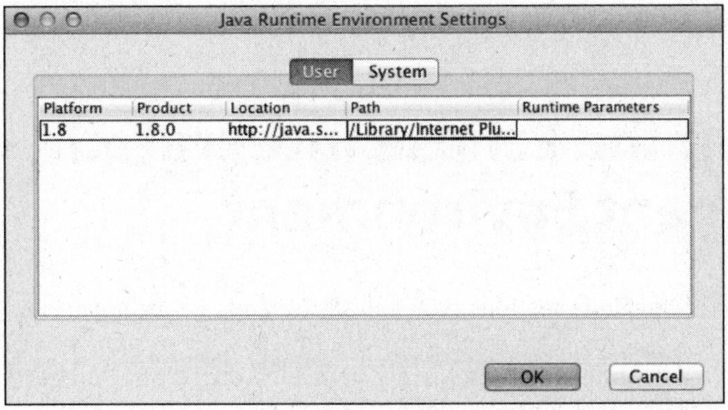

FIGURE 2-7:
The User tab in
the Java Runtime
Environment
Settings window.

6. **Look for versions of Java on the User tab and the System tab of the Java Runtime Environment Settings window.**

Figure 2-7 shows the User tab of the Java Runtime Environment Settings window. According to the figure, the computer runs Java 1.8. (Java's close friends call this version "Java 8.")

On Linux

To check your Java installation (or your lack of Java) on a Linux computer, do the following:

1. Poke around among the desktop's menus for something named Terminal (also known as Konsole).

A Terminal window opens (usually, with plain white text on a plain black background).

2. In the Terminal window, type the following text and then press Enter: java -version.

On one of my Linux computers, the Terminal window responds with the following text:

```
java version 1.8.0_111
```

On another Linux computer, I see this:

```
java version 9
```

Between Java 8 and Java 9, Oracle changed its version numbering system. So version 9 comes immediately after the 1.8.0 versions. Anyway, if your computer responds with the number 9 or higher, you can pop open the champagne and look forward to some good times running this book's examples. If the version number is 1.5 or greater, you can run many, but not all, of this book's examples. If your computer responds with something like command not found, most likely, Java isn't installed on your computer.

Setting Up the Eclipse Integrated Development Environment

In the previous sections, you get all the tools your *computer* needs for processing Java programs. This section is different. In this section, you get the tool that *you* need for composing and testing your Java programs. You get Eclipse — an integrated development environment for Java.

An *integrated development environment (IDE)* is a program that provides tools to help you create software easily and efficiently. You can create Java programs without an IDE, but the time and effort you save using an IDE makes the IDE worthwhile. (Some hard-core programmers disagree with me, but that's another matter.)

According to the Eclipse Foundation's website, *Eclipse* is "a universal tool platform — an open extensible IDE for anything and nothing in particular." Indeed, Eclipse is versatile. Programmers generally think of Eclipse as an IDE for developing Java programs, but Eclipse has tools for programming in C++, PHP, and many other languages.

I've even seen incarnations of Eclipse that have nothing to do with program development. For example, Dynatrace has an application that monitors the performance of large systems. When you run Dynatrace's application on a desktop computer, you're running a dressed-up version of Eclipse.

Downloading Eclipse

Here's how you download Eclipse:

1. **Visit** www.eclipse.org.

   Today, I visit www.eclipse.org and see a big button displaying the word *Download*. (See Figure 2-8.) Tomorrow, who knows what I'll see on this ever-changing website!

FIGURE 2-8: The home page for eclipse.org.

   One way or another, you probably see a Download button of some kind.

2. **Click the Download button.**

   After clicking the Download button, you might find a few download options. (See Figure 2-9.)

   A new version of Eclipse appears every year in June, and the version names are ordered alphabetically. In June 2016, the name is Neon. In June 2017, it's Oxygen. In June 2018, it's Photon. Get it? The names begin with N, and then O, and then P. (In Figure 2-9, don't let the *O* in *Orion* fool you. That's a different piece of software.)

Tool Platforms

Get Eclipse Neon

Install your favorite Eclipse packages.

DOWNLOAD 64 BIT

Download Packages

Eclipse Che

Eclipse Che is a developer workspace server and cloud IDE.

ORION

A modern, open source software development environment that runs in the cloud.

FIGURE 2-9:
In May 2017, I download Eclipse Neon.

3. **Click the button to download the current Eclipse version.**

In May 2017, I clicked the DOWNLOAD 64 BIT button in Figure 2-9. As a result, Eclipse's website showed me yet another button. This other button offered me a copy of Eclipse from one of many servers around the world.

4. **Click the appropriate button and follow the appropriate links to get the download to begin.**

The links you follow depend on which of Eclipse's many mirror sites is offering up your download. Just wade through the possibilities and get the download going.

Notice the Download Packages link in Figure 2-9. If you click that link, you can download a copy of Eclipse with certain features added. For example, the Eclipse IDE for Java EE Developers package includes heavyweight features for industrial-strength development. The Eclipse IDE for JavaScript and Web Developers package has features to help people create web pages.

If you land on a page that offers various packages, look for a package named Eclipse IDE for Java Developers (not Java EE Developers).

TIP

Eclipse's download page directs you to versions of Eclipse that are specific to your computer's operating system. For example, if you visit the page on a Windows computer, the page shows you downloads for Windows only. If you're download-ing Eclipse for use on another computer, you may want to override the automatic choice of operating system. Look for a little drop-down list containing the name of your computer's operating system. You can change the selected operating system on that drop-down list.

WARNING

If you know which Java version you have (32-bit or 64-bit), be sure to download the corresponding Eclipse version. If you don't know which Java version you have, download the 64-bit version of Eclipse and try to launch it. If you can launch 64-bit Eclipse, you're okay. But if you get a No Java virtual machine was found error message, try downloading and launching the 32-bit version of Eclipse. For the full lowdown on 32-bit and 64-bit word lengths, see this chapter's earlier sidebar "How many bits does your computer have?"

Installing Eclipse

Precisely how you install Eclipse depends on your operating system and on what kind of file you get when you download Eclipse. Here's a brief summary:

» **If you run Windows and the download is an** `.exe` **file:**

Double-click the `.exe` file's icon.

» **If you run Windows and the download is a** `.zip` **file:**

Extract the file's contents to the directory of your choice.

In other words, find the `.zip` file's icon in File Explorer (also known as *Windows Explorer*). Then double-click the `.zip` file's icon. (As a result, Explorer displays the contents of the `.zip` file, which consists of only one folder — a folder named `eclipse`.) Drag the `eclipse` folder to a convenient place on your computer's hard drive.

For more information about `.zip` files, see the "Compressed archive files" sidebar, earlier in this chapter.

My favorite place to drag the `eclipse` folder is directly onto the `C:` drive. So my `C:` drive has folders named `Program Files`, `Windows`, `eclipse`, and others. I avoid making the `eclipse` folder be a subfolder of `Program Files` because from time to time, I've had problems dealing with the blank space in the name `Program Files`.

» **If you run Mac OS X:**

When you download Eclipse, you get either a `.tar.gz` file or a `.dmg` file.

- A `.tar.gz` file is a compressed archive file. When you download the file, your web browser might automatically do some uncompressing for you. If so, you won't find a `.tar.gz` file in your `Downloads` folder. Instead, you'll find either a `.tar` file (because your web browser uncompressed the `.gz` part) or an `eclipse` folder (because your web browser uncompressed both the `.tar` and `.gz` parts).

  If you find a new `.tar` file or `.tar.gz` file in your `Downloads` folder, double-click the file until you see the `eclipse` folder. Drag this new `eclipse` folder to your `Applications` folder, and you're all set.

- If you download a `.dmg` file, your web browser may open the file for you. If not, find the `.dmg` file in your `Downloads` folder and double-click the file. Follow any instructions that appear after this double-click. If you're expected to drag Eclipse into your `Applications` folder, do so.

Running Eclipse for the first time

The first time you launch Eclipse, you perform a few extra steps. To get Eclipse running, do the following:

1. **Launch Eclipse.**

In Windows, the Start menu may not have an Eclipse icon. In that case, look in File Explorer (aka Windows Explorer) for the folder containing your extracted Eclipse files. Double-click the icon representing the `eclipse.exe` file. (If you see an `eclipse` file but not an `eclipse.exe` file, check this chapter's earlier sidebar "Those pesky filename extensions.")

On a Mac, go to the Spotlight and type **Eclipse** in the search field. When *Eclipse* appears as the top hit on the Spotlight's list, press Enter.

TIP

The first time you try to run Eclipse on a Mac, you might get a message telling you that Eclipse isn't from the App Store and isn't from an identified developer. Nothing in this world is 100 percent safe, but I've downloaded and installed Eclipse a zillion times, and I've never had a problem with it. So, to get around this stumbling block, find the Eclipse app entry in your `Applications` folder (or wherever else you installed Eclipse). Control-click the application entry and, on the resulting context menu, select Open. At this point, a dialog box appears. The dialog box asks whether you're sure that you want to open the application. You're sure, so click Open.

When you launch Eclipse, you see a Workspace Launcher dialog. (See Figure 2-10.) The dialog asks where, on your computer's hard drive, you want to store the code that you will create using Eclipse.

2. **In the Workspace Launcher dialog, click OK to accept the default (or don't accept the default!).**

One way or another, it's no big deal!

Because this is your first time using a particular Eclipse workspace, Eclipse starts with a Welcome screen. (See Figure 2-11.)

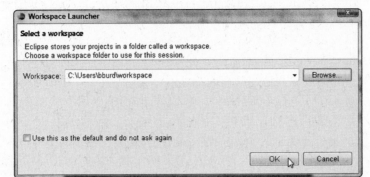

FIGURE 2-10:
Eclipse's
Workspace
Launcher.

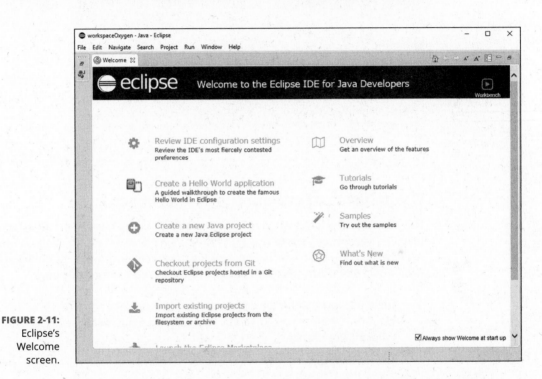

FIGURE 2-11:
Eclipse's
Welcome
screen.

3. **On the Welcome screen, look for a button or an icon labeled Workbench.**

In Figure 2-11, that button is in the upper-right corner.

TIP

Through the ages, many of the Eclipse Welcome screens have displayed icons along with little or no helpful text. If you don't see the word *Workbench* anywhere on the Welcome screen, hover the mouse over each icon until you find an icon whose tooltip contains the word *Workbench*.

4. **Click the Workbench icon to open Eclipse's main screen.**

A view of the main screen, after opening Eclipse with a brand-new workspace, is shown in Figure 2-12.

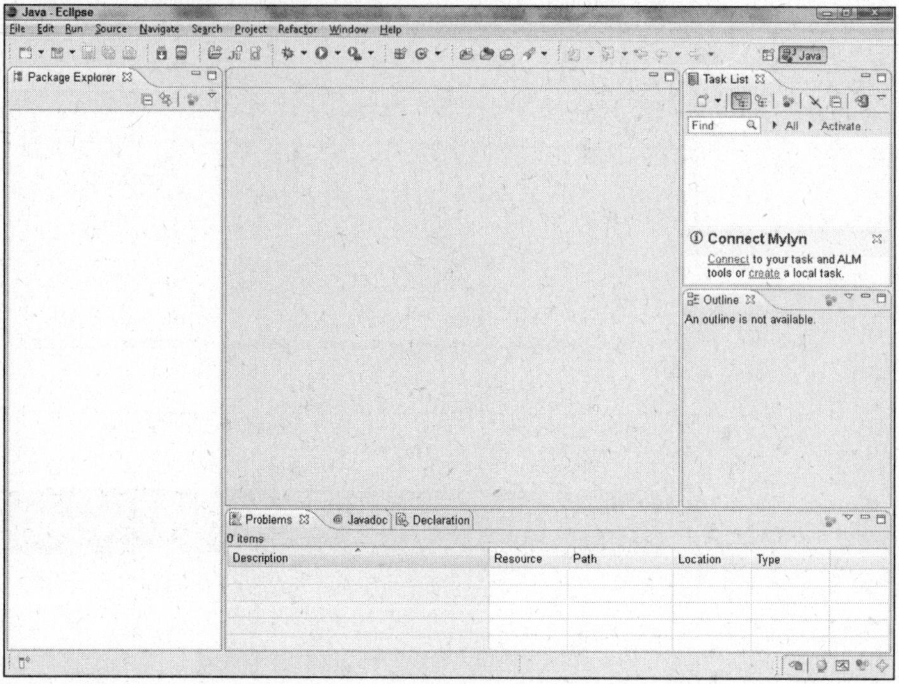

FIGURE 2-12:
FIGURE 2-12:
The Eclipse
workbench with
a brand-new
workspace.

If you have to configure Java in Eclipse . . .

Eclipse normally looks on your computer for Java installations and selects an installed version of Java to use for running your Java programs. Your computer may have more than one version of Java, so you may want to double-check Eclipse's choice of the Java version. The following steps show you how:

1. **On Windows or Linux: On Eclipse's main menu, select Window ⇨ Preferences. On a Mac: On Eclipse's main menu, select Eclipse ⇨ Preferences.**

   As a result, Eclipse's Preferences dialog appears. (You can follow along with Figure 2-13.)

2. **In the tree on the left side of the Preferences dialog, expand the** Java **branch.**

3. **Within the** Java **branch, select the** `Installed JREs` **subbranch.**

4. **Look at the list of Java versions (Installed JREs) in the main body of the Preferences dialog.**

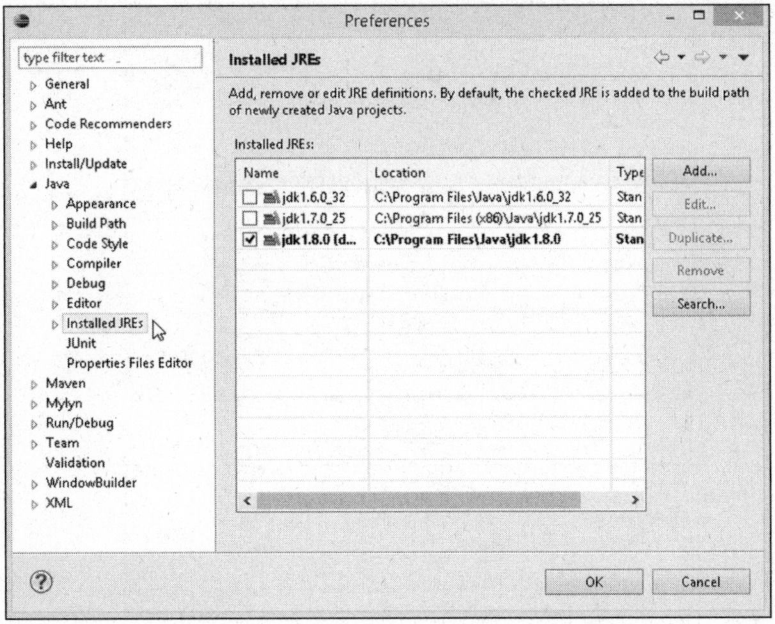

FIGURE 2-13:
Eclipse's
Preferences
dialog.

In the list, each version of Java has a check box. Eclipse uses the version whose box is checked. If the checked version isn't your preferred version (for example, if the checked version isn't version 9 or higher), you can make some changes.

5. **If your preferred version of Java appears on the Installed JREs list, put a check mark in that version's check box.**

6. **If your preferred version of Java doesn't appear in the Installed JREs list, click the Add button.**

When you click the Add button, a JRE Type dialog appears. (See Figure 2-14.)

7. **In the JRE Type dialog, double-click Standard VM.**

As a result, a JRE Definition dialog appears. (See Figure 2-15.) What you do next depends on a few different things.

8. **Fill in the dialog's JRE Home field.**

How you do this depends on your operating system.

- On Windows, browse to the directory in which you've installed your preferred Java version. On my many Windows computers, that directory is either `C:\Program Files\Java\jre-9`, `C:\Program Files\Java\jdk1.8.0`, `C:\Program Files (x86)\Java\jre-9`, or something of that sort.

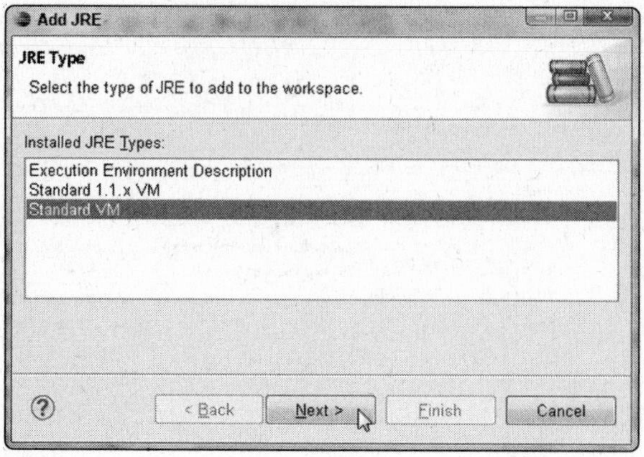

FIGURE 2-14:
The JRE Type dialog.

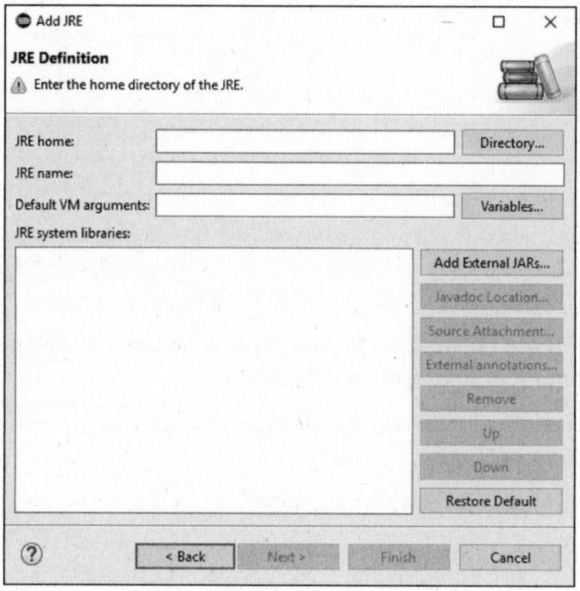

FIGURE 2-15:
The JRE Definition dialog.

- On a Mac, use the Finder to browse to the directory in which you've installed your preferred Java version. Type the name of the directory in the dialog's JRE Home field.

  My Mac has one Java directory named `/System/Library/Java/Java Virtual Machines/1.6.0.jdk/Contents/Home` and another Java directory named `/Library/Java/JavaVirtualMachines/jdk-9.jdk/Contents/Home`. (The first is for Apple's old version of Java; the second is for Oracle's new Java version.) You might also find Apple's old Java version in the `/System/Library/Frameworks/JavaVM.framework/Versions` directory, and find Oracle's Java in the `/Library/Internet Plug-Ins/JavaAppletPlugin.plugin/Contents/Home` directory.

Directories like /System and /Library don't normally appear in the Finder window. To browse to one of these directories (to the /Library directory, for example), choose Go ➪ Go to Folder in the Finder's menu bar. In the resulting dialog, type /Library and then press Go.

As you navigate to the directory containing your preferred Java version, you may encounter a JDK 1.8.0.jdk icon or some other item whose extension is .jdk. To see the contents of this item, Control-click the item's icon and then select Show Package Contents from the menu that appears.

- On Linux, browse to the directory in which you've installed your preferred Java version. When in doubt, search for a directory whose name starts with jre or jdk.

You might have one more thing to do back in the JRE Definition dialog.

9. **Look at the JRE Definition dialog's JRE Name field; if Eclipse hasn't filled in a name automatically, type a name (almost any text) in the JRE Name field.**

10. **Dismiss the JRE Definition dialog by clicking Finish.**

   Eclipse's Preferences dialog returns to the foreground. The box's Installed JREs list contains your newly added version of Java.

11. **Put a check mark in the check box next to your newly added version of Java.**

   You're almost done. (You have a few more steps to follow.)

12. **Within the** Java **branch on the left side of the Preferences dialog, select the** Compiler **subbranch.**

   In the main body of the Preferences dialog, you see a Compiler Compliance Level drop-down list.

13. **In the Compiler Compliance Level drop-down list, select a number that matches your preferred Java version.**

   For Java 8, I select compliance level 1.8. For Java 9, I select compliance level 1.9 or compliance level 9.

   Eclipse updates aren't always in sync with Java updates. If you're running Java 9 and the Eclipse's highest compliance level is 1.8, select 1.8. Take my word for it. Everything will be okay.

14. **Whew! Click the Preferences dialog's OK button to return to the Eclipse workbench.**

Importing This Book's Sample Programs

The import business in Eclipse can be tricky. As you move from one dialog to the next, many of the options have similar names. That's because Eclipse offers many different ways to import many different kinds of things. Anyway, if you follow these instructions, you'll be okay.

1. **Follow the steps in this chapter's earlier section "Getting This Book's Sample Programs."**

2. **On Eclipse's main menu, choose File ➪ Import. (See Figure 2-16.)**

    As a result, Eclipse displays an Import dialog.

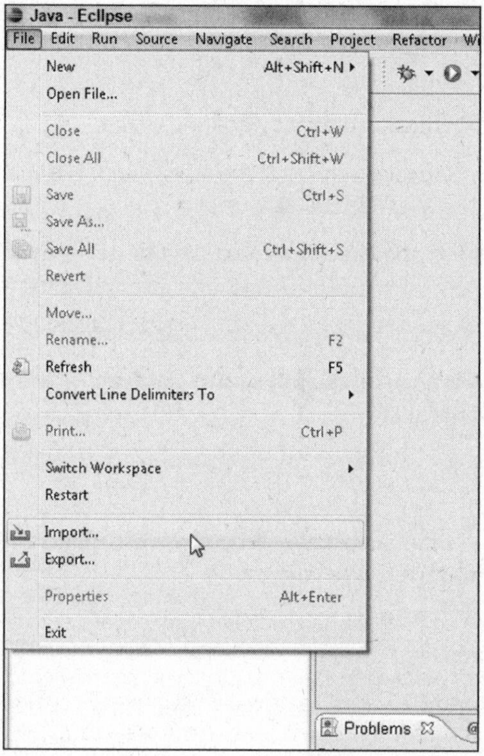

FIGURE 2-16:
Starting to import
this book's code.

3. **In the Import dialog's tree, expand the** General **branch.**

4. **In the** General **branch, double-click the** Existing Projects into Workspace **subbranch. (See Figure 2-17)**

    As a result, the Import Projects dialog appears.

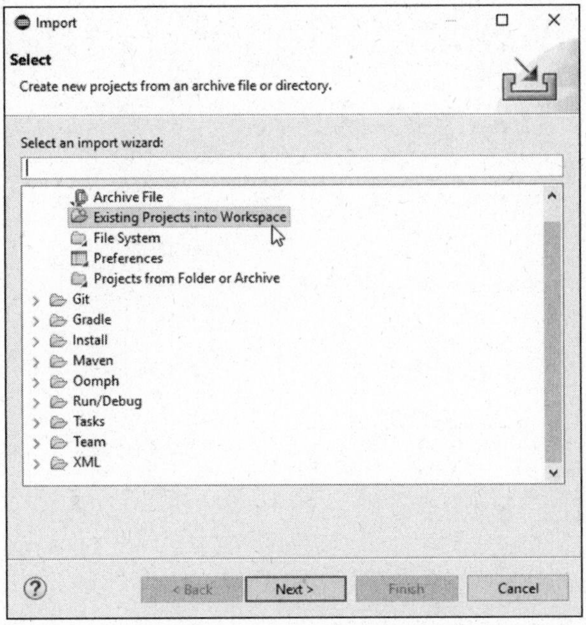

FIGURE 2-17:
Among all the
options, select
Existing Projects
into Workspace.

Look again at Figure 2-17. In that dialog box, don't select Archive File or File System. My book's download isn't set up for either of these options.

WARNING

5. **In the Import Projects dialog, choose either the Select Root Directory radio button or the Select Archive File radio button. (See Figure 2-18)**

Here's how you decide which radio button to choose:

First, make sure that you've heeded the advice that I give in the earlier sidebar entitled "Those pesky filename extensions." Then look in the folder containing the file that you downloaded from this book's website.

- If your web browser doesn't automatically uncompress downloaded .zip files, you'll find this book's code in an archive file named BeginProgJava Dummies5.zip. In that case, choose the Select Archive File radio button.

- If your web browser automatically uncompresses downloaded .zip files, you'll find this book's code in a directory (a folder) named BeginProgJavaDummies5. In that case, choose the Select Root Directory radio button.

REMEMBER

To ensure that you can distinguish between a folder and a .zip file, check this chapter's "Those pesky filename extensions" sidebar.

For the complete scoop on .zip files and other archive files, see the sidebar entitled "Compressed archive files."

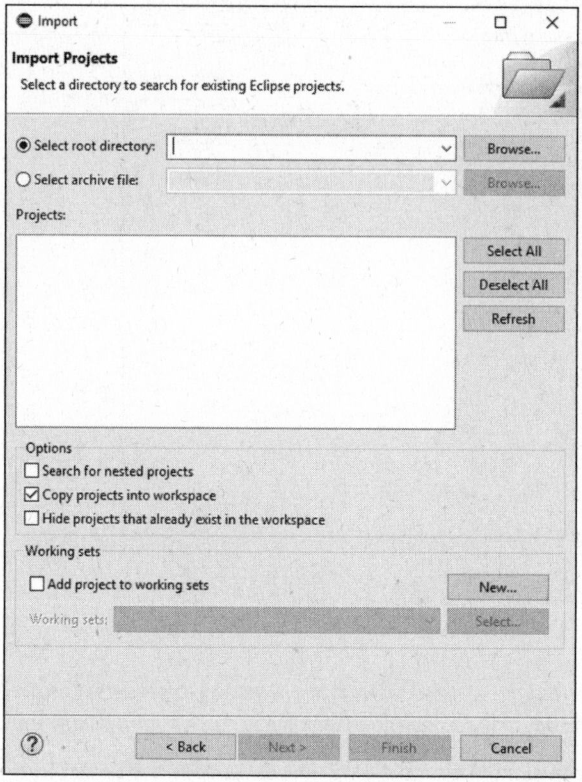

FIGURE 2-18:
The Import
Projects dialog.

6. **Click the Browse button to find the** `BeginProgJavaDummies5.zip` **file or the** `BeginProgDummies5` **directory on your computer's hard drive.**

   After you find the file or the directory, Eclipse's Import Projects dialog displays the names of the projects inside the file. (See Figure 2-19.)

7. **Click the Select All button.**

   This book's examples are so exciting that you want to import all of them!

8. **Click the Finish button.**

   As a result, the main Eclipse workbench reappears. The left side of the workbench displays the names of this book's Java projects. (See Figure 2-20.)

Now the real fun begins.

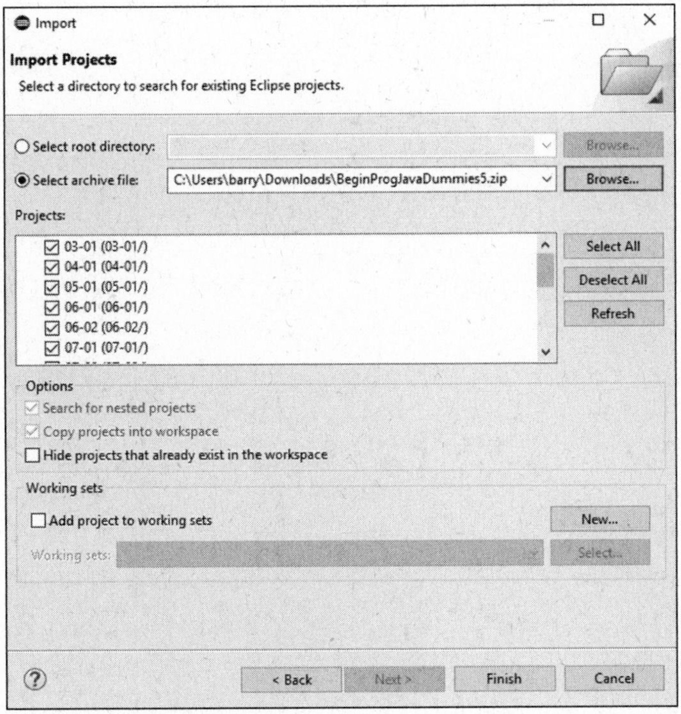

FIGURE 2-19:
Projects to be
imported.

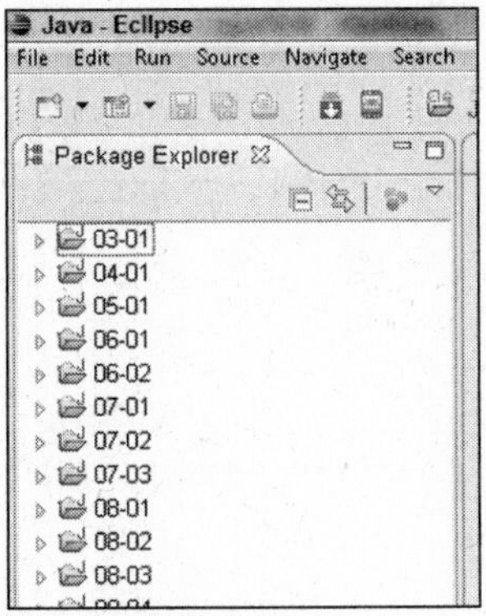

FIGURE 2-20:
Eclipse displays a
bunch of Java
projects.

What's Next?

If you're reading this paragraph, you've probably finished installing Java and
Eclipse on your computer. In Chapter 3, you start reaping the benefits of your
software installation efforts. You use Eclipse to run a brand-new Java program.

Chapter **3**

Running Programs

I f you're a programming newbie, for you, running a program probably means clicking a mouse. You want to run Microsoft Word, so you double-click the Microsoft Word icon. That's all there is to it.

When you create your own programs, the situation is a bit different. With a new program, the programmer (or someone from the programmer's company) creates the program's icon. Before that process, a perfectly good program may not even have an icon. So what do you do with a brand-new Java program? How do you get the program to run? This chapter tells you what you need to know.

Running a Canned Java Program

The best way to get to know Java is to do Java. When you're doing Java, you're writing, testing, and running your own Java programs. This section prepares you by describing how you run and test a program. Instead of writing your own program, you run a program that I've already written for you. The program calculates your monthly payments on a home mortgage loan.

The mortgage-calculating program doesn't open its own window. Instead, the program runs in Eclipse's Console view. The Console view is one of the tabs in the lower-right part of the Eclipse workbench. (See Figure 3-1.) A program that operates completely in this Console view is called a *text-based program*.

FIGURE 3-1:
A run of this
chapter's
text-based
mortgage
program.

```
20         .print( How much are you borrowing?
21    principal = Double.parseDouble(keyboard.nextLine());
```

| Problems | @ Javadoc | Declaration | Search | Console ⊠ |

<terminated> Mortgage [Java Application] C:\Program Files\Java\jre7\bin\ja

```
How much are you borrowing?            100000.00
What's the interest rate?              5.25
How many years are you taking to pay?  30
--------------------------------
Your monthly payment is                $552.20
```

TIP

You may not see a Console tab in the lower-right part of the Eclipse workbench. To coax the Console view out of hiding, choose Window⇨Show View⇨Other. In the resulting Show View dialog box, expand the General branch. Finally, within that General branch, double-click the Console item.

For more information about the Console view (and about Eclipse's workbench in general), see the "Views, editors, and other stuff" section, later in this chapter.

You can see GUI versions of the program in Figure 3-1, and of many other examples from this book, by visiting the book's website (http://allmycode.com/BeginProg).

Actually, as you run the mortgage program, you see two things in Eclipse's Console view:

>> **Messages and results that the mortgage program sends to you:** Messages include things like How much are you borrowing?, and results include lines like Your monthly payment is $552.20.

>> **Responses that you give to the mortgage program while it runs:** If you type 100000.00 in response to the program's question about how much you're borrowing, you see that number echoed in Eclipse's Console view.

Here's how you run the mortgage program:

1. **Make sure that you've followed the instructions in Chapter 2 — instructions for installing Java, for installing and configuring Eclipse, and for getting this book's sample programs.**

   Thank goodness! You don't have to follow those instructions more than once.

2. **Launch Eclipse.**

   The Eclipse Workspace Launcher dialog box appears. (See Figure 3-2.)

A *workspace* is a folder on your computer's hard drive. Eclipse stores your Java programs in one or more workspace folders. Along with these Java programs, each workspace folder contains some Eclipse settings. These settings store things like the version of Java that you're using, the colors that you prefer for words in the editor, and the size of the editor area when you drag the area's edges. You can have several workspaces with different programs and different settings in each workspace.

By default, the Workspace Launcher offers to open whatever workspace you opened the last time you ran Eclipse. You want to open the workspace that you used in Chapter 2, so don't modify the stuff in the Launcher's Workspace field.

3. **In the Workspace Launcher dialog box, click OK.**

The big Eclipse workbench stares at you from your computer screen. (See Figure 3-3.)

In Figure 3-3, the leftmost part of the workbench is Eclipse's Package Explorer, which contains numbers like 03-01, 04-01, and so on. Each number is actually the name of an Eclipse project. Formally, a *project* is a collection of files and folders inside a workspace. Intuitively, a project is a basic work unit. For example, a self-contained collection of Java program files to manage your CD collection (along with the files containing the data) may constitute a single Eclipse project.

Looking again at the Package Explorer in Figure 3-3, you see projects named 03-01, 04-01, and so on. My project 03-01 holds the code for Listing 3-1 (the first and only listing in this chapter, Chapter 3). Project 06-02 contains the Java program in Listing 6-2 (the second code listing in Chapter 6 of this book). Project names can include letters, digits, blank spaces, and other characters; for the names of this book's examples, I stick with digits and dashes.

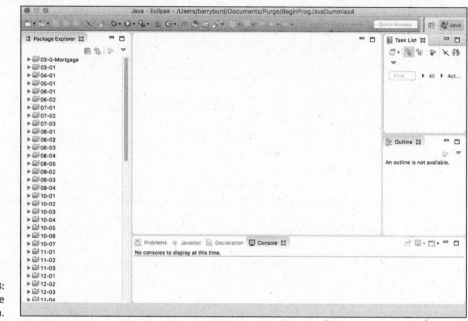

FIGURE 3-3:
The Eclipse
workbench.

To read more about topics like Eclipse's Package Explorer, see the upcoming section "What's All That Stuff in Eclipse's Window?"

WARNING

When you launch Eclipse, you may see something different from the stuff in Figure 3-3. You may see Eclipse's Welcome screen with only a few icons in an otherwise barren window. You may also see a workbench like the one in Figure 3-3, but without a list of numbers (03-01, 04-01, and so on) in the Package Explorer. If so, you may have missed some instructions on configuring Eclipse in Chapter 2. Alternatively, you may have modified the stuff in the Launcher's Workspace field in Step 2 of this section's instructions.

In any case, make sure that you see numbers like 03-01 and 04-01 in the Package Explorer. Seeing these numbers assures you that Eclipse is ready to run the sample programs from this book.

4. In the Package Explorer, click the 03-0-Mortgage **branch.**

The 03-0-Mortgage project is the only project whose name isn't two digits, a dash, and then two more digits.

TIP

You may want to see a sneak preview of some Java code. To see the Java program that you're running in Project 03-0-Mortgage, expand the 03-0-Mortgage branch in the Package Explorer. Inside the 03-0-Mortgage branch, you find a src branch, which in turn contains a (default package) branch. Inside the (default package) branch, you find the Mortgage.java branch. That `Mortgage.java` branch represents my Java program. Double-clicking the `Mortgage.java` branch makes my code appear in Eclipse's editor.

5. **Choose Run ⇨ Run As ⇨ Java Application from the main menu, as shown in Figure 3-4.**

When you choose Run As ⇨ Java Application, the computer runs the project's code. (In this example, the computer runs a Java program that I wrote.) As part of the run, the message `How much are you borrowing?` appears in Eclipse's Console view. (The Console view shares the lower-right area of Eclipse's workbench with the Problems view, the Javadoc view, the Declaration view, and possibly other views. Refer to Figure 3-1.)

FIGURE 3-4: One of the ways to run the code in Project 03-0-Mortgage.

6. **Click anywhere inside Eclipse's Console view and then type a number, like 100000.00, and press Enter.**

WARNING

When you type a number in Step 6, don't include your country's currency symbol and don't group the digits. (U.S. residents: Don't type a dollar sign and don't use any commas.) Things like $100000.00 and 1,000,000.00 cause the program to crash. You see a `NumberFormatException` message in the Console view.

Grouping separators vary from one country to another. The run shown in Figure 3-1 is for a computer configured in the United States where *100000.00* (with a dot) means "one hundred thousand." But the run might look different on a computer that's configured in what I call a "comma country" — a country where *100000,00* (with a comma) means "one hundred thousand." If you live in a comma country and you type 100000.00 exactly as it's shown in Figure 3-1, you probably get an error message (an `InputMismatchException`). If so, change the number amounts in your file to match your country's number format. When you do, you should be okay.

After you press Enter, the Java program displays another message (`What's the interest rate?`) in the Console view. (Again, refer to Figure 3-1.)

7. **In response to the interest rate question, type a number, like 5.25, and press Enter.**

After you press Enter, the Java program displays another message (`How many years ... ?`) in the Console view.

8. **Type a number, like 30, and press Enter.**

In response to the numbers that you type, the Java program displays a monthly payment amount. Again, refer to Figure 3-1.

Disclaimer: Your local mortgage company charges fees of all kinds. To get a mortgage in real life, you pay more than the amount that my Java program calculates. (A lot more.)

WARNING

When you type a number in Step 8, don't include a decimal point. Numbers like 30.0 cause the program to crash. You see a NumberFormatException message in the Console view.

TIP

Occasionally, you decide in the middle of a program's run that you've made a mistake of some kind. You want to stop the program's run dead in its tracks. Simply click the little red square above the Console view. (See Figure 3-5.)

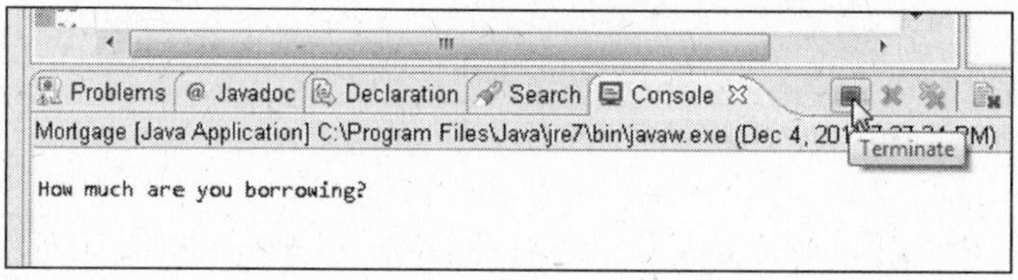

FIGURE 3-5:
How to prematurely terminate a program's run.

> ▲ ▶ Problems @ Javadoc 🔍 Declaration 🔍 Search 🖳 Console ✕ 🔲 ✕ 🔏 🔂
> Mortgage [Java Application] C:\Program Files\Java\jre7\bin\javaw.exe (Dec 4, 201▓▓▓▓▓▓ Terminate M)
>
> How much are you borrowing?

If you follow this section's instructions and you don't get the results that I describe, you can try three things. I list them in order from best to worst:

>> Check all the steps to make sure that you did everything correctly.

>> Send an email to me at BeginProg@allmycode.com, post to my Facebook wall (/allmycode), or tweet to the Burd (@allmycode). If you describe what happened, I can probably figure out what went wrong and tell you how to correct the problem.

>> Panic.

Typing and Running Your Own Code

The previous section is about running someone else's Java code (code that you download from this book's website). But eventually, you'll write code on your own. This section shows you how to create code with the Eclipse IDE.

Separating your programs from mine

In Chapter 2, you download this book's examples from my website. Then you create an Eclipse workspace and import the book's examples into your workspace.

You can create your own projects in the same workspace. But if you want to separate your code from mine, you can create a second workspace. Here are two ways to create a new workspace:

>> **When you launch Eclipse, type a new folder name in the Workspace field of Eclipse's Workspace Launcher dialog box.**

If the folder doesn't already exist, Eclipse creates the folder. If the folder already exists, Eclipse's Package Explorer lists any projects that the folder contains.

>> **On the Eclipse workbench's main menu, choose File ➪ Switch Workspace. (See Figure 3-6.)**

When you choose File ➪ Switch Workspace, Eclipse offers you a few of your previously opened workspace folders. If your choice of folder isn't in the list, select the Other option. In response, Eclipse reopens its Workspace Launcher dialog box.

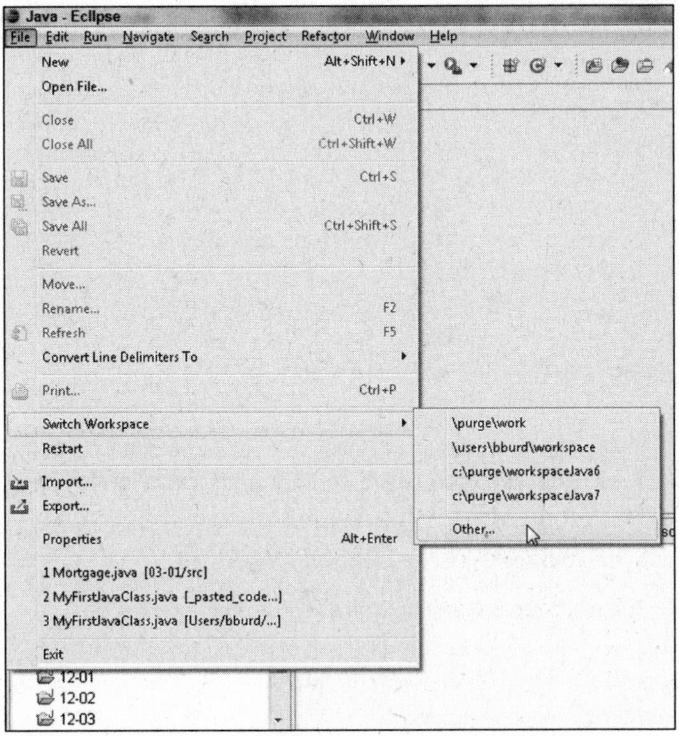

FIGURE 3-6:
Switching to a different Eclipse workspace.

Writing and running your program

Here's how you create a new Java project:

1. **Launch Eclipse.**

2. **From Eclipse's menu bar, choose File ➪ New ➪ Java Project.**

   A New Java Project dialog box appears.

3. **In the New Java Project dialog box, type a name for your project and then click Finish.**

   In Figure 3-7, I type the name `MyFirstProject`.

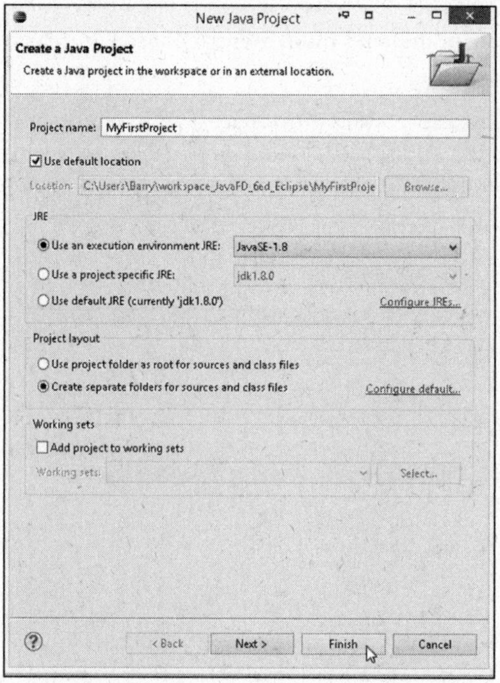

FIGURE 3-7:
Getting Eclipse
to create a new
project.

REMEMBER

If you click Next instead of Finish, you see some other options that you don't need right now. To avoid any confusion, just click Finish.

Clicking Finish brings you back to Eclipse's workbench, with `MyFirstProject` in the Package Explorer, as shown in Figure 3-8.

The next step is to create a new Java source code file.

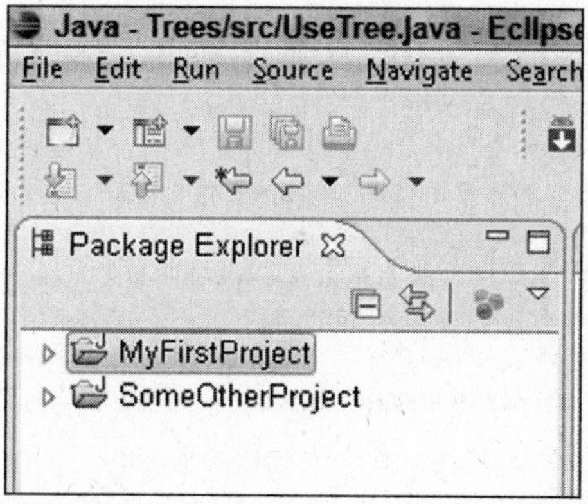

FIGURE 3-8:
Your project
appears in
Eclipse's Package
Explorer.

4. **Select your newly created project in the Package Explorer.**

   To create Figure 3-8, I selected MyFirstProject instead of
   SomeOtherProject.

5. **In Eclipse's main menu, choose File ⇨ New ⇨ Class.**

   Eclipse's New Java Class dialog box appears. (See Figure 3-9.)

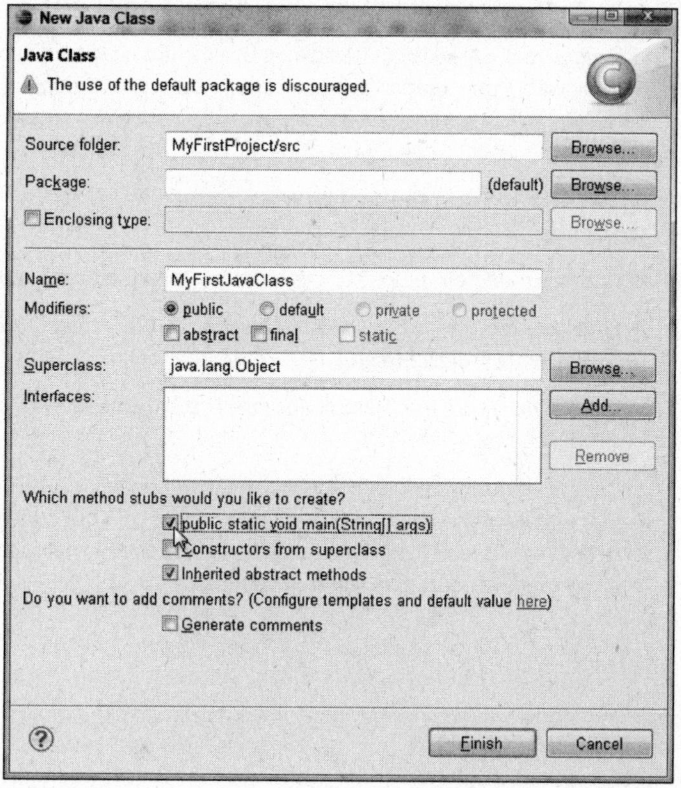

FIGURE 3-9:
Getting Eclipse
to create a new
Java class.

Java programmers normally divide their code into one or more *packages*. A typical package has a name like `java.util` or `org.allyourcode.images`. In Figure 3-9, Eclipse is warning me that I'm not naming a package to contain my project's code. So the code goes into a nondescript thing called Java's *default package*. Java's default package is a package with no name — a catchall location for code that isn't otherwise packaged. Packages are great for managing big programming projects, but this book contains no big programming projects. So, in this example (and in all of this book's examples), I choose to ignore the warning. For more info about Java packages, see Chapter 18.

Like every other windowed environment, Eclipse provides many ways to accomplish the same task. Instead of choosing File ⇨ New ⇨ Class, you can right-click `MyFirstProject` in the Package Explorer in Windows (or control-click `MyFirstProject` in the Package Explorer on a Mac). From the resulting context menu, choose New ⇨ Class. You can also start by pressing Alt+Shift+N in Windows (or Option+⌘+N on a Mac). The choice of clicks and keystrokes is up to you.

6. **In the New Java Class dialog box's Name field, type the name of your new class.**

In this example, I use the name `MyFirstJavaClass`, with no blank spaces between any of the words in the name. (Refer to Figure 3-9.)

The name in the New Java Class dialog box cannot have blank spaces. And the only allowable punctuation symbol is the underscore character (_). You can name your class `MyFirstJavaClass` or `My_First_Java_Class`, but you can't name it `My First Java Class` or `JavaClass,MyFirst`.

7. **Put a check mark in the** `public static void main(String[] args)` **check box.**

Your check mark tells Eclipse to create some boilerplate Java code.

8. **Accept the defaults for everything else in the New Java Class dialog box. (In other words, click Finish.)**

You can even ignore the "Default Package Is Discouraged" warning near the top of the dialog box.

Clicking Finish brings you back to Eclipse's workbench. Now `MyFirstProject` contains a file named `MyFirstJavaClass.java`. For your convenience, the `MyFirstJavaClass.java` file already has some code in it. Eclipse's editor displays the Java code. (See Figure 3-10.)

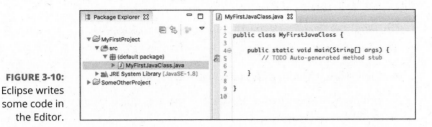

FIGURE 3-10:
Eclipse writes
some code in
the Editor.

9. **Replace an existing line of code in your new Java program.**

   Type a line of code in Eclipse's Editor. Replace the line

   ```
   // TODO Auto-generated method stub
   ```

   with the line

   ```
   System.out.println("Chocolate, royalties, sleep");
   ```

DO I SEE FORMATTING IN MY JAVA PROGRAM?

When you use Eclipse's editor to write a Java program, you see words in various colors. Certain words are always blue. Other words are always black. You even see some bold and italic phrases. You may think you see formatting, but you don't. Instead, what you see is called *syntax coloring* or *syntax highlighting*.

No matter what you call it, the issue is as follows:

- With Microsoft Word, things like bold formatting are marked inside a document. When you save MyPersonalDiary.docx, the instructions to make the words *love* and *hate* bold are recorded inside the MyPersonalDiary.docx file.

- With a Java program editor, things like bold and coloring aren't marked inside the Java program file. Instead, the editor displays each word in a way that makes the Java program easy to read.

For example, in a Java program, certain words (words like class, public, and void) have their own special meanings. So Eclipse's editor displays class, public, and void in bold, reddish letters. When I save my Java program file, the computer stores nothing about bold, colored letters in my Java program file. But the editor uses its discretion to highlight special words with reddish coloring.

Certain other editors may display the same words in a blue font. Another editor (like Windows Notepad) displays all words in plain old black.

Copy the new line of code exactly as you see it in Listing 3-1.

- Spell each word exactly the way I spell it in Listing 3-1.

- Capitalize each word exactly the way I do in Listing 3-1.

- Include all the punctuation symbols — the dots, the quotation marks, the semicolon — everything.

REMEMBER

- Distinguish between the lowercase letter l and the digit 1. The word println tells the computer to print a whole line. Each character in the word println is a lowercase letter. The word contains no digits.

LISTING 3-1: **A Program to Display the Things I Like**

```
public class MyFirstJavaClass {

    public static void main(String[] args) {
        System.out.println("Chocolate, royalties, sleep");

    }

}
```

WARNING

Java is *case-sensitive*, which means that system.out.printLn isn't the same as System.out.println. If yOu tyPe system.out.printLn, your progrAm won't worK. Be sUre to cAPItalize your codE eXactLy as it is in LiSTIng 3-1.

WARNING

If you copy and paste code from an ebook, check to make sure that the quotation marks in the code are straight quotation marks (" "), not curly quotation marks (""). In a Java program, straight quotation marks are good; curly quotation marks are troublesome.

If you typed everything correctly, you see the stuff in Figure 3-11.

FIGURE 3-11:
A Java program, in the Eclipse editor.

```
 J MyFirstJavaClass.java ⊠
 1
 2  public class MyFirstJavaClass {
 3
 4⊖     public static void main(String[] args) {
 5          System.out.println("Chocolate, royalties, sleep");
 6
 7      }
 8
 9  }
10
11
```

If you don't type the code exactly as it's shown in Listing 3-1, you may see jagged red underlines, tiny rectangles with X-like markings inside them, or other red marks in the editor. (See Figure 3-12.)

```
MyFirstJavaClass.java ⌧
 1
 2  public class MyFirstJavaClass {
 3
 4      public static void main(String[] args) {
 5          system.out.println("Chocolate, royalties, sleep");
 6
 7      }
 8
 9  }
10
11
```

FIGURE 3-12:
A Java program, typed incorrectly.

The red marks in Eclipse's editor refer to *compile-time errors* in your Java code. A compile-time error (also known as a *compiler error*) is an error that prevents the computer from translating your code. (See the talk about code translation in Chapter 1.)

TIP

The error marker in Figure 3-12 appears on line 5 of the Java program. Line numbers appear in the editor's left margin. To make Eclipse's editor display line numbers, choose Window ⇨ Preferences (in Windows) or Eclipse ⇨ Preferences (on a Mac). Then choose General ⇨ Editors ⇨ Text Editors. Finally, put a check mark in the Show Line Numbers check box.

To fix compile-time errors, you must become a dedicated detective. You join an elite squad known as *Law & Order: Java Programming Unit*. You seldom find easy answers. Instead, you comb the evidence slowly and carefully for clues. You compare everything you see in the editor, character by character, with my code in Listing 3-1. You don't miss a single detail, including spelling, punctuation, and uppercase-versus-lowercase.

Eclipse has a few nice features to help you find the source of a compile-time error. For example, you can hover the mouse pointer over the jagged red underline. When you do, you see a brief explanation of the error along with some suggestions for repairing the error — some *quick fixes*. (See Figure 3-13.)

In Figure 3-13, a pop-up message tells you that Java doesn't know what the word *system* means — that is, *system cannot be resolved*. Near the bottom of the figure, one of the quick fix options is to change *system* to *System*.

When you click that Change To 'System' (java.lang) option, Eclipse's editor replaces *system* with *System*. The editor's error markers disappear, and you go from the incorrect code in Figure 3-12 to the correct code back in Figure 3-11.

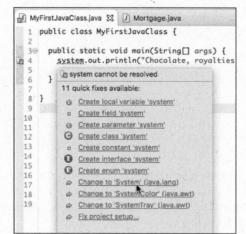

FIGURE 3-13: Eclipse offers some helpful suggestions.

10. **Make any changes or corrections to the code in Eclipse's editor.**

When at last you see no jagged underlines or blotches in the editor, you're ready to try running the program.

11. **Select** MyFirstJavaClass **either by clicking inside the editor or by clicking the** MyFirstProject **branch in the Package Explorer.**

12. **From Eclipse's main menu, choose Run ▷ Run As ▷ Java Application.**

That does the trick. Your new Java program runs in Eclipse's Console view. If you're running the code in Listing 3-1, you see the Chocolate, royalties, sleep message in Figure 3-14. It's like being in heaven!

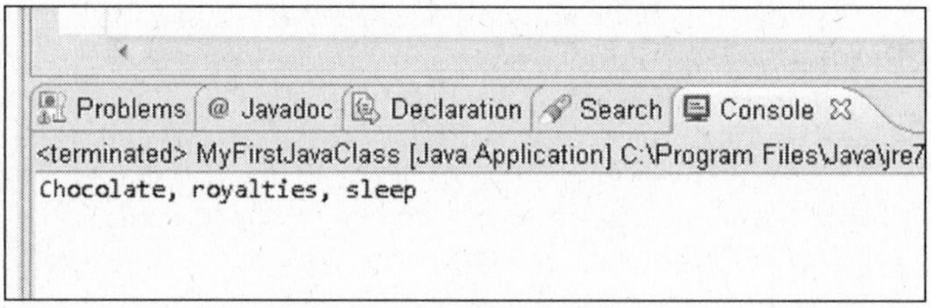

FIGURE 3-14: Running the program in Listing 3-1.

WHAT CAN POSSIBLY GO WRONG?

Ridding the editor of jagged underlines is cause for celebration. Eclipse likes the look of your code, so from that point on, it's smooth sailing. Right?

Well, it ain't necessarily so. In addition to some conspicuous compile-time errors, your code can have other, less obvious errors.

Imagine someone telling you to "go to the intersection, and then *run tight*." You notice immediately that the speaker made a mistake, and you respond with a polite "Huh?" The nonsensical *run tight* phrase is like a compile-time error. Your "Huh?" is like the jagged underlines in Eclipse's editor. As a listening human being, you may be able to guess what *run tight* means, but Eclipse's editor never dares to fix your code's mistakes.

In addition to compile-time errors, some other kinds of gremlins can hide inside a Java program:

- **Unchecked runtime exceptions:** You have no compile-time errors, but when you run your program, the run ends prematurely. Somewhere in the middle of the run, your instructions tell Java to do something that can't be done. For example, while you're running the Mortgage program in the "Running a Canned Java Program" section, you type 1,000,000.00 instead of 1000000.00. Java doesn't like the commas in the number, so your program crashes and displays a nasty-looking message, as shown in the figure.

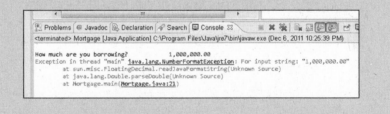

```
Problems  @ Javadoc  Declaration  Search  Console  ✕
<terminated> Mortgage [Java Application] C:\Program Files\Java\jre7\bin\javaw.exe (Dec 6, 2011 10:25:39 PM)

How much are you borrowing?      1,000,000.00
Exception in thread "main" java.lang.NumberFormatException: For input string: "1,000,000.00"
        at sun.misc.FloatingDecimal.readJavaFormatString(Unknown Source)
        at java.lang.Double.parseDouble(Unknown Source)
        at Mortgage.main(Mortgage.java:21)
```

  This is an example of an *unchecked runtime exception* — the equivalent of someone telling you to turn right at the intersection when the only thing to the right is a big brick wall. Eclipse's editor doesn't warn you about an unchecked runtime exception because, until you run the program, the computer can't predict that the exception will occur.

- **Logic errors:** You see no error markers in Eclipse's editor, and when you run your code, the program runs to completion. But the answer isn't correct. Instead of $552.20 in the figure, the output is $552,200,000.00. The program wrongly tells you to pay thousands of times what your house is worth and tells you to pay this amount each month! It's the equivalent of being told to turn right instead of turning left. You can drive in the wrong direction for a very long time.

(continued)

(continued)

```
Console 🔲    @ Javadoc    🔲 Declaration    🔎 Search
<terminated> Mortgage [Java Application] C:\Program Files\Java\jre7\

How much are you borrowing?            100000.00
What's the interest rate?              5.25
How many years are you taking to pay?  30
-------------------------------
Your monthly payment is                $552,200,000.00
```

Logic errors are the most challenging errors to find and to fix. And worst of all, logic errors often go unnoticed. In March 1985, I got a monthly home heating bill for $1,328,932.21. Clearly, some computer had printed the incorrect amount. When I called the gas company to complain about it, the telephone service representative said, "Don't be upset. Pay only half that amount."

- **Compile-time warnings:** A warning isn't as severe as an error message. So, when Eclipse notices something suspicious in your program, the editor displays a jagged yellow underline, a tiny yellow icon containing an exclamation point, and a few other not-so-intrusive clues.

For example, in the sidebar figure, I add something about amount = 10 to the code from Listing 3-1. (It's that bit on line 8.) The problem is, I never make use of amount or of the number 10 anywhere in my program. With its faint yellow markings, Eclipse effectively tells me "Your amount = 10 code isn't bad enough to be a showstopper. Eclipse can still manage to run your program. But are you sure you want amount = 10 (the stuff that seems to serve no purpose) in your program?"

```
🔲 MyFirstJavaClass.java 🔲
 1
 2  public class MyFirstJavaClass {
 3
 4⊖     public static void main(String[] args) {
 5          int amount = 10;
 6          System.out.println("Chocolate, royalties, sleep");
 7
 8      }
 9
10  }
11
```

Imagine being told to "turn when you reach the intersection." The direction may be just fine. But if you're suspicious, you ask, "Which way should I turn? Left or right?"

When you're sure that you know what you're doing, you can ignore warnings and worry about them at some later time. But a warning can be an indicator that something more serious is wrong with your code. My sweeping recommendation is this: Pay attention to warnings. But, if you can't figure out why you're getting a particular warning, don't let the warning prevent you from moving forward.

What's All That Stuff in Eclipse's Window?

Believe it or not, an editor once rejected one of my book proposals. In the margins, the editor scribbled, "This is not a word" next to things like *can't, it's,* and *I've.* To this day, I still do not know what this editor did not like about contractions. My own opinion is that language always needs to expand. Where would we be without a new words — words like *dot-com, infomercial,* and *vaporware?*

Even the *Oxford English Dictionary* (the last word in any argument about words) grows by more than 4,000 entries each year. That's an increase of more than 1 percent per year. It's about 11 new words per day!

The fact is, human thought is like a big high-rise building: You can't build the 50th floor until you've built at least part of the 49th. You can't talk about *spam* until you have a word like *email.* With all that goes on these days, you need verbal building blocks. That's why this section contains a bunch of new terms.

In this section, each newly defined term describes an aspect of the Eclipse IDE. So before you read all this Eclipse terminology, I provide the following disclaimers:

>> **This section is optional reading.** Refer to this section if you have trouble understanding some of this book's instructions. But if you have no trouble navigating the Eclipse IDE, don't complicate things by fussing over the terminology in this section.

>> **This section provides explanations of terms, not formal definitions of terms.** Yes, my explanations are fairly precise, but no, they're not airtight. Almost every description in this section has hidden exceptions, omissions, exemptions, and exclusions. Take the paragraphs in this section to be friendly reminders, not legal contracts.

>> **Eclipse is a very useful tool.** But Eclipse isn't officially part of the Java ecosystem. Although I don't describe details in this book, you can write Java programs without ever using Eclipse.

Understanding the big picture

Your tour of Eclipse begins with a big Burd's-eye view.

>> **Workbench:** The Eclipse Desktop. (Refer to Figure 3-3.) The workbench is the environment in which you develop code.

>> **Area:** A section of the workbench. The workbench in Figure 3-3 contains five areas. To illustrate the point, I've drawn borders around each of the areas. (See Figure 3-15.)

>> **Window:** A copy of the Eclipse workbench. With Eclipse, you can have several copies of the workbench open at once. Each copy appears in its own window.

>> **Action:** A choice that's offered to you — typically, when you click something. For example, when you choose File ⇨ New on Eclipse's main menu bar, you see a list of new things that you can create. The list usually includes Project, Folder, File, and Other, but it may also include things like Package, Class, and Interface. Each of these things (each item on the menu) is called an *action*.

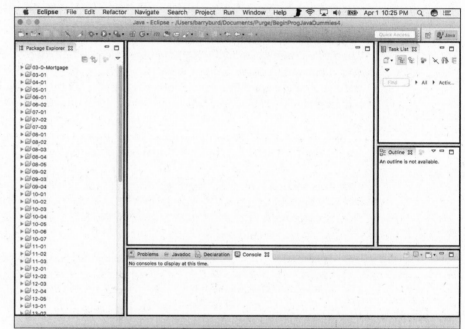

FIGURE 3-15: The workbench is divided into areas.

Views, editors, and other stuff

The next bunch of terms deals with things called views, editors, and tabs.

TIP

You may have difficulty understanding the difference between views and editors. (A view is like an editor, which is like a view, or something like that.) If views and editors seem the same to you and you're not sure that you can tell which is which, don't be upset. As an ordinary Eclipse user, the distinction between views and editors comes naturally as you gain experience using the workbench. You rarely have to decide whether the thing you're using is a view or an editor.

If you ever have to decide what a view is as opposed to an editor, here's what you need to know:

>> **View:** A part of the Eclipse workbench that displays information for you to browse. In the simplest case, a view fills up an area in the workbench. For example, in Figure 3-15 the Package Explorer view fills up the leftmost area.

Many views display information as lists or trees. For example, in Figure 3-10 the Package Explorer view contains a tree.

You can use a view to make changes to things. For example, to delete the 03–01 project listed on the left side in Figure 3-15, right-click the 03–01 branch in the Package Explorer view. (On a Mac, control-click the 03–01 branch.) Then, on the resulting context menu, choose Delete.

REMEMBER

When you use a view to change something, the change takes place immediately. For example, when you choose Delete on the Package Explorer's context menu, whatever item you've selected is deleted immediately. In a way, this behavior is nothing new. The same kind of thing happens when you recycle a file using Windows Explorer or trash a file using the Macintosh Finder.

>> **Editor:** A part of the Eclipse workbench that displays information for you to modify. A typical editor displays information in the form of text. This text can be the contents of a file. For example, an editor in Figure 3-11 displays the contents of the MyFirstJavaClass.java file.

REMEMBER

When you use an editor to change something, the change doesn't take place immediately. For example, look at the editor in Figure 3-11. This editor displays the contents of the MyFirstJavaClass.java file. You can type all kinds of things in the editor. Nothing happens to MyFirstJavaClass.java until you choose File ➪ Save from Eclipse's menu bar. Of course, this behavior is nothing new. The same kind of thing happens when you work in Microsoft Word or in any other word processing program.

TECHNICAL STUFF

Like other authors, I occasionally become lazy and use the word *view* when I really mean *view or editor*. When you catch me doing this, just shake your head and move onward. When I'm being very careful, I use the official Eclipse terminology. I refer to views and editors as *parts* of the Eclipse workbench. Unfortunately, this "parts" terminology doesn't stick in people's minds very well.

An area of the Eclipse workbench might contain several overlapping views or overlapping editors. To bring one view or editor to the forefront, you click a tab. Most Eclipse users get along fine without giving this "several views" business a second thought (or even a first thought). But if you care about the terminology surrounding tabs and active views, here's the scoop:

>> **Tab:** Something that's impossible to describe except by calling it a *tab*. That which we call a tab by any other name would move us as well from one view to another or from one editor to another. The important thing is, views can be *stacked* on top of one another. Eclipse displays stacked views as though they're pages in a tabbed notebook. For example, Figure 3-14 displays one area of the Eclipse workbench. The area contains five views (the Problems view, the Javadoc view, the Declaration view, the Search view, and the Console view). Each view has its own tab.

A bunch of stacked views is called a *tab group*. To bring a view in the stack to the forefront, you click that view's tab.

And, by the way, all this stuff about tabs and views holds true for tabs and editors. The only interesting thing is the way Eclipse uses the word *editor.* In Eclipse, each tabbed page of the editor area is an individual editor. For example, the Editor area in Figure 3-16 contains three editors (not three tabs belonging to a single editor).

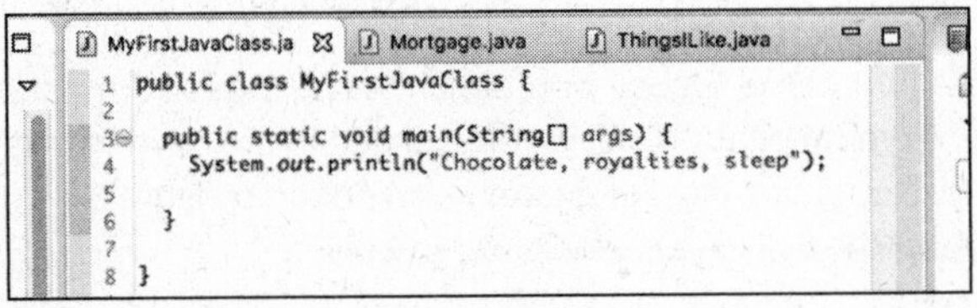

FIGURE 3-16:
The editor area
contains three
editors.

>> **Active view or active editor:** In a tab group, the view or editor that's in front.

In Figure 3-16, the MyFirstJavaClass.java editor is the active editor. The Mortgage.java and ThingsILike.java editors are inactive.

What's inside a view or an editor?

The next several terms deal with individual views, individual editors, and individual areas.

>> **Toolbar:** The bar of buttons (and other little things) at the top of a view. (See Figure 3-17.)

>> **Menu button:** A downward-pointing arrow in the toolbar. When you click the Menu button, a drop-down list of actions appears. (See Figure 3-18.) Which actions you see in the list varies from one view to another.

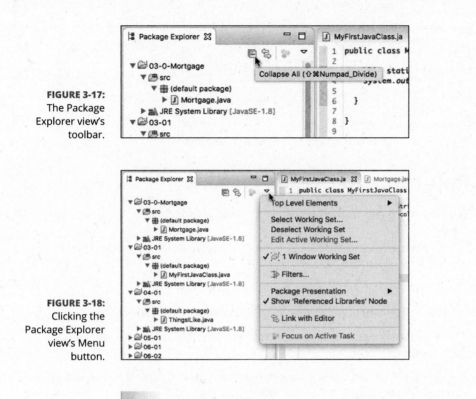

FIGURE 3-17:
The Package Explorer view's toolbar.

FIGURE 3-18:
Clicking the Package Explorer view's Menu button.

>> **Close button:** A button that gets rid of a particular view or editor. (See Figure 3-19.)

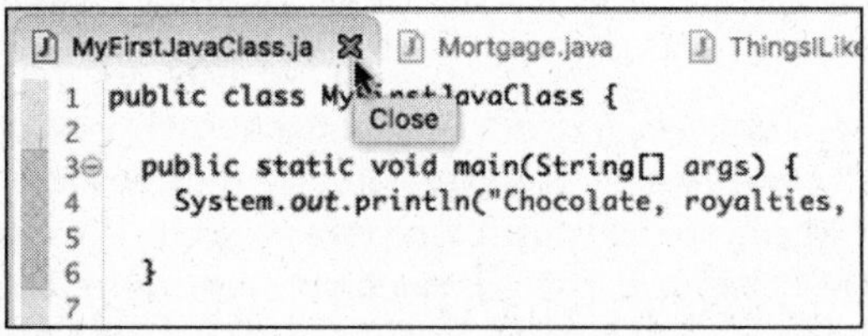

FIGURE 3-19:
An editor's Close button.

>> **Chevron:** A double arrow indicating that other tabs should appear in a particular area (but that the area isn't wide enough). The chevron in Figure 3-20 has a little number 2 beside it. The 2 tells you that, in addition to the two visible tabs, two tabs are invisible. Clicking the chevron brings up a hover tip containing the labels of all the tabs.

>> **Marker bar:** The vertical ruler on the left edge of the editor area. Eclipse displays tiny alert icons, called *markers*, inside the marker bar. (For an example, refer to Figure 3-12.)

FIGURE 3-20:
The chevron indicates that two editors are hidden.

```
MyFirstJavaClas ⊠    Mortgage.java    »₂       ─ ☐
  1  public class MyFirstJavaClass {  |ype filter text
  2
  3⊖    public static void main(Strin,  Ⓙ EchoLine.java
  4        System.out.println("Chocola  Ⓙ ThingsILike.java
  5                                     Ⓙ Mortgage.java
  6    }                                Ⓙ MyFirstJavaClass.java
  7
  8  }
  9
 10
```

Returning to the big picture

The next two terms deal with Eclipse's overall look and feel:

» **Layout:** An arrangement of certain views. The layout in Figure 3-3 has seven views, of which four are easily visible:

- At the far left, you see the Package Explorer view.

- On the far right, you have the Task List view and the Outline view.

- Near the bottom, you get the Problems, Javadoc, Declaration, and Console views.

Along with all these views, the layout contains a single *editor area*. Any and all open editors appear inside this editor area.

» **Perspective:** A very useful layout. If a particular layout is really useful, someone gives that layout a name. And if a layout has a name, you can use the layout whenever you want. For example, the workbench of Figure 3-3 displays Eclipse's Java perspective. By default, the *Java perspective* contains six views in an arrangement very much like the arrangement shown in Figure 3-3.

The Console view appears in Figure 3-3, but the Console view doesn't always appear as part of the Java perspective. Normally, the Console view appears automatically when you run a text-based Java program. If you want to force the Console view to appear, choose Window ➪ Show View ➪ Other. In the resulting Show View dialog box, expand the General branch. Finally, within that General branch, double-click the Console item.

Along with all these views, the Java perspective contains an editor area. (Sure, the editor area has several tabs, but the number of tabs has nothing to do with the Java perspective.)

You can switch among perspectives by choosing Window ➪ Open Perspective in Eclipse's main menu bar. This book focuses almost exclusively on Eclipse's Java perspective. But if you like poking around, visit some of the other perspectives to get a glimpse of Eclipse's power and versatility.

TIP

TRY IT OUT

Here are some things for you to try to help you understand the material in this chapter. If trying these things builds your confidence, that's good. If trying these things makes you question what you've read, that's good too. If trying these things makes you nervous, don't be discouraged. You can find answers and other help at this book's website (www.allmycode.com/BeginProg). You can also email me with your questions (BeginProg@allmycode.com).

Eclipse basics

Follow the instructions in this chapter's earlier section "Running a Canned Java Program." Then try the following tasks:

>> Make sure you can see the mortgage-calculating program's code in Eclipse's editor. If you don't see it, look for 03-0-Mortgage in the Package Explorer view on the left side of the Eclipse workbench. Expand the 03-0-Mortgage branch until you see a branch labeled Mortgage.java. Double-click the Mortgage.java branch.

>> In Eclipse's editor, make any change to the text in the mortgage-calculating program. After making the change, undo the change by selecting Edit ⇨ Undo from Eclipse's main menu.

>> Look for Eclipse's Console tab in the lower portion of the Eclipse workbench. If you don't see that tab, make the Console view appear by selecting Window ⇨ Show View ⇨ Console from Eclipse's main menu. (If Window ⇨ Show View ⇨ Console doesn't work, try Window ⇨ Show View ⇨ Other. In the resulting dialog box, double-click the General ⇨ Console item.)

>> The Eclipse workbench has several areas. Use the mouse to drag the boundaries between the areas (and thus resize each of the areas). To get the areas back to the way they were before resizing, select Window ⇨ Perspective ⇨ Reset Perspective from Eclipse's main menu.

>> The Eclipse workbench has several different perspectives. In this book, you use the Java perspective. Switch temporarily to the Debug perspective by selecting Window ⇨ Perspective ⇨ Open Perspective ⇨ Debug in Eclipse's main menu. Notice how the areas and views in the Eclipse workbench change. Switch back to the Java perspective by selecting Window ⇨ Perspective ⇨ Open Perspective ⇨ Java from Eclipse's main menu. (If, for some reason, Java isn't among the choices when you select Window ⇨ Perspective ⇨ Open Perspective, select Other and look for Java in the resulting dialog box.)

Experimenting with error messages

Follow the instructions in this chapter's earlier section "Running a Canned Java Program." Look for the 03-01 branch in Eclipse's Package Explorer. As you expand that 03-01 branch, look for a branch labeled MyFirstJavaClass.java. When you double-click the MyFirstJavaClass.java branch, the code for MyFirstJavaClass appears in Eclipse's editor.

>> In Eclipse's editor, change the lowercase letter c in the word class to an uppercase letter C. When you do this, notice that some red marks appear. These red marks indicate that your program has a compile-time error. Java is case-sensitive. So, in a Java program, the word Class (with an uppercase letter C) doesn't mean the same thing as the word class (with a lowercase letter c).

There are a few places in Project 03-01 where changing the capitalization doesn't cause errors. But for most of the text, a change in capitalization causes red error warnings to appear in the Eclipse editor.

>> In Eclipse's editor, change

```
System.out.println("You'll love Java!");
```

to

```
System.out.println(6/0);
```

No error markers appear in Eclipse's editor. But, when you try to run the program, you see red text in Eclipse's Console view. The red text indicates that a runtime exception has occurred. The exception occurs because Java can't divide a number by 0.

2

Writing Your Own Java Programs

Chapter **4**

Exploring the Parts of a Program

I work in the science building at a liberal arts college. When I walk past the biology lab, I always say a word of thanks under my breath. I'm thankful for not having to dissect small animals. In my line of work, I dissect computer programs instead. Computer programs smell much better than preserved dead animals. Besides, when I dissect a program, I'm not reminded of my own mortality.

In this chapter, I invite you to dissect a program with me. I have a small program, named `ThingsILike`. I cut apart the program and carefully investigate the program's innards. Get your scalpel ready. Here we go!

Checking Out Java Code for the First Time

I have a confession to make. The first time I look at somebody else's computer program, I feel a bit queasy. The realization that I don't understand something (or many things) in the code makes me nervous. I've written hundreds (maybe thousands) of programs, but I still feel insecure when I start reading someone else's code.

The truth is, learning about a computer program is a bootstrapping experience. First, I gawk in awe of the program. Then I run the program to see what it does. Then I stare at the program for a while or read someone's explanation of the program and its parts. Then I gawk a little more and run the program again. Eventually, I come to terms with the program. Don't believe the wise guys who say they never go through these steps. Even experienced programmers approach a new project slowly and carefully.

Behold! A program!

In Listing 4-1, you get a blast of Java code. Like all novice programmers, you're expected to gawk humbly at the code. But *don't be intimidated.* When you get the hang of it, programming is pretty easy. Yes, it's fun, too.

LISTING 4-1: **A Simple Java Program**

```
/*
 * A program to list the good things in life
 * Author: Barry Burd, BeginProg@allmycode.com
 * February 13, 2017
 */

class ThingsILike {

  public static void main(String args[]) {
    System.out.println("Chocolate, royalties, sleep");
  }
}
```

When I run the program in Listing 4-1, I get the result shown in Figure 4-1: The computer shows the words Chocolate, royalties, sleep on the screen. Now, I admit that writing and running a Java program is a lot of work just to get the words Chocolate, royalties, sleep to appear on somebody's computer screen, but every endeavor has to start somewhere.

FIGURE 4-1: Running the program in Listing 4-1.

```
Console 23
<terminated> ThingsILike [Java Application] C:\F
Chocolate, royalties, sleep
```

Most of the programs in this book are text-based programs. When you run one of these programs, the input and output appears in Eclipse's Console view. In contrast, a GUI (*graphical user interface*) program displays windows, buttons, text fields, and other widgets to interact with the user. You can see GUI versions of the program in Listing 4-1, and in many other examples from this book, by visiting the book's website (http://allmycode.com/BeginProg).

You can run the code in Listing 4-1 on your computer. Here's how:

1. **Follow the instructions in Chapter 2 for installing Eclipse.**

2. **Then follow the instructions in the first half of Chapter 3.**

   Those instructions tell you how to run the project named 03–01, which comes in a download from this book's website (http://allmycode.com/BeginProg). To run the code in Listing 4-1, follow the same instructions for the 04–01 project, which comes in the same download.

What the program's lines say

If the program in Listing 4-1 ever becomes famous, someone will write a *Cliffs Notes* book to summarize the program. The book will be really short because you can summarize the action of Listing 4-1 in just one sentence. Here's the sentence:

```
Display Chocolate, royalties, sleep
on the computer screen.
```

Now compare the preceding sentence with the bulk in Listing 4-1. Because Listing 4-1 has so many more lines, you may guess that it has lots of boilerplate code. Well, your guess is correct. You can't write a Java program without writing the boilerplate stuff, but, fortunately, the boilerplate text doesn't change much from one Java program to another. Here's my best effort at summarizing all the Listing 4-1 text in 66 words or fewer:

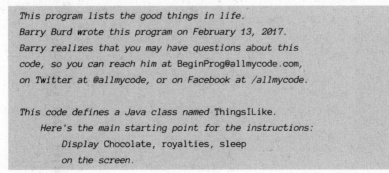
```
This program lists the good things in life.
Barry Burd wrote this program on February 13, 2017.
Barry realizes that you may have questions about this
code, so you can reach him at BeginProg@allmycode.com,
on Twitter at @allmycode, or on Facebook at /allmycode.

This code defines a Java class named ThingsILike.
    Here's the main starting point for the instructions:
        Display Chocolate, royalties, sleep
        on the screen.
```

The rest of this chapter (about 5,000 more words) explains the Listing 4-1 code in more detail.

The Elements in a Java Program

That both English and Java are called *languages* is no coincidence. You use a language to express ideas. English expresses ideas to people, and Java expresses ideas to computers. What's more, both English and Java have things like words, names, and punctuation. In fact, the biggest difference between the two languages is that Java is easier to learn than English. (If English were easy, computers would understand English. Unfortunately, they can't.)

Take an ordinary English sentence and compare it with the code in Listing 4-1. Here's the sentence:

Ann doesn't pronounce the "r" sound because she's from New York.

In your high school grammar class, you worried about verbs, adjectives, and other such things. But in this book, you think in terms of keywords and identifiers, as summarized in Figure 4-2.

Ann's sentence has all kinds of things in it. They're the same kinds of things that you find in a computer program. So here's the plan: Compare the elements in Figure 4-2 with similar elements in Listing 4-1. You already understand English, so you can use this understanding to figure out some new things about Java.

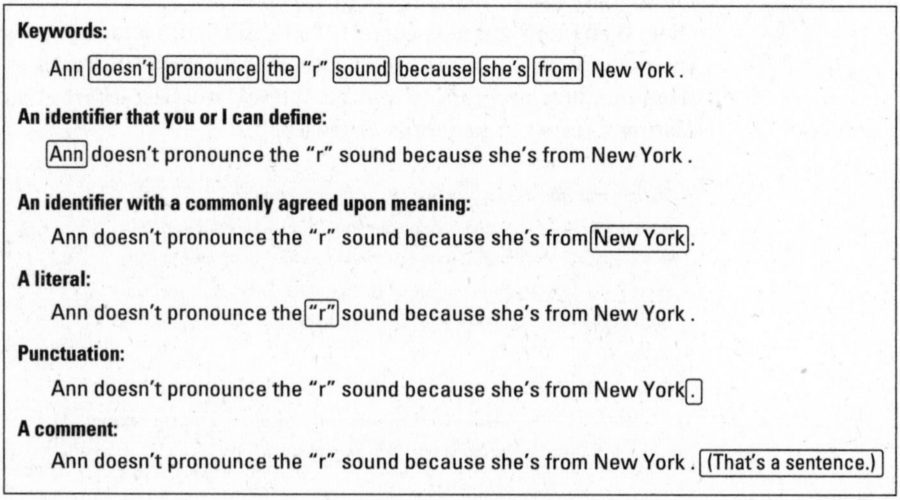

Keywords:

Ann doesn't pronounce the "r" sound because she's from New York .

An identifier that you or I can define:

Ann doesn't pronounce the "r" sound because she's from New York .

An identifier with a commonly agreed upon meaning:

Ann doesn't pronounce the "r" sound because she's from New York .

A literal:

Ann doesn't pronounce the "r" sound because she's from New York .

Punctuation:

Ann doesn't pronounce the "r" sound because she's from New York .

A comment:

Ann doesn't pronounce the "r" sound because she's from New York . (That's a sentence.)

FIGURE 4-2:
The things you find in a simple sentence.

But first, here's a friendly reminder: In the next several paragraphs, I draw comparisons between English and Java. As you read these paragraphs, keep an open mind. In comparing Java with English, I may write, "Names of things aren't the same as dictionary words." Sure, you can argue that some dictionaries list proper nouns and that some people have first names like Hope, Prudence, and Spike, but please don't. You'll get more out of the reading if you avoid nitpicking. Okay? Are we still friends?

Keywords

A *keyword* is a dictionary word — a word that's built right into a language.

In Figure 4-2, a word like "from" is a keyword because "from" plays the same role whenever it's used in an English sentence. The other keywords in Ann's sentence are "doesn't," "pronounce," "the," "sound," "because," and "she's."

Computer programs have keywords, too. In fact, the program in Listing 4-1 uses four of Java's keywords (shown in bold):

```
class ThingsILike {

    public static void main(String args[]) {
```

Each Java keyword has a specific meaning — a meaning that remains unchanged from one program to another. For example, whenever I write a Java program, the word public always signals a part of the program that's accessible to any other piece of code.

The java proGRAMMing lanGUage is *case-sensitive*. ThIS MEans that if you change a lowerCASE LETTer in a wORD TO AN UPPercase letter, you chANge the wORD'S MEaning. ChangiNG CASE CAN MakE the enTIRE WORD GO FROM BeiNG MEANINGFul to bEING MEaningless. In Listing 4-1, you can't replace public with Public. If you do, the WHOLE PROGRAM STOPS WORKING.

This chapter has little or no detail about the meanings of the keywords class, public, static, and void. You can peek ahead at the material in other chapters, or you can get along by cheating. When you write a program, just start with

```
class SomethingOrOther {
```

and then paste the text

```
public static void main(String args[]) {
```

into your code. In your first few programs, this strategy serves you well.

Table 4-1 has a complete list of Java keywords.

TABLE 4-1   ## Java Keywords

abstract	continue	for	new	switch
assert	default	goto	package	synchronized
boolean	do	if	private	this
break	double	implements	protected	throw
byte	else	import	public	throws
case	enum	instanceof	return	transient
catch	extends	int	short	try
char	final	interface	static	void
class	finally	long	strictfp	volatile
const	float	native	super	while

TECHNICAL STUFF

In Java, the words `true`, `false`, and `null` have specific meanings. As with the keywords in Table 4-1, you can't use `true`, `false`, and `null` to mean anything other than what they normally mean in a Java program. But for reasons that concern only the fussiest Java experts, `true`, `false`, and `null` are not called Java keywords. One way or another, if you scribble the words `true`, `false`, and `null` into Table 4-1, you'll be okay.

Here's one thing to remember about keywords: In Java, each keyword has an official, predetermined meaning. The people at Oracle, who have the final say on what constitutes a Java program, created all of Java's keywords. You can't make up your own meaning for any of the Java keywords. For example, you can't use the word `public` in a calculation:

```
//This is BAD, BAD CODE:
public = 6;
```

If you try to use a keyword this way, the compiler displays an error message and refuses to translate your source code. It works the same way in English. Have a baby and name it Because:

> "Let's have a special round of applause for tonight's master of ceremonies — Because O. Borel."

You can do it, but the kid will never lead a normal life.

TECHNICAL STUFF

Despite my ardent claims in this section, two of Java's keywords have no meaning in a Java program. Those keywords — const and goto — are reserved for nonuse in Java. If you try to create a variable named goto, Eclipse displays an Invalid VariableDeclaratorId error message. The creators of Java figure that if you use either of the words const or goto in your code, you should be told politely to move to the C++ programmers' table.

Identifiers that you or I can define

I like the name Ann, but if you don't like traditional names, make up a brand-new name. You're having a new baby. Call her Deneen or Chrisanta. Name him Belton or Merk.

A *name* is a word that identifies something, so I'll stop calling these things names and start calling them *identifiers*. In computer programming, an *identifier* is a noun of some kind. An identifier refers to a value, a part of a program, a certain kind of structure, or any number of things.

Listing 4-1 has two identifiers that you or I can define on our own. They're the made-up words ThingsILike and args.

```
class ThingsILike {

    public static void main(String args[]) {
```

Just as the names Ann and Chrisanta have no special meaning in English, the names ThingsILike and args have no special meaning in Java. In Listing 4-1, I use ThingsILike for the name of my program, but I could also have used a name like GooseGrease, Enzyme, or Kalamazoo. I have to put (String *someName*[]) in my program, but I could use (String args[]), (String commandLineArguments[]), or (String cheese[]).

TIP

Make up sensible, informative names for the things in your Java programs. Names like GooseGrease are legal, and they're certainly cute, but they don't help you keep track of your program-writing strategy.

REMEMBER

When I name my Java program, I can use ThingsILike or GooseGrease, but I can't use the word public. Words like class, public, static, and void are keywords in Java.

The args in (String args[]) holds anything extra that you type when you issue the command to run a Java program. For example, if you get the program to run by typing `java ThingsILike won too 3`, then `args` stores the extra values `won`, `too`, and `3`. As a beginning programmer, you don't need to think about this feature of Java. Just paste (`String args[]`) into each of your programs.

Identifiers with agreed-upon meanings

Many people are named Ann, but only one well-known city is named New York. That's because there's a standard, well-known meaning for the term "New York." It's the city that never sleeps. If you start your own city, you should avoid naming it New York because naming it New York would just confuse everyone. (I know, a town in Florida is named New York, but that doesn't count. Remember, you should ignore exceptions like this.)

Most programming languages have identifiers with agreed-upon meanings. In Java, almost all these identifiers are defined in the Java API. Listing 4-1 has five such identifiers. They're the words `main`, `String`, `System`, `out`, and `println`:

```
public static void main(String args[]) {
    System.out.println("Chocolate, royalties, sleep");
}
```

Here's a quick rundown on the meaning of each of these names (and more detailed descriptions appear throughout this book):

>> **main:** The main starting point for execution in every Java program.

>> **String:** A bunch of text; a row of characters, one after another.

>> **System:** A canned program in the Java API. This program accesses some features of your computer that are outside the direct control of the Java Virtual Machine (JVM).

>> **out:** The place where a text-based program displays its text. (For a program running in Eclipse, the word `out` represents the Console view. To read more about text-based programs, check the first several paragraphs of Chapter 3.)

>> **println:** Displays text on your computer screen.

REMEMBER

The name `println` comes from the words "print a *line*." If you were allowed to write the name in uppercase letters, it would be `PRINTLN`, with a letter `L` near the end of the word. When the computer executes `println`, the computer puts some text in Eclipse's Console view and then immediately *moves to the beginning of the next line* in preparation for whatever else will appear in the Console view.

TECHNICAL STUFF

Strictly speaking, the meanings of the identifiers in the Java API aren't cast in stone. Although you can make up your own meanings for words like `System` or `println`, doing so isn't a good idea — because you'd confuse the dickens out of other programmers, who are used to the standard API meanings for these familiar identifier names.

Literals

A *literal* is a chunk of text that looks like whatever value it represents. In Ann's sentence (refer to Figure 4-2), "r" is a literal because "r" refers to the letter *r*.

Programming languages have literals, too. For example, in Listing 4-1, the stuff in quotes is a literal:

```
System.out.println("Chocolate, royalties, sleep");
```

When you run the `ThingsILike` program, you see the words `Chocolate`, `royalties`, `sleep` on the screen. In Listing 4-1, the text `"Chocolate, royalties, sleep"` refers to these words, exactly as they appear on the screen (minus the quotation marks).

Most of the numbers that you use in computer programs are literals. If you put the statement

```
mySalary = 1000000.00;
```

in a computer program, then `1000000.00` is a literal. It stands for the number 1000000.00 (one million).

If you don't enjoy counting digits, you can put the following statement in your Java 7 program:

```
mySalary = 1_000_000.00;
```

Starting with Java 7, numbers with underscores are permissible as literals.

WARNING

In versions of Java before Java 7, you cannot use numbers such as `1_000_000.00` in your code.

TECHNICAL STUFF

Different countries use different number separators and different number formats. For example, in the United States, you write 1,234,567,890.55. In France, you write 1234567890,55. In India, you group digits in sets of two and three. You write 1,23,45,67,890.55. You can't put a statement like `mySalary = 1,000,000.00` in your Java program. Java's numeric literals don't have any commas in them. But you can write `mySalary = 10_00_000.00` for easy-to-read programming in India. And for a program's output, you can display numbers like 1234567890,55 using Java's `Locale` and `NumberFormat` classes. (For more on `Locale` and `NumberFormat`, check out Chapter 18.)

Punctuation

A typical computer program has lots of punctuation. For example, consider the program in Listing 4-1:

```
class ThingsILike {

  public static void main(String args[]) {
    System.out.println("Chocolate, royalties, sleep");
  }
}
```

Each bracket, each brace, each squiggle of any kind plays a role in making the program meaningful.

In English, you write all the way across one line and then you wrap the text to the start of the next line. In programming, you seldom work this way. Instead, the code's punctuation guides the indenting of certain lines. The indentation shows which parts of the program are subordinate to which other parts. It's as though, in English, you wrote a sentence like this:

Ann doesn't pronounce the "r" sound because

,

    as we all know

,

she's from New York.

The diagrams in Figures 4-3 and 4-4 show you how parts of the `ThingsILike` program are contained inside other parts. Notice how a pair of curly braces acts like a box. To make the program's structure visible at a glance, you indent all the stuff inside of each box.

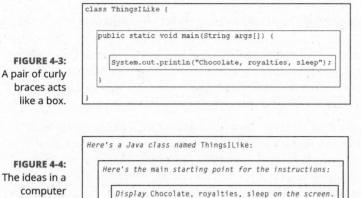

```
class ThingsILike {

    public static void main(String args[]) {

        System.out.println("Chocolate, royalties, sleep");

    }

}
```

FIGURE 4-3:
A pair of curly braces acts like a box.

```
Here's a Java class named ThingsILike:

    Here's the main starting point for the instructions:

        Display Chocolate, royalties, sleep on the screen.
```

FIGURE 4-4:
The ideas in a computer program are nested inside one another.

REMEMBER

I can't emphasize this point enough: If you don't indent your code or if you indent but you don't do it carefully, your code still compiles and runs correctly. But this successful run gives you a false sense of confidence. The minute you try to update some poorly indented code, you become hopelessly confused. Take my advice: Keep your code carefully indented at every step in the process. Make its indentation precise, whether you're scratching out a quick test program or writing code for a billionaire customer.

TIP

Eclipse can indent your code automatically for you. Select the `.java` file whose code you want to indent. Then, on Eclipse's main menu, choose Source ⇨ Format. Eclipse rearranges the lines in the editor, indenting things that should be indented and generally making your code look good.

Comments

A *comment* is text that's outside the normal flow. In Figure 4-2, the words "That's a sentence" aren't part of the Ann sentence. Instead, these words are about the Ann sentence.

The same is true of comments in computer programs. The first five lines in Listing 4-1 form one big comment. The computer doesn't act on this comment. There are no instructions for the computer to perform inside this comment. Instead, the comment tells other programmers something about your code.

Comments are for your own benefit, too. Imagine that you set aside your code for a while and work on something else. When you return later to work on the code again, the comments help you remember what you were doing.

The Java programming language has three kinds of comments:

>> **Traditional comments:** The comment in Listing 4-1 is a *traditional* comment. The comment begins with /* and ends with */. Everything between the opening /* and the closing */ is for human eyes only. Nothing between /* and */ gets translated by the compiler.

The second, third, and fourth lines in Listing 4-1 have extra asterisks. I call them "extra" because these asterisks aren't required when you create a comment. They just make the comment look pretty. I include them in Listing 4-1 because, for some reason that I don't entirely understand, most Java programmers add these extra asterisks.

>> **End-of-line comments:** Here's some code with end-of-line comments:

```
class ThingsILike {                    //Two things are missing

    public static void main(String args[]) {
        System.out.println("sleep");     // Missing from here
    }
}
```

An *end-of-line* comment starts with two slashes and extends to the end of a line of type.

TIP

You may hear programmers talk about *commenting out* certain parts of their code. When you're writing a program and something's not working correctly, it often helps to try removing some of the code. If nothing else, you find out what happens when that suspicious code is removed. Of course, you may not like what happens when the code is removed, so you don't want to delete the code completely. Instead, you turn your ordinary Java statements into comments. For example, turn System.out.println("Sleep"); into /* System.out.println("Sleep"); */. This keeps the Java compiler from seeing the code while you try to figure out what's wrong with your program.

>> **Javadoc comments:** A special *Javadoc* comment is any traditional comment that begins with an extra asterisk:

```
/**
 * Print a String and then terminate the line.
 */
```

This is a cool Java feature. The Java SE software that you download from Oracle's website includes a little program called javadoc. The javadoc program looks for these special comments in your code. The program uses these comments to create a brand-new web page — a customized documentation page for your code. To find out more about turning Javadoc comments into web pages, visit this book's website (`http://allmycode.com/BeginProg`).

Understanding a Simple Java Program

The following sections present, explain, analyze, dissect, and otherwise demystify the Java program in Listing 4-1.

What is a method?

You're working as an auto mechanic in an upscale garage. Your boss, who's always in a hurry and has a habit of running words together, says, "fixTheAlternator on that junkyOldFord." Mentally, you run through a list of tasks. "Drive the car into the bay, lift the hood, get a wrench, loosen the alternator belt," and so on. Three things are going on here:

>> **You have a name for the thing you're supposed to do.** The name is fixTheAlternator.

>> **In your mind, you have a list of tasks associated with the name fixTheAlternator.** The list includes "Drive the car into the bay, lift the hood, get a wrench, loosen the alternator belt," and so on.

>> **You have a grumpy boss who's telling you to do all this work.** Your boss gets you working by saying, "fixTheAlternator." In other words, your boss gets you working by saying the name of the thing you're supposed to do.

In this scenario, using the word *method* wouldn't be a big stretch. You have a method for doing something with an alternator. Your boss calls that method into action, and you respond by doing all the things in the list of instructions that you've associated with the method.

Java methods

If you believe all that stuff in the preceding section, you're ready to read about Java methods. In Java, a *method* is a list of things to do. Every method has a name, and you tell the computer to do the things in the list by using the method's name in your program.

I've never written a program to get a robot to fix an alternator. But, if I were to, the program might include a method named fixTheAlternator. The list of instructions in my fixTheAlternator method would look something like the text in Listing 4-2.

LISTING 4-2: **A Method Declaration**

```
void fixTheAlternator(onACertainCar) {
    driveInto(car, bay);
    lift(hood);
    get(wrench);
    loosen(alternatorBelt);
    ...
}
```

Somewhere else in my Java code (somewhere outside of Listing 4-2), I need an instruction to call my fixTheAlternator method into action. The instruction to call the fixTheAlternator method into action may look like the line in Listing 4-3.

LISTING 4-3: **Calling a Method**

```
fixTheAlternator(junkyOldFord);
```

WARNING

Don't scrutinize Listings 4-2 and 4-3 too carefully. All the lines of code in Listings 4-2 and 4-3 are fakes! I made up this code so that it looks a lot like real Java code, but it's not real. What's more important, the code in Listings 4-2 and 4-3 isn't meant to illustrate all the rules about Java. So if you have a grain of salt handy, take it with Listings 4-2 and 4-3.

TECHNICAL STUFF

Almost every computer programming language has something akin to Java's methods. If you've worked with other languages, you may remember things like subprograms, procedures, functions, subroutines, Sub procedures, or PERFORM statements. Whatever you call it in your favorite programming language, a *method* is a bunch of instructions collected together and given a new name.

The declaration, the header, and the call

If you have a basic understanding of what a method is and how it works (see preceding section), you can dig a little deeper into some useful terminology:

>> If I'm being lazy, I refer to the code in Listing 4-2 as a *method*. If I'm not being lazy, I refer to this code as a *method declaration*.

>> The method declaration in Listing 4-2 has two parts. The first line (the part with the name `fixTheAlternator` in it, up to but not including the open curly brace) is called a *method header*. The rest of Listing 4-2 (the part surrounded by curly braces) is a *method body*.

>> The term *method declaration* distinguishes the list of instructions in Listing 4-2 from the instruction in Listing 4-3, which is known as a method call.

For a handy illustration of all the method terminology, see Figure 4-5.

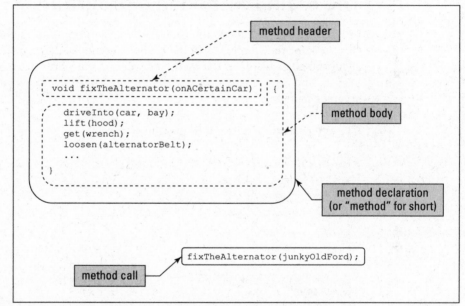

FIGURE 4-5:
The terminology describing methods.

A method's header and body are like an entry in a dictionary. An entry doesn't really use the word that it defines. Instead, an entry tells you what happens if and when you use the word:

> **chocolate** (choc-o-late) *n.* **1.** The most habit-forming substance on earth. **2.** Something you pay for with money from royalties. **3.** The most important nutritional element in a person's diet.

> **fixTheAlternator(onACertainCar)** Drive the car into the bay, lift the hood, get the wrench, loosen the alternator belt, and then eat some chocolate.

In contrast, a method call is like the use of a word in a sentence. A method call sets some code in motion:

"I want some chocolate, or I'll throw a fit."

"fixTheAlternator on that junkyOldFord."

REMEMBER

A *method's declaration* tells the computer what will happen if you call the method into action. A *method call* (a separate piece of code) tells the computer to actually call the method into action. A method's declaration and the method's call tend to be in different parts of the Java program.

The main method in a program

In Listing 4-1, the bulk of the code is the declaration of a method named main. (Just look for the word main in the code's method header.) For now, don't worry about the other words in the method header — the words public, static, void, String, and args. I explain these words (on a need-to-know basis) in the next several chapters.

Like any Java method, the main method is a recipe:

```
How to make biscuits:
    Preheat the oven.
    Roll the dough.
    Bake the rolled dough.
```

or

```
How to follow the main instructions in
the ThingsILike code:
    Display Chocolate, royalties, sleep on the screen.
```

The word main plays a special role in Java. In particular, you never write code that explicitly calls a main method into action. The word main is the name of the method that is called into action automatically when the program begins running.

When the ThingsILike program runs, the computer automatically finds the program's main method and executes any instructions inside the method's body. In the ThingsILike program, the main method's body has only one instruction. That instruction tells the computer to print Chocolate, royalties, sleep on the screen.

REMEMBER

None of the instructions in a method is executed until the method is called into action. But if you give a method the name `main`, that method is called into action automatically.

How you finally tell the computer to do something

Buried deep in the heart of Listing 4-1 is the single line that actually issues a direct instruction to the computer. The line

```
System.out.println("Chocolate, royalties, sleep");
```

tells the computer to display the words `Chocolate, royalties, sleep`. (If you use Eclipse, the computer displays `Chocolate, royalties, sleep` in the Console view.) I can describe this line of code in at least two different ways:

>> **It's a statement.** In Java, a direct instruction that tells the computer to do something is called a *statement*. The statement in Listing 4-1 tells the computer to display some text. The statements in other programs may tell the computer to put 7 in a certain memory location or make a window appear on the screen. The statements in computer programs do all kinds of things.

>> **It's a method call.** Earlier in this chapter, I describe something named a method call. The statement

```
fixTheAlternator(junkyOldFord);
```

is an example of a method call, and so is

```
System.out.println("Chocolate, royalties, sleep");
```

Java has many different kinds of statements. A method call is just one kind.

Ending a statement with a semicolon

In Java, each statement ends with a semicolon. The code in Listing 4-1 has only one statement in it, so only one line in Listing 4-1 ends with a semicolon.

Take any other line in Listing 4-1 — the method header, for example. The method header (the line with the word `main` in it) doesn't directly tell the computer to do anything. Instead, the method header describes some action for future reference. The header announces "Just in case someone ever calls the `main` method, the next few lines of code tell you what to do in response to that call."

REMEMBER

Every complete Java statement ends with a semicolon. A method call is a statement, so it ends with a semicolon, but neither a method header nor a method declaration is a statement.

The method named System.out.println

The statement in the middle of Listing 4-1 calls a method named `System.out.println`. This method is defined in the Java API. Whenever you call the `System.out.println` method, the computer displays text on its screen.

Think about names. Believe it or not, I know two people named Pauline Ott. One of them is a nun; the other is a physicist. Of course, there are plenty of Paulines in the English-speaking world, just as there are several things named `println` in the Java API. To distinguish the physicist Pauline Ott from the film critic Pauline Kael, I write the full name Pauline Ott. And to distinguish the nun from the physicist, I write "Sister Pauline Ott." In the same way, I write either `System.out.println` or `DriverManager.println`. The first (which you use often) writes text on the computer's screen. The second (which you don't use at all in this book) writes to a database log file.

Just as Pauline and Ott are names in their own right, so `System`, `out` and `println` are names in the Java API. But to use `println`, you must write the method's full name. You never write `println` alone. It's always `System.out.println` or another combination of API names.

WARNING

The Java programming language is cAsE-sEnSiTiVe. If you change a lowercase letter to an uppercase letter (or vice versa), you change a word's meaning. You can't replace `System.out.println` with `system.out.Println`. If you do, your program won't work.

Methods, methods everywhere

Two methods play roles in the `ThingsILike` program. Figure 4-6 illustrates the situation, and the next few bullets give you a guided tour.

> » **There's a declaration for a** `main` **method.** I wrote the `main` method myself. This `main` method is called automatically whenever I start running the `ThingsILike` program.

> » **There's a call to the** `System.out.println` **method.** The method call for the `System.out.println` method is the only statement in the body of the `main` method. In other words, calling the `System.out.println` method is the only thing on the `main` method's to-do list.
>
> The declaration for the `System.out.println` method is buried inside the official Java API. For a refresher on the Java API, refer to Chapter 1.

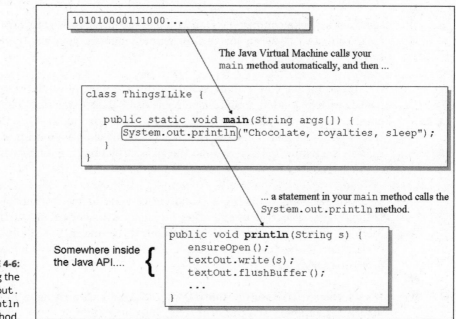

```
101010000111000...
```

The Java Virtual Machine calls your
main method automatically, and then ...

```
class ThingsILike {

    public static void main(String args[]) {
        System.out.println("Chocolate, royalties, sleep");
    }
}
```

... a statement in your main method calls the
System.out.println method.

Somewhere inside
the Java API.... {

```
public void println(String s) {
    ensureOpen();
    textOut.write(s);
    textOut.flushBuffer();
    ...
}
```

FIGURE 4-6:
Calling the
System.out.
println
method.

When I say things like "System.out.println is buried inside the API," I'm not doing justice to the API. True, you can ignore all the nitty-gritty Java code inside the API. All you need to remember is that System.out.println is defined somewhere inside that code. But I'm not being fair when I make the API code sound like something magical. The API is just another bunch of Java code. The statements in the API that tell the computer what it means to carry out a call to System.out. println look a lot like the Java code in Listing 4-1.

The Java class

Have you heard the term *object-oriented programming* (also known as *OOP*)? OOP is a way of thinking about computer programming problems — a way that's supported by several different programming languages. OOP started in the 1960s with a language called Simula. It was reinforced in the 1970s with another language, named Smalltalk. In the 1980s, OOP took off big-time with the language C++.

Some people want to change the acronym and call it COP — class-oriented programming. That's because object-oriented programming begins with something called a *class*. In Java, everything starts with classes, everything is enclosed in classes, and everything is based on classes. You can't do anything in Java until you've created a class of some kind. It's like being on *Jeopardy*, hearing Alex Trebek say, "Let's go to a commercial," and then interrupting him by saying, "I'm sorry, Alex. You can't issue an instruction without putting your instruction inside a class."

It's important for you to understand what a class really is, so I dare not give a haphazard explanation in this chapter. Instead, I devote much of Chapter 17 to the question "What is a class?" Anyway, in Java, your `main` method has to be inside a class. I wrote the code in Listing 4-1, so I got to make up a name for my new class. I chose the name `ThingsILike`, so the code in Listing 4-1 starts with the words `class ThingsILike`.

Take another look at Listing 4-1 and notice what happens after the line `class ThingsILike`. The rest of the code is enclosed in curly braces. These braces mark all the stuff inside the class. Without these braces, you'd know where the declaration of the `ThingsILike` class starts, but you wouldn't know where the declaration ends.

It's as though the stuff inside the `ThingsILike` class is in a box. (Refer to Figure 4-3.) To box off a chunk of code, you do two things:

>> **You use curly braces.** These curly braces tell the compiler where a chunk of code begins and ends.

>> **You indent code.** Indentation tells your human eye (and the eyes of other programmers) where a chunk of code begins and ends.

Don't forget. You have to do both.

THE WORDS IN A PROGRAM

TRY IT OUT

Listing 4-1 contains several kinds of words. Find out what happens when you change some of these words.

>> Change one of the keywords. For example, change the word `class` to the word `bologna`. Look for an error message in Eclipse's editor.

>> Change one of the identifiers that you or I can define. For example, change the word `args` to the word `malarkey`. After doing so, can your program still run?

The word `ThingsILike` is also a word that you or I can make up. So you can try changing the word `ThingsILike` to a different word. If you've copied the code exactly as it is in Listing 4-1, your program still runs. But if your program starts with the word `public`, as in

```
public class SomeOtherWord {
```

you might have some trouble. If you do, simply remove the word `public`.

>> Change an identifier that has an agreed-upon meaning. For example, change `println` to `display`. Look for an error message in Eclipse's editor.

>> Change the program's punctuation. For example, remove a pair of curly braces. Look for an error message in Eclipse's editor.

>> Comment out the entire `System.out.println("Chocolate, royalties, sleep");` line. (Use the end-of-line commenting style.) What happens when you run the program?

>> Comment out the entire `System.out.println("Chocolate, royalties, sleep");` line. (Use the traditional commenting style.) What happens when you run the program?

VALID IDENTIFIERS

There are limits to the kinds of names you can make up. For example, a person's name might include a dash, but it can't include a question mark. (At least it can't where I come from.) A well-known celebrity's name can be an unpronounceable symbol. But for most of us, plain old letters, dashes, and hyphens are all we can use.

What kinds of names can you make up as part of a Java program? Find out by changing the word `args` to these other words in Eclipse's editor. Which of the changes are okay, and which are not?

>> `helloThere`

>> `hello_there`

>> `args7`

>> `ar7gs`

>> `75`

>> `7args`

>> `hello there`

>> `hello-there`

>> `public`

>> `royalties`

>> @args

>> #args

>> /args

YOUR FAVORITE THINGS

Change the code in Listing 4-1 so that it displays things that *you* like. Run the program to make sure that it displays these things in the Eclipse Console view.

Chapter **5**

Composing a Program

J ust yesterday, I was chatting with my servant, RoboJeeves. (RoboJeeves is an upscale model in the RJ-3000 line of personal robotic life-forms.) Here's how the discussion went:

Me: RoboJeeves, tell me the velocity of an object after it's been falling for three seconds in a vacuum.

RoboJeeves: All right, I will. "The velocity of an object after it's been falling for three seconds in a vacuum." There, I told it to you.

Me: RoboJeeves, don't give me that smart-alecky answer. I want a number. I want the actual velocity.

RoboJeeves: Okay! "A number; the actual velocity."

Me: RJ, these cheap jokes are beneath your dignity. Can you or can't you tell me the answer to my question?

RoboJeeves: Yes.

Me: "Yes," what?

RoboJeeves: Yes, I either can or can't tell you the answer to your question.

Me: Well, which is it? Can you?

RoboJeeves: Yes, I can.

Me: Then do it. Tell me the answer.

RoboJeeves: The velocity is 153,984,792 miles per hour.

Me: (After pausing to think. . . .) RJ, I know you never make a mistake, but that number, 153,984,792, is much too high.

RoboJeeves: Too high? That's impossible. Things fall very quickly on the giant planet Mangorrrrkthongo. Now, if you wanted to know about objects falling on Earth, you should have said so in the first place.

Sometimes that robot rubs me the wrong way. The truth is, RoboJeeves does whatever I tell him to do — nothing more and nothing less. If I say "Feed the cat," then RJ says, "Feed it to whom? Which of your guests will be having cat for dinner?"

Computers Are Stupid

Handy as they are, all computers do the same darn thing. They do *exactly* what you tell them to do, and that's sometimes very unfortunate. For example, in 1962, a Mariner spacecraft to Venus was destroyed just four minutes after its launch. Why? It was destroyed because of a missing keystroke in a FORTRAN program. Around the same time, NASA scientists caught an error that could have trashed the Mercury space flights. (Yup! These were flights with people on board!) The error was a line with a period instead of a comma. (A computer programmer wrote `DO 10 I=1.10` instead of `DO 10 I=1,10`.)

With all due respect to my buddy RoboJeeves, he and his computer cousins are all incredibly stupid. Sometimes they look as though they're second-guessing us humans, but actually they're just doing what other humans told them to do. They can toss virtual coins and use elaborate schemes to mimic creative behavior, but they never really think on their own. If you say, "Jump," they do what they're programmed to do in response to the letters J-u-m-p.

So, when you write a computer program, you have to imagine that a genie has granted you three wishes. Don't ask for eternal love because, if you do, the genie will give you a slobbering, adoring mate — someone you don't like at all. And don't ask for a million dollars unless you want the genie to turn you into a bank robber.

Everything you write in a computer program has to be *precise*. Take a look at an example. . . .

A Program to Echo Keyboard Input

Listing 5-1 contains a small Java program. The program lets you type one line of characters on the keyboard. As soon as you press Enter, the program displays a second line that copies whatever you typed.

LISTING 5-1: **A Java Program**

```java
import java.util.Scanner;

class EchoLine {

    public static void main(String args[]) {
        Scanner keyboard = new Scanner(System.in);

        System.out.println(keyboard.nextLine());

        keyboard.close();
    }
}
```

REMEMBER

Most of the programs in this book are text-based programs. When you run one of these programs, the input and output appears in Eclipse's Console view. You can see GUI versions of the program in Listing 5-1 — and of many other examples from this book — by visiting the book's website (http://allmycode.com/BeginProg).

Figure 5-1 shows a run of the EchoLine code (the code in Listing 5-1). The text in the figure is a mixture of my own typing and the computer's responses.

FIGURE 5-1:
What part of the word *don't* do you not understand?

```
🖳 Console ⊠
<terminated> EchoLine [Java Application] C:
Please don't repeat this to anyone.
Please don't repeat this to anyone.
```

In Figure 5-1, I type the first line (the first Please don't repeat this to anyone line), and the computer displays the second line. Here's what happens when you run the code in Listing 5-1:

1. **At first, the computer does nothing.**

The computer is waiting for you to type something.

2. **You click inside Eclipse's Console view.**

   As a result, you see a cursor on the left edge of Eclipse's Console view, as shown in Figure 5-2.

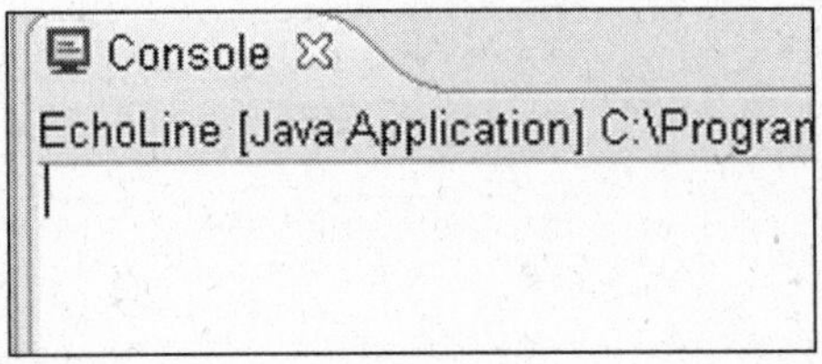

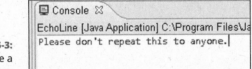

FIGURE 5-2:
The computer waits for you to type something.

3. **You type one line of text — any text at all. (See Figure 5-3.)**

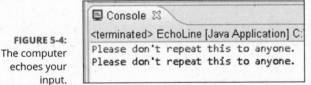

FIGURE 5-3:
You type a sentence.

4. **You press Enter, and the computer displays another copy of the line that you typed, as shown in Figure 5-4.**

FIGURE 5-4:
The computer echoes your input.

After a copy of your input is displayed, the program's run comes to an end.

Typing and running a program

This book's website (http://allmycode.com/BeginProg) has a link for downloading all the book's Java programs. After you download the programs, you can follow the instructions in Chapter 2 to add the programs to your Eclipse workspace. Then, to test the code in Listing 5-1, you can run the ready-made 05-01 project.

But instead of running the ready-made code, I encourage you to start from scratch — to type Listing 5-1 yourself and then to test your newly created code. Just follow these steps:

1. **Launch Eclipse.**

2. **From Eclipse's menu bar, choose File ➪ New ➪ Java Project.**

   Eclipse's New Java Project dialog box appears.

3. **In the dialog box's Project Name field, type** MyNewProject.

4. **Click Finish.**

   Clicking Finish brings you back to the Eclipse workbench, with MyNewProject in the Package Explorer. The next step is to create a new Java source code file.

5. **In the Package Explorer, select** MyNewProject **and then, on Eclipse's main menu, choose File ➪ New ➪ Class.**

   Eclipse's New Java Class dialog box appears.

6. **In the New Java Class dialog box's Name field, type the name of your new class.**

   In this example, use the name EchoLine. Spell EchoLine exactly the way I spell it in Listing 5-1, with a capital E, a capital L, and no blank space.

   In Java, consistent spelling and capitalization are very important — if you're not consistent within a particular program, the program will probably have some nasty, annoying compile-time errors.

WARNING

TIP

   Optionally, you can put a check mark in the box labeled public static void main(String[] args}. If you leave the box unchecked, you'll have a bit more typing to do when you get to Step 8. Either way (checked or unchecked), it's no big deal.

7. **Click Finish.**

   Clicking Finish brings you back to the Eclipse workbench. An editor in this workbench has a tab named EchoLine.java.

8. **Type the program of Listing 5-1 in the EchoLine.java editor.**

   Copy the code exactly as you see it in Listing 5-1.

   - Spell each word exactly the way I spell it in Listing 5-1.

   - Capitalize each word exactly the way I do in Listing 5-1.

   - Include all the punctuation symbols: the dots, the semicolons — everything.

   - Double-check the spelling of the word println. Make sure that each character in the word println is a lowercase letter. (In particular, the l in ln is a letter, not a digit.)

REMEMBER

The name `println` comes from the words "print a *line*." If you were allowed to write the name in uppercase letters, it would be PRINTLN, with a letter *L* near the end of the word. (Unfortunately, Java is case-sensitive. So you have to type `println`, which might look as though it contains a digit 1. It doesn't.)

If you typed everything correctly, you don't see any error markers in the editor.

If you see error markers, go back and compare everything you typed with the stuff in Listing 5-1. Compare every letter, every word, every squiggle, every smudge.

TIP

If you're reading an electronic version of this book, you might try copying directly from Listing 5-1 and pasting it into Eclipse's editor. This strategy might be okay, but you might also find that the book's electronic image contains characters that don't belong in a Java program. For example, many books use curly quotation marks (" and "), which are different from Java's straight quotation mark ("). And remember, you can download *bona fide* electronic copies of the examples in this book by visiting the book's website, `http://allmycode.com/BeginProg`.

9. **Make any changes or corrections to the code in the editor.**

When at last you see no error markers, you're ready to run the program.

10. **Select the** `EchoLine` **class by either clicking inside the editor or clicking the** `MyNewProject` **branch in the Package Explorer.**

11. **On Eclipse's main menu, choose Run ⇨ Run As ⇨ Java Application.**

Your new Java program runs, but nothing much happens.

12. **Click inside Eclipse's Console view.**

As a result, a cursor sits on the left edge of Eclipse's Console view. (Refer to Figure 5-2.) The computer is waiting for you to type something.

WARNING

If you forget to click inside the Console view, Eclipse may not send your keystrokes to the running Java program. Instead, Eclipse may send your keystrokes to the editor or (strangely enough) to the Package Explorer.

13. **Type a line of text and then press Enter.**

In response, the computer displays a second copy of your line of text. Then the program's run comes to an end. (Refer to Figure 5-4.)

If this list of steps seems a bit sketchy, you can find much more detail in Chapter 3. (Look first at the "Typing and Running Your Own Code" section in Chapter 3.) For the most part, the steps here are a quick summary of the material in Chapter 3.

So, what's the big deal when you type the program yourself? Well, lots of interesting things can happen when you apply fingers to keyboard. That's why the second half of this chapter is devoted to troubleshooting.

How the EchoLine program works

When you were a tiny newborn, resting comfortably in your mother's arms, she told you how to send characters to the computer screen:

```
System.out.println(whatever text you want displayed);
```

What she didn't tell you was how to fetch characters from the computer keyboard. There are lots of ways to do it, but the one I recommend in this chapter is

```
keyboard.nextLine()
```

Now, here's the fun part. Calling the nextLine method doesn't just scoop characters from the keyboard. When the computer runs your program, the computer *substitutes whatever you type on the keyboard* in place of the text keyboard.nextLine().

To understand this, look at the statement in Listing 5-1:

```
System.out.println(keyboard.nextLine());
```

When you run the program, the computer sees your call to nextLine and stops dead in its tracks. (Refer to Figure 5-2.) The computer waits for you to type a line of text. So (refer to Figure 5-3) you type this line:

```
Hey, there's an echo in here.
```

The computer substitutes this entire Hey line for the keyboard.nextLine() call in your program. The process is illustrated in Figure 5-5.

The call to keyboard.nextLine() is nestled inside the System.out.println call. So, when all is said and done, the computer behaves as though the statement in Listing 5-1 looks like this:

```
System.out.println("Hey, there's an echo in here.");
```

The computer displays another copy of the text Hey, there's an echo in here. on the screen. That's why you see two copies of the Hey line in Figure 5-4.

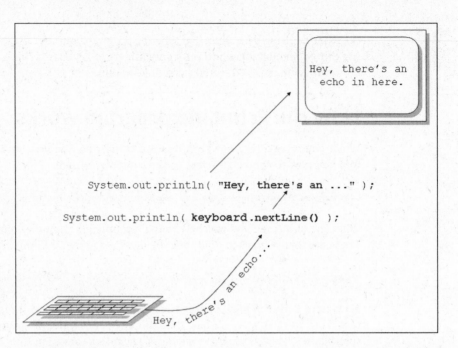

FIGURE 5-5:
The computer
substitutes text in
place of the
nextLine call.

Getting numbers, words, and other things

In Listing 5-1, the words `keyboard.nextLine()` get an entire line of text from the computer keyboard. If you type

```
Testing 1 2 3
```

the program in Listing 5-1 echoes back the entire `Testing 1 2 3` line of text.

Sometimes you don't want a program to get an entire line of text. Instead, you want the program to get a piece of a line. For example, when you type **1 2 3**, you may want the computer to get the number 1. (Maybe the number 1 stands for one customer or something like that.) In such situations, you don't put `keyboard.nextLine()` in your program. Instead, you use `keyboard.`**nextInt()**.

Table 5-1 shows you a few variations on the `keyboard.next` business. Unfortunately, the table's entries aren't very predictable. To read a line of input, you call `nextLine`. But to read a word of input, you don't call `nextWord`. (The Java API has no `nextWord` method.) Instead, to read a word, you call `next`.

Also, the table's story has a surprise ending. To read a single character, you don't call `next`*Something*. Instead, you can call the bizarre `findWithinHorizon(".",0).charAt(0)` combination of methods. (You'll have to excuse the folks who created the `Scanner` class. They created `Scanner` from a specialized point of view.)

TABLE 5-1 Some Scanner Methods

To Read This . . .	. . . Make This Method Call
A number with no decimal point in it	`nextInt()`
A number with a decimal point in it	`nextDouble()`
A word (ending in a blank space, for example)	`next()`
A line (or what remains of a line after you've already read some data from the line)	`nextLine()`
A single character (such as a letter, digit, or punctuation character)	`findWithinHorizon(".",0).charAt(0)`

To see some of the table's methods in action, check other program listings in this book. Chapters 6, 7, and 8 have some particularly nice examples.

GETTING SINGLE WORDS AND ENTIRE LINES OF TEXT

Follow the instructions in this chapter's "Typing and running a program" section, but make these two changes:

» In Step 6, type **GetInput** in the Name field of the New Java Class dialog box.

» Instead of typing the code in Listing 5-1, type the following program:

```java
import java.util.Scanner;

public class GetInput {

    public static void main(String[] args) {
        Scanner keyboard = new Scanner(System.in);

        System.out.println(keyboard.next());
        System.out.println(keyboard.next());
        System.out.println(keyboard.nextLine());

        keyboard.close();
    }
}
```

When the program runs, type the following text (all on one line) in Eclipse's Console view, and then press Enter. How does the computer respond? Why?

```
I enjoy learning Java.
```

Type three lines of code and don't look back

Buried innocently inside Listing 5-1 are three extra lines of code. These lines help the computer read input from the keyboard. The three lines are

```java
import java.util.Scanner;

        Scanner keyboard = new Scanner(System.in);

        keyboard.close();
```

Concerning these three lines, I have bad news and good news:

>> **The bad news is, the reasoning behind these lines is difficult to understand.** That's especially true here in Chapter 5, where I introduce Java's most fundamental concepts.

>> **The good news is, you don't have to understand the reasoning behind these three lines.** You can copy and paste these lines into any program that gets input from the keyboard. You don't have to change the lines in any way. These lines work without any modifications in all kinds of Java programs.

Just be sure to put these lines in the right places:

>> Make the `import java.util.Scanner` line the first line in your program.

>> Put the `Scanner keyboard = new Scanner(System.in)` line inside the `main` method immediately after the `public static void main(String args[]) {` line.

>> Make the `keyboard.close()` line the last line in your program.

At some point in the future, you may have to be more careful about the positioning of these three lines. But for now, the rules I give will serve you well.

A QUICK LOOK AT THE SCANNER

In this chapter, I advise you to ignore any of the meanings behind the lines `import java.util.Scanner` and `Scanner keyboard`, etc. Just paste these two lines mindlessly in your code and then move on.

Of course, you may not want to take my advice. You may not like ignoring things in your code. If you happen to be such a stubborn person, I have a few quick facts for you:

- **The word** Scanner **is defined in the Java API.**

  A Scanner is something you can use for getting input.

  This Scanner class belongs to Java versions 5.0 and higher. If you use version Java 1.4.2, you don't have access to the Scanner class. (You see an error marker when you type Listing 5-1.)

- **The words** System **and** in **are defined in the Java API.**

  Taken together, the words System.in stand for the computer keyboard.

  In later chapters, you see things like new Scanner(new File("myData.txt")). In those chapters, I replace System.in with the words new File("myData.txt") because I'm not getting input from the keyboard. Instead, I'm getting input from a file on the computer's hard drive.

- **The word** keyboard **doesn't come from the Java API.**

  The word keyboard is a Barry Burd creation. Instead of keyboard, you can use readingThingie (or any other name you want to use as long as you use the name consistently). So, if you want to be creative, you can write

  ```
  Scanner readingThingie = new Scanner(System.in);

  System.out.println(readingThingie.nextLine());
  ```

  The revised Listing 5-1 (with readingThingie instead of keyboard) compiles and runs without a hitch.

- **The line** import java.util.Scanner **is an example of an** *import declaration.*

  The optional import declaration allows you to abbreviate names in the rest of your program. You can remove the import declaration from Listing 5-1. But if you do, you must use the Scanner class's *fully qualified name* throughout your code. Here's how:

  ```
  class EchoLine {

    public static void main(String args[]) {

      java.util.Scanner keyboard = new java.util.Scanner(System.in);

      System.out.println(keyboard.nextLine());

      keyboard.close();
    }
  }
  ```

Expecting the Unexpected

Not long ago, I met an instructor with an interesting policy. He said, "Sometimes when I'm lecturing, I compose a program from scratch on the computer. I do it right in front of my students. If the program compiles and runs correctly on the first try, I expect the students to give me a big round of applause."

At first, you may think this guy has an enormous ego, but you have to put things in perspective. It's unusual for a program to compile and run correctly the first time. There's almost always a typo or another error of some kind.

So this section deals with the normal, expected errors that you see when you compile and run a program for the first time. Everyone makes these mistakes, even the most seasoned travelers. The key is keeping a cool head. Here's my general advice:

>> **Don't expect a program that you type to compile the first time.**

   Be prepared to return to your editor and fix some mistakes.

>> **Don't expect a program that compiles flawlessly to run correctly.**

   Even with no error markers in Eclipse's editor, your program might still contain flaws. After Eclipse compiles your program, you still have to run it successfully. That is, your program should finish its run and display the correct output.

   You compile and then you run. Getting a program to compile without errors is the easier of the two tasks.

>> **Read what's in the Eclipse editor, not what you assume is in the Eclipse editor.**

   Don't assume that you've typed words correctly, that you've capitalized words correctly, or that you've matched curly braces or parentheses correctly. Compare the code you typed with any sample code that you have. Make sure that every detail is in order.

>> **Be patient.**

   Every good programming effort takes a long time to get right. If you don't understand something right away, be persistent. Stick with it (or put it away for a while and come back to it). There's nothing you can't understand if you put in enough time.

>> **Don't become frustrated.**

   Don't throw your pie crust. Frustration (not lack of knowledge) is your enemy. If you're frustrated, you can't accomplish anything.

> » **Don't think you're the only person who's slow to understand.**
>
> I'm slow, and I'm proud of it. (Katie, Chapter 6 will be a week late.)
>
> » **Don't be timid.**
>
> If your code isn't working and you can't figure out why it's not working, ask someone. Post a message in an online forum. And don't be afraid of anyone's snide or sarcastic answer. (For a list of gestures you can make in response to peoples' snotty answers, see Appendix Z.)
>
> To ask me directly, send me an email message, tweet me, or post to me on Facebook. (Send email to BeginProg@allmycode.com, tweets to @allmycode, or posts to Facebook at /allmycode.)

Diagnosing a problem

The "Typing and running a program" section, earlier in this chapter, tells you how to run the EchoLine program. If all goes well, your screen ends up looking like the one shown in Figure 5-1. But things don't always go well. Sometimes your finger slips, inserting a typo into your program. Sometimes you ignore one of the details in Listing 5-1, and you get a nasty error message.

Of course, some things in Listing 5-1 are okay to change. Not every word in Listing 5-1 is cast in stone. Here's a nasty wrinkle: I can't tell you that you must always retype Listing 5-1 exactly as it appears. Some changes are okay; others are not. Keep reading for some "f'rinstances."

Case sensitivity

Java is case-sensitive. Among other things, *case-sensitive* means that, in a Java program, the letter P isn't the same as the letter p. If you send me some fan mail and start with "Dear barry" instead of "Dear Barry," I still know what you mean. But Java doesn't work that way.

Change just one character in a Java program and, instead of an uneventful compilation, you get a big headache! Change p to P like so:

```
//The following line is incorrect:
System.out.Println(keyboard.nextLine());
```

When you type the program in Eclipse's editor, you get the ugliness shown in Figure 5-6.

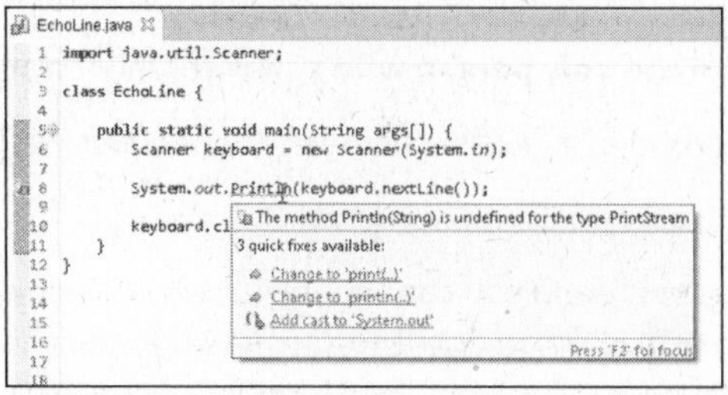

FIGURE 5-6:
The Java compiler understands `println`, but not `Println`.

When you see error markers like the ones in Figure 5-6, your best bet is to stay calm and read the messages carefully. Sometimes the messages contain useful hints. (Of course, sometimes they don't.) The message in Figure 5-6 is `The method Println(String) is undefined for the type PrintStream`. In plain English, this means "The Java compiler can't interpret the word `Println`." (The message stops short of saying, "Don't type the word `Println`, you Dummy!" In any case, if the computer says you're one of us Dummies, you should take it as a compliment.) Now, there are plenty of reasons why the compiler may not be able to understand a word like `Println`. But, for a beginning programmer, you should check two important things right away:

>> **Have you spelled the word correctly?**

Did you accidentally type `print1n` with the digit 1, instead of `println` with the lowercase letter l?

>> **Have you capitalized all letters correctly?**

Did you incorrectly type `Println` or `PrintLn` instead of `println`?

Either of these errors can send the Java compiler into a tailspin. So compare your typing with the approved typing word for word (and letter for letter). When you find a discrepancy, go back to the editor and fix the problem. Then try compiling the program again.

TIP

As you type a program in Eclipse's editor, Eclipse tries to compile the program. When Eclipse finds a compile-time error, the editor usually displays at least three red error markers. (Refer to Figure 5-6.) The marker in the editor's left margin has an X-like marking and sometimes a tiny light bulb. The marker in the right margin is a small square. The marker in the middle is a jagged red underline.

If you hover the mouse cursor over any of these markers, Eclipse displays a message that attempts to describe the nature of the error. If you hover over the jagged line, Eclipse displays a message and possibly a list of suggested solutions. (Each suggested solution is called a *quick fix*.) If you right-click the left margin's marker (or control-click on a Mac) and choose Quick Fix in the resulting context menu, Eclipse displays the suggested solutions. To have Eclipse modify your code automatically (using a suggestion from the quick-fix list), either single-click or double-click the item in the quick-fix list. (That is, single-click anything that looks like a link; double-click anything that doesn't look like a link.)

Not enough punctuation

In English and in Java, using the; proper! punctuation is important)

Take, for example, the semicolons in Listing 5-1. What happens if you forget to type a semicolon?

```
//The following code is incorrect:

    System.out.println(keyboard.nextLine())

    keyboard.close();
```

If you leave off the semicolon, you see the message shown in Figure 5-7.

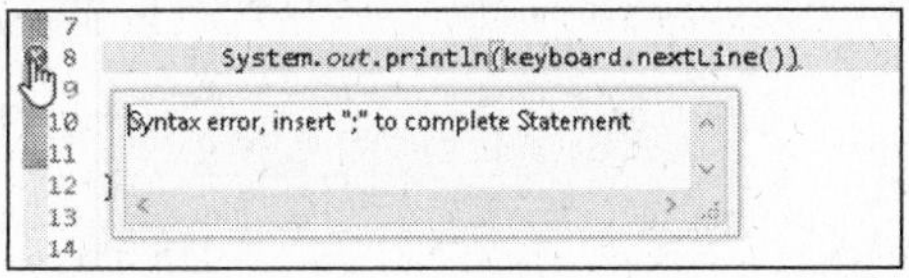

FIGURE 5-7:
A helpful error
message.

A message like the one in Figure 5-7 makes your life much simpler. I don't have to explain the message, and you don't have to puzzle over the message's meaning. Just take the message insert ";" to complete Statement at its face value. Insert the semicolon between the end of the System.out.println(keyboard. nextLine()) statement and whatever code comes after the statement. (For code that's easier to read and understand, tack on the semicolon at the end of the System.out.println(keyboard.nextLine()) statement.)

Too much punctuation

In junior high school, my English teacher said I should use a comma whenever I would normally pause for a breath. This advice doesn't work well during allergy season, when my sentences have more commas in them than words. Even as a paid author, I have trouble deciding where the commas should go, so I often add extra commas for good measure. This makes more work for my copy editor, Becky, who has a trash can full of commas by the desk in her office.

WHY CAN'T THE COMPUTER FIX IT?

How often do you get to finish someone else's sentence? "Please," says your supervisor, "go over there and connect the . . ."

"Wires," you say. "I'll connect the wires." If you know what someone means to say, why wait for her to say it?

This same question comes up in connection with computer error messages. Take a look at the message in Figure 5-7. The computer expects a semicolon after the statement on line 8. Well, Mr. Computer, if you know where you want a semicolon, just add the semicolon and be done with it. Why are you bothering me about it?

The answer is simple. The computer isn't interested in taking any chances. What if you *don't* really want a semicolon after the statement on line 8? What if the missing semicolon represents a more profound problem? If the computer added the extra semicolon, it could potentially do more harm than good.

Returning to you and your supervisor. . . .

Boom! A big explosion. "Not the wires, you Dummy. The dots. I wanted you to connect the dots."

"Sorry," you say.

It's the same way in a Java program. You can get carried away with punctuation. Consider, for example, the `main` method header in Listing 5-1. This line is a dangerous curve for novice programmers.

For information on the terms *method header* and *method body*, refer to Chapter 4.

Normally, you shouldn't end a method header with a semicolon. But people add semicolons anyway. (Maybe, in some subtle way, a method header looks like it should end with a semicolon.)

```
//The following line is incorrect:
public static void main(String args[]); {
```

If you add this extraneous semicolon to the code in Listing 5-1, you get the message shown in Figure 5-8.

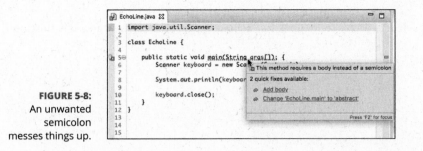

FIGURE 5-8:
An unwanted
semicolon
messes things up.

The error message and quick fixes in Figure 5-8 are a bit misleading. The message starts with `This method requires a body`. But the method has a body. Doesn't it?

When the computer tries to compile `public static void main(String args[]);` (ending with a semicolon), the computer gets confused. I illustrate the confusion in Figure 5-9. Your eye sees an extra semicolon, but the computer's eye interprets this as a method without a body. So that's the error message — the computer says `This method requires a body instead of a semicolon`.

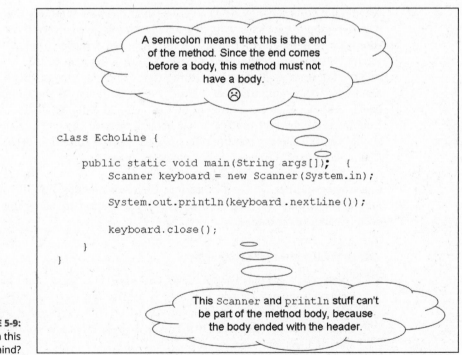

FIGURE 5-9:
What's on this
computer's mind?

If you select the Add Body quick fix, Eclipse creates the following (really horrible) code:

```java
import java.util.Scanner;

class EchoLine {

    public static void main(String args[]) {
    } {
        Scanner keyboard = new Scanner(System.in);
        System.out.println(keyboard.nextLine());
        keyboard.close();
    }
}
```

This "fixed" code has no compile-time errors. But when you run this code, nothing happens. The program starts running and then stops running with nothing in Eclipse's Console view.

We all know that a computer is a very patient, very sympathetic machine. That's why the computer looks at your code and decides to give you one more chance. The computer remembers that Java has an advanced feature in which you write a method header without writing a method body. When you do this, you get what's called an *abstract method* — something that I don't use in this book. Anyway, in Figure 5-9, the computer sees a header with no body. So the computer says to itself, "I know! Maybe the programmer is trying to write an abstract method. The trouble is, an abstract method's header has to have the word abstract in it. I should remind the programmer about that." So the computer offers the Change 'EchoLine.main' to 'abstract' quick fix in Figure 5-9.

One way or another, you can't interpret the error message and the quick fixes in Figure 5-9 without reading between the lines. So here are some tips to help you decipher murky messages:

>> **Avoid the knee-jerk response.**

Some people see the Change 'EchoLine.main' to 'abstract' quick fix in Figure 5-9 and wonder how to change EchoLine.main so that it's abstract. Unfortunately, this isn't the right approach. If you don't know what abstract means, chances are that you didn't mean to make EchoLine.main be abstract in the first place.

>> **Stare at the bad line of code for a long, long time.**

If you look carefully at the public static ... line in Figure 5-9, eventually you'll notice that it's different from the corresponding line in Listing 5-1. The line in Listing 5-1 has no semicolon, but the line in Figure 5-9 has one.

Of course, you won't always start with some prewritten code like the stuff in Listing 5-1. That's where practice makes perfect. The more code you write, the more sensitive your eyes will become to things like extraneous semicolons and other programming goofs.

Too many curly braces

You're looking for the nearest gas station, so you ask one of the locals. "Go to the first traffic light and make a left," says the local. You go straight for a few streets and see a blinking yellow signal. You turn left at the signal and travel for a mile or so. What? No gas station? Maybe you mistook the blinking signal for a real traffic light.

You come to a fork in the road and say to yourself, "The directions said nothing about a fork. Which way should I go?" You veer right, but a minute later you're forced onto a highway. You see a sign that says, Next Exit 24 Miles. Now you're really lost, and the gas gauge points to S. (The *S* stands for Stranded.)

Here's what happened: You made an honest mistake. You shouldn't have turned left at the yellow blinking light. That mistake alone wasn't so terrible. But that first mistake led to more confusion, and eventually, your choices made no sense at all. If you hadn't turned at the blinking light, you'd never have encountered that stinking fork in the road. Then getting on the highway was sheer catastrophe.

Is there a point to this story? Of course there is. A computer can get itself into the same sort of mess. The computer notices an error in your program. Then, metaphorically speaking, the computer takes a fork in the road — a fork based on the original error — a fork for which none of the alternatives leads to good results.

Here's an example. You're retyping the code in Listing 5-1, and you mistakenly type an extra curly brace:

```java
//The following code is incorrect:
import java.util.Scanner;

class EchoLine {

    public static void main(String args[]) {
        Scanner keyboard = new Scanner(System.in);
    }


        System.out.println(keyboard.nextLine());
        keyboard.close();
    }
}
```

In Eclipse's editor, you hover over the leftmost marker. You see the messages shown in Figure 5-10.

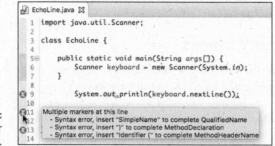

```
EchoLine.java ✕
 1  import java.util.Scanner;
 2
 3  class EchoLine {
 4
 5⊖     public static void main(String args[]) {
 6          Scanner keyboard = new Scanner(System.in);
 7      }
 8
 9          System.out.println(keyboard.nextLine());
10
11  Multiple markers at this line
12    - Syntax error, insert "SimpleName" to complete QualifiedName
13    - Syntax error, insert ")" to complete MethodDeclaration
14    - Syntax error, insert "Identifier (" to complete MethodHeaderName
```

FIGURE 5-10: Three error messages.

Eclipse is confused because some of the program's code is completely out of place. Eclipse displays three messages — something about a SimpleName, something about the parenthesis, and something concerning the MethodHeaderName. None of these messages addresses the cause of the problem. Eclipse is trying to make the best of a bad situation, but at this point, you shouldn't believe a word that Eclipse says.

Computers aren't smart animals, and if someone programs Eclipse to say insert "SimpleName" to complete QualifiedName, that's exactly what Eclipse says. (Some people say that computers make them feel stupid. For me, it's the opposite. A computer reminds me how dumb a machine can be and how smart a person can be. I like that.)

When you see a bunch of error messages, read each error message carefully. Ask yourself what you can learn from each message. But don't take each message as the authoritative truth. When you've exhausted your efforts with Eclipse's messages, return to your efforts to stare carefully at the code.

REMEMBER

If you get more than one error message, always look carefully at each message in the bunch. Sometimes a helpful message hides among a bunch of not-so-helpful messages.

Misspelling words (and other missteps)

You've found an old family recipe for deviled eggs (one of my favorites). You follow every step as carefully as you can, but you leave out the salt because of your grandmother's high blood pressure. You hand your grandmother an egg (a finished masterpiece). "Not enough pepper," she says, and she walks away.

The next course is beef bourguignon. You take an unsalted slice to dear old Granny. "Not sweet enough," she groans, and she leaves the room. "But that's impossible," you think. "There's no sugar in beef bourguignon. I left out the salt." Even so, you go back to the kitchen and prepare mashed potatoes. You use unsalted butter, of course. "She'll love it this time," you think.

"Sour potatoes! Yuck!" Granny says, as she goes to the sink to spit it all out. Because you have a strong ego, you're not insulted by your grandmother's behavior. But you're somewhat confused. Why is she saying such different things about three unsalted recipes? Maybe there are some subtle differences that you don't know about.

Well, the same kind of thing happens when you're writing computer programs. You can make the same kind of mistake twice (or at least, make what you think is the same kind of mistake twice) and get different error messages each time.

For example, if you change the spelling or capitalization of `println` in Listing 5-1, Eclipse tells you the method `is undefined for the type PrintStream`. But if you change `System` to `system`, Eclipse says that `system cannot be resolved`. And with `System` misspelled, Eclipse doesn't notice whether `println` is spelled correctly.

In Listing 5-1, if you change the spelling of `args`, nothing goes wrong. The program compiles and runs correctly. But if you change the spelling of `main`, you face some unusual difficulties. (If you don't believe me, read the "Runtime error messages" section, a little later in this chapter.)

Still in Listing 5-1, change the number of equal signs in the `Scanner keyboard = new Scanner(System.in)` line. With one equal sign, everybody's happy. If you accidentally type two equal signs (`Scanner keyboard == new Scanner(System.in)`), Eclipse steers you back on course, telling you `Syntax error on token "==", = expected`. (See Figure 5-11.) But if you go crazy and type four equal signs or if you type no equal signs, Eclipse misinterprets everything and suggests that you `insert ";" to complete BlockStatements`. Unfortunately, inserting a semicolon is no help at all. (See Figure 5-12.)

REMEMBER

Java responds to errors in many different ways. Two changes in your code might look alike, but similar changes don't always lead to similar results. Each problem in your code requires its own individualized attention.

TIP

Here's a useful exercise: Start with a working Java program. After successfully running the code, make a change that intentionally introduces errors. Look carefully at each error message and ask yourself whether the message would help you diagnose the problem. This exercise is useful because it helps you think of errors as normal occurrences and gives you practice in analyzing messages when you're not under pressure to get your program to run correctly.

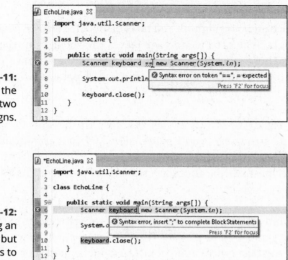

FIGURE 5-11:
Remove the second of two equal signs.

FIGURE 5-12:
You're missing an equal sign, but Eclipse fails to notice.

Runtime error messages

Up to this point in the chapter, I describe errors that crop up when you compile a program. Another category of errors hides until you run the program. A case in point is the improper spelling or capitalization of the word main.

Assume that, in a moment of wild abandon, you incorrectly spell main with a capital M:

```
//The following line is incorrect:
public static void Main(String args[]) {
```

When you type the code, everything is hunky-dory. You don't see any error markers.

But then you try to run your program. At this point, the bits hit the fan. The catastrophe is illustrated in Figure 5-13.

Sure, your program has something named Main, but does it have anything named main? (Yes, I've heard of a famous poet named e. e. cummings, but who the heck is E. E. Cummings?) The computer doesn't presume that your word Main means the same thing as the expected word main. You need to change Main back to main. Then everything will be okay.

But in the meantime (or in the "maintime"), how does this improper capitalization make it past the compiler? Why don't you get error messages when you compile the program? And if a capital M doesn't upset the compiler, why does this capital M mess everything up at runtime?

FIGURE 5-13:
Whadaya mean
"Selection does
not contain a
main type"?

```
EchoLine.java
1  import java.util.Scanner;
2
3  class EchoLine {
4
5      public static void Main(String args[]) {
6          Scanner keyboard = new Scanner(System.in);
7
8          System.out.println(keyboard.nextLine());
9
10         keyboard.close();
11     }
12 }
```

Launch Error

Selection does not contain a main type

OK

The answer goes back to the different kinds of words in the Java programming language. As I say in Chapter 4, Java has identifiers and keywords.

The keywords in Java are cast in stone. If you change `class` to `Class` or `public` to `Public`, you get something new — something that the computer probably can't understand. That's why the compiler chokes on improper keyword capitalizations. It's the compiler's job to make sure that all the keywords are used properly.

On the other hand, the identifiers can bounce all over the place. Sure, there's an identifier named `main`, but you can make up a new identifier named `Main`. (You shouldn't do it, though. It's too confusing to people who know Java's usual meaning for the word `main`.) When the compiler sees a mistyped line, like `public static void Main`, the compiler just assumes that you're making up a brand-new name. So the compiler lets the line pass. You get no complaints from your old friend, the compiler.

But then, when you try to run the code, the computer goes ballistic. The Java Virtual Machine (JVM) runs your code. (For details, see Chapter 1.) The JVM needs to find a place to start executing statements in your code, so the JVM looks for a starting point named `main`, with a small `m`. If the JVM doesn't see anything named `main`, the JVM gets upset. "Main method not found in class EchoLine," says the JVM. So at runtime, the JVM, and not the compiler, gives you an error message.

A better error message would be *main* `method not found in class EchoLine`, with a lowercase letter *m* in *main*. Here and there, the people who create the error messages overlook a detail or two.

TIP

What problem? I don't see a problem

I end this chapter on an upbeat note by showing you some of the things you can change in Listing 5-1 without rocking the boat.

The identifiers that you create

If you create an identifier, that name is up for grabs. For example, in Listing 5-1, you can change EchoLine to RepeatAfterMe:

```
class RepeatAfterMe {


    public static void main ... etc.
```

This presents no problem at all, as long as you're willing to be consistent. Just follow most of the steps in this chapter's earlier section "Typing and running a program."

>> In Step 6, instead of typing **EchoLine**, type **RepeatAfterMe** in the New Java Class dialog box's Name field.

>> In Step 8, when you copy the code from Listing 5-1, don't type

```
    class EchoLine {
```

near the top of the listing. Instead, type the words

```
    class RepeatAfterMe {
```

Rather than start your program with only the word class, you can start your program with the words public class. If you do, changing the word EchoLine to RepeatAfterMe might get you into a bit of trouble. For you, the novice programmer, the easiest solution is to remove the word public.

Spaces and indentation

Java isn't fussy about the use of spaces and indentation. All you need to do is keep your program well-organized and readable. Here's an alternative to spacing and indentation of the code in Listing 5-1:

```java
import java.util.Scanner;
class EchoLine
{
  public static void main( String args[] )
  {
    Scanner keyboard =
        new Scanner( System.in );
    System.out.println
        ( keyboard.nextLine() );
    keyboard.close();
  }
}
```

How you choose to do things

A program is like a fingerprint. No two programs look much alike. Say that I discuss a programming problem with a colleague. Then we go our separate ways and write our own programs to solve the same problem. Sure, we're duplicating the effort. But will we create the exact same code? Absolutely not. Everyone has his or her own style, and everyone's style is unique.

I asked fellow Java programmer David Herst to write his own EchoLine program without showing him my code from Listing 5-1. Here's what he wrote:

```java
import java.io.BufferedReader;
import java.io.InputStreamReader;
import java.io.IOException;

public class EchoLine {
    public static void main(String[] args) throws IOException {
        InputStreamReader isr = new InputStreamReader(System.in);
        BufferedReader br = new BufferedReader(isr);
        String input = br.readLine();
        System.out.println(input);
    }
}
```

Don't worry about BufferedReader, InputStreamReader, or things like that. Just notice that, like snowflakes, no two programs are written exactly alike, even if they accomplish the same task. That's nice. It means that your code, however different, can be as good as the next person's. That's encouraging.

COMPILE-TIME ERRORS

TRY IT OUT

The MCV vaccine helps you build an immunity to measles by giving you a mild case of measles. In the same way, you can enhance your immunity against programming errors by making mistakes intentionally in small, throwaway Java programs.

No matter how many years you spend writing code, you'll always have some programming errors in any new code you write. Even the most experienced professional programmers make mistakes. But by practicing with some simple errors, you can discover some errors that beginners make most often, and become accustomed to the "code, test, fix, code again" cycle.

Try these ways of introducing errors in Listing 5-1:

» In the word `println`, change the lowercase letter l to a digit 1.

» Move the entire `System.out.println` line so that it's above the `public static void main` line.

» Delete the parentheses around `("Chocolate, royalties, sleep")`.

» Delete the quotation marks around `"Chocolate, royalties, sleep"`.

» Break the quoted text between lines as follows:

```
System.out.println("Chocolate,
                    royalties,
                    sleep");
```

» Open your favorite word processing program (Microsoft Word, Apple Pages, or whatever) and create a document containing only the text "Chocolate, royalties, sleep". Most likely, your word processor will automatically use curly quotation marks ("") instead of straight quotation marks (""), and curly quotation marks aren't good for a Java program. So copy this curly-quoted text from your word processor. In Eclipse's editor, paste the curly-quoted text into Listing 3-1 (over in Chapter 3). Replace the original `"Chocolate, royalties, sleep"` text in that listing, straight quotation marks and all. See the kind of error messages that Eclipse displays.

ALLOWABLE CHANGES IN SPACING AND INDENTATION

You can't break a quoted string (such as `"Chocolate, royalties, sleep"`) into two or three lines. But in other parts of a Java program, line breaks don't matter. Experiment by changing the spacing and indentation in Listing 5-1. Try running this code:

```
import java.util.Scanner;
class ThingsILike
{
    public static void main (String[] args)
    {
        Scanner keyboard = new Scanner (System.in);
        System.out.println ("Chocolate, royalties, sleep");
        keyboard.close ();
    }

}
```

Chapter **6**

Using the Building Blocks: Variables, Values, and Types

Back in 1946, John von Neumann wrote a groundbreaking paper about the newly emerging technology of computers and computing. Among other things, he established one fundamental fact: For all their complexity, the main business of computers is to move data from one place to another. Take a number — the balance in a person's bank account. Move this number from the computer's memory to the computer's processing unit. Add a few dollars to the balance and then move it back to the computer's memory. The movement of data . . . that's all there is; there ain't no more.

Good enough! This chapter shows you how to move your data around.

Using Variables

Here's an excerpt from a software company's website:

> SnitSoft recognizes its obligation to the information technology community. For that reason, SnitSoft is making its most popular applications available for a nominal charge. For just $5.95 plus shipping and handling, you receive a flash drive containing SnitSoft's premier products.

Go ahead. Click the Order Now! link. Just see what happens. You get an order form with two items on it. One item is labeled $5.95 (Flash drive), and the other item reads $25.00 (Shipping and handling). What a rip-off! Thanks to Snit-Soft's generosity, you can pay $30.95 for ten cents' worth of software.

Behind the scenes of the SnitSoft web page, a computer program does some scoundrel's arithmetic. The program looks something like the code in Listing 6-1.

LISTING 6-1: **SnitSoft's Grand Scam**

```java
class SnitSoft {

    public static void main(String args[]) {
        double amount;

        amount = 5.95;
        amount = amount + 25.00;

        System.out.print("We will bill $");
        System.out.print(amount);
        System.out.println(" to your credit card.");
    }
}
```

When I run the Listing 6-1 code on my own computer (not on the SnitSoft computer), I get the output shown in Figure 6-1.

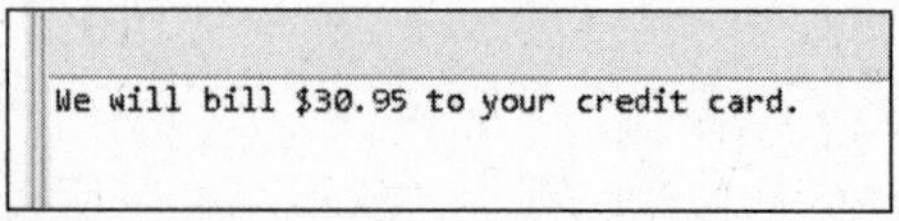

FIGURE 6-1:
Running the code
from Listing 6-1.

```
We will bill $30.95 to your credit card.
```

Using a variable

The code in Listing 6-1 makes use of a variable named amount. A *variable* is a placeholder. You can stick a number like 5.95 into a variable. After you've placed a number in the variable, you can change your mind and put a different number, like 30.95, into the variable. (That's what varies in a variable.) Of course, when you put a new number in a variable, the old number is no longer there. If you didn't save the old number somewhere else, the old number is gone.

Figure 6-2 gives a before-and-after picture of the code in Listing 6-1. When the computer executes amount = 5.95, the variable amount has the number 5.95 in it. Then, after the amount = amount + 25.00 statement is executed, the variable amount suddenly has 30.95 in it. When you think about a variable, picture a place in the computer's memory where wires and transistors store 5.95, 30.95, or whatever. In Figure 6-2, imagine that each box is surrounded by millions of other such boxes.

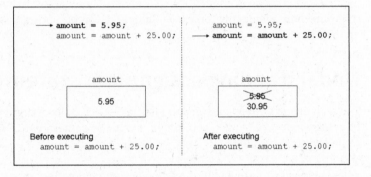

FIGURE 6-2: A variable (before and after).

Now you need some terminology. (You can follow along in Figure 6-3.) The thing stored in a variable is called a *value*. A variable's value can change during the run of a program (when SnitSoft adds the shipping and handling cost, for example). The value stored in a variable isn't necessarily a number. (You can, for example, create a variable that always stores a letter.) The kind of value stored in a variable is a variable's *type*. (You can read more about types in the rest of this chapter and in the next two chapters.)

TECHNICAL STUFF

There's a subtle, almost unnoticeable difference between a variable and a variable's *name*. Even in formal writing, I often use the word *variable* when I mean *variable name*. Strictly speaking, amount is the variable name, and all the memory storage associated with amount (including the value and type of amount) is the variable itself. If you think this distinction between *variable* and *variable name* is too subtle for you to worry about, join the club.

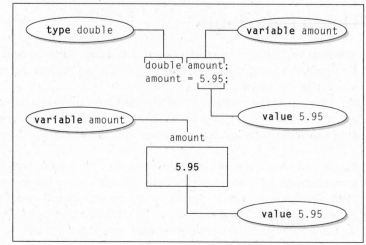

FIGURE 6-3:
A variable, its
value, and its
type.

Every variable name is an identifier — a name that you can make up in your own code (for more about this topic, see Chapter 4). In preparing Listing 6-1, I made up the name amount.

Understanding assignment statements

The statements with equal signs in Listing 6-1 are called assignment statements. In an *assignment statement*, you assign a value to something. In many cases, this something is a variable.

You should get into the habit of reading assignment statements from right to left. For example, the first assignment statement in Listing 6-1 says, "Assign 5.95 to the amount variable." The second assignment statement is just a bit more complicated. Reading the second assignment statement from right to left, you get "Add 25.00 to the value that's already in the amount variable, and make that number (30.95) be the new value of the amount variable." For a graphic, hit-you-over-the-head illustration of this, see Figure 6-4.

REMEMBER

In an assignment statement, the thing being assigned a value is always on the left side of the equal sign.

To wrap or not to wrap?

The last three statements in Listing 6-1 use a neat trick. You want the program to display just one line on the screen, but this line contains three different things:

>> The line starts with We will bill $.

>> The line continues with the `amount` variable's value.

>> The line ends with `to your credit card`.

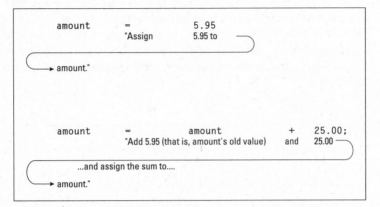

FIGURE 6-4:
Reading an assignment statement from right to left.

FORGET WHAT YOU'VE SEEN

In Listing 6-1, and in other examples throughout this book, I do something that experienced programmers avoid doing. I put actual numbers, such as 5.95 and 25.00 in my Java code. This is called *hard-coding* the values. I hard-coded values to keep these introductory programming examples as simple as possible.

But in most real-life applications, hard-coding is bad. Imagine a day when SnitSoft raises its shipping and handling fee from $25.00 to $35.00. Then the program in Listing 6-1 no longer works correctly. Someone has to launch Eclipse, look over the code, change the code, test the new code, and distribute the new code to the people who run it. What a pain! For the ten-line program in Listing 6-1, this process takes minutes. For a 10,000-line program in a real-life setting, this process might take days, weeks or months.

Instead of hard-coding values, you should type values on the keyboard during the run of the program. If that's not practical, your program can read values from a computer's hard disk. (Chapter 13 has the scoop on reading from disk files.) One way or another, you should design your program to work with all values, not only with specific values such as 5.95 and 25.00.

Keep reading this book's examples. When you see my hard-coded values, remember that I use hard-coded values to keep you from being distracted by input and output problems. I keep you focused on whatever new ideas each example has to offer. I don't do hardcoding to convince you that hard-coding is good programming practice. In fact, it's not.

These are three separate things, so you put these things in three separate statements. The first two statements are calls to System.out.print. The last statement is a call to System.out.println.

Calls to System.out.print display text on part of a line and then leave the cursor at the end of the current line. After executing System.out.print, the cursor is still at the end of the same line, so the next System.out.*whatever* can continue printing on that same line. With several calls to print capped off by a single call to println, the result is just one nice-looking line of output, as Figure 6-5 illustrates.

FIGURE 6-5:
The roles played
by System.
out.print and
System.out.
println.

```
                   print            print
We will bill $  --------→  30.95  --------→  to your credit card.  ⌐
←──────────────────────────────────────────────────────────────────┘
                                                        println
```

REMEMBER

A call to System.out.print writes some things and leaves the cursor sitting at the end of the line of output. A call to System.out.println writes things and then finishes the job by moving the cursor to the start of a brand-new line of output.

What Do All Those Zeros and Ones Mean?

Here's a word:

gift

The question for discussion is, what does that word mean? Well, it depends on who looks at the word. For example, an English-speaking reader would say that *gift* stands for something one person bestows upon another in a box covered in bright paper and ribbons:

Look! I'm giving you a **gift**!

But in German, the word *gift* means "poison:"

Let me give you some **gift**, my dear.

And in Swedish, *gift* can mean either "married" or "poison:"

As soon as they got **gift**, she slipped a **gift** into his drink.

Then there's French. In France, there's a candy bar named "Gift":

He came for the holidays, and all he gave me was a bar of **Gift**.

What do the letters g-i-f-t really mean? Well, they don't mean anything until you decide on a way to interpret them. The same is true of the zeros and ones inside a computer's circuitry.

Take, for example, the sequence 01001010. This sequence can stand for the letter *J*, but it can also stand for the number 74. That same sequence of zeros and ones can stand for $1.0369608636003646 \times 10^{-43}$. And when interpreted as screen pixels, the same sequence can represent the dots shown in Figure 6-6. The meaning of 01001010 depends entirely on the way the software interprets this sequence.

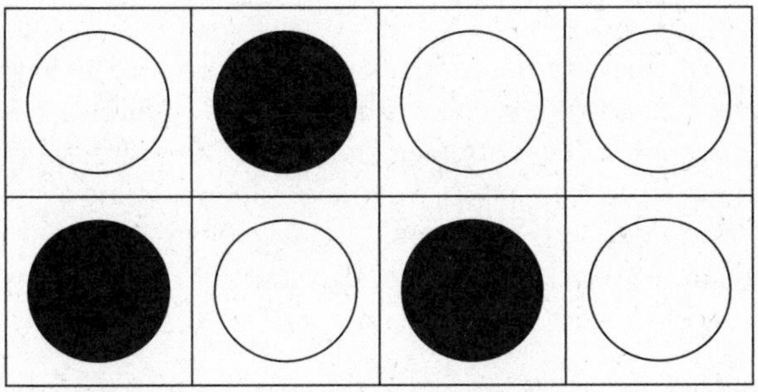

FIGURE 6-6: An extreme close-up of eight black-and-white screen pixels.

Types and declarations

How do you tell the computer what 01001010 stands for? The answer is in the concept called type. The *type* of a variable describes the kinds of values that the variable is permitted to store.

In Listing 6-1, look at the first line in the body of the `main` method:

```
double amount;
```

This line is called a *variable declaration*. Putting this line in your program is like saying, "I'm declaring my intention to have a variable named `amount` in my program." This line reserves the name `amount` for your use in the program.

In this variable declaration, the word *double* is a Java keyword. This word `double` tells the computer what kinds of values you intend to store in `amount`. In particular, the word `double` stands for numbers between -1.8×10^{308} and 1.8×10^{308}. That's an enormous range of numbers. Without the fancy ×10 notation, the second of these numbers is

```
18000000000000000000000000000000000000000000000000000000000
00000000000000000000000000000000000000000000000000000000000
00000000000000000000000000000000000000000000000000000000000
00000000000000000000000000000000000000000000000000000000000
00000000000000000000000000000000000000000000000000000000000
000000000000000000000000000000000000000000000.0
```

If the folks at SnitSoft ever charge that much for shipping and handling, they can represent the charge with a variable of type `double`.

What's the point?

More important than the humongous range of the `double` keyword's numbers is the fact that a `double` value can have digits to the right of the decimal point. After you declare `amount` to be of type `double`, you can store all sorts of numbers in `amount`. You can store 5.95, 0.02398479, or −3.0. In Listing 6-1, if I hadn't declared `amount` to be of type `double`, I wouldn't have been able to store 5.95. Instead, I would have had to store plain old 5 or dreary old 6, without any digits beyond the decimal point.

For more info on numbers without decimal points, see Chapter 7.

TECHNICAL
STUFF

This paragraph deals with a really picky point, so skip it if you're not in the mood. People often use the phrase *decimal number* to describe a number with digits to the right of the decimal point. The problem is, the syllable "dec" stands for the number 10, so the word *decimal* implies a base-10 representation. Because computers store base-2 (not base-10) representations, the word *decimal* to describe such a number is a misnomer. But in this book, I just can't help myself. I'm calling them decimal numbers, whether the techies like it or not.

TRY IT OUT

Here are some things for you to try:

NUMBER CRUNCHING

Change the number values in Listing 6-1, and run the program with the new numbers.

VARYING A VARIABLE

In Listing 6-1, change the variable name `amount` to another name. Change the name consistently throughout the Listing 6-1 code. Then run the program with its new variable name.

USING UNDERSCORES

Modify the code in Listing 6-1 so that shipping and handling costs 1 million dollars. Use 1_000_000.00 (with underscores) to represent the million-dollar amount.

MORE INFORMATION, PLEASE

Modify the code in Listing 6-1 so that it displays three values: the original price of the flash drive, the cost of shipping and handling, and the combined cost.

Reading Decimal Numbers from the Keyboard

I don't believe it! SnitSoft is having a sale! For one week only, you can get the SnitSoft flash drive for the low price of just $5.75! Better hurry up and order one.

No, wait! Listing 6-1 has the price fixed at $5.95. I have to revise the program.

I know. I'll make the code more versatile. I'll input the amount from the keyboard. Listing 6-2 has the revised code, and Figure 6-7 shows a run of the new code.

LISTING 6-2:   **Getting a Double Value from the Keyboard**

```java
import java.util.Scanner;

class VersatileSnitSoft {

    public static void main(String args[]) {
        Scanner keyboard = new Scanner(System.in);
        double amount;

        System.out.print("What's the price of a flash drive? ");
        amount = keyboard.nextDouble();
        amount = amount + 25.00;

        System.out.print("We will bill $");
        System.out.print(amount);
        System.out.println(" to your credit card.");

        keyboard.close();
    }
}
```

FIGURE 6-7:
Getting the value
of a double
variable.

```
What's the price of a flash drive? 5.75
We will bill $30.75 to your credit card.
```

WARNING

Grouping separators vary from one country to another. The run shown in Figure 6-7 is for a computer configured in the United States where 5.75 means "five and seventy-five hundredths." But the run might look different on a computer that's configured in what I call a "comma country" — a country where 5,75 means "five and seventy-five hundredths." If you live in a comma country and you type 5.75 exactly as it's shown in Figure 6-7, you probably get an error message (an InputMismatchException). If so, change the number amounts in your file to match your country's number format. When you do, you should be okay.

Though these be methods, yet there is madness in 't

Notice the call to the nextDouble method in Listing 6-2. Over in Listing 5-1, in Chapter 5, I use nextLine; but here in Listing 6-2, I use nextDouble.

In Java, each type of input requires its own, special method. If you're getting a line of text, then nextLine works just fine. But if you're reading stuff from the keyboard and you want that stuff to be interpreted as a number, you need a method like nextDouble.

To go from Listing 6-1 to Listing 6-2, I added an import declaration and some stuff about new Scanner(System.in). You can find out more about these things by reading the "Getting numbers, words, and other things" section in Chapter 5. (You can find out even more about input and output by visiting Chapter 13.) And more examples (more keyboard.next*Something* methods) are in Chapters 7 and 8.

Methods and assignments

Note how I use keyboard.nextDouble in Listing 6-2. The call to method keyboard.nextDouble is part of an assignment statement. If you look in Chapter 5 at the section on how the EchoLine program works, you see that the computer can substitute something in place of a method call. The computer does this in Listing 6-2. When you type **5.75** on the keyboard, the computer turns

```
amount = keyboard.nextDouble();
```

into

```
amount = 5.75;
```

WHO DOES WHAT, AND HOW?

When you write a program, you're called a *programmer,* but when you run a program, you're called a *user.* So when you test your own code, you're being both the programmer and the user.

Suppose that your program contains a keyboard.next*Something*( ) call, like the calls in Listings 5-1 (in Chapter 5) and 6-2. Then your program gets input from the user. But, when the program runs, how does the user know to type something on the keyboard? If the user and the programmer are the same person, and the program is fairly simple, knowing what to type is no big deal. For example, when you start running the code in Listing 5-1, you have this book in front of you, and the book says "The computer is waiting for you to type something. . . . You type one line of text. . . ." So you type the text and press Enter. Everything is fine.

But very few programs come with their own books. In many instances, when a program starts running, the user has to stare at the screen to figure out what to do next. The code in Listing 6-2 works in this stare-at-the-screen scenario. In Listing 6-2, the first call to print puts an informative message (What's the price of a flash drive?) on the user's screen. A message of this kind is called a *prompt.*

When you start writing programs, you can easily confuse the roles of the prompt and the user's input. *Remember:* No preordained relationship exists between a prompt and the subsequent input. To create a prompt, you call print or println. Then, to read the user's input, you call nextLine, nextDouble, or one of the Scanner class's other next*Something* methods. These print and next calls belong in two separate statements. Java has no commonly used, single statement that does both the prompting and the "next-ing."

As the programmer, your job is to combine the prompting and the next-ing. You can combine prompting and next-ing in all kinds of ways. Some ways are helpful to the user, and some ways aren't, as described in this list:

- **If you don't have a call to** print **or** println**, the user sees no prompt.** A blinking cursor sits quietly and waits for the user to type something. The user has to guess what kind of input to type. Occasionally that's okay, but usually it isn't.

- **If you call** print **or** println **but you don't call a** keyboard.next*Something* **method, the computer doesn't wait for the user to type anything.** The program races to execute whatever statement comes immediately after the print or println.

- **If your prompt displays a misleading message, you misled the user.** Java has no built-in feature that checks the appropriateness of a prompt. That's not surprising. Most computer languages have no prompt-checking feature.

Be careful with your prompts. Be nice to your user. Remember that you were once a humble computer user, too.

(The computer doesn't really rewrite the code in Listing 6-2. This `amount = 5.75` line simply illustrates the effect of the computer's action.) In the second assignment statement in Listing 6-2, the computer adds 25.00 to the 5.75 that's stored in `amount`.

Some method calls have this substitution effect, and others (like `System.out.println`) don't. To find out more about this topic, see Chapter 19.

Variations on a Theme

In Listing 6-1, it takes two lines to give the `amount` variable its first value:

```
double amount;
amount = 5.95;
```

You can do the same thing with just one line:

```
double amount = 5.95;
```

When you do this, you don't say that you're "assigning" a value to the `amount` variable. The line `double amount=5.95` isn't called an "assignment statement." Instead, this line is called a declaration with an *initialization*. You're *initializing* the `amount` variable. You can do all sorts of things with initializations, even arithmetic:

```
double gasBill  = 174.59;
double elecBill =  84.21;
double H2OBill  =  22.88;
double total    = gasBill + elecBill + H2OBill;
```

Moving variables from place to place

It helps to remember the difference between initializations and assignments. For one thing, you can drag a declaration with its initialization outside of a method:

```
//This is okay:
class SnitSoft {
    static double amount = 5.95;

    public static void main(String args[]) {
        amount = amount + 25.00;
```

```
        System.out.print("We will bill $");
        System.out.print(amount);
        System.out.println(" to your credit card.");
    }
}
```

You can't do the same thing with assignment statements (see the following code
and Figure 6-8):

```
//This does not compile:
class BadSnitSoftCode {
    static double amount;


    amount = 5.95;              //Misplaced statement


    public static void main(String args[]) {
        amount = amount + 25.00;

        System.out.print("We will bill $");
        System.out.print(amount);
        System.out.println(" to your credit card.");
    }
}
```

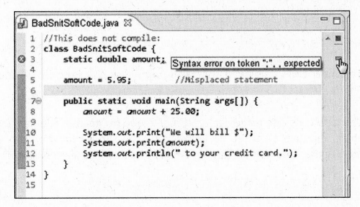

FIGURE 6-8:
A failed
attempt to
compile
BadSnit
SoftCode.

You can't drag statements outside of methods. (Even though a variable declaration
ends with a semicolon, a variable declaration isn't considered to be a statement.
Go figure!)

The advantage of putting a declaration outside of a method is illustrated in
Chapter 17. While you wait impatiently to reach that chapter, notice how I added
the word static to each declaration that I pulled out of the main method. I had to

do this because the `main` method's header has the word `static` in it. Not all methods are static. In fact, most methods aren't static. But whenever you pull a declaration out of a `static` method, you have to add the word `static` at the beginning of the declaration. All the mystery surrounding the word `static` is resolved in Chapter 18.

Combining variable declarations

The code in Listing 6-1 has only one variable (as if variables are in short supply). You can get the same effect with several variables:

```
class SnitSoftNew {

    public static void main(String args[]) {
        double flashDrivePrice;
        double shippingAndHandling;
        double total;

        flashDrivePrice = 5.95;
        shippingAndHandling = 25.00;
        total = flashDrivePrice + shippingAndHandling;

        System.out.print("We will bill $");
        System.out.print(total);
        System.out.println(" to your credit card.");
    }
}
```

This new code gives you the same output as the code in Listing 6-1. (Refer to Figure 6-1.)

The new code has three declarations — one for each of the program's three variables. Because all three variables have the same type (the type `double`), I can modify the code and declare all three variables in one fell swoop:

```
double flashDrivePrice, shippingAndHandling, total;
```

Which is better — one declaration or three declarations? Neither is better. It's a matter of personal style.

You can even add initializations to a combined declaration. When you do, each initialization applies to only one variable. For example, with the line

```
double flashDrivePrice, shippingAndHandling = 25.00, total;
```

the value of `shippingAndHandling` becomes `25.00`, but the variables `flashDrive-Price` and `total` get no particular value.

Would you like some practice with this section's concepts? You got it!

TRY IT OUT

TIP THE PARKING ATTENDANT

An online blog advises a $2 tip when a parking attendant fetches your car in a New York City garage. Write a program like the one Listing 6-2. When the program runs, you type the garage's posted price for parking your car. The program tells you how much you'll pay after adding the $2 tip.

DOUBLE PRICE

Modify the code in Listing 6-2 so that, whatever a flash drive normally costs, the program charges twice that amount. In other words, the price for a $5 flash drive ends up being $10, and the price for a $100 flash drive becomes $200.

Experimenting with JShell

The programs in this book all begin with the same old tiresome refrain:

```
class SomethingOrOther {

    public static void main(String args[]) {
```

Retyping this boilerplate code into Eclipse's editor can be annoying, especially when your goal is to test the effect of executing a few simple statements. To fix this problem, the stewards of Java came up with a new tool in Java 9. They call it JShell.

When you use JShell, you hardly ever type an entire program. Instead, you type a Java statement, and then JShell responds to your statement, and then you type a second statement, and then JShell responds to your second statement, and then you type a third statement, and so on. A single statement is enough to get a response from JShell.

JShell is only one example of a language's *Read Evaluate Print Loop* (REPL). Many programming languages have REPLs and, with Java 9, the Java language finally has a REPL of its own.

Launching the JShell program

To run JShell, make sure you have Java 9 (or a higher version of Java when it becomes available) on your computer.

To launch JShell on a Windows computer

1. Open a Command Prompt window.

In Windows 7: Press Win+R, and then type **cmd**, and then press Enter.

In Windows 8: On the Start screen, press Win+Q. In the resulting search field, type **command prompt**, and then press Enter.

In Windows 10: Choose Start ➪ Windows System ➪ Command Prompt.

2. In the Command Prompt window, type the following commands:

```
cd "\Program Files\Java"
dir jdk*
```

TIP

On some computers, you might have better luck typing cd "\Program Files (x86)\Java" for the first of the two commands. Whatever works!

The Command Prompt window responds by listing some directory names.

3. In the Command Prompt window's response, look for a directory named jdk-9, **or something like that.**

Directories whose names start with jdk1.8 or lower won't work. You must have Java 9 or higher installed in order to run JShell.

In the next step, I assume that you've found a directory named jdk-9. If your directory has a different name, adjust your typing to match that name.

4. In the Command Prompt window, type the following commands:

```
cd jdk-9\bin
jshell
```

If all goes well, the Command Prompt window displays the JShell> prompt. That's how you know that you've successfully launched JShell.

To launch JShell on a Mac

1. Press Command+spacebar, and then type Terminal, **and then press Enter.**

As a result, your computer's Terminal application starts running.

2. **In the Terminal application's window, type the following commands:**

```
cd /Library/Java/JavaVirtualMachines
dir jdk*
```

The Terminal application responds by listing some directory names.

3. **In the Terminal application's response, look for a directory named** jdk-9. jdk**, or something like that.**

Directories whose names start with jdk1.8 or lower won't work. You must have Java 9 or higher installed in order to run JShell.

In the next step, I assume that you've found a directory named jdk-9.jdk. If your directory has a different name, adjust your typing to match that name.

4. **In the Terminal application's window, type the following commands:**

```
cd jdk-9.jdk/Contents/Home/bin
./jshell
```

If all goes well, the Terminal application displays the JShell> prompt. That's how you know that you've successfully launched JShell.

Using JShell

In Figure 6-9, I use JShell to experiment with this chapter's Java concepts.

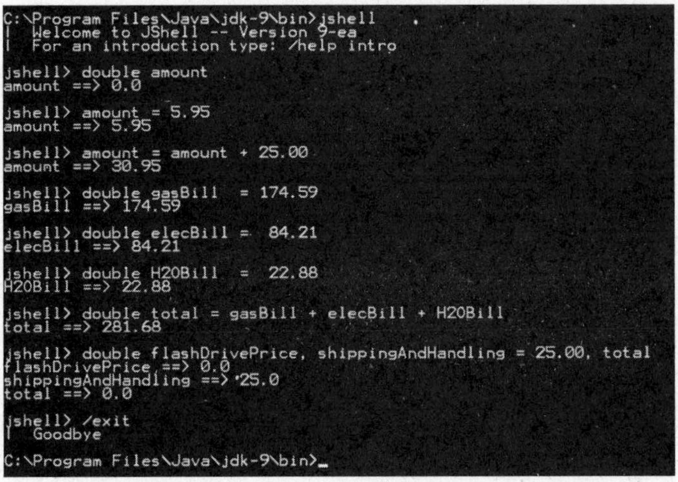

FIGURE 6-9:
An intimate
conversation
between me and
JShell.

When you run JShell, the dialogue goes something like this:

```
jshell> You type a statement
JShell responds

jshell> You type another statement
JShell responds
```

For example, in Figure 6-9, I type double amount and then press Enter. JShell responds by displaying

```
amount ==> 0.0
```

Then I type amount = 5.95, and JShell responds with

```
amount ==> 5.95
```

And then, when I type amount = amount + 25.00, JShell comes back with a friendly

```
amount ==> 30.95
```

Here are a few things to notice about JShell:

>> **You don't have to type an entire Java program.**

Typing a few statements such as

```
double amount
amount = 5.95
amount = amount + 25.00
```

does the trick. It's like running the code snippet in Listing 4-1 (except that Listing 4-1 doesn't declare amountInAccount to be a double).

>> **In JShell, semicolons are (to some extent) optional.**

In Figure 6-9, I don't bother to end any lines with semicolons.

>> **JShell responds immediately after you type each line.**

After I declare amount to be double, JShell responds by telling me that the amount variable has the value 0.0. After I type amount = amount + 25.00, JShell tells me that the new value of amount is 30.95.

Figure 6-10 illustrates a few more of JShell's nice features.

```
jshell> double gasBill = 174.59
gasBill ==> 174.59

jshell> double elecBill = 84.21
elecBill ==> 84.21

jshell> gasBill + elecBill
$3 ==> 258.8

jshell> 42 + 7
$4 ==> 49

jshell> $4 + 1
$5 ==> 50
```

FIGURE 6-10:
Using JShell to evaluate expressions.

>> **You can ask JShell for the value of an expression.**

You don't have to assign the expression's value to a variable. For example, in Figure 6-10, I type

```
gasBill + elecBill
```

JShell responds by telling me that the value of gasBill + elecBill is 258.8. JShell makes up a temporary name for that value. In Figure 6-10, the name happens to be $3.

>> **You can even get answers from JShell without using variables.**

In Figure 6-10, I ask for the value of 42 + 7, and JShell generously answers with the value 49. JShell makes up the temporary name $4 for that value 49. So, on the next line in Figure 6-10, I ask for the value of $4 +1, and JShell gives me the answer 50.

TIP

While you're running JShell, you don't have to retype commands that you've already typed. If you press the up-arrow key once, JShell shows you the command that you typed most recently. If you press the up-arrow key twice, JShell shows you the next-to-last command that you typed. And so on. When JShell shows you a command, you can use the left- and right-arrow keys to move to any character in the middle of the command. You can modify characters in the command. Finally, when you press Enter, JShell executes your newly modified command.

To end your run of JShell, you type **/exit** (starting with a slash). But /exit is only one of many commands you can give to JShell. To ask JShell what other kinds of commands you can use, type **/help**.

With JShell, you can test your statements before you put them into a full-blown Java program. That makes JShell a truly useful tool.

FUN WITH JShell

TRY IT OUT

Launch the JShell application on your computer. Type the following statements, one after another, into the JShell application, and watch how JShell responds:

```
jshell> double bananaCalories = 100.0

jshell> double appleCalories = 95.0

jshell> double dietSodaCalories = 0.0

jshell> double cheeseburgerCalories = 500.0

jshell> bananaCalories + appleCalories +
   ...> dietSodaCalories + cheeseburgerCalories
```

Notice that, in JShell, a statement can straddle two or more lines. After typing the first part of a statement

```
bananaCalories + appleCalories +
```

you press Enter. Then, on the next line, JShell doesn't display its usual `jshell>` prompt. Instead, JShell `displays` `...>`, which indicates that you should continue typing more of the same statement.

Keep JShell running in preparation for the next experiment.

MOVING WITHIN JShell

In the previous experiment, you entered the calorie counts for four food items. But because you performed that experiment, you've revised your estimate of the number of calories in a cheeseburger.

With JShell still running, press your keyboard's up-arrow key until you see the statement

```
double cheeseburgerCalories = 500.0
```

Then press the left-arrow key until the cursor is next to the 5 digit. Press your keyboard's Backspace or Delete key to get rid of the 5 digit, and then type a 7 digit in its place. Now the statement reads as follows:

```
double cheeseburgerCalories = 700.0
```

Press Enter to confirm that you want JShell to execute that revised statement.

With the value of cheeseburgerCalories changed to 700.0, use your keyboard's up arrow and down arrow to make JShell sum up the calorie counts a second time:

```
jshell> bananaCalories + appleCalories +
   ...> dietSodaCalories + cheeseburgerCalories
```

Don't retype the variable names. Let your arrow keys do the work!

Chapter **7**

Numbers and Types

Not so long ago, people thought computers did nothing but big, number-crunching calculations. Computers solved arithmetic problems, and that was the end of the story.

In the 1980s, with the widespread use of word processing programs, the myth of the big metal math brain went by the wayside. But even then, computers made great calculators. After all, computers are very fast and very accurate. Computers never need to count on their fingers. Best of all, computers don't feel burdened when they do arithmetic. I hate ending a meal in a good restaurant by worrying about the tax and tip, but computers don't mind that stuff at all. (Even so, computers seldom go out to eat.)

Using Whole Numbers

Let me tell you, it's no fun being an adult. Right now I have four little kids in my living room. They're all staring at me because I have a bag full of gumballs in my hand. With 30 gumballs in the bag, the kids are all thinking, "Who's the best? Who gets more gumballs than the others? And who's going to be treated unfairly?" They insist on a complete, official gumball count, with each kid getting exactly the same number of tasty little treats. I must be careful. If I'm not, I'll never hear the end of it.

With 30 gumballs and four kids, there's no way to divide the gumballs evenly. Of course, if I get rid of a kid, I can give 10 gumballs to each kid. The trouble is, gumballs are disposable; kids are not. So my only alternative is to divvy up what gumballs I can and dispose of the rest. "Okay, think quickly," I say to myself. "With 30 gumballs and 4 kids, how many gumballs can I promise to each kid?"

I waste no time in programming my computer to figure out this problem for me. When I'm finished, I have the code in Listing 7-1.

LISTING 7-1: **How to Keep Four Kids from Throwing Tantrums**

```java
class KeepingKidsQuiet {

    public static void main(String args[]) {
        int gumballs;
        int kids;
        int gumballsPerKid;

        gumballs = 30;
        kids = 4;
        gumballsPerKid = gumballs / kids;

        System.out.print("Each kid gets ");
        System.out.print(gumballsPerKid);
        System.out.println(" gumballs.");
    }
}
```

Figure 7-1 shows a run of the KeepingKidsQuiet program. If each kid gets seven gumballs, then the kids can't complain that I'm playing favorites. They'll have to find something else to squabble about.

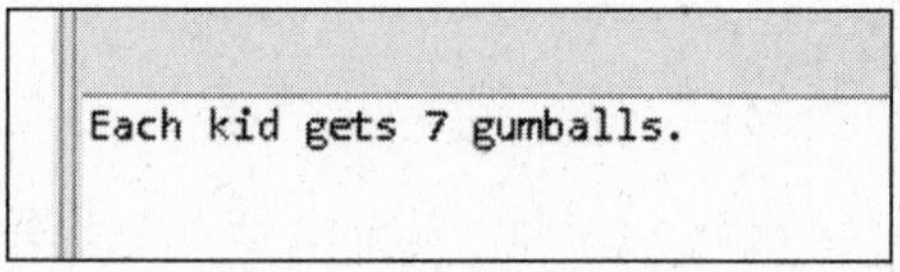

FIGURE 7-1:
Fair and square.

```
Each kid gets 7 gumballs.
```

At the core of the gumball problem, I've got whole numbers — numbers with no digits beyond the decimal point. When I divide 30 by 4, I get 7½, but I can't take the ½ seriously. No matter how hard I try, I can't divide a gumball in half, at least not without hearing "my half is bigger than his half." This fact is reflected nicely in Java. In Listing 7-1, all three variables (gumballs, kids, and gumballsPerKid) are of type int. An int value is a whole number. When you divide one int value by another (as you do with the slash in Listing 7-1), you get another int. When you divide 30 by 4, you get 7 — not 7½. You see this in Figure 7-1. Taken together, the statements

```
gumballsPerKid = gumballs/kids;

System.out.print(gumballsPerKid);
```

put the number 7 on the computer screen.

Reading whole numbers from the keyboard

What a life! Yesterday there were four kids in my living room, and I had 30 gumballs. Today there are six kids in my house, and I have 80 gumballs. How can I cope with all this change? I know! I'll write a program that reads the numbers of gumballs and kids from the keyboard. The program is in Listing 7-2, and a run of the program is shown in Figure 7-2.

LISTING 7-2:   **A More Versatile Program for Kids and Gumballs**

```java
import java.util.Scanner;

class KeepingMoreKidsQuiet {

    public static void main(String args[]) {
        Scanner keyboard = new Scanner(System.in);
        int gumballs;
        int kids;
        int gumballsPerKid;

        System.out.print("How many gumballs? How many kids? ");
        gumballs = keyboard.nextInt();
        kids = keyboard.nextInt();

        gumballsPerKid = gumballs / kids;
        System.out.print("Each kid gets ");
        System.out.print(gumballsPerKid);
        System.out.println(" gumballs.");

        keyboard.close();
    }
}
```

FIGURE 7-2:
Next thing you
know, I'll have
70 kids and 1,000
gumballs.

```
How many gumballs? How many kids? 80 6
Each kid gets 13 gumballs.
```

You should notice a couple of things about Listing 7-2. First, you can read an int value with the nextInt method. (Refer to the table in Chapter 5.) Second, you can issue successive calls to Scanner methods. In Listing 7-2, I call nextInt twice. All I have to do is separate the numbers I type by blank spaces. In Figure 7-2, I put one blank space between my 80 and my 6, but more blank spaces would work as well.

This blank-space rule applies to many of the Scanner methods. For example, here's some code that reads three numeric values:

```java
gumballs = keyboard.nextInt();
costOfGumballs = keyboard.nextDouble();
kids = keyboard.nextInt();
```

Figure 7-3 shows valid input for these three method calls.

FIGURE 7-3:
Three numbers
for three
Scanner
method calls.

```
80          7.35 6
```

What you read is what you get

When you're writing your own code, you should never take anything for granted. Suppose that you accidentally reverse the order of the gumballs and kids assignment statements in Listing 7-2:

```java
//This code is misleading:
System.out.print("How many gumballs? How many kids? ");

kids = keyboard.nextInt();
gumballs = keyboard.nextInt();
```

Here, the line How many gumballs? How many kids? is misleading. Because the kids assignment statement comes before the gumballs assignment statement, the first number you type becomes the value of kids, and the second number you type becomes the value of gumballs. It doesn't matter that your program displays the message How many gumballs? How many kids?. What matters is the order of the assignment statements in the program.

If the `kids` assignment statement accidentally comes first, you can get a strange answer, like the zero answer in Figure 7-4. That's how `int` division works. It just cuts off any remainder. Divide a small number (like 6) by a big number (like 80), and you get 0.

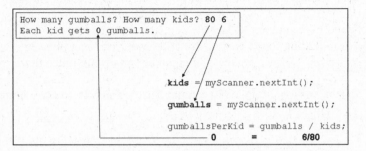

Like the mad scientist in an old horror movie, try these fascinating experiments!

TRY IT OUT

MAKE IT AND BREAK IT

Run the program in Listing 7-2. When the program asks How many gumballs? How many kids?, type **80.5 6**. (Actually, if you live in a country where 80,5 represents eighty-and-a-half, type 80,5 instead of 80.5.)

What unpleasant message do you see during this run of the program? Why do you see this message?

BREAK IT AGAIN

Run the program in Listing 7-2. When the program asks How many gumballs? How many kids?, type **"80" "6"** (quotation marks and all).

What unpleasant message do you see during this run of the program? Why do you see this message?

A TINY ADDING MACHINE

Write a program that gets two numbers from the keyboard and displays the sum of the two numbers.

Creating New Values by Applying Operators

What could be more comforting than your old friend, the plus sign? It was the first thing you learned about in elementary school math. Almost everybody knows how to add two and two. In fact, in English usage, adding two and two is a metaphor for something that's easy to do. Whenever you see a plus sign, one of your brain cells says, "Thank goodness, it could be something much more complicated."

So Java has a plus sign. You can use the plus sign to add two numbers:

```
int apples, oranges, fruit;
apples = 5;
oranges = 16;
fruit = apples + oranges;
```

Of course, the old minus sign is available, too:

```
apples = fruit - oranges;
```

Use an asterisk for multiplication and a forward slash for division:

```
double rate, pay, withholding;
int hours;

rate = 6.25;
hours = 35;
pay = rate * hours;
withholding = pay / 3.0;
```

TIP

When you divide an `int` value by another `int` value, you get an `int` value. The computer doesn't round. Instead, the computer chops off any remainder. If you put `System.out.println(11 / 4)` in your program, the computer prints 2, not 2.75. If you need a decimal answer, make either (or both) of the numbers you're dividing `double` values. For example, if you put `System.out.println(11.0 / 4)` in your program, the computer divides a `double` value, 11.0, by an `int` value, 4. Because at least one of the two values is `double`, the computer prints 2.75.

Finding a remainder

There's a useful arithmetic operator called the *remainder* operator. The symbol for the remainder operator is the percent sign (%). When you put `System.out.println(11 % 4)` in your program, the computer prints 3. It does so because 4 goes into 11 who-cares-how-many times, with a remainder of 3.

Another name for the remainder operator is the *modulus* operator.

The remainder operator turns out to be fairly useful. After all, a remainder is the amount you have left over after you divide two numbers. What if you're making change for $1.38? After dividing 138 by 25, you have 13 cents left over, as shown in Figure 7-5.

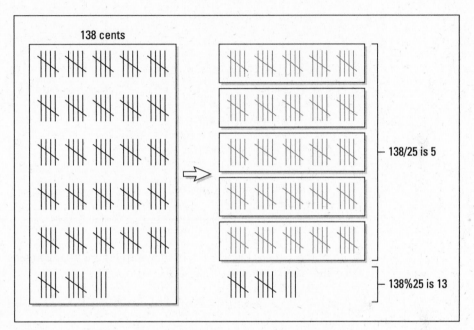

138 cents

138/25 is 5

138%25 is 13

FIGURE 7-5:
Hey, bud! Got change for 138 sticks?

The code in Listing 7-3 makes use of this remainder idea.

LISTING 7-3: **Making Change**

```java
import java.util.Scanner;

class MakeChange {

    public static void main(String args[]) {
        Scanner keyboard = new Scanner(System.in);
        int quarters, dimes, nickels, cents;
        int whatsLeft, total;

        System.out.print("How many cents do you have? ");
        total = keyboard.nextInt();
```

(continued)

LISTING 7-3: **(continued)**

```
        quarters = total / 25;
        whatsLeft = total % 25;

        dimes = whatsLeft / 10;
        whatsLeft = whatsLeft % 10;

        nickels = whatsLeft / 5;
        whatsLeft = whatsLeft % 5;

        cents = whatsLeft;

        System.out.println();
        System.out.println("From " + total + " cents you get");
        System.out.println(quarters + " quarters");
        System.out.println(dimes + " dimes");
        System.out.println(nickels + " nickels");
        System.out.println(cents + " cents");

        keyboard.close();
    }
}
```

A run of the code in Listing 7-3 is shown in Figure 7-6. You start with a total of 138 cents. The statement

```
quarters = total / 25;
```

divides 138 by 25, giving 5. That means you can make 5 quarters from 138 cents. Next, the statement

```
whatsLeft = total % 25;
```

divides 138 by 25 again, and puts only the remainder, 13, into whatsLeft. Now you're ready for the next step, which is to take as many dimes as you can out of 13 cents.

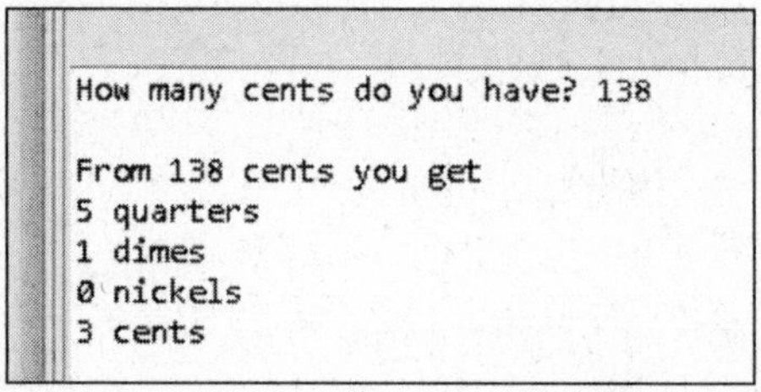

```
How many cents do you have? 138

From 138 cents you get
5 quarters
1 dimes
0 nickels
3 cents
```

FIGURE 7-6:
Change for $1.38.

You keep going like this until you've divided away all the nickels. At that point, the value of `whatsLeft` is just 3 (meaning 3 cents).

The code in Listing 7-3 makes change in U.S. currency with the following coin denominations: 1 cent, 5 cents (one nickel), 10 cents (one dime), and 25 cents (one quarter). With these denominations, the `MakeChange` program gives you more than simply a set of coins adding up to 138 cents. The `MakeChange` class gives you the *smallest number of coins* that add up to 138 cents. With some minor tweaking, you can make the code work in any country's coinage. You can always get a set of coins adding up to a total. But, for the denominations of coins in some countries, you won't always get the *smallest number of coins* that add up to a total. In fact, I'm looking for examples. If your country's coinage prevents `MakeChange` from always giving the best answer, please, send me an email (`BeginProg@allmycode.com`), tweet to `@allmycode`, or post on Facebook at `/allmycode`. Thanks.

IF THINE INT OFFENDS THEE, CAST IT OUT

The run in Figure 7-6 seems artificial. Why would you start with 138 cents? Why not use the more familiar $1.38? The reason is that the number 1.38 isn't a whole number, and whole numbers are more accurate than other kinds of numbers. In fact, without whole numbers, the remainder operator isn't very useful. For example, the value of `1.38 % 0.25` is `0.1299999999999999`. All those nines are tough to work with. Imagine reading your credit card statement and seeing that you owe $0.1299999999999999. You'd probably pay $0.13 and let the credit card company keep the change. But after years of rounding numbers, the credit card company would make a fortune! Chapter 8 describes, in a bit more detail, inaccuracies that may come from using `double` values.

Throughout this book, I illustrate Java's `double` type with programs about money. Many authors do the same thing. But for greater accuracy, avoid using `double` values for money. Instead, you should use `int` values or use the `long` values that I describe in the last section of this chapter. Even better, look up `BigInteger` and `BigDecimal` in Java's API documentation. These `BigSomethingOrOther` types are cumbersome to use, but they provide industrial-strength numeric range and accuracy.

Now, what if you want to input `1.38` and then have the program take your 1.38 and turn it into 138 cents? How can you get your program to do this?

My first idea is to multiply 1.38 by 100:

```
//This doesn't quite work.
double amount;
```

(continued)

(continued)

```
int total;
amount=keyboard.nextDouble();
total=amount*100;
```

In everyday arithmetic, multiplying by 100 does the trick. But computers are fussy. With a computer, you have to be very careful when you mix int values and double values. (See the first figure in this sidebar.)

To cram a double value into an int variable, you need something called *casting*. When you *cast* a value, you essentially say, "I'm aware that I'm trying to squish a double value into an int variable. It's a tight fit, but I want to do it anyway."

To do casting, you put the name of a type in parentheses, as follows:

```
//This works!
total = (int) (amount * 100);
```

This casting notation turns the double value 138.00 into the int value 138, and everybody's happy. (See the second figure in this sidebar.)

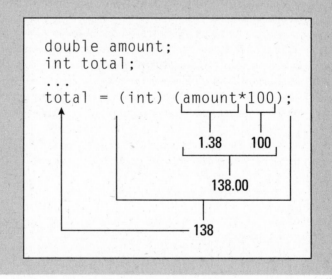

When two or more variables have similar types, you can create the variables with combined declarations. For example, Listing 7-3 has two combined declarations — one for the variables quarters, dimes, nickels, and cents (all of type int); another for the variables whatsLeft and total (both of type int). But to create variables of different types, you need separate declarations. For example, to create an int variable named total and a double variable named amount, you need one declaration int total; and another declaration double amount;.

Listing 7-3 has a call to System.out.println() with nothing in the parentheses. When the computer executes this statement, the cursor jumps to a new line on the screen. (I often use this statement to put a blank line in a program's output.)

JAVA ARITHMETIC

What's the value of each of the following expressions? Type each expression on a separate line in JShell to find out whether your answers are correct:

```
10 / 3

10 % 3

3 / 10

3 % 10

8 * 3 + 4

4 + 8 * 3

8 * (3 + 4)

34 % 5 - 2 * 2 + 21 / 5
```

VARIABLE VALUES

What's the value of each of the following variables (a, b, c, and so on)? Type each statement on a separate line in JShell to find out whether your answers are correct:

```
int a = 8

int b = 3

int c = b / a
```

```
int d = a / b

int e = a % b

int f = 5 + e * d - 2
```

HIRING A PLUMBER

A local plumber charges $75 to come to my house. In addition, for every hour the plumber works at my house, the plumber charges an additional $125. Write a program that inputs the number of hours that a plumber works at my house, and outputs the total amount that the plumber charges.

MAKING CHANGE AGAIN

Modify the code in Listing 7-3 so that it starts by getting a number of dollars and a number of cents from the keyboard. For example, instead of typing **138** (meaning 138 cents), the user types **1 38** (1 dollar and 38 cents).

HOW TALL AM I?

Where I come from, we don't use metric measurements. Instead, we measure each person's height in feet and inches. A foot is 12 inches, and I'm five-and-a-half feet tall. (My height in feet is the double value 5.5.) Write a program to find my height in inches. (That is, from 5.5 feet, calculate 66 inches.)

Modify the program so that it asks for the user's height in feet and then reports the person's height in inches.

Modify the program so that it asks for the user's height in feet and inches. For example, a person who's five-and-a-half feet tall types the number **5** (for five feet) followed by the number **6** (for six more inches). The program reports the person's height in inches.

HOW MANY ANNIVERSARIES?

My wife and I were married on February 29, so we have one anniversary every four years. Write a program with a variable named years. Based on the value of the years variable, the program displays the number of anniversaries we've had. For example, if the value of years is 4, the program displays the sentence Number of anniversaries: 1. If the value of years is 7, the program still displays Number of anniversaries: 1. But if the value of years is 8, the program displays Number of anniversaries: 2.

The increment and decrement operators

Java has some neat little operators that make life easier (for the computer's processor, for your brain, and for your fingers). Altogether, there are four such operators — two increment operators and two decrement operators. The increment operators add one, and the decrement operators subtract one. To see how they work, you need some examples.

Using preincrement

The first example is in Figure 7-7.

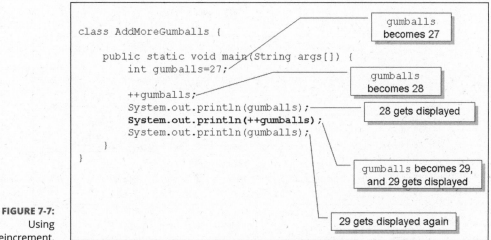

```
class AddMoreGumballs {

    public static void main(String args[]) {
        int gumballs=27;

        ++gumballs;
        System.out.println(gumballs);
        System.out.println(++gumballs);
        System.out.println(gumballs);
    }
}
```

gumballs becomes 27

gumballs becomes 28

28 gets displayed

gumballs becomes 29, and 29 gets displayed

29 gets displayed again

FIGURE 7-7:
Using preincrement.

A run of the program in Figure 7-7 is shown in Figure 7-8. In this horribly uneventful run, the count of gumballs is displayed three times.

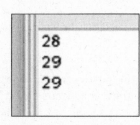

FIGURE 7-8:
A run of the preincrement code (the code in Figure 7-7).

```
28
29
29
```

The double plus sign goes under two different names, depending on where you put it. When you put the ++ before a variable, the ++ is called the *preincrement* operator.

In the word *preincrement,* the *pre* stands for *before.* In this setting, the word *before* has two different meanings:

» You're putting ++ before the variable.

» The computer adds 1 to the variable's value before the variable is used in any other part of the statement.

Figure 7-9 has a slow-motion, instant replay of the preincrement operator's action. In Figure 7-9, the computer encounters the `System.out.println(++gumballs)` statement. First, the computer adds 1 to `gumballs` (raising the value of `gumballs` to 29). Then the computer executes `System.out.println`, using the new value of `gumballs` (29).

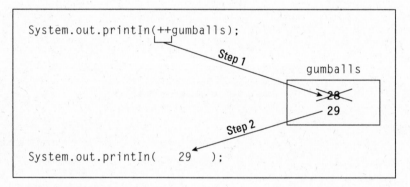

FIGURE 7-9:
The preincrement operator in action.

Using postincrement

An alternative to preincrement is *postincrement.* With postincrement, the *post* stands for *after.* The word *after* has two different meanings:

» You put ++ after the variable.

» The computer adds 1 to the variable's value after the variable is used in any other part of the statement.

Figure 7-10 shows a close-up view of the postincrement operator's action. In Figure 7-10, the computer encounters the `System.out.println(gumballs++)` statement. First, the computer executes `System.out.println`, using the old value of `gumballs` (28). Then the computer adds 1 to `gumballs` (raising the value of `gumballs` to 29).

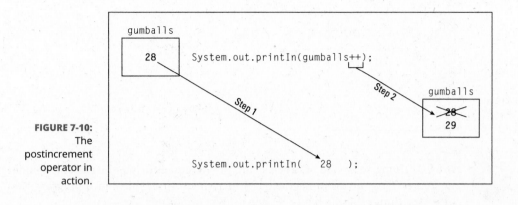

FIGURE 7-10:
The postincrement operator in action.

Look at the bold line of code in Figure 7-11. The computer prints the old value of gumballs (28) on the screen. Only after printing this old value does the computer add 1 to gumballs (raising the gumballs value from 28 to 29).

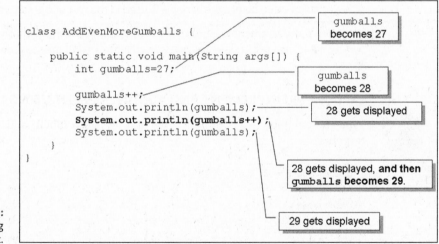

FIGURE 7-11:
Using postincrement.

REMEMBER

With System.out.println(gumballs++), the computer adds 1 to gumballs *after* printing the old value that gumballs already had.

A run of the code in Figure 7-11 is shown in Figure 7-12. Compare Figure 7-12 with the run in Figure 7-8.

>> With preincrement in Figure 7-8, the second number that's displayed is 29.

>> With postincrement in Figure 7-12, the second number that's displayed is 28.

In Figure 7-12, the number 29 doesn't show up on the screen until the end of the run, when the computer executes one last System.out.println(gumballs).

```
28
28
29
```

FIGURE 7-12:
A run of the
postincrement
code (the code in
Figure 7-11).

TIP

Are you trying to decide between using preincrement or postincrement? Ponder no longer. Most programmers use postincrement. In a typical Java program, you often see things like `gumballs++`. You seldom see things like `++gumballs`.

In addition to preincrement and postincrement, Java has two operators that use `--`. These operators are called *predecrement* and *postdecrement:*

>> With predecrement (`--gumballs`), the computer subtracts 1 from the variable's value before the variable is used in the rest of the statement.

>> With postdecrement (`gumballs--`), the computer subtracts 1 from the variable's value after the variable is used in the rest of the statement.

EXPLORE PREINCREMENT AND POSTINCREMENT USING JShell

TRY IT OUT

Type the boldface text, one line after another, into JShell, and see how JShell responds:

```
jshell> int i = 8

jshell> i++

jshell> i

jshell> i

jshell> i++

jshell> i

jshell> ++i

jshell> i
```

STATEMENTS AND EXPRESSIONS

Any part of a computer program that has a value is called an *expression*. If you write

```
gumballs = 30;
```

then 30 is an expression (an expression whose value is the quantity 30). If you write

```
amount = 5.95 + 25.00;
```

then 5.95 + 25.00 is an expression (because 5.95 + 25.00 has the value 30.95). If you write

```
gumballsPerKid = gumballs / kids;
```

then gumballs / kids is an expression. (The value of the expression gumballs / kids depends on whatever values the variables gumballs and kids have when the statement with the expression in it is executed.)

This brings us to the subject of the pre- and postincrement and decrement operators. There are two ways to think about these operators: the way everyone understands it and the right way. The way I explain it in most of this section (in terms of time, with *before* and *after*) is the way everyone understands the concept. Unfortunately, the way everyone understands the concept isn't really the right way. When you see ++ or −−, you can think in terms of time sequence. But occasionally some programmer uses ++ or −− in a convoluted way, and the notions of before and after break down. So if you're ever in a tight spot, you should think about these operators in terms of statements and expressions.

First, remember that a statement tells the computer to do something, and an expression has a value. (Statements are described in Chapter 4, and expressions are described earlier in this sidebar.) Which category does gumballs++ belong to? The surprising answer is both. The Java code gumballs++ is both a statement and an expression.

Suppose that, before executing the code System.out.println(gumballs++), the value of gumballs is 28:

As a statement, gumballs++ tells the computer to add 1 to gumballs.

As an expression, the value of gumballs++ is 28, not 29.

So, even though gumballs gets 1 added to it, the code System.out.println (gumballs++) really means System.out.println(28). (See the figure in this sidebar.)

(continued)

(continued)

Postincrement

```
System.out.println(   gumballs++  );
```
28

... and, by the way, add 1 to
gumballs, changing the value
of gumballs from 28 to 29.

Preincrement

```
System.out.println(  ++gumballs  );
```
29

... and, by the way, add 1 to
gumballs, changing the value
of gumballs from 28 to 29.

Now, almost everything you've just read about gumballs++ is true about ++gumballs. The only difference is, as an expression, ++gumballs behaves in a more intuitive way. Suppose that before executing the code System.out.println(++gumballs), the value of gumballs is 28:

- As a statement, ++gumballs tells the computer to add 1 to gumballs.

- As an expression, the value of ++gumballs is 29.

So, with System.out.println(++gumballs), the variable gumballs gets 1 added to it, and the code System.out.println(++gumballs) really means System.out.println(29).

EXPLORE PREINCREMENT AND POSTINCREMENT IN A JAVA PROGRAM

Before you run the following code, try to predict what the code's output will be. Then run the code to find out whether your prediction is correct:

```java
public class Main {

   public static void main(String[] args) {
      int i = 10;
      System.out.println(i++);
      System.out.println(--i);
```

```
    --i;
    i--;
    System.out.println(i);
    System.out.println(++i);
    System.out.println(i--);
    System.out.println(i);
  }
}
```

Assignment operators

If you've read the previous section — the section about operators that add 1 — you may be wondering whether you can manipulate these operators to add 2, or add 5, or add 1000000. Can you write gumballs++++ and still call yourself a Java programmer? Well, you can't. If you try it, Eclipse will give you an error message:

```
Invalid argument to operation ++/--
```

If you don't use Eclipse, you may see a different error message:

```
unexpected type
required: variable
found   : value
    gumballs++++;
          ^
```

Eclipse or no Eclipse, the bottom line is the same: Namely, your code contains an error, and you have to fix it.

How can you add values other than 1? As luck would have it, Java has plenty of assignment operators you can use. With an *assignment operator,* you can add, subtract, multiply, or divide by anything you want. You can do other cool operations, too.

For example, you can add 1 to the kids variable by writing

```
kids += 1;
```

Is this better than kids++ or kids = kids + 1? No, it's not better. It's just an alternative. But you can add 5 to the kids variable by writing

```
kids += 5;
```

You can't easily add 5 with preincrement or postincrement. And what if the kids get stuck in an evil scientist's cloning machine? The statement

```
kids *= 2;
```

multiplies the number of kids by 2.

With the assignment operators, you can add, subtract, multiply, or divide a variable by any number. The number doesn't have to be a literal. You can use a number-valued expression on the right side of the equal sign:

```
double amount = 5.95;
double shippingAndHandling = 25.00, discount = 0.15;
amount += shippingAndHandling;
amount -= discount * 2;
```

The preceding code adds 25.00 (shippingAndHandling) to the value of amount. Then the code subtracts 0.30 (discount * 2) from the value of amount. How generous!

If the word *literal* doesn't ring any bells for you, refer to Chapter 4.

CROSS REFERENCE

EXPERIMENT WITH ASSIGNMENT OPERATORS

Before you run the following code, try to predict what the code's output will be. Then run the code to find out whether your prediction is correct:

TRY IT OUT

```java
public class Main {

  public static void main(String[] args) {
    int i = 10;

    i += 2;
    i -= 5;
    i *= 6;

    System.out.println(i);
    System.out.println(i += 3);
    System.out.println(i /= 2);
  }
}
```

MAKING CHANGE YET AGAIN

In addition to the assignment operators that I describe in this section, Java also has a %= operator. The %= operator does for remainders what the += operator does for addition. Modify the code in Listing 7-3 so that it uses the %= assignment operator wherever possible.

Size Matters

Here are today's new vocabulary words:

foregift (fore-gift) *n.* A premium that a lessee pays to the lessor upon the taking of a lease.

hereinbefore (here-in-be-fore) *adv.* In a previous part of this document.

Now imagine yourself scanning some compressed text. In this text, all blanks have been removed to conserve storage space. You come upon the following sequence of letters:

hereinbeforegiftedit

The question is, what do these letters mean? If you knew each word's length, you could answer the question:

here in be foregift edit

hereinbefore gifted it

herein before gift Ed it

A computer faces the same kind of problem. When a computer stores several numbers in memory or on a disk, the computer doesn't put blank spaces between the numbers. So imagine that a small chunk of the computer's memory looks like the stuff in Figure 7-13. (The computer works exclusively with zeros and ones, but Figure 7-13 uses ordinary digits. With ordinary digits, it's easier to see what's going on.)

FIGURE 7-13:
Storing the
digits 4221.

| 4 | 2 | 2 | 1 |

What number or numbers are stored in Figure 7-13? Is it two numbers, 42 and 21? Or is it one number, 4,221? And what about storing four numbers, 4, 2, 2, and 1? It all depends on the amount of space each number consumes.

Imagine a variable that stores the number of paydays in a month. This number never gets bigger than 31. You can represent this small number with just eight zeros and ones. But what about a variable that counts stars in the universe? That number could easily be more than a trillion, and to represent 1 trillion accurately, you need 64 zeros and ones.

At this point, Java comes to the rescue. Java has four types of whole numbers. Just as in Listing 7-1, I declare

```
int gumballsPerKid;
```

I can also declare

```
byte paydaysInAMonth;
short sickDaysDuringYourEmployment;
long numberOfStars;
```

Each of these types (byte, short, int, and long) has its own range of possible values. (See Table 7-1.)

TABLE 7-1

Java's Primitive Numeric Types

Type Name	Range of Values
Whole Number Types	
byte	–128 to 127
short	–32768 to 32767
int	–2147483648 to 2147483647
long	–9223372036854775808 to 9223372036854775807
Decimal Number Types	
float	-3.4×10^{38} to 3.4×10^{38}
double	-1.8×10^{308} to 1.8×10^{308}

Java has two types of decimal numbers (numbers with digits to the right of the decimal point). Just as in Listing 6-1 (over in Chapter 6), I declare

```
double amount;
```

I can also declare

```
float monthlySalary;
```

Given the choice between double and float, I always choose double. A variable of type double has a greater possible range of values and much greater accuracy. (See Table 7-1.)

Table 7-1 lists six of Java's *primitive* types (also known as *simple* types). Java has only eight primitive types, so only two of Java's primitive types are missing from Table 7-1.

Chapter 8 describes the two remaining primitive types. Chapter 17 introduces types that aren't primitive.

As a beginning programmer, you don't have to choose among the types in Table 7-1. Just use int for whole numbers and double for decimal numbers. If, in your travels, you see something like short or float in someone else's program, just remember the following:

>> The types byte, short, int, and long represent whole numbers.

>> The types float and double represent decimal numbers.

Most of the time, that's all you need to know.

Chapter **8**

Numbers? Who Needs Numbers?

don't particularly like fax machines. They're so inefficient. Send a short fax, and what do you have? You have two slices of a tree — one at the sending end and another at the receiving end. You also have millions of dots — dots that scan tiny little lines across the printed page. The dots distinguish patches of light from patches of darkness. What a waste!

Compare a fax with an email message. Using email, I can send a 25-word contest entry with just 2,500 zeros and ones, and I don't waste any paper. Best of all, an email message doesn't describe light dots and dark dots. An email message contains codes for each of the letters — a short sequence of zeros and ones for the letter *A*, a different sequence of zeros and ones for the letter *B*, and so on. What could be simpler?

Now imagine sending a one-word fax. The word is *true,* which is understood to mean, "True, I accept your offer to write *Beginning Programming with Java For Dummies,* 5th Edition." A fax with this message sends a picture of the four letters t-r-u-e, with fuzzy lines where dirt gets on the paper and little white dots where the cartridge runs short on toner.

But really, what's the essence of the "true" message? There are just two possibilities, aren't there? The message could be "true" or "false," and to represent those possibilities, I need very little fanfare. How about 0 for "false" and 1 for "true?"

They ask, "Do you accept our offer to write *Beginning Programming with Java For Dummies,* 5th Edition?"

"1," I reply.

Too bad I didn't think of that a few months ago. Anyway, this chapter deals with letters, truth, falsehood, and other such things.

Characters

In Chapters 6 and 7, you store numbers in all your variables. That's fine, but there's more to life than numbers. For example, I wrote this book with a computer, and this book contains thousands and thousands of nonnumeric things called *characters.*

The Java type that's used to store characters is *char.* Listing 8-1 has a simple program that uses the char type, and a run of the Listing 8-1 program is shown in Figure 8-1.

LISTING 8-1: **Using the char Type**

```
class LowerToUpper {

    public static void main(String args[]) {
        char smallLetter, bigLetter;

        smallLetter = 'b';
        bigLetter = Character.toUpperCase(smallLetter);
        System.out.println(bigLetter);
    }
}
```

FIGURE 8-1:
Exciting program output!

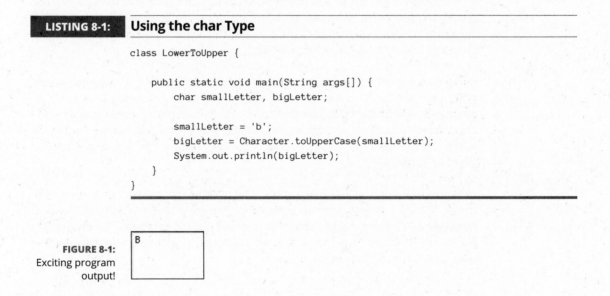

In Listing 8-1, the first assignment statement stores the letter b in the smallLetter variable. In that statement, notice how b is surrounded by single quote marks (' '). In a Java program, every char literal starts and ends with a single quote mark.

When you surround a letter with quote marks, you tell the computer that the letter isn't a variable name. For example, in Listing 8-1, the incorrect statement small-Letter = b would tell the computer to look for a variable named b. Because there's no variable named b, you'd get a b cannot be resolved to a variable message.

In the second assignment statement of Listing 8-1, the program calls an API method whose name is Character.toUpperCase. The method Character.toUp-perCase does what its name suggests — the method produces the uppercase equivalent of a lowercase letter. In Listing 8-1, this uppercase equivalent (the letter B) is assigned to the variable bigLetter, and the B that's in bigLetter is printed on the screen, as illustrated in Figure 8-2.

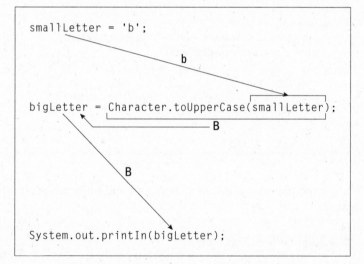

FIGURE 8-2: The action in Listing 8-1.

When the computer displays a char value on the screen, the computer doesn't surround the character with single quote marks.

I digress . . .

A while ago, I wondered what would happen if I called the Character.toUpper-Case method and fed the method a character that isn't lowercase to begin with. I yanked out the Java API documentation, but I found no useful information. The documentation said that toUpperCase "converts the character argument to uppercase using case mapping information from the UnicodeData file." Thanks, but that's not useful to me.

Silly as it seems, I asked myself what I'd do if I were the toUpperCase method. What would I say if someone handed me a capital R and told me to capitalize that letter? I'd say, "Take back your stinking capital R." In the lingo of computing, I'd send that person an error message. So I wondered whether I'd get an error message if I applied Character.toUpperCase to the letter R.

I tried it. I cooked up the experiment in Listing 8-2.

LISTING 8-2: **Investigating the Behavior of toUpperCase**

```java
class MyExperiment {

    public static void main(String args[]) {
        char smallLetter, bigLetter;

        smallLetter = 'R';
        bigLetter = Character.toUpperCase(smallLetter);
        System.out.println(bigLetter);

        smallLetter = '3';
        bigLetter = Character.toUpperCase(smallLetter);
        System.out.println(bigLetter);
    }
}
```

In my experiment, I didn't mix chemicals and blow things up. Here's what I did instead:

>> **I assigned** 'R' **to** smallLetter.

The toUpperCase method took the uppercase R and gave me back another uppercase R. (See Figure 8-3.) I got no error message. This told me what the toUpperCase method does with a letter that's already uppercase. The method does nothing.

>> **I assigned** '3' **to** smallLetter.

The toUpperCase method took the digit 3 and gave me back the same digit 3. (See Figure 8-3.) I got no error message. This told me what the toUpperCase method does with a character that's not a letter. It does nothing — zip, zilch, bupkis.

FIGURE 8-3:
Running the code
in Listing 8-2.

I write about this experiment to make an important point. When you don't understand something about computer programming, it often helps to write a test program. Make up an experiment and see how the computer responds.

I guessed that handing a capital R to the `toUpperCase` method would give me an error message, but I was wrong. See? The answers to questions aren't handed down from heaven. The people who created the Java API made decisions. They made some obvious choices, and they also made some unexpected choices. No one knows everything about Java's features, so don't expect to cram all the answers into your head.

The Java documentation is great, but for every question that the documentation answers, it ignores three other questions. So be bold. Don't be afraid to tinker. Write lots of short, experimental programs. You can't break the computer, so play tough with it. Your inquisitive spirit will always pay off.

Reading and understanding Java's API documentation is an art, not a science. For advice on making the most of these docs, read my article "Making Sense of Java's API Documentation," at `www.dummies.com/programming/java/making-sense-of-javas-api-documentation`.

One character only, please

A `char` variable stores only one character. So if you're tempted to write the following statements

```
char smallLetters;
smallLetters = 'barry';   //Don't do this
```

please resist the temptation. You can't store more than one letter at a time in a `char` variable, and you can't put more than one letter between a pair of single quotes. If you're trying to store words or sentences (not just single letters), then you need to use something called a *String*. For a look at Java's `String` type, see Chapter 18.

Variables and recycling

In Listing 8-2, I use `smallLetter` twice, and I use `bigLetter` twice. That's why they call these things *variables*. First, the value of `smallLetter` is R. Later, I vary the value of `smallLetter` so that the value of `smallLetter` becomes 3.

When I assign a new value to smallLetter, the old value of smallLetter gets obliterated. For example, in Figure 8-4, the second smallLetter assignment puts 3 into smallLetter. When the computer executes this second assignment statement, the old value R is gone.

Is that okay? Can you afford to forget the value that smallLetter once had? Yes, in Listing 8-2, it's okay. After you've assigned a value to bigLetter with the statement

```
bigLetter = Character.toUpperCase(smallLetter);
```

you can forget all about the existing smallLetter value. You don't need to do this:

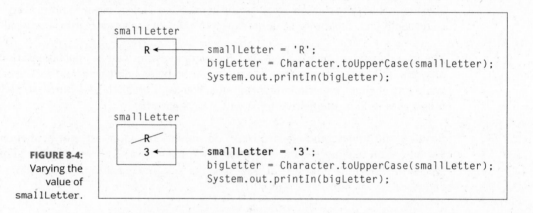

FIGURE 8-4:
Varying the
value of
smallLetter.

```
// This code is cumbersome.
// The extra variables are unnecessary.
char smallLetter1, bigLetter1;
char smallLetter2, bigLetter2;


smallLetter1 = 'R';
bigLetter1 = Character.toUpperCase(smallLetter1);
System.out.println(bigLetter1);


smallLetter2 = '3';
bigLetter2 = Character.toUpperCase(smallLetter2);
System.out.println(bigLetter2);
```

You don't need to store the old and new values in separate variables. Instead, you can reuse the variables smallLetter and bigLetter as in Listing 8-2.

This reuse of variables doesn't save you from a lot of extra typing. It doesn't save much memory space, either. But reusing variables keeps the program uncluttered. When you look at Listing 8-2, you can see at a glance that the code has two parts, and you see that both parts do roughly the same thing.

The code in Listing 8-2 is simple and manageable. In such a small program, simplicity and manageability don't matter much. But in a large program, it helps to think carefully about the use of each variable.

When not to reuse a variable

The previous section discusses the reuse of variables to make a program slick and easy to read. This section shows you the flip side. In this section, the problem at hand forces you to create new variables.

Suppose that you're writing code to reverse the letters in a four-letter word. You store each letter in its own, separate variable. Listing 8-3 shows the code, and Figure 8-5 shows the code in action.

LISTING 8-3: **Making a Word Go Backward**

```java
import java.util.Scanner;

class ReverseWord {

  public static void main(String args[]) {
    Scanner keyboard = new Scanner(System.in);
    char c1, c2, c3, c4;

    c1 = keyboard.findWithinHorizon(".", 0).charAt(0);
    c2 = keyboard.findWithinHorizon(".", 0).charAt(0);
    c3 = keyboard.findWithinHorizon(".", 0).charAt(0);
    c4 = keyboard.findWithinHorizon(".", 0).charAt(0);

    System.out.print(c4);
    System.out.print(c3);
    System.out.print(c2);
    System.out.print(c1);
    System.out.println();

    keyboard.close();
  }
}
```

FIGURE 8-5:
Stop those pots!

```
pots
stop
```

The trick in Listing 8-3 is as follows:

» Assign values to variables c1, c2, c3, and c4 in that order.

» Display these variables' values on the screen in reverse order: c4, c3, c2, and then c1, as illustrated in Figure 8-6.

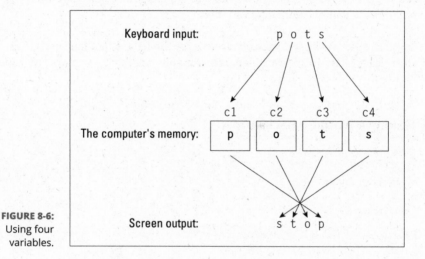

FIGURE 8-6:
Using four variables.

If you don't use four separate variables, you don't get the result that you want. For example, imagine that you store characters in only one variable. You run the program and type the word pots. When it's time to display the word in reverse, the computer remembers the final s in the word pots. But the computer doesn't remember the p, the o, or the t, as shown in Figure 8-7.

I wish I could give you 12 simple rules to help you decide when and when not to reuse variables. The problem is, I can't. It all depends on what you're trying to accomplish. So, how do you figure out on your own when and when not to reuse variables? Like the guy says to the fellow who asks how to get to Carnegie Hall, "Practice, practice, practice."

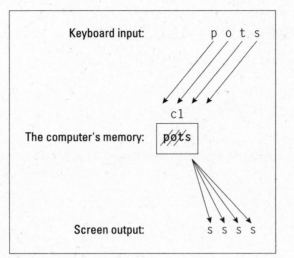

FIGURE 8-7:
Getting things
wrong because
you used only
one variable.

Reading characters

The people who created Java's Scanner class didn't create a next method for reading a single character. So, to input a single character, I paste two Java API methods together. I use the findWithinHorizon and charAt methods.

Table 5-1 (over in Chapter 5) introduces this findWithinHorizon(".", 0). charAt(0) technique for reading a single input character, and Listing 8-3 uses the technique to read one character at a time. (In fact, Listing 8-3 uses the technique four times to read four individual characters.)

Notice the format for the input in Figure 8-5. To enter the characters in the word pots, I type four letters, one after another, with no blank spaces between the letters and no quote marks. The findWithinHorizon(".", 0).charAt(0) technique works that way, but don't blame me or my technique. Other developers' character-reading methods work the same way. No matter whose methods you use, reading a character differs from reading a number. Here's how:

>> **With methods like** nextDouble **and** nextInt, **you type blank spaces between numbers.**

If I type **80 6**, then two calls to nextInt read the number 80, followed by the number 6. If I type **806**, then a single call to nextInt reads the number 806 (eight hundred six), as illustrated in Figure 8-8.

WHAT'S BEHIND ALL THIS findWithinHorizon NONSENSE?

Without wallowing in too much detail, here's how the `findWithinHorizon` (`"."`, `0`).`charAt(0)` technique works:

Java's `findWithinHorizon` method looks for things in the input. The things the method finds depend on the stuff you put in parentheses. For example, a call to `findWithinHorizon("\\d\\d\\d", 0)` looks for a group consisting of three digits. With the following line of code

```
System.out.println(keyboard.findWithinHorizon("\\d\\d\\d", 0));
```

I can type

```
Testing 123 Testing Testing
```

and the computer responds by displaying

```
123
```

In the call `findWithinHorizon("\\d\\d\\d", 0)`, each `\\d` stands for a single digit. This `\\d` business is one of many abbreviations in special code called *regular expressions*.

Now here's something strange. In the world of regular expressions, a dot stands for any character at all. (That is, a dot stands for "any character, not necessarily a dot.") So `findWithinHorizon(".", 0)` tells the computer to find the next character of any kind that the user types on the keyboard. When you're trying to input a single character, `findWithinHorizon(".", 0)` is mighty useful.

In the call `findWithinHorizon("\\d\\d\\d", 0)`, the 0 tells `findWithinHorizon` to keep searching until the end of the input. This value 0 is a special case because anything other than 0 limits the search to a certain number of characters. (That's why the method name contains the word *horizon*. The *horizon* is as far as the method sees.) Here are a few examples:

- With the same input `Testing 123 Testing Testing`, the call `findWithinHorizon("\\d\\d\\d", 9)` returns `null`. It returns `null` because the first nine characters of the input (the characters `Testing 1` — seven letters, a blank space, and a digit) don't contain three consecutive digits. These nine characters don't match the pattern `\\d\\d\\d`.

- With the same input, the call findWithinHorizon("\\d\\d\\d", 10) also returns null. It returns null because the first ten characters of the input (the characters Testing 12) don't contain three consecutive digits.

- With the same input, the call findWithinHorizon("\\d\\d\\d", 11) returns 123. It returns 123 because the first 11 characters of the input (the characters Testing 123) contain these three consecutive digits.

- With the input A57B442123 Testing, the call findWithinHorizon("\\d\\d\\d", 12) returns 442. It returns 442 because, among the first 12 characters of the input (the characters A57B442123 Test), the first sequence consisting of three consecutive digits is the sequence 442.

But wait! To grab a single character from the keyboard, I call findWithinHorizon(".", 0).charAt(0). What's the role of charAt(0) in reading a single character? Unfortunately, any findWithinHorizon call behaves as though it's finding a bunch of characters, not just a single character. Even when you call findWithinHorizon(".", 0), and the computer fetches just one letter from the keyboard, the Java program treats that letter as one of possibly many input characters.

The call to charAt(0) takes care of the multicharacter problem. This charAt(0) call tells Java to pick the initial character from any of the characters that findWithinHorizon fetches.

Yes, it's complicated. And yes, I don't like having to explain it. But no, you don't have to understand any of the details in this sidebar. Just read the details if you want to read them and skip the details if you don't care.

» **With** findWithinHorizon(".", 0).charAt(0), **you don't type blank spaces between characters.**

    If I type **po**, then two successive calls to findWithinHorizon(".", 0).charAt(0) read the letter p, followed by the letter o. If I type **p o**, then two calls to findWithinHorizon(".", 0).charAt(0) read the letter p, followed by a blank space character. (Yes, the blank space is a character!) Again, see Figure 8-8.

REMEMBER

To represent a lone character in the text of a computer program, you surround the character with single quote marks. But, when you type a character as part of a program's input, you don't surround the character with quote marks.

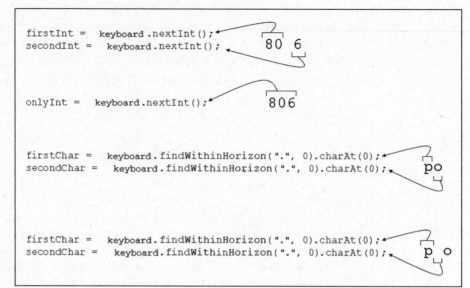

FIGURE 8-8:
Reading numbers and characters.

WARNING

Suppose that your program calls `nextInt` and then `findWithinHorizon(".", 0).charAt(0)`. If you type **80x** on the keyboard, you get an error message. (The message says `InputMismatchException`. The `nextInt` method expects you to type a blank space after each `int` value.) Now what happens if, instead of typing **80x**, you type **80 x** on the keyboard? Then the program gets 80 for the `int` value, followed by a blank space for the character value. For the program to get the x, the program has to call `findWithinHorizon(".", 0).charAt(0)` one more time. It seems wasteful, but it makes sense in the long run.

WHAT'S IN A NAME?

TRY IT OUT

In addition to its `Character.toUpperCase` method. Java has a `Character.toLowerCase` method. With that in mind, write a program that reads a three-letter word and outputs the word as it's capitalized when it's a person's name. For example, if the program reads the letters ann, the program outputs Ann. If the program inputs BoB, the program outputs Bob.

ARRANGEMENTS OF LETTERS

Write a program that reads three letters from the keyboard and outputs all possible arrangements of the three letters. For example, if the program reads the letters

box

the program outputs

```
box
bxo
obx
oxb
xbo
xob
```

The boolean Type

I'm in big trouble. I have 140 gumballs, and 15 kids are running around and screaming in my living room. They're screaming because each kid wants 10 gumballs, and they're running because that's what kids do in a crowded living room. I need a program that tells me whether I can give 10 gumballs to each kid.

I need a variable of type *boolean*. A boolean variable stores one of two values — true or false (true, I can give ten gumballs to each kid; or false, I can't give ten gumballs to each kid). Anyway, the kids are going berserk, so I've written a short program and put it in Listing 8-4. The output of the program is shown in Figure 8-9.

LISTING 8-4: **Using the boolean Type**

```
class CanIKeepKidsQuiet {

    public static void main(String args[]) {
        int gumballs;
        int kids;
        int gumballsPerKid;
        boolean eachKidGetsTen;

        gumballs = 140;
        kids = 15;
        gumballsPerKid = gumballs / kids;

        System.out.print("True or false? ");
        System.out.println("Each kid gets 10 gumballs.");
        eachKidGetsTen = gumballsPerKid >= 10;
        System.out.println(eachKidGetsTen);
    }

}
```

FIGURE 8-9:
Oh, no!

```
True or false? Each kid gets 10 gumballs.
false
```

In Listing 8-4, the variable eachKidGetsTen is of type boolean. So the value stored in the eachKidGetsTen variable can be either true or false. (I can't store a number or a character in the eachKidGetsTen variable.)

To find a value for the variable eachKidGetsTen, the program checks to see whether gumballsPerKid is greater than or equal to ten. (The symbols >= stand for "greater than or equal to." What a pity! There's no ≥ key on the standard computer keyboard.) Because gumballsPerKid is only nine, gumballsPerKid >= 10 is false. So eachKidGetsTen becomes false. Yikes! The kids will tear the house apart! (Before they do, take a look at Figure 8-10.)

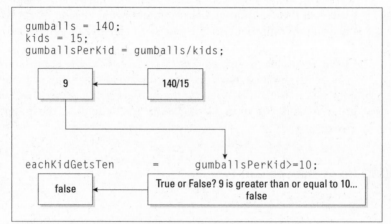

FIGURE 8-10:
Assigning a value to the eachKidGetsTen variable.

Expressions and conditions

In Listing 8-4, the code gumballsPerKid >= 10 is an expression. The expression's value depends on the value stored in the variable gumballsPerKid. On a bad day, the value of gumballsPerKid >= 10 is false. So the variable eachKidGetsTen is assigned the value false.

An expression like gumballsPerKid >= 10, whose value is either true or false, is sometimes called a *condition*.

TECHNICAL STUFF

Values like `true` and `false` may look as though they contain characters, but they really don't. Internally, the Java Virtual Machine doesn't store `boolean` values with the letters t-r-u-e or f-a-l-s-e. Instead, the JVM stores codes, like 0 for false and 1 for true. When the computer displays a `boolean` value (as in `System.out.println(eachKidGetsTen)`), the Java Virtual Machine converts a code like 0 into the five-letter word `false`.

Comparing numbers; comparing characters

In Listing 8-4, I compare a variable's value with the number 10. I use the `>=` operator in the expression

```
gumballsPerKid >= 10
```

Of course, the greater-than-or-equal-to comparison gets you only so far. Table 8-1 shows you the operators you can use to compare things with one another.

TABLE 8-1 **Comparison Operators**

Operator Symbol	Meaning	Example
==	is equal to	myGuess == winningNumber
!=	is not equal to	5 != numberOfCows
<	is less than	strikes < 3
>	is greater than	numberOfBoxtops > 1000
<=	is less than or equal to	lowNumber + highNumber <= 25
>=	is greater than or equal to	gumballsPerKid >= 10

With the operators in Table 8-1, you can compare both numbers and characters.

WARNING

Notice the double equal sign in the first row of Table 8-1. Don't try to use a single equal sign to compare two values. The expression `myGuess = winningNumber` (with a single equal sign) doesn't compare `myGuess` with `winningNumber`. Instead, `myGuess = winningNumber` changes the value of `myGuess`. (It assigns the value of `winningNumber` to the variable `myGuess`.)

You can compare other things (besides numbers and characters) with the `==` and `!=` operators. But when you do, you have to be careful. For more information, see Chapter 18.

Comparing numbers

Nothing is more humdrum than comparing numbers. "True or false? Five is greater than or equal to ten." False. Five is neither greater than nor equal to ten. See what I mean? Bo-ring.

Comparing whole numbers is an open-and-shut case. But unfortunately, when you compare decimal numbers, there's a wrinkle. Take a program for converting from Celsius to Fahrenheit. Wait! Don't take just any such program; take the program in Listing 8-5.

LISTING 8-5: **It's Warm and Cozy in Here**

```java
import java.util.Scanner;

class CelsiusToFahrenheit {

  public static void main(String args[]) {
    Scanner keyboard = new Scanner(System.in);
    double celsius, fahrenheit;

    System.out.print("Enter the Celsius temperature: ");
    celsius = keyboard.nextDouble();

    fahrenheit = 9.0 / 5.0 * celsius + 32.0;

    System.out.print("Room temperature? ");
    System.out.println(fahrenheit == 69.8);

    keyboard.close();
  }
}
```

If you run the code in Listing 8-5 and input the number 21, the computer finds the value of `9.0 / 5.0 * 21 + 32.0`. Believe it or not, you want to check the computer's answer. (Who knows? Maybe the computer gets it wrong!) You need to do some arithmetic, but please don't reach for your calculator. A calculator is just a small computer, and machines of that kind stick up for one another. To check the computer's work, you need to do the arithmetic by hand. What? You say you're math-phobic? Well, don't worry. I've done all the math in Figure 8-11.

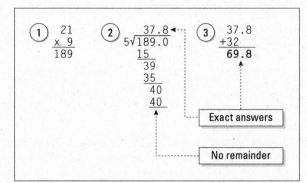

FIGURE 8-11:
The Fahrenheit
temperature is
exactly 69.8.

If you do the arithmetic by hand, the value you get for 9.0 / 5.0 * 21 + 32.0 is exactly 69.8. So run the code in Listing 8-5 and give celsius the value 21. You should get true when you display the value of fahrenheit == 69.8, right?

Well, no. Take a look at the run in Figure 8-12. When the computer evaluates fahrenheit == 69.8, the value turns out to be false, not true. What's going on here?

FIGURE 8-12:
A run of the code
in Listing 8-5.

```
Enter the Celsius temperature: 21
Room temperature? false
```

REMEMBER

Grouping separators vary from one country to another. The run shown in Figure 8-12 works almost everywhere in the world. But if the Celsius temperature is twenty-one-and-a-half degrees, you type **21.5** (with a dot) in some countries and **21,5** (with a comma) in others. Your computer's hardware doesn't have a built-in "country-ometer," but when you install the computer's operating system, you tell it which country you live in. Java programs access this information and use it to customize the way the nextDouble method works.

A little detective work can go a long way. Review the facts:

>> **Fact:** The value of fahrenheit should be exactly 69.8.

>> **Fact:** If fahrenheit is 69.8, then fahrenheit == 69.8 is true.

>> **Fact:** In Figure 8-12, the computer displays the word false. So the expression fahrenheit == 69.8 isn't true.

How do you reconcile these facts? There can be little doubt that fahrenheit == 69.8 is false, so what does that say about the value of fahrenheit? Nowhere in Listing 8-5 is the value of fahrenheit displayed. Could that be the problem?

At this point, I use a popular programmer's trick. I add statements to display the value of `fahrenheit`:

```
fahrenheit = 9.0 / 5.0 * celsius + 32.0;
System.out.print("fahrenheit: ");          //Added
System.out.println(fahrenheit);            //Added
```

A run of the enhanced code is shown in Figure 8-13. As you can see, the computer misses its mark. Instead of the expected value `69.8`, the computer's value for `9.0 / 5.0 * 21 + 32.0` is `69.80000000000001`. That's just the way the cookie crumbles. The computer does all its arithmetic with zeros and ones, so the computer's arithmetic doesn't look like the base-10 arithmetic in Figure 8-11. The computer's answer isn't wrong. The answer is just slightly inaccurate.

FIGURE 8-13:
The fahrenheit variable's full value.

```
Enter the Celsius temperature: 21
fahrenheit: 69.80000000000001
Room temperature? false
```

In an example in Chapter 7, Java's remainder operator (%) gives you the answer `0.1299999999999999` instead of the `0.13` that you expect. The same strange kind of thing happens in this section's example. But this section's code doesn't use an exotic remainder operator. This section's code uses your old friends: division, multiplication, and addition.

Be careful when you compare two numbers for equality (with `==`) or for inequality (with `!=`). Little inaccuracies can creep in almost anywhere when you work with Java's `double` type or with Java's `float` type. And several little inaccuracies can build on one another to become very large inaccuracies. When you compare two `double` values or two `float` values, the values are almost never dead-on equal to one another.

REMEMBER

If your program isn't doing what you think it should do, check your suspicions about the values of variables. Add `print` and `println` statements to your code.

TECHNICAL STUFF

When you compare `double` values, give yourself some leeway. Instead of comparing for exact equality, ask whether a particular value is reasonably close to the expected value. For example, use a condition like `fahrenheit >= 69.8 - 0.01 && fahrenheit <= 69.8 + 0.01` to find out whether `fahrenheit` is within 0.01 of the value `69.8`. To read more about conditions containing Java's `&&` operator, see Chapter 10.

AUTOMATED DEBUGGING

If your program isn't working correctly, you can try something called a debugger. A *debugger* automatically adds invisible `print` and `println` calls to your suspicious code. In fact, debuggers have all kinds of features to help you diagnose problems. For example, a debugger can pause a run of your program and accept special commands to display variables' values. With some debuggers, you can pause a run and change a variable's value (just to see whether things go better when you do).

An Eclipse *perspective* is a collection of views intended to help you with a certain aspect of program development. By default, Eclipse starts in the *Java perspective* — the arrangement of views to help you create Java programs. Another perspective — the *Debug perspective* — helps you diagnose errors in your code.

In this book, I don't promote the use of an automated debugger. But for any large programming project, automated debugging is an essential tool. If you plan to write bigger and better programs, please give Eclipse's Debug perspective a try. For a small sample of the Debug perspective's capabilities, do the following:

1. **In the editor (where you see your Java code), double-click in the margin to the left of a line of code.**

   A little blue dot appears in the margin. (See the first sidebar figure.) This dot indicates a *breakpoint* in the code. In the steps that follow, you'll make the run of the program pause at this breakpoint. In the figure, I click the last line of code from Listing 8-5.

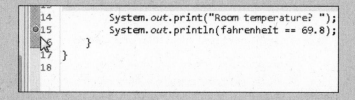

2. **On Eclipse's main menu, click Window ⇨ Open Perspective ⇨ Debug.**

   As a result, Eclipse displays a new layout. The new layout contains some familiar views, such as the Console view and the Outline view. The layout also contains some new views, such as the Debug view, the Variables view, and the Breakpoints view. (See the next sidebar figure.)

(continued)

(continued)

3. **On Eclipse's main menu, choose Run ⇨ Debug As ⇨ Java Application.**

   Remember to select the Debug As menu item. Selecting this item enables all the debugging tools.

   Your code begins running. Because you're working with the program in Listing 8-5, the code prompts you to enter the Celsius temperature.

4. **Type the number 21 and then press Enter.**

   Your code continues running until execution reaches the breakpoint. At the breakpoint, the execution pauses to allow you to examine the program's state.

5. **In the upper-right corner of Eclipse's window, look for the Variables view.**

   The Variables view displays the values of the program's variables. (That's not surprising.) In this sidebar's third figure, the `fahrenheit` variable's value is 69.80000000000001. How nice! Using the debugging tools, you can examine variables' values in the middle of a run!

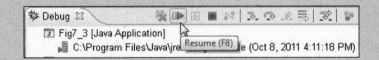

Debug screenshot: Eclipse IDE showing the CelsiusToFahrenheit.java debug session.

6. **To finish running your program, click the Resume button at the top of the Debug view. (See this sidebar's final figure.)**

7. **To return to the Java perspective, choose Window ➪ Open Perspective ➪ Java.**

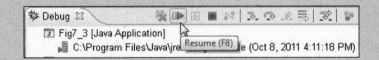

Comparing characters

The comparison operators in Table 8-1 work overtime for characters. Roughly speaking, the operator ‹ means "comes earlier in the alphabet." But you have to be careful of the following:

» Because B comes alphabetically before H, the condition 'B' ‹ 'H' is true. That's not surprising.

» Because b comes alphabetically before h, the condition 'b' ‹ 'h' is true. That's no surprise, either.

> ❯❯ Every uppercase letter comes before any of the lowercase letters, so the condition 'b' < 'H' is false. Now, that's a surprise. (See Figure 8-14.)

FIGURE 8-14:
The ordering
of the letters.

ABCDEFGHIJKLMNOPQRSTUVWXYZabcdefghijklmnopqrstuvwxyz

lesser ◀──▶ greater

In practice, you seldom have reason to compare one letter with another. But in Chapter 18, you can read about Java's String type. With the String type, you can compare words, names, and other good stuff. At that point, you have to think carefully about alphabetical ordering, and the ideas in Figure 8-14 come in handy.

TECHNICAL
STUFF

Under the hood, the letters A through Z are stored with numeric codes 65 through 90. The letters a through z are stored with codes 97 through 122. That's why each uppercase letter is "less than" any of the lowercase letters.

The Remaining Primitive Types

In Chapter 7, I tell you that Java has eight primitive types, but Table 7-1 lists only six of eight types. Table 8-2 describes the remaining two types — the types char and boolean. Table 8-2 isn't too exciting, but I can't just leave you with the incomplete story in Table 7-1.

TABLE 8-2   ## Java's Primitive Non-Numeric Types

Type Name	Range of Values
Character Type	
char	Thousands of characters, glyphs, and symbols
Logical Type	
boolean	Only true or false

TECHNICAL
STUFF

If you dissect parts of the Java Virtual Machine, you find that Java considers char to be a numeric type. That's because Java represents characters with something called *Unicode* — an international standard for representing alphabets of the world's many languages. For example, the Unicode representation of an uppercase letter C is 67. The representation of a Hebrew letter Aleph is 1488. And (to take a more obscure example) the representation for the voiced retroflex approximant in phonetics is 635. But don't worry about all of this. The only reason I'm writing about the char type's being numeric is to save face among my techie friends.

TECHNICAL STUFF

After looking at Table 8-2, you may be wondering what a glyph is. (In fact, I'm proud to be writing about this esoteric concept, whether you have any use for the information or not.) A *glyph* is a particular representation of a character. For example, a and *a* are two different glyphs, but both of these glyphs represent the same lowercase letter of the Roman alphabet. (Because these two glyphs have the same meaning, the glyphs are called *allographs*. If you want to sound smart, find a way to inject the words *glyph* and *allograph* into a casual conversation!)

MORE CHARACTER METHODS

TRY IT OUT

Type the boldface text, one line after another, into JShell, and see how JShell responds.

```
jshell> Character.isDigit('a')

jshell> Character.isDigit('2')

jshell> Character.isLetter('a')

jshell> Character.isLetter('2')

jshell> Character.isLetterOrDigit('4')

jshell> Character.isLetterOrDigit('@')

jshell> Character.isLowerCase('b')

jshell> Character.isLowerCase('B')

jshell> Character.isLowerCase('7')

jshell> Character.isJavaIdentifierPart('x')

jshell> Character.isJavaIdentifierPart('7')

jshell> Character.isJavaIdentifierPart('-')

jshell> Character.isJavaIdentifierPart(' ')
```

3
Controlling the Flow

Chapter **9**

Forks in the Road

Here's an excerpt from *Beginning Programming with Java For Dummies*, 5th Edition, Chapter 8:

> If you're trying to store words or sentences (not just single letters), then you need to use something called a *String*.*

This excerpt illustrates two important points: First, you may have to use something called a *String*. Second, your choice of action can depend on something being true or false:

> If it's true that you're trying to store words or sentences,
>
> you need to use something called a *String*.

This chapter deals with decision-making, which plays a fundamental role in the creation of instructions. With the material in this chapter, you expand your programming power by leaps and bounds.

---

* This excerpt is reprinted with permission from John Wiley & Sons, Inc. If you can't find a copy of *Beginning Programming with Java For Dummies*, 5th Edition, in your local bookstore, visit www.dummies.com.

Decisions, Decisions!

Picture yourself walking along a quiet country road. You're enjoying a pleasant summer day. It's not too hot, and a gentle breeze from the north makes you feel fresh and alert. You're holding a copy of this book, opened to Chapter 9. You read the paragraph about storing words or sentences, and then you look up.

You see a fork in the road. You see two signs — one pointing to the right and the other pointing to the left. One sign reads, "Storing words or sentences? True." The other sign reads, "Storing words or sentences? False." You evaluate the words-or-sentences situation and march on, veering right or left depending on your software situation. A diagram of this story is shown in Figure 9-1.

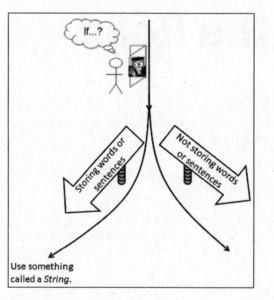

FIGURE 9-1:
Which way to go?

Life is filled with forks in the road. Take an ordinary set of directions for heating up a frozen snack:

> **» Microwave cooking directions:**
>
> Place on microwave-safe plate.
>
> Microwave on high for 2 minutes.
>
> Turn product.
>
> Microwave on high for 2 more minutes.

>> **Conventional oven directions:**

> Preheat oven to 350 degrees.
>
> Place product on baking sheet.
>
> Bake for 25 minutes.

Again, you choose between alternatives. If you use a microwave oven, do this. Otherwise, do that.

In fact, it's hard to imagine useful instructions that don't involve choices. If you're a homeowner with two dependents earning more than $30,000 per year, check here. If you don't remember how to use curly braces in Java programs, see Chapter 4. Did the user correctly type his password? If yes, then let the user log in; if no, then kick the bum out. If you think the market will go up, then buy stocks; otherwise, buy bonds. And if you buy stocks, which should you buy? And when should you sell?

Making Decisions (Java if Statements)

When you work with computer programs, you make one decision after another. Almost every programming language has a way of branching in one of two directions. In Java (and in many other languages), the branching feature is called an *if statement*. Check out Listing 9-1 to see an if statement.

LISTING 9-1: **An if Statement**

```
if (randomNumber > 5) {
    System.out.println("Yes. Isn't it obvious?");
} else {
    System.out.println("No, and don't ask again.");
}
```

To see a complete program containing the code from Listing 9-1, skip to Listing 9-2 (or, if you prefer, walk, jump, or run to Listing 9-2).

The `if` statement in Listing 9-1 represents a branch, a decision, two alternative courses of action. In plain English, this statement has the following meaning:

```
If the randomNumber variable's value is greater than 5,
    display "Yes. Isn't it obvious?" on the screen.
Otherwise,
    display "No, and don't ask again." on the screen.
```

Pictorially, you get the fork shown in Figure 9-2.

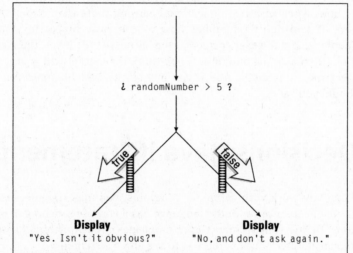

FIGURE 9-2:
A random number decides your fate.

Looking carefully at if statements

An `if` statement can take the following form:

```
if (Condition) {
    SomeStatements
} else {
    OtherStatements
}
```

To get a real-life `if` statement, substitute meaningful text for the three place-holders *Condition*, *SomeStatements*, and *OtherStatements*. Here's how I make the substitutions in Listing 9-1:

>> I substitute randomNumber > 5 for *Condition*.

» I substitute `System.out.println("Yes. Isn't it obvious?");` for *SomeStatements*.

» I substitute `System.out.println("No, and don't ask again.");` for *OtherStatements*.

The substitutions are illustrated in Figure 9-3.

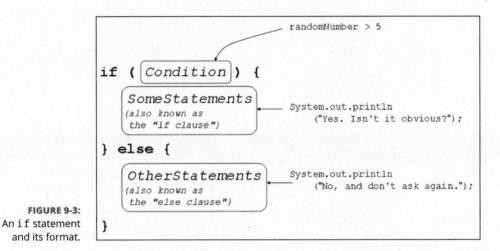

FIGURE 9-3:
An `if` statement
and its format.

Sometimes I need alternate names for parts of an `if` statement. I call them the *if clause* and the *else clause:*

```
if (Condition) {
    if clause
} else {
    else clause
}
```

An `if` statement is an example of a *compound statement* — a statement that includes other statements within it. The `if` statement in Listing 9-1 includes two `println` calls, and these calls to `println` are statements.

Notice how I use parentheses and semicolons in the `if` statement of Listing 9-1. In particular, notice the following:

» The condition must be in parentheses.

» Statements inside the `if` clause end with semicolons. So do statements inside the `else` clause.

>> There's no semicolon immediately after the condition.

>> There's no semicolon immediately after the word else.

As a beginning programmer, you may think these rules are arbitrary. But they're not. These rules belong to a carefully crafted grammar. They're like the grammar rules for English sentences, but they're even more logical! (Sorry, Becky.)

Table 9-1 shows you the kinds of things that can go wrong when you break the if statement's punctuation rules. The table's last two items are the most notorious. In these two situations, the compiler doesn't catch the error. This lulls you into a false sense of security. The trouble is, when you run the program, the code's behavior isn't what you expect it to be.

TABLE 9-1   **Common if Statement Error Messages**

Error	Example	Most Likely Messages or Results
Missing parentheses surrounding the condition	`if randomNumber > 5 {`	`Syntax error on token "if", ( expected after this token`

Missing semicolon after a statement that's inside the if clause or the else clause	`if (randomNumber > 5) {`
	`    System.out.println("Y")`
	
	`}`
		`Syntax error, insert ";" to complete BlockStatements`

Semicolon immediately after the condition	`if (randomNumber > 5); {`
	`    System.out.println("Y");`
	
	`} else {`
		`Syntax error on token "else", delete this token`

Semicolon immediately after the word else	`} else; {`	The program compiles without errors, but the statement after the word else is always executed, whether the condition is true or false.

Missing curly braces	`if (randomNumber > 5)`
	
	`otherValue = 7;`
	
	`System.out.println("Y");`
	
	`else`
	
	`otherValue = 9;`
	
	`System.out.println("N");`
		The program sometimes compiles without errors, but the program's run may not do what you expect it to do. (The bottom line: Don't omit the curly braces.)

As you compose your code, it helps to think of an if statement as one indivisible unit. Instead of typing the whole first line (condition and all), try typing the if statement's skeletal outline:

```
if () {            //To do: Fill in the condition.
                   //To do: Fill in the if clause.
} else {
                   //To do: Fill in the else clause.
}
```

With the entire outline in place, you can start working on the items on your to-do list. When you apply this kind of thinking to a compound statement, it's harder to make a mistake.

A complete program

Listing 9-2 contains a complete program with a simple if statement. The listing's code behaves like an electronic oracle. Ask the program a yes-or-no question, and the program answers you back. Of course, the answer to your question is randomly generated. But who cares? It's fun to ask anyway.

LISTING 9-2: **I Know Everything**

```
import java.util.Scanner;
import java.util.Random;

class AnswerYesOrNo {

  public static void main(String args[]) {
    Scanner keyboard = new Scanner(System.in);
    Random myRandom = new Random();
    int randomNumber;

    System.out.print("Type your question, my child:  ");
    keyboard.nextLine();

    randomNumber = myRandom.nextInt(10) + 1;

    if (randomNumber > 5) {
      System.out.println("Yes. Isn't it obvious?");
    } else {
      System.out.println("No, and don't ask again.");
    }

    keyboard.close();
  }
}
```

Figure 9-4 shows several runs of the program in Listing 9-2. The program's action has four parts:

1. **Prompt the user.**

   Call System.out.print, telling the user to type a question.

2. **Get the user's question from the keyboard.**

   In Figure 9-4, I run the AnswerYesOrNo program four times, and I type a different question each time. Meanwhile, back in Listing 9-2, the statement

   ```
   keyboard.nextLine();
   ```

   swallows up my question and does absolutely nothing with it. This is an anomaly, but you're smart, so you can handle it.

```
Type your question, my child:  Will I write a bestseller?
Yes. Isn't it obvious?
```

```
Type your question, my child:  Will I earn lots of money?
No, and don't ask again.
```

```
Type your question, my child:  Is "no" the correct answer to this question?
Yes. Isn't it obvious?
```

```
Type your question, my child:  Fritz ate air meow swimmingly crackers
Yes. Isn't it obvious?
```

FIGURE 9-4:
The all-knowing Java program in action.

Normally, when a program gets input from the keyboard, the program does something with the input. For example, the program can assign the input to a variable:

```
amount = keyboard.nextDouble();
```

Alternatively, the program can display the input on the screen:

```
System.out.println(keyboard.nextLine());
```

But the code in Listing 9-2 is different. When this AnswerYesOrNo program runs, the user has to type something. (The call to nextLine waits for the user to type some stuff and then press Enter.) But the AnswerYesOrNo program has no need to store the input for further analysis. (The computer does what I do when my wife asks me whether I plan to clean up after myself — I ignore the question and make up an arbitrary answer.) So the program doesn't do anything with the user's input. The call to keyboard.nextLine just sits there in a statement of its own, doing nothing, behaving like a big, black hole. It's unusual for a program to do this, but an electronic oracle is an unusual thing. It calls for some slightly unusual code.

3. **Get a random number — any int value from 1 to 10.**

Okay, wise guys. You've just trashed the user's input. How will you answer yes or no to the user's question?

No problem! None at all! You'll display an answer randomly. The user won't know the difference. (Ha ha!) You can do this as long as you can generate random numbers. The numbers from 1 to 10 will do just fine.

In Listing 9-2, the stuff about Random and myRandom looks much like the familiar Scanner code. From a beginning programmer's point of view, Random and Scanner work almost the same way. Of course, there's an important difference: A call to the Random class's nextInt(10) method doesn't fetch anything from the keyboard. Instead, this nextInt(10) method gets a number out of the blue.

The name Random is defined in the Java API. The call to myRandom.nextInt(10) in Listing 9-2 gets a number from 0 to 9. Then my code adds 1 (making a number from 1 to 10) and assigns that number to the variable randomNumber. When that's done, you're ready to answer the user's question.

TECHNICAL STUFF

In Java's API, the word Random is the name of a Java class, and nextInt is the name of a Java method. For more information on the relationship between classes and methods, see Chapters 17, 18, and 19.

4. **Answer yes or no.**

Calling myRandom.nextInt(10) is like spinning a wheel on a TV game show. The wheel has slots numbered 1 to 10. The if statement in Listing 9-2 turns your number into a yes-or-no alternative. If you roll a number that's greater than 5, the program answers *yes*. Otherwise (if you roll a number that's less than or equal to 5), the program answers *no*.

You can trust me on this one. I've made lots of important decisions based on my AnswerYesOrNo program.

RANDOMNESS MAKES ME DIZZY

When you call `myRandom.nextInt(10) + 1`, you get a number from 1 to 10. As a test, I wrote a program that calls `myRandom.nextInt(10) + 1` 20 times:

```
Random myRandom=new Random();
System.out.print(myRandom.nextInt(10) + 1);
System.out.print(" ");
System.out.print(myRandom.nextInt(10) + 1);
System.out.print(" ");
System.out.print(myRandom.nextInt(10) + 1);
// ... And so on.
```

I ran the program several times and got the results shown in the following figure. (Actually, I copied the results from Eclipse's Console view to Windows Notepad.) Stare briefly at the figure and notice two trends:

- There's no obvious way to predict what number comes next.

- No number occurs much more often than any of the others.

The Java Virtual Machine jumps through hoops to maintain these trends. That's because cranking out numbers in a random fashion is a tricky business. Here are some interesting facts about the process:

- Scientists and nonscientists use the term *random number*. But in reality, there's no such thing as a single random number. After all, how random is a number like 9?

  A number is *random* only when it's one in a disorderly collection of numbers. More precisely, a number is *random* if the process used to generate the number follows the two preceding trends. When they're being careful, scientists avoid the term *random number* and use the term *randomly generated number* instead.

- It's hard to generate numbers randomly. Computer programs do the best they can, but ultimately, today's computer programs follow a pattern, and that pattern isn't truly random.

To generate numbers in a truly random fashion, you need a big tub of ping-pong balls, like the kind they use in state lottery drawings. The problem is, most computers don't come with big tubs of ping-pong balls among their peripherals. So, strictly speaking, the numbers generated by Java's Random class aren't random. Instead, scientists call these numbers *pseudorandom*.

- It surprises us all, but knowing one randomly generated value is of no help in predicting the next randomly generated value.

  For example, if you toss a coin twice, and get heads both times, are you more likely to get tails on the third flip? No. It's still 50-50.

  If you have three sons, and you're expecting a fourth child, is the fourth child more likely to be a girl? No. A child's gender has nothing to do with the genders of the older children. (I'm ignoring any biological effects, which I know absolutely nothing about. Wait! I do know some biological trivia: A newborn child is more likely to be a boy than a girl. For every 21 newborn boys, there are only 20 newborn girls. Boys are weaker, so we die off faster. That's why nature makes more of us at birth.)

Indenting if statements in your code

Notice how, in Listing 9-2, the `println` calls inside the `if` statement are indented. Strictly speaking, you don't have to indent the statements that are inside an `if` statement. For all the compiler cares, you can write your whole program on a single line or place all your statements in an artful, misshapen zigzag. The problem is, if you don't indent your statements in some logical fashion, neither you nor anyone else can make sense of your code. In Listing 9-2, the indenting of the `println` calls helps your eyes (and brain) see quickly that these statements are subordinate to the overall `if`/`else` flow.

In a small program, unindented or poorly indented code is barely tolerable. But in a complicated program, indentation that doesn't follow a neat, logical pattern is a big, ugly nightmare.

Always indent your code to make the program's flow apparent at a glance.

REMEMBER

You don't have to think about indenting your code, because Eclipse can indent your code automatically. For details, see Chapter 4.

TIP

Variations on the Theme

I don't like to skin cats. But I've heard that, if I ever need to skin one, I have a choice of several techniques. I'll keep that in mind the next time my cat Histamine mistakes the carpet for a litter box.*

Anyway, whether you're skinning catfish, skinning kitties, or writing computer programs, the same principle holds true. You always have alternatives. Listing 9-2 shows you one way to write an `if` statement. The rest of this chapter (and all of Chapter 10) shows you some other ways to create `if` statements.

. . . Or else what?

You can create an `if` statement without an `else` clause. For example, imagine a web page on which one in ten randomly chosen visitors receives a special offer. To keep visitors guessing, I call the `Random` class's `nextInt` method and make the offer to anyone whose number is lucky 7:

>> If `myRandom.nextInt(10) + 1` generates the number 7, display a special offer message.

>> If `myRandom.nextInt(10) + 1` generates any number other than 7, do nothing. Don't display a special offer message and don't display a discouraging, "Sorry, no offer for you," message.

---

* Rick Ross, who read about skinning cats in one of my other books, sent me this information via email: " . . . you refer to 'skinning the cat' and go on to discuss litter boxes and whatnot. Please note that the phrase 'more than one way to skin a cat' refers to the difficulty in removing the inedible skin from catfish, and that there is more than one way to do same. These range from nailing the critter's tail to a board and taking a pair of pliers to peel it down, to letting the furry kind of cat have the darn thing and just not worrying about it. I grew up on The River (the big one running north/south down the U.S. that begins with *M* and has so many repeated letters), so it's integral to our experience there." Another reader, Alan Wilson, added his two cents to this discussion: " . . . the phrase 'Skinning a Cat' . . . actually has an older but equally interesting British Naval origin. It refers to the activity of attaching the nine ropes to the whip used to punish recalcitrant sailors up to a couple of hundred years ago. The 'Cat-O'-Nine-Tails' was the name of the whip and there was more than one way to attach the ropes or 'skin' the whip." One way or another, it's time for me to apologize to my little house pet.

The code to implement such a strategy is shown in Listing 9-3. A few runs of the code are shown in Figure 9-5.

Aren't You Lucky?

```java
import java.util.Random;

class SpecialOffer {

    public static void main(String args[]) {
        Random myRandom = new Random();
        int randomNumber = myRandom.nextInt(10) + 1;

        if (randomNumber == 7) {
            System.out.println("An offer just for you!");
        }
        System.out.println(randomNumber);
    }
}
```

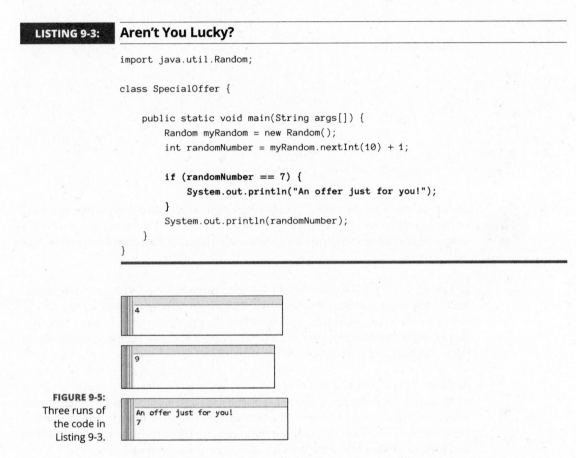

FIGURE 9-5: Three runs of the code in Listing 9-3.

The `if` statement in Listing 9-3 has no `else` clause. This `if` statement has the following form:

```
if (Condition) {
    SomeStatements
}
```

When `randomNumber` is 7, the computer displays An offer just for you! When `randomNumber` isn't 7, the computer doesn't display An offer just for you! The action is illustrated in Figure 9-6.

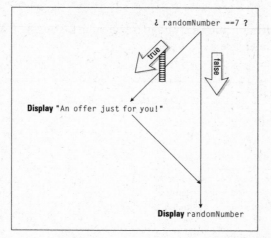

¿ randomNumber ==7 ?

true

false

Display "An offer just for you!"

Display randomNumber

FIGURE 9-6:
If you have
nothing good to
say, don't say
anything.

REMEMBER

Always (I mean *always*) use a double equal sign when you compare two numbers or characters in an if statement's condition. Never (that's *never, ever, ever*) use a single equal sign to compare two values. A single equal sign does assignment, not comparison.

In Listing 9-3, I took the liberty of adding an extra println. This println (at the end of the main method) displays the random number generated by my call to nextInt. On a web page with special offers, you probably wouldn't see the randomly generated number, but I can't test my SpecialOffer code without knowing what numbers the code generates.

Anyway, notice that the value of randomNumber is displayed in every run. The println for randomNumber isn't inside the if statement. (This println comes after the if statement.) So the computer always executes this println. Whether randomNumber == 7 is true or false, the computer takes the appropriate if action and then marches on to execute System.out.println(randomNumber).

Packing more stuff into an if statement

Here's an interesting situation: You have two baseball teams — the Hankees and the Socks. You want to display the teams' scores on two separate lines, with the winner's score coming first. (On the computer screen, the winner's score is displayed above the loser's score. In case of a tie, you display the two identical scores, one above the other.) Listing 9-4 has the code.

LISTING 9-4: **May the Best Team Be Displayed First**

```java
import java.util.Scanner;
import static java.lang.System.in;
import static java.lang.System.out;

class TwoTeams {

    public static void main(String args[]) {
        Scanner keyboard = new Scanner(in);
        int hankees, socks;

        out.print("Hankees and Socks scores?  ");
        hankees = keyboard.nextInt();
        socks = keyboard.nextInt();
        out.println();

        if (hankees > socks) {
            out.print("Hankees: ");
            out.println(hankees);
            out.print("Socks:    ");
            out.println(socks);
        } else {
            out.print("Socks:    ");
            out.println(socks);
            out.print("Hankees: ");
            out.println(hankees);
        }

        keyboard.close();
    }
}
```

Figure 9-7 has a few runs of the code. (To show a few runs in one figure, I copied the results from Eclipse's Console view to Windows Notepad.)

With curly braces, a bunch of print and println calls are tucked away safely inside the if clause. Another group of print and println calls are squished inside the else clause. This creates the forking situation shown in Figure 9-8.

```
Hankees and Socks scores?   9 4

Hankees:  9
Socks:    4




Hankees and Socks scores?   3 8

Socks:    8
Hankees:  3




Hankees and Socks scores?   0 0

Socks:    0
Hankees:  0
```

FIGURE 9-7:
See? The code in
Listing 9-4 really
works!

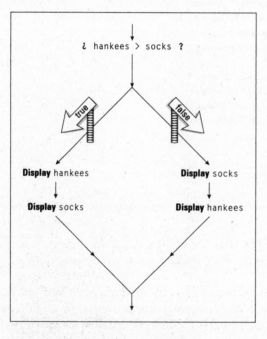

FIGURE 9-8:
Cheer for your
favorite team.

Some handy import declarations

When I wrote this section's example, I was tired of writing the word System. After
all, Listing 9-4 has ten System.out.print lines. By this point in the book,
shouldn't my computer remember what out.print means?

STATEMENTS AND BLOCKS

An elegant way to think about if statements is to realize that you can put only one statement inside each clause of an if statement:

```
if (Condition)
    aStatement
else
    anotherStatement
```

On your first reading of this 1-statement rule, you're probably thinking that there's a misprint. After all, in Listing 9-4, each clause (the if clause and the else clause) seems to contain four statements, not just one.

But technically, the if clause in Listing 9-4 has only one statement, and the else clause in Listing 9-4 has only one statement. The trick is, when you surround a bunch of statements with curly braces, you get what's called a *block*, and a block behaves, in all respects, like a single statement. In fact, the official Java documentation lists a block as a kind of statement (one of many different kinds of statements). So, in Listing 9-4, the block

```
{
    out.print("Hankees: ");
    out.println(hankees);
    out.print("Socks:   ");
    out.println(socks);
}
```

is a single statement. It's a statement that has four smaller statements within it. So this big block, this single statement, serves as the one and only statement inside the if clause in Listing 9-4.

That's how the 1-statement rule works. In an if statement, when you want the computer to execute several statements, you combine those statements into one big statement. To do this, you make a block using curly braces.

Of course, computers don't work that way. If you want a computer to "know" what out.print means, you have to code that knowledge somewhere inside the Java compiler.

Fortunately for me, the ability to abbreviate things like System.out.print is available from Java 5.0 onward. (An older Java compiler simply chokes on the code in Listing 9-4.) This ability to abbreviate things is called *static import*. It's illustrated in the second and third lines of Listing 9-4.

Whenever I start a program with the line

```
import static java.lang.System.out;
```

I can replace System.out with plain out in the remainder of the program. The same holds true of System.in. With an import declaration near the top of Listing 9-4, I can replace new Scanner(System.in) with the simpler new Scanner(in).

You may be wondering what all the fuss is about. If I can abbreviate java.util. Scanner by writing Scanner, what's so special about abbreviating System.out? And why do I have to write out.print? Can I trim System.out.print to the single word print? Look again at the first few lines of Listing 9-4. When do you need the word static? And what's the difference between java.util and java.lang?

I'm sorry. My response to these questions won't thrill you. The fact is, I can't explain away any of these issues until Chapter 18. Before I can explain static import declarations, I need to introduce some ideas. I need to describe classes, packages, and static members.

Until you reach Chapter 18, please bear with me. Just paste three import declarations to the top of your Java programs and trust that everything will work well.

REMEMBER

You can abbreviate System.out with the single word out. And you can abbreviate System.in with the single word in. Just be sure to copy the import declarations *exactly* as you see them in Listing 9-4. With any deviation from the lines in Listing 9-4, you may get a compiler error.

TRY IT OUT

Get some practice writing if statements!

OOPS!

What's wrong with the following code? How can the code be fixed?

```
System.out.println("How many donuts are in a dozen?");
int number = keyboard.nextInt();

if (number = 12) {
    System.out.println("That's correct.");
} else {
    System.out.println("Sorry. That's incorrect");
}
```

DON'T WRITE CODE THIS WAY

When I wrote the following code, I didn't indent the code properly. What's the output of this bad code? Why?

```
int n = 100;

if (n > 100)
System.out.println("n is big");
System.out.println("Will Java display this line of text?");
if (n <= 100)
System.out.println("n is small");
System.out.println("How about this line of text?");
```

THE WORLD SMILES WITH YOU

Write a program that asks the users whether they want to see a smiley face. If the user replies Y (meaning "yes"), the code displays this:

```
:-)
```

Otherwise, the code displays this:

```
:-(
```

SUCCESSIVE IF STATEMENTS

Modify the previous program (the smiley face program) to take three possibilities into account:

>> If the user replies Y (meaning "yes"), the code displays :-).

>> If the user replies N (meaning "no"), the code displays :-(.

>> If the user replies ? (meaning "I don't know"), the code displays :-|.

Use three separate if statements, one after another.

GUESSING GAME

Write a program that randomly generates a number from 1 to 10. The program then reads a number that the user enters on the keyboard. If the user's number is the same as the randomly generated number, the program displays You win!. Otherwise, the program displays You lose.

CONVERTING LENGTHS

Write a program that reads a number of meters from the keyboard. The program also reads a letter from the keyboard. If the letter is c, the program converts the number of meters into centimeters and displays the result. If the letter is m, the program converts the number of meters into millimeters and displays the result. For any other number, the program doesn't display any result.

PUTTING SEVERAL STATEMENTS INSIDE AN IF STATEMENT

Find a short poem (maybe four or five lines long). Write a program that asks the users whether they want to read the poem. If the user replies Y (meaning "yes"), display the poem in Eclipse's Console view. If the user's reply is anything other than Y, display the following:

```
Sorry!
I thought you were a poetry buff.
Maybe you'll want to see the poem the next time you run this program.
```

Chapter **10**

Which Way Did He Go?

t's tax time again. At the moment, I'm working on Form 12432-89B. Here's what it says:

> If you're married with fewer than three children, and your income is higher than the EIQ (Estimated Income Quota), or if you're single and living in a non-residential area (as defined by Section 10, Part iii of the Uniform Zoning Act), and you're either self-employed as an LLC (Limited Liability Company) or you qualify for veterans' benefits, then skip Steps 3 and 4 or 4, 5, and 6, depending on your answers to Questions 2a and 3d.

No wonder I have no time to write! I'm too busy interpreting these tax forms.

Anyway, this chapter deals with the potential complexity of `if` statements. This chapter has nothing as complex as Form 12432-89B, but if you ever encounter something that complicated, you'll be ready for it.

Forming Bigger and Better Conditions

In Listing 9-2 (refer to Chapter 9), the code chooses a course of action based on one call to the Random class's nextInt method. That's fine for the electronic oracle program described in Chapter 9, but what if you're rolling a pair of dice?

In backgammon and other dice games, rolling 3 and 5 isn't the same as rolling 4 and 4, even though the total for both rolls is 8. The next move varies, depending on whether you roll doubles. To get the computer to roll two dice, you execute `myRandom.nextInt(6) + 1` two times. Then you combine the two rolls into a larger, more complicated `if` statement.

To simulate a backgammon game (and many other, more practical situations) you need to combine conditions:

```
If die1 + die2 equals 8 and die1 equals die2, ...
```

You need things like *and* and *or* — things that can wire conditions together. Java has operators to represent these concepts, which are described in Table 10-1 and illustrated in Figure 10-1.

TABLE 10-1

Logical Operators

Operator Symbol	Meaning	Example	Illustration
&&	and	4 < age && age < 8	Figure 10-1(a)
||	or	age < 4 || 8 < age	Figure 10-1(b)
!	not	!eachKidGetsTen	Figure 10-1(c)

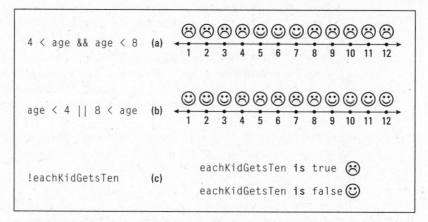

FIGURE 10-1:
When you satisfy a condition, you're happy.

Combined conditions, like the ones in Table 10-1, can be mighty confusing. That's why I tread carefully when I use such things. Here's a short explanation of each example in the table:

>> `4 < age && age < 8`

The value of the age variable is greater than 4 *and* is less than 8. The numbers 5, 6, 7, 8, 9 . . . are all greater than 4. But among these numbers, only 5, 6, and 7 are less than 8. So only the numbers 5, 6, and 7 satisfy this combined condition.

>> `age < 4 || 8 < age`

The value of the age variable is less than 4 *or* is greater than 8. To create the *or* condition, you use two pipe symbols. On many U.S. English keyboards, you can find the pipe symbol immediately above the Enter key (the same key as the backslash, but shifted).

In this combined condition, the value of the age variable is either less than 4 or greater than 8. For example, if a number is less than 4, the number satisfies the condition. Numbers like 1, 2, and 3 are all less than 4, so these numbers satisfy the combined condition.

Also, if a number is greater than 8, the number satisfies the combined condition. Numbers like 9, 10, and 11 are all greater than 8, so these numbers satisfy the condition.

>> `!eachKidGetsTen`

If I weren't experienced with computer programming languages, I'd be confused by the exclamation point. I'd think that `!eachKidGetsTen` means, "Yes, each kid *does* get ten." But that's not what this expression means. This expression says, "The variable `eachKidGetsTen` does *not* have the value `true`." In Java and other programming languages, an exclamation point stands for *negative,* for *no way,* for *not.*

Listing 8-4 (refer to Chapter 8) has a `boolean` variable named `eachKidGetsTen`. A `boolean` variable's value is either `true` or `false`. Because `!` means *not,* the expressions `eachKidGetsTen` and `!eachKidGetsTen` have opposite values. So when `eachKidGetsTen` is `true`, `!eachKidGetsTen` is `false` (and vice versa).

Java's `||` operator is *inclusive.* This means that you get `true` whenever the thing on the left side is `true`, the thing on the right side is `true`, or both things are `true`. For example, the condition `2 < 10 || 20 < 30` is true.

In Java, you can't combine comparisons the way you do in ordinary English. In English, you may say, "We'll have between three and ten people at the dinner table." But in Java, you get an error message if you write `3 <= people <= 10`. To do this comparison, you need something like `3 <= people && people <= 10`.

Combining conditions: An example

Here's a handy example of the use of logical operators. A movie theater posts its prices for admission:

Regular price: $9.25

Kids under 12: $5.25

Seniors (65 and older): $5.25

Because the kids' and seniors' prices are the same, you can combine these prices into one category. (That's not always the best programming strategy, but do it anyway for this example.) To find a particular moviegoer's ticket price, you need one or more `if` statements. You can structure the conditions in many ways, and I chose one of these ways for the code in Listing 10-1.

LISTING 10-1: Are You Paying Too Much?

```java
import java.util.Scanner;

class TicketPrice {

    public static void main(String args[]) {
        Scanner keyboard = new Scanner(System.in);
        int age;
        double price = 0.00;

        System.out.print("How old are you? ");
        age = keyboard.nextInt();

        if (age >= 12 && age < 65) {
            price = 9.25;
        }
        if (age < 12 || age >= 65) {
            price = 5.25;
        }

        System.out.print("Please pay $");
        System.out.print(price);
        System.out.print(". ");
        System.out.println("Enjoy the show!");

        keyboard.close();
    }
}
```

Several runs of the TicketPrice program (refer to Listing 10-1) are shown in Figure 10-2. (For your viewing pleasure, I've copied the runs from Eclipse's Console view to Windows Notepad.) When you turn 12, you start paying full price. You keep paying the full price until you become 65. At that point, you pay the reduced price again.

The pivotal part of Listing 10-1 is the lump of if statements in the middle, which are illustrated in Figure 10-3.

```
How old are you? 11
Please pay $5.25. Enjoy the show!

How old are you? 12
Please pay $9.25. Enjoy the show!

How old are you? 35
Please pay $9.25. Enjoy the show!

How old are you? 64
Please pay $9.25. Enjoy the show!

How old are you? 65
Please pay $5.25. Enjoy the show!
```

FIGURE 10-2: Admission prices for *Beginning Programming with Java For Dummies: The Movie.*

```
age >= 12 && age < 65
```

```
age < 12 || age >= 65
```

FIGURE 10-3: The meanings of the conditions in Listing 10-1.

>> The first if statement's condition tests for the regular-price group. Anyone who's at least 12 years of age *and* is under 65 belongs in this group.

>> The second if statement's condition tests for the fringe ages. A person who's under 12 *or* is 65 or older belongs in this category.

TIP

When you form the opposite of an existing condition, you can often follow the pattern in Listing 10-1. Change >= to <. Change < to >=. Change && to ||.

WARNING

If you change the dollar amounts in Listing 10-1, you can get into trouble. For example, with the statement `price = 5.00`, the program displays `Please pay $5.0. Enjoy the show!` This happens because Java doesn't store the two zeros to the right of the decimal point (and Java doesn't know or care that 5.00 is a dollar amount). To fix this kind of thing, see the discussion of `NumberFormat.getCurrencyInstance` in Chapter 18.

When to initialize?

Take a look at Listing 10-1 and notice the `price` variable's initialization:

```
double price = 0.00;
```

This line declares the `price` variable and sets the variable's starting value to `0.00`. When I omit this initialization, I get an error message:

```
The local variable price may not have been initialized
```

What's the deal here? I don't initialize the `age` variable, but the compiler doesn't complain about that. Why is the compiler fussing over the `price` variable?

The answer is in the placement of the code's assignment statements. Consider the following two facts:

>> **The statement that assigns a value to the** `age` **variable** (`age = keyboard.nextInt()`) **isn't inside an** `if` **statement.**

   That assignment statement always gets executed, and (as long as nothing extraordinary happens) the variable age is sure to be assigned a value.

>> **Both statements that assign a value to the** `price` **variable** (`price = 9.25` **and** `price = 5.25`) **are inside** `if` **statements.**

   If you look at Figure 10-3, you see that every age group is covered. No one shows up at the ticket counter with an age that forces both `if` conditions to be `false`. So, whenever you run the `TicketPrice` program, either the first or the second `price` assignment is executed.

   The problem is that the compiler isn't smart enough to check all of this. The compiler just sees the structure in Figure 10-4 and becomes scared that the computer won't take either of the `true` detours.

   If (for some unforeseen reason) both of the `if` statements' conditions are `false`, then the variable `price` isn't assigned a value. So without an initialization, `price` has no value. (More precisely, `price` has no value that's intentionally given to it in the code.)

Eventually, the computer reaches the `System.out.print(price)` statement. It can't display `price` unless `price` has a meaningful value. At that point, the compiler throws up its virtual hands in disgust.

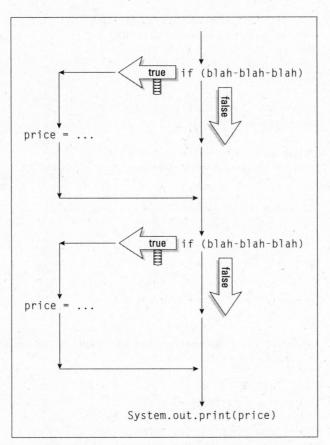

FIGURE 10-4:
The choices in
Listing 10-1.

More and more conditions

Last night I had a delicious meal at the neighborhood burger joint. As part of a promotion, I got a discount coupon along with the meal. The coupon is good for $2.00 off the price of a ticket at the local movie theater.

To make use of the coupon in the `TicketPrice` program, I have to tweak the code in Listing 10-1. The revised code is in Listing 10-2. In Figure 10-5, I take that new code around the block a few times.

LISTING 10-2: **Do You Have a Coupon?**

```java
import java.util.Scanner;

class TicketPriceWithDiscount {

    public static void main(String args[]) {
        Scanner keyboard = new Scanner(System.in);
        int age;
        double price = 0.00;
        char reply;

        System.out.print("How old are you? ");
        age = keyboard.nextInt();

        System.out.print("Have a coupon? (Y/N) ");
        reply = keyboard.findWithinHorizon(".", 0).charAt(0);

        if (age >= 12 && age < 65) {
            price = 9.25;
        }
        if (age < 12 || age >= 65) {
            price = 5.25;
        }

        if (reply == 'Y' || reply == 'y') {
            price -= 2.00;
        }
        if (reply != 'Y' && reply != 'y' && reply!='N' && reply!='n') {
            System.out.println("Huh?");
        }

        System.out.print("Please pay $");
        System.out.print(price);
        System.out.print(". ");
        System.out.println("Enjoy the show!");

        keyboard.close();
    }
}
```

```
How old are you? 51
Have a coupon? (Y/N) Y
Please pay $7.25. Enjoy the show!

How old are you? 51
Have a coupon? (Y/N) y
Please pay $7.25. Enjoy the show!

How old are you? 51
Have a coupon? (Y/N) N
Please pay $9.25. Enjoy the show!

How old are you? 51
Have a coupon? (Y/N) X
Huh?
Please pay $9.25. Enjoy the show!
```

FIGURE 10-5:
Running the code
in Listing 10-2.

Listing 10-2 has two `if` statements whose conditions involve characters:

>> In the first such statement, the computer checks to see whether the `reply` variable stores the letter Y *or* the letter y. If either is the case, it subtracts 2.00 from the `price`. (For information on operators like `-=`, see Chapter 7.)

>> The second such statement has a hefty condition. The condition tests to see whether the `reply` variable stores any reasonable value at all. If the reply *isn't* Y, *and isn't* y, *and isn't* N, *and isn't* n, the computer expresses its concern by displaying, "Huh?" (As a paying customer, the word *Huh?* on the automated ticket teller's screen will certainly get your attention.)

TIP

When you create a big multipart condition, you always have several ways to think about the condition. For example, you can rewrite the last condition in Listing 10-2 as `if (!(reply == 'Y' || reply == 'y' || reply == 'N' || reply == 'n'))`. "*If it's not the case that* the `reply` is *either* Y, y, N, *or* n, then display 'Huh?'" So which way of writing the condition is better — the way I do it in Listing 10-2 or the way I do it in this tip? It depends on your taste. Whichever makes the logic easier for you to understand is the better way.

Using boolean variables

No matter how good a program is, you can always make it a little bit better. Take the code in Listing 10-2. Does the forest of `if` statements make you nervous? Do you slow to a crawl when you read each condition? Wouldn't it be nice if you could glance at a condition and make sense of it very quickly?

To some extent, you can. If you're willing to create some additional variables, you can make your code easier to read. Listing 10-3 shows you how.

LISTING 10-3: **George Boole Would Be Proud**

```java
import java.util.Scanner;

class NicePrice {

    public static void main(String args[]) {
        Scanner keyboard = new Scanner(System.in);
        int age;
        double price = 0.00;
        char reply;
        boolean isKid, isSenior, hasCoupon, hasNoCoupon;

        System.out.print("How old are you? ");
        age = keyboard.nextInt();

        System.out.print("Have a coupon? (Y/N) ");
        reply = keyboard.findWithinHorizon(".", 0).charAt(0);

        isKid = age < 12;
        isSenior = age >= 65;
        hasCoupon = reply == 'Y' || reply == 'y';
        hasNoCoupon = reply == 'N' || reply == 'n';

        if (!isKid && !isSenior) {
            price = 9.25;
        }
        if (isKid || isSenior) {
            price = 5.25;
        }
        if (hasCoupon) {
            price -= 2.00;
        }
        if (!hasCoupon && !hasNoCoupon) {
            System.out.println("Huh?");
        }

        System.out.print("Please pay $");
        System.out.print(price);
        System.out.print(". ");
        System.out.println("Enjoy the show!");

        keyboard.close();
    }
}
```

Runs of the Listing 10-3 code look like the stuff in Figure 10-5. The only difference between Listings 10-2 and 10-3 is the use of `boolean` variables. In Listing 10-3, you get past all the less-than signs and double equal signs before the start of any `if` statements. By the time you encounter the two `if` statements, the conditions can use simple words — words like `isKid`, `isSenior`, and `hasCoupon`. With all these `boolean` variables, expressing each `if` statement's condition is a snap. You can read more about `boolean` variables in Chapter 8.

Adding a `boolean` variable can make your code more manageable. But because some programming languages don't have `boolean` variables, many programmers prefer to create `if` conditions on the fly. That's why I mix the two techniques (conditions with and without `boolean` variables) in this book.

Mixing different logical operators together

If you read about Listing 10-2, you know that my local movie theater offers discount coupons. The trouble is, I can't use a coupon along with any other discount. I tried to convince the ticket taker that I'm under 12 years of age, but he didn't buy it. When that didn't work, I tried combining the coupon with the senior citizen discount. That didn't work, either.

Apparently, the theater uses some software that checks for people like me. It looks something like the code in Listing 10-4. To watch the code run, take a look at Figure 10-6.

LISTING 10-4: **No Extra Break for Kids or Seniors**

```java
import java.util.Scanner;

class CheckAgeForDiscount {

    public static void main(String args[]) {
        Scanner keyboard = new Scanner(System.in);
        int age;
        double price = 0.00;
        char reply;

        System.out.print("How old are you? ");
        age = keyboard.nextInt();

        System.out.print("Have a coupon? (Y/N) ");
        reply = keyboard.findWithinHorizon(".", 0).charAt(0);
```

(continued)

LISTING 10-4: *(continued)*

```
        if (age >= 12 && age < 65) {
            price = 9.25;
        }
        if (age < 12 || age >= 65) {
            price = 5.25;
        }

        if ((reply == 'Y' || reply == 'y') &&
            (age >= 12 && age < 65)) {
            price -= 2.00;
        }

        System.out.print("Please pay $");
        System.out.print(price);
        System.out.print(". ");
        System.out.println("Enjoy the show!");

        keyboard.close();
    }
}
```

```
How old are you? 7
Have a coupon? (Y/N) Y
Please pay $5.25. Enjoy the show!

How old are you? 25
Have a coupon? (Y/N) y
Please pay $7.25. Enjoy the show!

How old are you? 25
Have a coupon? (Y/N) n
Please pay $9.25. Enjoy the show!

How old are you? 85
Have a coupon? (Y/N) y
Please pay $5.25. Enjoy the show!

How old are you? 85
Have a coupon? (Y/N) Y
Please pay $5.25. Enjoy the show!
```

FIGURE 10-6:
Running the code
in Listing 10-4.

Listing 10-4 is a lot like its predecessors, Listings 10-1 and 10-2. The big difference is the bolded if statement. This if statement tests two things, and each thing has two parts of its own:

>> **Does the customer have a coupon?**

That is, did the customer reply with either Y *or* y?

>> **Is the customer in the regular age group?**

That is, is the customer at least 12 years old *and* younger than 65?

In Listing 10-4, I join items 1 and 2 using the && operator. I do this because both items (item 1 *and* item 2) must be true in order for the customer to qualify for the $2.00 discount, as illustrated in Figure 10-7.

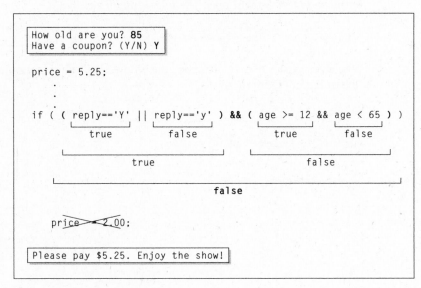

FIGURE 10-7: Both the reply and the age criteria must be true.

Using parentheses

Listing 10-4 demonstrates something important about conditions. Sometimes, you need parentheses to make a condition work correctly. Take, for example, the following incorrect if statement:

```
//This code is incorrect:
if (reply == 'Y' || reply == 'y' && age >= 12 && age < 65) {
    price -= 2.00;
}
```

Compare this code with the correct code in Listing 10-4. This incorrect code has no parentheses to group reply == 'Y' with reply == 'y', or to group age >= 12 with age < 65. The result is the bizarre pair of runs in Figure 10-8.

```
How old are you? 85
Have a coupon? (Y/N) y
Please pay $5.25. Enjoy the show!

How old are you? 85
Have a coupon? (Y/N) Y
Please pay $3.25. Enjoy the show!
```

FIGURE 10-8: A capital offense.

In Figure 10-8, notice that the y and Y inputs yield different ticket prices, even though the age is 85 in both runs. This happens because, without parentheses, any && operator gets evaluated before any || operator. (That's the rule in the Java programming language — evaluate && before ||.) When reply is Y, the condition in the bad if statement takes the following form:

```
reply == 'Y' || some-other-stuff-that-does-not-matter
```

Whenever reply == 'Y' is true, the whole condition is automatically true, as illustrated in Figure 10-9.

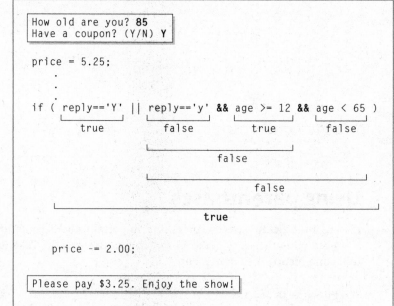

FIGURE 10-9: "True or false" makes "true."

Building a Nest

The year is 1968, and *The Prisoner* is on TV. In the last episode, the show's hero meets his nemesis, "Number One." At first, Number One wears a spooky happy-face/sad-face mask, and when the mask comes off, there's a monkey mask underneath. To find out what's behind the monkey mask, you have to rent the series and watch it yourself. But in the meantime, notice the layering: a mask within a mask. You can do the same kind of thing with if statements. This section's example shows you how.

But first, take a look at Listing 10-4. In that code, the condition age >= 12 &&
age < 65 is tested twice. Both times, the computer sends the numbers 12 and 65,
and the age value through its jumble of circuits; and both times, the computer
gets the same answer. This is wasteful, but waste isn't your only concern.

What if you decide to change the age limit for senior tickets? From now on, no one
under 100 gets a senior discount. You fish through the code and see the first
age >= 12 && age < 65 test. You change 65 to 100, pat yourself on the back, and
go home. The problem is, you've changed one of the two age >= 12 && age < 65
tests, but you haven't changed the other. Wouldn't it be better to keep all the
age >= 12 && age < 65 testing in just one place?

Listing 10-5 comes to the rescue. In Listing 10-5, I smoosh all my if statements
together into one big glob. The code is dense, but it gets the job done nicely.

LISTING 10-5: **Nested if Statements**

```java
import java.util.Scanner;

class AnotherAgeCheck {

    public static void main(String args[]) {
        Scanner keyboard = new Scanner(System.in);
        int age;
        double price = 0.00;
        char reply;

        System.out.print("How old are you? ");
        age = keyboard.nextInt();

        System.out.print("Have a coupon? (Y/N) ");
        reply = keyboard.findWithinHorizon(".", 0).charAt(0);

        if (age >= 12 && age < 65) {
            price = 9.25;
            if (reply == 'Y' || reply == 'y') {
                price -= 2.00;
            }
        } else {
            price = 5.25;
        }

        System.out.print("Please pay $");
        System.out.print(price);
```

(continued)

LISTING 10-5: *(continued)*

```
        System.out.print(". ");
        System.out.println("Enjoy the show!");

        keyboard.close();
    }
}
```

Nested if statements

A run of the code in Listing 10-5 looks identical to a run for Listing 10-4. You can see several runs in Figure 10-6. The main idea in Listing 10-5 is to put an if statement inside another if statement. After all, Chapter 9 says that an if statement can take the following form:

```
if (Condition) {
    SomeStatements
} else {
    OtherStatements
}
```

Who says *SomeStatements* can't contain an if statement? For that matter, *OtherStatements* can also contain an if statement. And, yes, you can create an if statement within an if statement within an if statement. There's no predefined limit on the number of if statements that you can have.

```
if (age >= 12 && age < 65) {
    price = 9.25;
    if (reply == 'Y' || reply == 'y') {
        if (isSpecialFeature) {
            price -= 1.00;
        } else {
            price -= 2.00;
        }
    }
} else {
    price = 5.25;
}
```

When you put one if statement inside another, you create *nested* if statements. Nested statements aren't difficult to write, as long as you take things slowly and keep a clear picture of the code's flow in your mind. If it helps, draw yourself a diagram like the one shown in Figure 10-10.

When you nest statements, you must be compulsive about the use of indentation and braces. (See Figure 10-11.) When code has misleading indentation, no one (not even the programmer who wrote the code) can figure out how the code works. A nested statement with sloppy indentation is a programmer's nightmare.

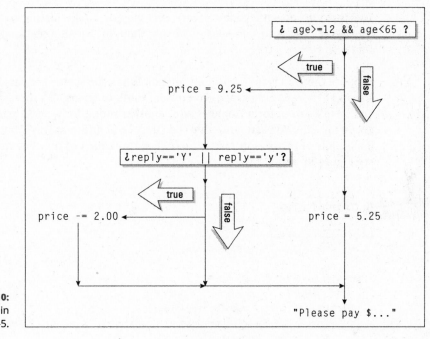

FIGURE 10-10:
The flow in
Listing 10-5.

FIGURE 10-11:
Be careful about
adding the
proper
indentation and
braces.

Cascading if statements

Here's a riddle: You have two baseball teams — the Hankees and the Socks. You want to display the teams' scores on two separate lines, with the winner's score listed first. (On the computer screen, the winner's score is displayed above the loser's score.) What happens when the scores are tied?

Do you give up? The answer is, there's no right answer. What happens depends on the way you write the program. Take a look at Listing 9-4, in Chapter 9. When the scores are equal, the condition hankees > socks is false. So the program's flow of execution drops down to the else clause. That clause displays the Socks score first and the Hankees score second. (Refer to Figure 9-7, in Chapter 9.)

The program doesn't have to work this way. If I take Listing 9-4 and change hankees > socks to hankees >= socks, then, in case of a tie, the Hankees score comes first.

Suppose that you want a bit more control. When the scores are equal, you want to see an It's a tie message. To do this, think in terms of a three-pronged fork. You have a prong for a Hankees win, another prong for a Socks win, and a third prong for a tie. You can write this code in several different ways, but one way that makes lots of sense is in Listing 10-6. For three runs of the code in Listing 10-6, see Figure 10-12.

LISTING 10-6: **In Case of a Tie . . .**

```java
import java.util.Scanner;
import static java.lang.System.out;

class WinLoseOrTie {

    public static void main(String args[]) {
        Scanner keyboard = new Scanner(System.in);
        int hankees, socks;

        out.print("Hankees and Socks scores?  ");
        hankees = keyboard.nextInt();
        socks = keyboard.nextInt();
        out.println();

        if (hankees > socks) {
            out.println("Hankees win...");
            out.print("Hankees: ");
            out.println(hankees);
            out.print("Socks:   ");
            out.println(socks);
        } else if (socks > hankees) {
            out.println("Socks win...");
            out.print("Socks:   ");
            out.println(socks);
            out.print("Hankees: ");
            out.println(hankees);
```

```
        } else {
            out.println("It's a tie...");
            out.print("Hankees: ");
            out.println(hankees);
            out.print("Socks:   ");
            out.println(socks);
        }

        keyboard.close();
    }
}
```

```
Hankees and Socks scores?  9 4

Hankees win...
Hankees: 9
Socks:   4

Hankees and Socks scores?  3 8

Socks win...
Socks:   8
Hankees: 3

Hankees and Socks scores?  0 0

It's a tie...
Hankees: 0
Socks:   0
```

FIGURE 10-12:
Go, team, go!

Listing 10-6 illustrates a way of thinking about a problem. You have one question with more than two answers. (In this section's baseball problem, the question is "Who wins?" and the answers are "Hankees," "Socks," or "Neither.") The problem begs for an if statement, but an if statement has only two branches — the true branch and the false branch. So you combine alternatives to form *cascading if statements*.

In Listing 10-6, the format for the cascading if statements is

```
if (Condition1) {
    SomeStatements
} else if (Condition2) {
    OtherStatements
} else {
    EvenMoreStatements
}
```

In general, you can use else if as many times as you want:

```java
if (hankeesWin) {
    out.println("Hankees win...");
    out.print("Hankees: ");
    out.println(hankees);
    out.print("Socks:   ");
    out.println(socks);
} else if (socksWin) {
    out.println("Socks win...");
    out.print("Socks:   ");
    out.println(socks);
    out.print("Hankees: ");
    out.println(hankees);
} else if (isATie) {
    out.println("It's a tie...");
    out.print("Hankees: ");
    out.println(hankees);
    out.print("Socks:   ");
    out.println(socks);
} else if (gameCancelled) {
    out.println("Sorry, sports fans.");
} else {
    out.println("The game isn't over yet.");
}
```

Nothing is special about cascading if statements. This isn't a new programming language feature. Cascading if statements take advantage of a loophole in Java — a loophole about omitting curly braces in certain circumstances. Other than that, cascading if statements just give you a new way to think about decisions within your code.

Note: Listing 10-6 uses a static import declaration to avoid needless repetition of the words System.out. To read a little bit about the static import declaration (along with an apology for my not explaining this concept more thoroughly), see Chapter 9. Then to get the real story on static import declarations, see Chapter 18.

Enumerating the Possibilities

Chapter 8 describes Java's boolean type — the type with only two values (true and false). The boolean type is very handy, but sometimes you need more values. After all, a traffic light's values can be green, yellow, or red. A playing card's suit can be spade, club, heart, or diamond. And a weekday can be Monday, Tuesday, Wednesday, Thursday, or Friday.

Life is filled with small sets of possibilities, and Java has a feature that can reflect these possibilities. The feature is called an enum type. It's available from Java version 5.0 onward.

Creating an enum type

The story in Listing 10-6 has three possible endings — the Hankees win, the Socks win, or the game is tied. You can represent the possibilities with the following line of Java code:

```
enum WhoWins {home, visitor, neither}
```

This week's game is played at Hankeeville's SnitSoft Stadium, so the value home represents a win for the Hankees, and the value visitor represents a win for the Socks.

One of the goals in computer programming is for each program's structure to mirror whatever problem the program solves. When a program reminds you of its underlying problem, the program is easy to understand and inexpensive to maintain. For example, a program to tabulate customer accounts should use names like customer and account. And a program that deals with three possible outcomes (home wins, visitor wins, and tie) should have a variable with three possible values. The line enum WhoWins {home, visitor, neither} creates a type to store three values.

The WhoWins type is called an *enum type.* Think of the new WhoWins type as a boolean on steroids. Instead of two values (true and false), the WhoWins type has three values (home, visitor, and neither). You can create a variable of type WhoWins:

```
WhoWins who;
```

and then assign a value to the new variable:

```
who = WhoWins.home;
```

In the next section, I put the WhoWins type to good use.

Using an enum type

Listing 10-7 shows you how to use the brand-new WhoWins type.

LISTING 10-7: **Proud Winners and Sore Losers**

```
import java.util.Scanner;
import static java.lang.System.out;

class Scoreboard {

    enum WhoWins {home, visitor, neither}

    public static void main(String args[]) {
        Scanner keyboard = new Scanner(System.in);
        int hankees, socks;
        WhoWins who;

        out.print("Hankees and Socks scores?   ");
        hankees = keyboard.nextInt();
        socks = keyboard.nextInt();
        out.println();

        if (hankees > socks) {
            who = WhoWins.home;
            out.println("The Hankees win :-)");
        } else if (socks > hankees) {
            who = WhoWins.visitor;
            out.println("The Socks win :-(");
        } else {
            who = WhoWins.neither;
            out.println("It's a tie :-|");
        }

        out.println();
        out.println("Today's game is brought to you by");
        out.println("SnitSoft, the number one software");
        out.println("vendor in the Hankeeville area.");
        out.println("SnitSoft is featured proudly in");
        out.println("Chapter 6. And remember, four out");
        out.println("of five doctors recommend");
        out.println("SnitSoft to their patients.");
        out.println();

        if (who == WhoWins.home) {
            out.println("We beat 'em good. Didn't we?");
        }

        if (who == WhoWins.visitor) {
            out.println("The umpire made an unfair call.");
        }
```

```
    if (who == WhoWins.neither) {
        out.println("The game goes into overtime.");
    }

    keyboard.close();
  }
}
```

Three runs of the program in Listing 10-7 are pictured in Figure 10-13.

Here's what happens in Listing 10-7:

>> **I create a variable to store values of type** WhoWins.

Just as the line

```
double amount;
```

declares amount to store double values (values like 5.95 and 30.95), the line

```
WhoWins who;
```

declares who to store WhoWins values (values like home, visitor, and neither).

>> **I assign a value to the** who **variable.**

I execute one of the

```
who = WhoWins.something;
```

assignment statements. The statement that I execute depends on the outcome of the if statement's hankees > socks comparison.

Notice that I refer to each of the WhoWins values in Listing 10-7. I write WhoWins.home, WhoWins.visitor, or WhoWins.neither. If I forget the WhoWins prefix and type

```
who = home;   //This assignment doesn't work!
```

the compiler gives me a home cannot be resolved to a variable error message. That's just the way enum types work.

>> **I compare the variable's value with each of the** WhoWins **values.**

In one if statement, I check the who == WhoWins.home condition. In the remaining two if statements, I check for the other WhoWins values.

```
Hankees and Socks scores?  9 4

The Hankees win :-)

Today's game is brought to you by
SnitSoft, the number one software
vendor in the Hankeeville area.
SnitSoft is featured proudly in
Chapter 6. And remember, four out
of five doctors recommend
SnitSoft to their patients.

We beat 'em good. Didn't we?


Hankees and Socks scores?  3 8

The Socks win :-(

Today's game is brought to you by
SnitSoft, the number one software
vendor in the Hankeeville area.
SnitSoft is featured proudly in
Chapter 6. And remember, four out
of five doctors recommend
SnitSoft to their patients.

The umpire made an unfair call.


Hankees and Socks scores?  0 0

It's a tie :-|

Today's game is brought to you by
SnitSoft, the number one software
vendor in the Hankeeville area.
SnitSoft is featured proudly in
Chapter 6. And remember, four out
of five doctors recommend
SnitSoft to their patients.

The game goes into overtime.
```

FIGURE 10-13:
Joy in
Hankeeville?

Near the end of Listing 10-7, I could have done without enum values. I could have tested things like hankees > socks a second time:

```java
if (hankees > socks) {
    out.println("The Hankees win :-)");
}


// And later in the program ...

if (hankees > socks) {
    out.println("We beat 'em good. Didn't we?");
}
```

But that tactic would be clumsy. In a more complicated program, I may end up checking hankees > socks a dozen times. It would be like asking the same question over and over again.

Instead of repeatedly checking the hankees > socks condition, I store the game's outcome as an enum value. Then I check the enum value as many times as I want. That's a tidy way to solve the repeated checking problem.

TRY IT OUT

It's okay to read about Java, but it's even better if you work with Java. Here are some things you can do to flex your Java muscles:

MYSTERIOUS WAYS

Explain why the following code always displays The first is smaller, no matter what numbers the user types. For example, if the user types 7 and then 5, the program displays The first is smaller:

```
int firstNumber = keyboard.nextInt();
int secondNumber = keyboard.nextInt();
boolean firstSmaller = firstNumber < secondNumber;

if (firstSmaller = true) {
    System.out.println("The first is smaller.");
}
```

WHAT KIND OF NUMBER?

Write a program that reads a number from the keyboard and displays one of the words positive, negative, or zero to describe that number. Use cascading if statements.

APPROACHING A TRAFFIC SIGNAL

Your driver's handbook says, "When approaching a green light, proceed through the intersection unless it's unsafe to do so, or unless a police officer directs you to do otherwise."

Write a program that asks the user three questions:

>> Are you approaching a green light?

>> Is it safe to proceed through the intersection?

>> Is a police officer directing you not to proceed?

In response to each question, the user replies Y or N. Based on the three replies, the program displays either Go or Stop.

Needless to say, you shouldn't run this program while you drive a vehicle.

"YES" AND "YES" AGAIN

Modify the "Approaching a traffic signal" program so that the program allows the user to reply "yes" with either an uppercase letter Y or a lowercase letter y.

RED OR YELLOW LIGHT

Modify the "Approaching a traffic signal" program so that the program asks What color is the traffic light? (G/Y/R). When the user replies Y or R, and either it's not safe to proceed or an office is directing drivers not to proceed, the program displays Stop. Otherwise, the program doesn't display anything.

WHAT? ANOTHER TRAFFIC SIGNAL PROGRAM?

You can use System.out.println to display an enum value. For example, in Listing 10-7, if you add the statement

```
System.out.println(who);
```

to the end of the main method, the program displays one of the words home, visitor, or neither. Try this by creating an enum named Color with values green, yellow, and red. Write a program that asks What color is the traffic light? (G/Y/R). Use the user's response to assign one of the values Color.green, Color.yellow, or Color.red to a variable named signal. Use System.out.println to display the value of the signal variable.

BUYING 3D GLASSES

My local movie theater charges an extra three dollars for a movie showing in 3D. (The theater makes me buy a new pair of 3D glasses. I can't bring the pair that I bought the last time I saw a 3D movie.) Modify the code in Listing 10-5 so that the program asks How many dimensions: 2 or 3? For a 3D movie, the program adds three dollars to the price of admission. (*Note:* The old *Twilight Zone* television series began with narrator Rod Serling talking about a fifth dimension. I wonder what I'd have to pay nowadays to see the *Twilight Zone* in my local movie theater!)

Chapter **11**

How to Flick a Virtual Switch

Imagine playing *Let's Make a Deal* with ten different doors. "Choose door number 1, door number 2, door number 3, door number 4 . . . Wait! Let's break for a commercial. When we come back, I'll say the names of the other six doors."

What Monty Hall (the show's host) needs is Java's `switch` statement.

Meet the switch Statement

The code in Listing 9-2 (refer to Chapter 9) simulates a fortune-telling toy — an electronic oracle. Ask the program a question, and the program randomly generates a yes or no answer. But, as toys go, the code in Listing 9-2 isn't much fun. The code has only two possible answers. There's no variety. Even the earliest talking dolls could say about ten different sentences.

Suppose that you want to enhance the code of Listing 9-2. The call to `myRandom.nextInt(10) + 1` generates numbers from 1 to 10. So maybe you can display a different sentence for each of the ten numbers. A big pile of if statements should do the trick:

```java
if (randomNumber == 1) {
    System.out.println("Yes. Isn't it obvious?");
}
if (randomNumber == 2) {
    System.out.println("No, and don't ask again.");
}
if (randomNumber == 3) {
    System.out.print("Yessir, yessir!");
    System.out.println(" Three bags full.");
}
if (randomNumber == 4)

       .

       .

       .

if (randomNumber < 1 || randomNumber > 10) {
    System.out.print("Sorry, the electronic oracle");
    System.out.println(" is closed for repairs.");
}
```

But that approach seems wasteful. Why not create a statement that checks the value of randomNumber just once and then takes an action based on the value that it finds? Fortunately, just such a statement exists: the *switch* statement. Listing 11-1 has an example of a switch statement.

LISTING 11-1: **An Answer for Every Occasion**

```java
import java.util.Scanner;
import java.util.Random;
import static java.lang.System.out;

class TheOldSwitcheroo {

    public static void main(String args[]) {
        Scanner keyboard = new Scanner(System.in);
        Random myRandom = new Random();
        int randomNumber;

        out.print("Type your question, my child:   ");
        keyboard.nextLine();
```

```java
randomNumber = myRandom.nextInt(10) + 1;

switch (randomNumber) {
case 1:
    out.println("Yes. Isn't it obvious?");
    break;

case 2:
    out.println("No, and don't ask again.");
    break;

case 3:
    out.print("Yessir, yessir!");
    out.println(" Three bags full.");
    break;

case 4:
    out.println("What part of 'no' don't you understand?");
    break;

case 5:
    out.println("No chance, Lance.");
    break;

case 6:
    out.println("Sure, whatever.");
    break;

case 7:
    out.println("Yes, but only if you're nice to me.");
    break;

case 8:
    out.println("Yes (as if I care).");
    break;

case 9:
    out.println("No, not until Cromwell seizes Dover.");
    break;

case 10:
    out.println("No, not until Nell squeezes Rover.");
    break;

default:
    out.print("You think you have problems?");
    out.print(" My random number generator is broken!");
```

(continued)

LISTING 11-1: *(continued)*

```
            break;
    }

    out.println("Goodbye");

    keyboard.close();
  }
}
```

The cases in a switch statement

Figure 11-1 shows three runs of the program in Listing 11-1. Here's what happens during one of these runs:

 >> The user types a heavy question, and the variable randomNumber gets a value. In the second run of Figure 11-1, this value is 2.

 >> Execution of the code in Listing 11-1 reaches the top of the switch statement, so the computer starts checking this statement's case clauses. The value 2 doesn't match the topmost case clause (the case 1 clause), so the computer moves on to the next case clause.

 >> The value in the next case clause (the number 2) matches the value of the randomNumber variable, so the computer executes the statements in this case 2 clause. These two statements are

```
out.println("No, and don't ask again.");
break;
```

The first of the two statements displays No, and don't ask again on the screen. The second statement is called a break statement. (What a surprise!) When the computer encounters a break statement, the computer jumps out of whatever switch statement it's in. So, in Listing 11-1, the computer skips right past case 3, case 4, and so on. The computer jumps to the statement just after the end of the switch statement.

 >> The computer displays Goodbye because that's what the statement after the switch statement tells the computer to do.

Type your question, my child: Is the Continuum Hypothesis true?
Sure, whatever.

?

...ring machine T halt on input i?

FIGURE 1
Running the
of Listing

...isting 11-1 is illustrated in Figure 11-2.

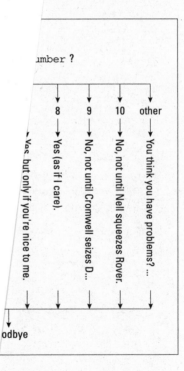

...mber ?

8 | 9 | 10 | other

Yes, but only if you're nice to me.

Yes (as if I care).

No, not until Cromwell seizes D...

No, not until Nell squeezes Rover.

You think you have problems? ...

...odbye

...switch statement

...y wrong during a run of the Listing 11-1 program? ...myRandom.nextInt(10) + 1 generates a number ...e. Then the computer responds by dropping past all ...anding on a case clause, the computer jumps to the ...ult clause, the computer displays You think you ...n breaks out of the switch statement. After the com- ...atement, the computer displays Goodbye.

TIP

You don't really need to put a break at the very end of a switch statement. In Listing 11-1, the last break (the break that's part of the default clause) is just for the sake of overall tidiness.

Picky details about the switch statement

A switch statement can take the following form:

```
switch (Expression) {
case FirstValue:
    Statements

case SecondValue:
    MoreStatements

// ... more cases ...

default:
    EvenMoreStatements
}
```

Here are some tidbits about switch statements:

>> The *Expression* doesn't have to have an int value. It can be char, byte, short, or int.

For example, the following code works in Java 5 and later:

```
char letterGrade;
letterGrade = keyboard.findWithinHorizon(".",0).charAt(0);

switch (letterGrade) {
case 'A':
    System.out.println("Excellent");
    break;

case 'B':
    System.out.println("Good");
    break;

case 'C':
    System.out.println("Average");
    break;
}
```

In fact, if you avoid using the Scanner class and its findWithinHorizon method, this bullet's switch statement works with all versions of Java — old and new.

» If you use Java 7 or later, the *Expression* can be a String. For example, the following code doesn't work with Java 6, but works well in Java 7:

```
String description;
description = keyboard.next();

switch (description) {
case "Excellent":
    System.out.println('A');
    break;

case "Good":
    System.out.println('B');
    break;

case "Average":
    System.out.println('C');
    break;
}
```

CROSS REFERENCE

I introduce Java's String type briefly in Chapter 8. I describe the String class with gusto in Chapter 18.

» The *Expression* doesn't have to be a single variable. It can be any expression of type char, byte, short, int, or String. For example, you can simulate the rolling of two dice with the following code:

```
int die1, die2;

die1 = myRandom.nextInt(6) + 1;
die2 = myRandom.nextInt(6) + 1;

switch (die1 + die2) {
    // ... etc.
```

» The cases in a switch statement don't have to be in order. Here's some acceptable code:

```
switch (randomNumber) {
case 2:
    System.out.println("No, and don't ask again.");
    break;
```

```
case 1:
    System.out.println("Yes. Isn't it obvious?");
    break;

case 3:
    System.out.print("Yessir, yessir!");
    System.out.println(" Three bags full.");
    break;

// ... etc.
```

This mixing of cases may slow you down when you're trying to read and understand a program, but it's legal nonetheless.

» You don't need a case for each expected value of the *Expression*. You can leave some expected values to the default. Here's an example:

```
switch (randomNumber) {
case 1:
    System.out.println("Yes. Isn't it obvious?");
    break;

case 5:
    System.out.println("No chance, Lance.");
    break;

case 7:
    System.out.println("Yes, but only if you're nice to me.");
    break;

case 10:
    System.out.println("No, not until Nell squeezes Rover.");
    break;

default:
    System.out.println("Sorry, I just can't decide.");
    break;
}
```

» The default clause is optional.

```
switch (randomNumber) {
case 1:
    System.out.println("Yes. Isn't it obvious?");
    break;
```

```
case 2:
    System.out.println("No, and don't ask again.");
    break;

case 3:
    System.out.print("I'm too tired.");
    System.out.println(" Go ask somebody else.");
}


System.out.println("Goodbye");
```

If you have no default clause, and a value that's not covered by any of the cases comes up, the switch statement does nothing. For example, if random-Number is 4, the preceding code displays Goodbye and nothing else.

» In some ways, if statements are more versatile than switch statements. For example, you can't use a condition in a switch statement's *Expression*:

```
//You can't do this:
switch (age >= 12 && age < 65)
```

You can't use a condition as a case value, either:

```
//You can't do this:
switch (age) {
case age <= 12:      // ... etc.
```

To break or not to break

At one time or another, every Java programmer forgets to use break statements. At first, the resulting output is confusing, but then the programmer remembers fall-through. The term *fall-through* describes what happens when you end a case without a break statement. What happens is that execution of the code falls right through to the next case in line. Execution keeps falling through until you eventually reach a break statement or the end of the entire switch statement.

If you don't believe me, just look at Listing 11-2. This listing's code has a switch statement gone bad.

LISTING 11-2: **Please, Gimme a Break!**

```
/*
 * This isn't good code. The programmer forgot some
 * of the break statements.
 */
import java.util.Scanner;
import java.util.Random;
import static java.lang.System.out;

class BadBreaks {

    public static void main(String args[]) {
        Scanner keyboard = new Scanner(System.in);
        Random myRandom = new Random();
        int randomNumber;

        out.print("Type your question, my child:  ");
        keyboard.nextLine();

        randomNumber = myRandom.nextInt(10) + 1;

        switch (randomNumber) {
        case 1:
            out.println("Yes. Isn't it obvious?");

        case 2:
            out.println("No, and don't ask again.");

        case 3:
            out.print("Yessir, yessir!");
            out.println(" Three bags full.");

        case 4:
            out.println("What part of 'no' don't you understand?");
            break;

        case 5:
            out.println("No chance, Lance.");

        case 6:
            out.println("Sure, whatever.");

        case 7:
            out.println("Yes, but only if you're nice to me.");

        case 8:
            out.println("Yes (as if I care).");
```

```
        case 9:
            out.println("No, not until Cromwell seizes Dover.");

        case 10:
            out.println("No, not until Nell squeezes Rover.");

        default:
            out.print("You think you have problems?");
            out.println(" My random number generator is broken!");
        }

        out.println("Goodbye");

        keyboard.close();
    }
}
```

I've put two runs of this code in Figure 11-3. In the first run, the randomNumber is 7. The program executes cases 7 through 10, and the default. In the second run, the randomNumber is 3. The program executes cases 3 and 4. Then, because case 4 has a break statement, the program jumps out of the switch and displays Goodbye.

```
Type your question, my child:  Do good things happen to good people?
Yes, but only if you're nice to me.
Yes (as if I care).
No, not until Cromwell seizes Dover.
No, not until Nell squeezes Rover.
You think you have problems? My random number generator is broken!
Goodbye

Type your question, my child:  Is your switch statement missing some breaks?
Yessir, yessir! Three bags full.
What part of 'no' don't you understand?
Goodbye
```

FIGURE 11-3:
Please make up
your mind.

REMEMBER

The switch statement in Listing 11-2 is missing some break statements. Even without these break statements, the code compiles with no errors. But when you run the code in Listing 11-2, you don't get the results that you want.

Using Fall-Through to Your Advantage

Often, when you're using a switch statement, you don't want fall-through, so you pepper break statements throughout the switch. But, sometimes, fall-through is just the thing you need.

Take the number of days in a month. Is there a simple rule for this? Months containing the letter *r* have 31 days? Months in which *i* comes before *e* except after *c* have 30 days?

You can fiddle with `if` conditions all you want. But to handle all the possibilities, I prefer a `switch` statement. Listing 11-3 demonstrates the idea.

LISTING 11-3: **Finding the Number of Days in a Month**

```
import java.util.Scanner;

class DaysInEachMonth {

    public static void main(String args[]) {

        Scanner keyboard = new Scanner(System.in);
        int month, numberOfDays = 0;
        boolean isLeapYear;
        System.out.print("Which month? ");
        month = keyboard.nextInt();

        switch (month) {
        case 1:
        case 3:
        case 5:
        case 7:
        case 8:
        case 10:
        case 12:
            numberOfDays = 31;
            break;

        case 4:
        case 6:
        case 9:
        case 11:
            numberOfDays = 30;
            break;

        case 2:
            System.out.print("Leap year (true/false)? ");
            isLeapYear = keyboard.nextBoolean();
            if (isLeapYear) {
                numberOfDays = 29;
            } else {
                numberOfDays = 28;
            }
```

```
        }

        System.out.print(numberOfDays);
        System.out.println(" days");

        keyboard.close();
    }
}
```

Figure 11-4 shows several runs of the program in Listing 11-3. For month number 6, the computer jumps to case 6. There are no statements inside the case 6 clause, so that part of the program's run is pretty boring.

```
Which month? 1
31 days

Which month? 6
30 days

Which month? 2
Leap year (true/false)? false
28 days

Which month? 2
Leap year (true/false)? true
29 days
```

FIGURE 11-4:
How many days until the next big deadline?

But with no break in the case 6 clause, the computer marches right along to case 9. Once again, the computer finds no statements and no break, so the computer ventures to the next case, which is case 11. At that point, the computer hits pay dirt. The computer assigns 30 to numberOfDays and breaks out of the entire switch statement. (See Figure 11-5.)

February is the best month of all. For one thing, the February case in Listing 11-3 contains a call to the Scanner class's nextBoolean method. The method expects me to type either true or false. The code uses whatever word I type to assign a value to a boolean variable. (In Listing 11-3, I assign true or false to the isLeapYear variable.)

February also contains its own if statement. In Chapter 10, I nest if statements within other if statements. But in February, I nest an if statement within a switch statement. That's cool.

TRY IT OUT

Here's where you get practice using switch statements.

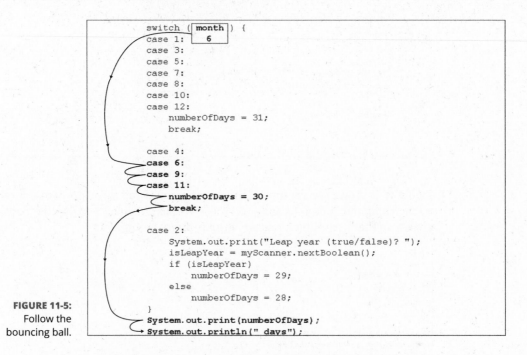

```
switch ( month ) {
                6
case 1:
case 3:
case 5:
case 7:
case 8:
case 10:
case 12:
    numberOfDays = 31;
    break;

case 4:
case 6:
case 9:
case 11:
    numberOfDays = 30;
    break;

case 2:
    System.out.print("Leap year (true/false)? ");
    isLeapYear = myScanner.nextBoolean();
    if (isLeapYear)
        numberOfDays = 29;
    else
        numberOfDays = 28;
}
System.out.print(numberOfDays);
System.out.println(" days");
```

FIGURE 11-5:
Follow the
bouncing ball.

DON'T DO THIS AT HOME (OR ANYWHERE ELSE)

What's wrong with the following code, and how can you fix it?

```
switch (amount) {
case 1:
    System.out.println("US cent");
case 5:
    System.out.println("US nickel");
case 10:
    System.out.println("US dime");
case 25:
    System.out.println("US quarter");
case 50:
    System.out.println("US half dollar");
case 100:
    System.out.println("US dollar");
default:
    System.out.println("Not a US coin");
}
```

DAYS OF THE WEEK

Write a program that reads a number (from 1 to 7) and displays the day of the week corresponding to that number. For example, in the United States, Sunday is counted as the first day of the week. So, if the user types 1, my program displays Sunday. If the user types 2, my program displays Monday. And so on.

TIME TO EAT

Write a program that asks the user what the current hour is, and uses a switch statement to inform the user about mealtime. If the hour is between 6 a.m. and 9 a.m., tell the user, "Breakfast is served." If the hour is between 11 a.m. and 1 p.m., tell the user, "Time for lunch." If the hour is between 5 p.m. and 8 p.m., tell the user, "It's dinnertime." For any other hours, tell the user, "Sorry, you'll have to wait, or go get a snack."

A TINY CALCULATOR

Write a program that prompts the user for two numbers and a character. In a switch statement, the program applies the character's operation to the two numbers and displays the result. A run of the program might look like this:

```
First number: 21.0
Second number: 8.0
Operation (+ - * or /): +
29.0
```

The program accepts any one of the characters +, -, *, or /. For an additional challenge, enhance the program's output as follows:

```
First number: 31.0
Second number: 10.0
Operation (+- * or /): *
31.0 * 10.0 = 310.0
```

Remember that you can't use Java's + sign to display a char value next to a numeric value. If you execute System.out.println(5 + ' ' + '*'), Java doesn't display 5 *. Instead, Java displays 79. (If you don't believe me, try it in JShell.)

COLOR BY NUMBERS

In the RGB color model, numeric values indicate amounts of red, green, and blue. If you mix red, green, and blue to show only eight colors, 0 is black, 1 is blue, 2 is green, 3 is cyan, 4 is red, 5 is magenta, 6 is yellow, and 7 is white. Write a program that reads a number from the keyboard and displays the name of that number's color.

Using a Conditional Operator

Java has a neat feature that I can't resist writing about. Using this feature, you can think about alternatives in a natural way.

And what do I mean by "a natural way"? If I think out loud as I imitate the if statement near the end of Listing 11-3, I come up with this:

```
//The thinking in Listing 11-3:
What should I do next?
If this is a leap year,
    I'll make the numberOfDays be 29;
Otherwise,
    I'll make the numberOfDays be 28.
```

I'm wandering into an if statement without a clue about what I'm doing next. That seems silly. It's February, and everybody knows what you do in February. You ask how many days the month has.

In my opinion, the code in Listing 11-3 doesn't reflect the most natural way to think about February. Here's a more natural way:

```
//A more natural way to think about the problem:
The value of numberOfDays is...
    Wait! Is this a leap year?
        If yes, 29
        If no, 28
```

In this second, more natural way of thinking, I know from the start that I'm picking a number of days. So by the time I reach a fork in the road (Is this a leap year?), the only remaining task is to choose between 29 and 28.

I can make the choice with finesse:

```
case 2:
    System.out.print("Leap year (true/false)? ");
    isLeapYear = keyboard.nextBoolean();
    numberOfDays = isLeapYear ? 29 : 28;
```

The ? : combination is called a *conditional operator*. In Figure 11-6, I show you how my natural thinking about February can morph into the conditional operator's format.

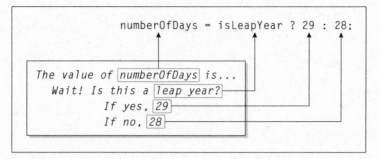

FIGURE 11-6:
From your mind
to the computer's
code.

Taken as a whole, `isLeapYear ? 29 : 28` is an expression with a value. And what value does this expression have? Well, the value of `isLeapYear ? 29 : 28` is either 29 or 28. It depends on whether `isLeapYear` is or isn't `true`. That's how the conditional operator works:

>> If the stuff before the question mark is `true`, the whole expression's value is whatever comes between the question mark and the colon.

>> If the stuff before the question mark is `false`, the whole expression's value is whatever comes after the colon.

Figure 11-7 gives you a goofy way to visualize these ideas.

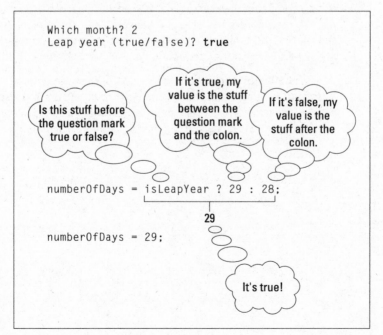

FIGURE 11-7:
Have you ever
seen an
expression
talking to itself?

The conditional operator's overall effect is as though the computer is executing

```
numberOfDays = 29;
```

or

```
numberOfDays = 28;
```

One way or another, `numberOfDays` gets a value, and the code solves the problem with style.

Get some practice using Java's conditional operator.

TRY IT OUT

DRESSED TO THE NINES

Take another look at the Try It Out programs in Chapter 9. Rewrite some of those programs using conditional operators.

» Ask the user if he or she wants to see a smiley face. Display :-) if the user replies Y; display :-(otherwise.

» Randomly generate one number and have the user enter a number. Display You win! if the numbers match, and You lose otherwise.

» Read a number of meters from the keyboard. Then read a letter (either c or m) from the keyboard. If the letter is c, convert meters to centimeters and display the result. If the letter is m, convert meters to millimeters and display the result. (Assume that the user always types either the letter c or the letter m.)

» Read a number of meters from the keyboard. Then read a letter from the keyboard. If the letter is c, convert meters to centimeters and display the result. If the letter is m, convert meters to millimeters and display the result. For any other letters, display the original number of meters.

Chapter **12**

Around and Around It Goes

C hapter 8 has code to reverse the letters in a four-letter word that the user enters. In case you haven't read Chapter 8 or you just don't want to flip to it, here's a quick recap of the code:

```
c1 = keyboard.findWithinHorizon(".",0).charAt(0);
c2 = keyboard.findWithinHorizon(".",0).charAt(0);
c3 = keyboard.findWithinHorizon(".",0).charAt(0);
c4 = keyboard.findWithinHorizon(".",0).charAt(0);

System.out.print(c4);
System.out.print(c3);
System.out.print(c2);
System.out.print(c1);
```

The code is just dandy for words with exactly four letters, but how do you reverse a five-letter word? As the code stands, you have to add two new statements:

```
c1 = keyboard.findWithinHorizon(".",0).charAt(0);
c2 = keyboard.findWithinHorizon(".",0).charAt(0);
c3 = keyboard.findWithinHorizon(".",0).charAt(0);
c4 = keyboard.findWithinHorizon(".",0).charAt(0);
c5 = keyboard.findWithinHorizon(".",0).charAt(0);
```

```
System.out.print(c5);
System.out.print(c4);
System.out.print(c3);
System.out.print(c2);
System.out.print(c1);
```

What a drag! You add statements to a program whenever the size of a word changes! You remove statements when the input shrinks! That can't be the best way to solve the problem. Maybe you can command a computer to add statements automatically. (But then again, maybe you can't.)

As luck would have it, you can do something that's even better: You can write a statement once and tell the computer to execute the statement many times. How many times? You can tell the computer to execute a statement as many times as it needs to be executed.

That's the big idea. The rest of this chapter has the details.

Repeating Instructions over and over Again (Java while Statements)

Here's a simple dice game: Keep rolling two dice until you roll 7 or 11. Listing 12-1 has a program that simulates the action in the game, and Figure 12-1 shows two runs of the program.

```
3 1
4 3
Rolled 7

2 1
4 6
5 3
6 4
4 6
1 5
2 2
1 5
1 3
2 6
1 4
6 5
Rolled 11
```

FIGURE 12-1:
Momma needs
a new pair
of shoes.

LISTING 12-1: **Roll 7 or 11**

```java
import java.util.Random;
import static java.lang.System.out;

class SimpleDiceGame {

    public static void main(String args[]) {
        Random myRandom = new Random();
        int die1 = 0, die2 = 0;

        while (die1 + die2 != 7 && die1 + die2 != 11) {
            die1 = myRandom.nextInt(6) + 1;
            die2 = myRandom.nextInt(6) + 1;
            out.print(die1);
            out.print(" ");
            out.println(die2);
        }

        out.print("Rolled ");
        out.println(die1 + die2);
    }
}
```

At the core of Listing 12-1 is a thing called a *while statement* (also known as a *while loop*). A `while` statement has the following form:

```
while (Condition) {
    Statements
}
```

Rephrased in English, the `while` statement in Listing 12-1 would say

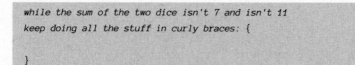

```
while the sum of the two dice isn't 7 and isn't 11
keep doing all the stuff in curly braces: {


}
```

The stuff in curly braces (the stuff that's repeated over and over) is the code that gets two new random numbers and displays those random numbers' values. The statements in curly braces are repeated as long as `die1 + die2 != 7 && die1 + die2 != 11` keeps being true.

Each repetition of the statements in the loop is called an *iteration* of the loop. In Figure 12-1, the first run has 2 iterations, and the second run has 12 iterations.

When `die1 + die2 != 7 && die1 + die2 != 11` is no longer true (that is, when the `sum` is either 7 or 11), the repeating of statements stops dead in its tracks. The computer marches on to the statements that come after the loop.

Following the action in a loop

To trace the action of the code in Listing 12-1, I'll borrow numbers from the first run in Figure 12-1:

>> At the start, the values of `die1` and `die2` are both `0`.

>> The computer gets to the top of the `while` statement and checks to see whether `die1 + die2 != 7 && die1 + die2 != 11` is true. (See Figure 12-2.) The condition is true, so the computer takes the `true` path in Figure 12-3.

The computer performs an iteration of the loop. During this iteration, the computer gets new values for `die1` and `die2` and prints those values on the screen. In the first run of Figure 12-1, the new values are 3 and 1.

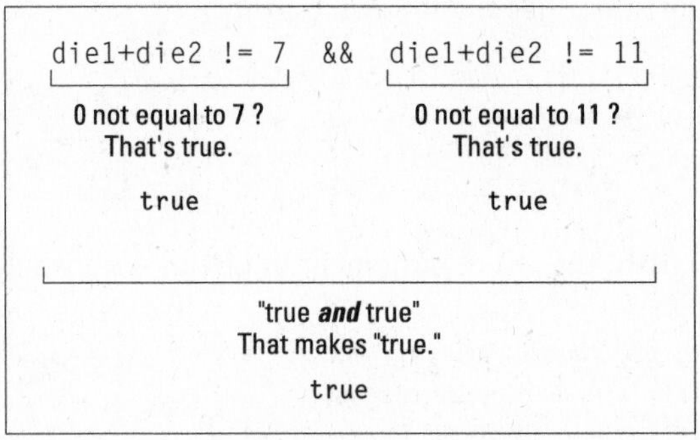

FIGURE 12-2:
Two wrongs don't make a right, but two trues make a true.

```
die1+die2 != 7    &&   die1+die2 != 11
└──────┬──────┘        └──────┬──────┘
  0 not equal to 7 ?      0 not equal to 11 ?
    That's true.            That's true.

       true                    true
└─────────────────────────────────────────┘
              "true and true"
           That makes "true."
                  true
```

>> The computer returns to the top of the `while` statement and checks to see whether `die1 + die2 != 7 && die1 + die2 != 11` is still true. The condition is true, so the computer takes the `true` path in Figure 12-3.

The computer performs another iteration of the loop. During this iteration, the computer gets new values for `die1` and `die2` and prints those values on the screen. In Figure 12-1, the new values are 4 and 3.

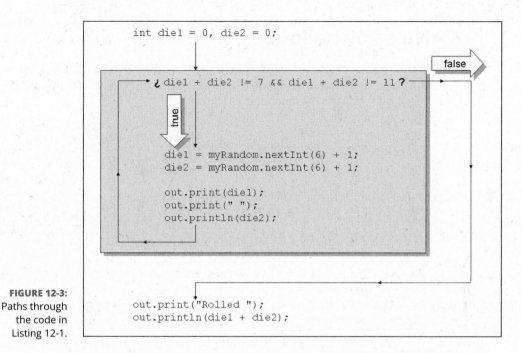

```
int die1 = 0, die2 = 0;
```
```
¿ die1 + die2 != 7 && die1 + die2 != 11 ?
```
false

true

```
die1 = myRandom.nextInt(6) + 1;
die2 = myRandom.nextInt(6) + 1;

out.print(die1);
out.print(" ");
out.println(die2);
```

```
out.print("Rolled ");
out.println(die1 + die2);
```

FIGURE 12-3:
Paths through
the code in
Listing 12-1.

» The computer returns to the top of the `while` statement and checks to see
whether `die1 + die2 != 7 && die1 + die2 != 11` is still true. Lo and
behold! This condition has become false! (See Figure 12-4.) The computer
takes the `false` path in Figure 12-3.

The computer leaps to the statements after the loop. The computer displays
`Rolled 7` and ends its run of the program.

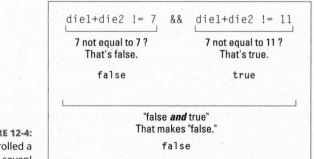

```
die1+die2 != 7    &&    die1+die2 != 11
```

7 not equal to 7 ?   7 not equal to 11 ?
That's false.   That's true.

false   true

"false **and** true"
That makes "false."
false

FIGURE 12-4:
Look! I rolled a
seven!

No early bailout

In Listing 12-1, when the computer finds `die1 + die2 != 7 && die1 + die2 != 11` to be true, the computer marches on and executes all five statements inside the loop's curly braces. The computer executes

```
die1 = myRandom.nextInt(6) + 1;
die2 = myRandom.nextInt(6) + 1;
```

STATEMENTS AND BLOCKS (PLAGIARIZING MY OWN SENTENCES FROM CHAPTER 9)

Java's `while` statements have a lot in common with `if` statements. Like an `if` statement, a `while` statement is a *compound statement* — that is, a `while` statement includes other statements within it. Also, both `if` statements and `while` statements typically include *blocks* of statements. When you surround a bunch of statements with curly braces, you get what's called a *block,* and a block behaves, in all respects, like a single statement.

In a typical `while` statement, you want the computer to repeat several smaller statements over and over again. To repeat several smaller statements, you combine those statements into one big statement. To do this, you make a block using curly braces.

In Listing 12-1, the block

```
{
    die1=myRandom.nextInt(6)+1;
    die2=myRandom.nextInt(6)+1;

    out.print(die1);
    out.print(" ");
    out.println(die2);
}
```

is a single statement. It's a statement that has, within it, five smaller statements. So this big block (this single statement) serves as one big statement inside the `while` statement in Listing 12-1.

That's the story about `while` statements and blocks. To find out how this stuff applies to `if` statements, see the "Statements and blocks" sidebar near the end of Chapter 9.

Maybe (just maybe), the new values of die1 and die2 add up to 7. Even so, the computer doesn't jump out in mid-loop. The computer finishes the iteration and executes

```
out.print(die1);
out.print(" ");
out.println(die2);
```

one more time. The computer performs the test again (to see whether die1 + die2 != 7 && die1 + die2 != 11 is still true) only after it fully executes all five statements in the loop.

Thinking about Loops (What Statements Go Where)

Here's a simplified version of the card game Twenty-One: You keep taking cards until the total is 21 or higher. Then, if the total is 21, you win. If the total is higher, you lose. (By the way, each face card counts as a 10.) To play this game, you want a program whose runs look like the runs in Figure 12-5.

```
Card     Total
8        8
6        14
3        17
4        21
You win :-)


Card     Total
1        1
7        8
3        11
4        15
2        17
2        19
3        22
You lose :-(
```

FIGURE 12-5: You win sum; you lose sum.

In most sections of this book, I put a program's listing before the description of the program's features. But this section is different. This section deals with strategies for composing code. So in this section, I start by brainstorming about strategies.

Finding some pieces

How do you write a program that plays a simplified version of Twenty-One? I start by fishing for clues in the game's rules, spelled out in this section's first paragraph. The big fishing expedition is illustrated in Figure 12-6.

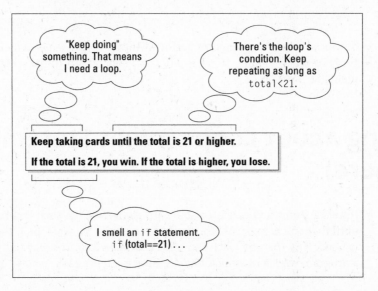

FIGURE 12-6:
Thinking about a programming problem.

With the reasoning in Figure 12-6, I need a loop and an `if` statement:

```
while (total < 21) {
    //do stuff
}

if (total == 21) {
    //You win
} else {
    //You lose
}
```

What else do I need to make this program work? Look at the sample output in Figure 12-5. I need a heading with the words `Card` and `Total`. That's a call to `System.out.println`:

```
System.out.println("Card    Total");
```

I also need several lines of output — each containing two numbers. For example, in Figure 12-5, the line 6 14 displays the values of two variables. One variable stores the most recently picked card; the other variable stores the total of all cards picked so far:

```
System.out.print(card);
System.out.print("        ");
System.out.println(total);
```

Now I have four chunks of code, but I haven't decided how they all fit together. Well, you can go right ahead and call me crazy. But at this point in the process, I imagine those four chunks of code circling around one another, like part of a dream sequence in a low-budget movie. As you may imagine, I'm not very good at illustrating circling code in dream sequences. Even so, I handed my idea to the art department folks at John Wiley & Sons, Inc., and they came up with the picture in Figure 12-7.

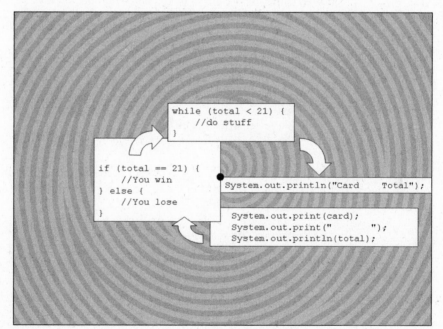

FIGURE 12-7:
. . . and where
they stop,
nobody knows.

Assembling the pieces

Where should I put each piece of code? The best way to approach the problem is to ask how many times each piece of code should be executed:

» **The program displays** card **and** total **values more than once.** For example, in the first run of Figure 12-5, the program displays these values four times (first 8 8, and then 6 14, and so on). To get this repeated display, I put the code that creates the display inside the loop:

```
while (total < 21) {
    System.out.print(card);
    System.out.print("        ");
    System.out.println(total);
}
```

» **The program displays the** Card Total **heading only once per run.** This display comes before any of the repeated number displays, so I put the heading code before the loop:

```
System.out.println("Card     Total");

while (total < 21) {
    System.out.print(card);
    System.out.print("        ");
    System.out.println(total);
}
```

» **The program displays** You win **or** You lose **only once per run.** This message display comes after the repeated number displays. So I put the win/lose code after the loop:

```
//Preliminary draft code -- NOT ready for prime time:
System.out.println("Card     Total");

while (total < 21) {
    System.out.print(card);
    System.out.print("        ");
    System.out.println(total);
}

if (total == 21) {
    System.out.println("You win :-)");
} else {
    System.out.println("You lose :-(");
}
```

Getting values for variables

I almost have a working program. But if I take the code that I've developed for a mental test run, I face a few problems. To see what I mean, picture yourself in the computer's shoes for a minute. (Well, a computer doesn't have shoes. Picture yourself in the computer's boots.)

You start at the top of the code shown in the previous section (the code that starts with the Preliminary draft comment). In the code's first statement, you display the words Card Total. So far, so good. But then you encounter the while loop and test the condition total < 21. Well, is total less than 21, or isn't it? Honestly, I'm tempted to make up an answer because I'm embarrassed about not knowing what the total variable's value is. (I'm sure the computer is embarrassed, too.)

The variable total must have a known value before the computer reaches the top of the while loop. Because a player starts with no cards at all, the initial total value should be 0. That settles it. I declare int total = 0 at the top of the program.

But what about my friend, the card variable? Should I set card to zero also? No. There's no zero-valued card in a deck (at least, not when I'm playing fair). Besides, card should get a new value several times during the program's run.

Wait! In the previous sentence, the phrase *several times* tickles a neuron in my brain. It stimulates the *inside a loop* reflex. So I place an assignment to the card variable inside my while loop:

```java
//This is a DRAFT -- still NOT ready for prime time:
int card, total = 0;

System.out.println("Card      Total");

while (total < 21) {
    card = myRandom.nextInt(10) + 1;

    System.out.print(card);
    System.out.print("        ");
    System.out.println(total);
}

if (total == 21) {
    System.out.println("You win :-)");
} else {
    System.out.println("You lose :-(");
}
```

The code still has an error, and I can probably find the error with more computer role-playing. But instead, I get daring. I run this beta code to see what happens. Figure 12-8 shows part of a run.

```
Card    Total
5       0
10       0
3       0
4       0
8       0
5       0
5       0
1       0
6       0
7       0
2       0
1       0
3       0
4       0
8       0
3       0
9       0
```

FIGURE 12-8:
An incorrect run.

Unfortunately, the run in Figure 12-8 doesn't stop on its own. This kind of processing is called an *infinite loop.* The loop runs and runs until someone trips over the computer's extension cord.

REMEMBER

You can stop a program's run dead in its tracks. Look for the tiny red rectangle at the top of Eclipse's Console view. When you hover the cursor over the rectangle, the tooltip says *Terminate.* When you click the rectangle, the active Java program stops running and the rectangle turns gray.

From infinity to affinity

For some problems, an infinite loop is normal and desirable. Consider, for example, a real-time mission-critical application — air traffic control, or the monitoring of a heart-lung machine. In these situations, a program should run and run and run.

But a game of Twenty-One should end pretty quickly. In Figure 12-8, the game doesn't end, because the total never reaches 21 or higher. In fact, the total is always zero. The problem is that my code has no statement to change the total variable's value. I should add each card's value to the total:

```
total += card;
```

Again, I ask myself where this statement belongs in the code. How many times should the computer execute this assignment statement? Once at the start of the program? Once at the end of the run? Repeatedly?

The computer should repeatedly add a card's value to the running total. In fact, the computer should add to the total each time a card gets drawn. So the preceding assignment statement should be inside the `while` loop, right alongside the statement that gets a new `card` value:

```
card = myRandom.nextInt(10) + 1;
total += card;
```

With this revelation, I'm ready to see the complete program. The code is in Listing 12-2, and two runs of the code are shown in Figure 12-5.

LISTING 12-2: A Simplified Version of the Game Twenty-One

```java
import java.util.Random;

class PlayTwentyOne {

    public static void main(String args[]) {
        Random myRandom = new Random();
        int card, total = 0;

        System.out.println("Card    Total");

        while (total < 21) {
            card = myRandom.nextInt(10) + 1;
            total += card;

            System.out.print(card);
            System.out.print("        ");
            System.out.println(total);
        }

        if (total == 21) {
            System.out.println("You win :-)");
        } else {
            System.out.println("You lose :-(");
        }
    }
}
```

If you've read this whole section, you're probably exhausted. Creating a loop can be a lot of work. Fortunately, the more you practice, the easier it becomes.

Thinking about Loops (Priming)

I remember when I was a young boy. We lived on Front Street in Philadelphia, near where the El train turned onto Kensington Avenue. Come early morning, I'd have to go outside and get water from the well. I'd pump several times before any water would come out. Ma and Pa called it "priming the pump."

These days I don't prime pumps. I prime while loops. Consider the case of a busy network administrator. She needs a program that extracts a username from an email address. For example, the program reads

```
John@BurdBrain.com
```

and writes

```
John
```

How does the program do it? Like other examples in this chapter, this problem involves repetition:

```
Repeatedly do the following:
    Read a character.
    Write the character.
```

The program then stops the repetition when it finds the @ sign. I take a stab at writing this program. My first attempt doesn't work, but it's a darn good start. It's in Listing 12-3.

LISTING 12-3: **Trying to Get a Username from an Email Address**

```
/*
 * This code does NOT work, but I'm not discouraged.
 */
import java.util.Scanner;

class FirstAttempt {

    public static void main(String args[]) {
        Scanner keyboard = new Scanner(System.in);
        char symbol = ' ';

        while (symbol != '@') {
            symbol = keyboard.findWithinHorizon(".",0).charAt(0);
            System.out.print(symbol);
        }
        System.out.println();

        keyboard.close();
    }
}
```

When you run the code in Listing 12-3, you get the output shown in Figure 12-9. The user types one character after another — the letter J, then o, then h, and so on. At first, the program in Listing 12-3 does nothing. (The computer doesn't send any of the user's input to the program until the user presses Enter.) After the user types a whole email address and presses Enter, the program gets its first character (the J in John).

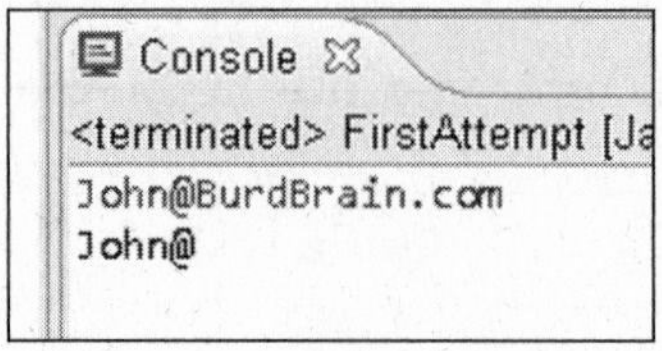

FIGURE 12-9:
Oops! Got the @
sign, too.

Unfortunately, the program's output isn't what you expect. Instead of just the username John, you get the username and the @ sign.

```
To find out why this happens, follow the computer's actions as it reads the
    input John@BurdBrain.com:Set symbol to ' ' (a blank space).

Is that blank space the same as an @ sign?
No, so perform a loop iteration.
    Input the letter 'J'.
    Print the letter 'J'.

Is that 'J' the same as an @ sign?
No, so perform a loop iteration.
    Input the letter 'o'.
    Print the letter 'o'.

Is that 'o' the same as an @ sign?
No, so perform a loop iteration.
    Input the letter 'h'.
    Print the letter 'h'.

Is that 'h' the same as an @ sign?
No, so perform a loop iteration.
    Input the letter 'n'.
    Print the letter 'n'.

Is that 'n' the same as an @ sign?  //Here's the problem.
No, so perform a loop iteration.
    Input the @ sign.
    Print the @ sign.                //Oops!

Is that @ sign the same as an @ sign?
Yes, so stop iterating.
```

Near the end of the program's run, the computer compares the letter n with the @ sign. Because n isn't an @ sign, the computer dives right into the loop:

>> The first statement in the loop reads an @ sign from the keyboard.

>> The second statement in the loop doesn't check to see whether it's time to stop printing. Instead, that second statement just marches ahead and displays the @ sign.

After you've displayed the @ sign, there's no going back. You can't change your mind and undisplay the @ sign. So the code in Listing 12-3 doesn't quite work.

Working on the problem

You learn from your mistakes. The problem with Listing 12-3 is that, between reading and writing a character, the program doesn't check for an @ sign. Instead of doing "Test, Input, Print," it should do "Input, Test, Print." That is, instead of doing this:

```
Is that 'o' the same as an @ sign?
No, so perform a loop iteration.
    Input the letter 'h'.
    Print the letter 'h'.

Is that 'h' the same as an @ sign?
No, so perform a loop iteration.
    Input the letter 'n'.
    Print the letter 'n'.

Is that 'n' the same as an @ sign?  //Here's the problem.
No, so perform a loop iteration.
    Input the @ sign.
    Print the @ sign.              //Oops!
```

the program should do this:

```
    Input the letter 'o'.
Is that 'o' the same as an @ sign?
No, so perform a loop iteration.
    Print the letter 'o'.

    Input the letter 'n'.
Is that 'n' the same as an @ sign?
No, so perform a loop iteration.
    Print the letter 'n'.

    Input the @ sign.
Is that @ sign the same as an @ sign?
Yes, so stop iterating.
```

This cycle is shown in Figure 12-10.

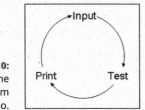

FIGURE 12-10:
What the
program
needs to do.

You can try to imitate the following informal pattern:

```
    Input a character.
Is that character the same as an @ sign?
If not, perform a loop iteration.
    Print the character.
```

The problem is, you can't put a `while` loop's test in the middle of the loop:

```
//This code doesn't work the way you want it to work:
{
    symbol = keyboard.findWithinHorizon(".",0).charAt(0);
while (symbol != '@')
    System.out.print(symbol);
}
```

You can't sandwich a `while` statement's condition between two of the statements that you intend to repeat. So what can you do? You need to follow the flow in Figure 12-11. Because every `while` loop starts with a test, that's where you jump into the circle, First Test, and then Print, and then, finally, Input.

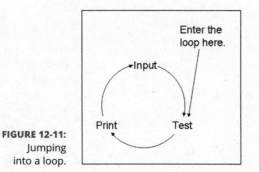

FIGURE 12-11:
Jumping
into a loop.

Listing 12-4 shows the embodiment of this "test, then print, then input" strategy.

Nice Try, But . . .

```java
/*
 * This code almost works, but there's one tiny error:
 */
import java.util.Scanner;

class SecondAttempt {

    public static void main(String args[]) {
        Scanner keyboard = new Scanner(System.in);
        char symbol = ' ';

        while (symbol != '@') {
            System.out.print(symbol);
            symbol = keyboard.findWithinHorizon(".",0).charAt(0);
        }

        System.out.println();

        keyboard.close();
    }
}
```

A run of the Listing 12-4 code is shown in Figure 12-12. The code is almost correct, but I still have a slight problem. Notice the blank space before the user's input. The program races prematurely into the loop. The first time the computer executes the statements

```java
System.out.print(symbol);
symbol = keyboard.findWithinHorizon(".",0).charAt(0);
```

the computer displays an unwanted blank space. Then the computer gets the J in John. In some applications, an extra blank space is no big deal. But in other applications, extra output can be disastrous.

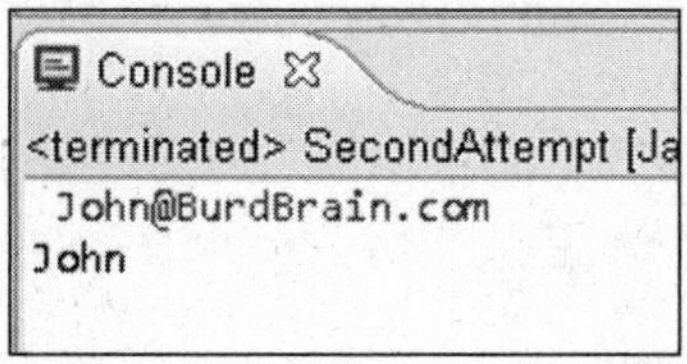

FIGURE 12-12:
The computer displays an extra blank space.

```
Console ⊠
<terminated> SecondAttempt [Ja
 John@BurdBrain.com
John
```

Fixing the problem

Disastrous or not, an unwanted blank space is the symptom of a logical flaw. The program shouldn't display results before it has any meaningful results to display. The solution to this problem is called . . . (drumroll, please) . . . *priming the loop.* You pump `findWithinHorizon(".",0).charAt(0)` once to get some values flowing. Listing 12-5 shows you how to do it.

LISTING 12-5: **How to Prime a Loop**

```
/*
 * This code works correctly!
 */
import java.util.Scanner;

class GetUserName {

    public static void main(String args[]) {
        Scanner keyboard = new Scanner(System.in);
        char symbol;

        symbol = keyboard.findWithinHorizon(".",0).charAt(0);

        while (symbol != '@') {
            System.out.print(symbol);
            symbol = keyboard.findWithinHorizon(".",0).charAt(0);
        }

        System.out.println();

        keyboard.close();
    }
}
```

Listing 12-5 follows the strategy shown in Figure 12-13. First you get a character (the letter J in John, for example), and then you enter the loop. After you're in the loop, you test the letter against the @ sign and print the letter if it's appropriate to do so. Figure 12-14 shows a beautiful run of the GetUserName program.

The priming of loops is an important programming technique. But it's not the end of the story. In Chapters 14, 15, and 16, you can read about some other useful looping tricks.

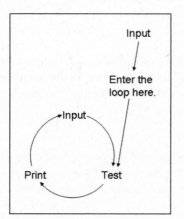

FIGURE 12-13:
The strategy in
Listing 12-5.

FIGURE 12-14:
A run of the code
in Listing 12-5.

```
Console ⊠
<terminated> GetUserName [Java Ap
John@BurdBrain.com
John
```

Face Java's loops head-on with these programming challenges.

TRY IT OUT

LIVING LARGE

Write a program that repeatedly reads numbers from the user's keyboard. The program stops looping when the user types a number that's larger than 100.

ARE WE THERE YET?

Write a program that repeatedly prompts the user with the same question: Are we there yet? The program stops looping when the user replies with the uppercase letter Y or the lowercase letter y. Here's a sample run:

```
Are we there yet? N
Are we there yet? n
Are we there yet? N
Are we there yet? N
Are we there yet? N
Are we there yet? y
Whew!
```

TALLY UP

Write a program that uses a loop to repeatedly read numbers from the keyboard. The program stops reading numbers when the user enters a negative number. The program reports the sum of the numbers, excluding the last (negative) number.

GUESS AGAIN

In Chapter 9, you write a Guessing Game program. The program compares whatever number the user enters with a number that the program generates randomly. The user wins if the two numbers are equal, and loses otherwise.

Modify this program as follows:

» As in the original version, the program generates a number randomly only once, but . . .

» . . . the program repeatedly asks the user for guesses until the user guesses correctly.

TWO IN A ROW

Write a program that repeatedly reads numbers from the user's keyboard. The program stops looping when the user types the same number twice in a row. Here's a sample run of the program:

```
5
13
21
5
4
5
5
Done!
```

Chapter **13**

Piles of Files: Dealing with Information Overload

Consider these scenarios:

» You're a business owner who handles hundreds of invoices each day. You store invoice data in a file on your hard drive. You need customized code to sort and classify the invoices.

» You're an astronomer with data from scans of the night sky. When you're ready to analyze a chunk of data, you load the chunk onto your computer's hard drive.

» You're the author of a popular self-help book. Last year's fad was called the Self Mirroring Method. This year's craze is the Make Your Cake System. You can't modify your manuscript without converting to the publisher's new specifications. You need software to make the task bearable.

Each situation calls for a new computer program, and each program reads from a large data file. On top of all of that, each program creates a brand-new file containing bright, shiny results.

In previous chapters, the examples get input from the keyboard and send output to the Eclipse Console view. That's fine for small tasks, but you can't have the computer prompt you for each bit of night sky data. For big problems, you need lots of data, and the best place to store the data is on a computer's hard drive.

Running a Disk-Oriented Program

To deal with volumes of data, you need tools for reading from (and writing to) disk files. At the mere mention of disk files, some people's hearts start to palpitate with fear. After all, a disk file is elusive and invisible. It's stored somewhere inside your computer, with some magic magnetic process.

The truth is, getting data from a disk is much like getting data from the keyboard. And printing data to a disk is like printing data to the computer screen.

TECHNICAL STUFF

In this book, displaying a program's text output "on the computer screen" means displaying text in Eclipse's Console view. If you shun Eclipse in favor of a different IDE (such as NetBeans or IntelliJ IDEA) or you shun all IDEs in favor of your system's command window, then, for you, "on the computer screen" means something slightly different. Please read between the lines as necessary. Also, I'm well aware that some computers have SSD drives with no honest-to-goodness disks inside them. So terms like *disk-oriented* and *disk files* are showing signs of age. But let's face facts: A "record store" no longer focuses on vinyl records, and in U.S. measurement units, 12 inches is no longer the length the of the king's foot. Today's LCD screens no longer need saving. And, unlike the old mechanical car radios, a web page's radio buttons don't mark your favorite stations.

Consider the scenario when you run the code in earlier chapters. You type some stuff on the keyboard. The program takes this stuff and spits out some stuff of its own. The program sends this new stuff to the Console view. In effect, the flow of data goes from the keyboard to the computer's innards and then to the screen, as shown in Figure 13-1.

Of course, the goal in this chapter is illustrated in Figure 13-2. There's a file containing data on your hard drive. The program takes data from the disk file and spits out some brand-new data. The program then sends the new data to another file on the hard drive. In effect, the flow of data goes from a disk file to the computer's innards and on to another disk file.

The scenarios in Figures 13-1 and 13-2 are similar. In fact, it helps to remember these fundamental points:

> » **The stuff in a disk file is no different from the stuff that you type on a keyboard.**

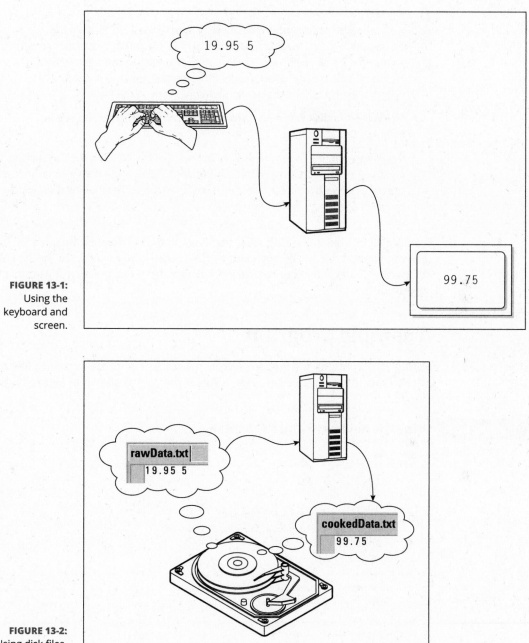

FIGURE 13-1:
Using the
keyboard and
screen.

FIGURE 13-2:
Using disk files.

If a keyboard-reading program expects you to type 19.95 5, then the corresponding disk-reading program expects a file containing those same characters, 19.95 5. If a keyboard-reading program expects you to press Enter and type more characters, then the corresponding disk-reading program expects more characters on the next line in the file.

>> **The stuff in a disk file is no different from the stuff that you see in Eclipse's Console view.**

If a screen-printing program displays the number 99.75, then the corresponding disk-writing program writes the number 99.75 to a file. If a screen-printing program moves the cursor to the next line, then the corresponding disk-writing program creates a new line in the file.

If you have trouble imagining what you have in a disk file, just imagine the text that you would type on the keyboard or the text that you would see on the computer screen (that is, in Eclipse's Console view). That same text can appear in a file on your disk.

A sample program

Listing 13-1 contains a keyboard/screen program. The program multiplies unit price by quantity to get a total price. A run of the code is shown in Figure 13-3.

LISTING 13-1: Using the Keyboard and the Screen

```java
import java.util.Scanner;

class ComputeTotal {

    public static void main(String args[]) {
        Scanner keyboard = new Scanner(System.in);
        double unitPrice, total;
        int quantity;

        unitPrice = keyboard.nextDouble();
        quantity = keyboard.nextInt();

        total = unitPrice * quantity;

        System.out.println(total);

        keyboard.close();
    }
}
```

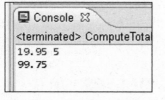

FIGURE 13-3:
Read from the
keyboard; write
to the screen.

REMEMBER

Grouping separators vary from one country to another. The run shown in Figure 13-3 works almost everywhere in the world. But if the unit price is nineteen and ninety-five hundredths, you type 19.95 (with a dot) in some countries and 19,95 (with a comma) in others. When you install the computer's operating system, you tell it which country you live in. Java programs access this information and use it to customize the way the nextDouble method works.

The goal is to write a program like the one in Listing 13-1. But, rather than talk to your keyboard and screen, this new program talks to your hard drive. The new program reads unit price and quantity from your hard drive and writes the total back to your hard drive.

Java's API has everything you need for interacting with a hard drive. A nice example is in Listing 13-2.

LISTING 13-2: **Using Input and Output Files**

```java
import java.util.Scanner;
import java.io.File;
import java.io.FileNotFoundException;
import java.io.PrintStream;

class ReadAndWrite {

    public static void main(String args[]) throws FileNotFoundException {
        Scanner diskScanner = new Scanner(new File("rawData.txt"));
        PrintStream diskWriter = new PrintStream("cookedData.txt");
        double unitPrice, total;
        int quantity;

        unitPrice = diskScanner.nextDouble();
        quantity = diskScanner.nextInt();

        total = unitPrice * quantity;

        diskWriter.println(total);

        diskScanner.close();
        diskWriter.close();
    }
}
```

For a guide to the care and feeding of the rawData.txt file (whose name appears in Listing 13-2), see the upcoming "Creating an input file" section.

Creating code that messes with your hard drive

"I _____ (print your name)_____ agree to pay $_____each month on the ____th day of the month."

Fill in the blanks. That's all you have to do. Reading input from a disk can work the same way. Just fill in the blanks in Listing 13-3.

LISTING 13-3: **A Template to Read Data from a Disk File**

```
/*
 * Before Eclipse can compile this code,
 * you must fill in the blanks.
 */
import java.util.Scanner;
import java.io.File;
import java.io.FileNotFoundException;

class _____ {

    public static void main(String args[]) throws FileNotFoundException {

        Scanner diskScanner = new Scanner(new File("_____"));

        _____ = diskScanner.nextInt();
        _____ = diskScanner.nextDouble();
        _____ = diskScanner.nextLine();
        _____ = diskScanner.findWithinHorizon(".",0).charAt(0);

        // Etc.

        diskScanner.close();
    }
}
```

To use Listing 13-3, make up a name for your class. Insert that name into the first blank space. Type the name of the input file in the second space (between the quotation marks). Then, to read a whole number from the input file, call `diskScanner.nextInt`. To read a number that has a decimal point, call `diskScanner.nextDouble`. You can call any of the `Scanner` methods in Chapter 5's Table 5-1 — the same methods you call when you get keystrokes from the keyboard.

The stuff in Listing 13-3 isn't a complete program. Instead, it's a *code template* — a half-baked piece of code, with spaces for you to fill in.

With the template in Listing 13-3, you can input data from a disk file. With a similar template, you can write output to a file. The template is in Listing 13-4.

LISTING 13-4: A Template to Write Data to a Disk File

```
/*
 * Before Eclipse can compile this code,
 * you must fill in the blanks.
 */
import java.io.File;
import java.io.FileNotFoundException;
import java.io.PrintStream;

class _____ {

    public static void main(String args[]) throws FileNotFoundException {

        PrintStream diskWriter = new PrintStream("_____");

        diskWriter.print(_____);
        diskWriter.println(_____);

        // Etc.

        diskWriter.close();
    }
}
```

To use Listing 13-4, insert the name of your class into the first blank space. Type the name of the output file in the space between the quotation marks. Then, to write part of a line to the output file, call `diskWriter.print`. To write the remainder of a line to the output file, call `diskWriter.println`.

TIP

Eclipse has a built-in feature for creating and inserting code templates. To get started using Eclipse templates, choose Window ⇨ Preferences (in Windows) or Eclipse ⇨ Preferences (on a Mac). In the resulting Preferences dialog box, choose Java ⇨ Editor ⇨ Templates. Creating new templates isn't simple. But if you poke around a bit, you accomplish a lot.

If your program gets input from one disk file and writes output to another, combine the stuff from Listings 13-3 and 13-4. When you do, you get a program like the one in Listing 13-2.

A QUICK LOOK AT JAVA'S DISK ACCESS FACILITIES

Templates like the ones in Listings 13-3 and 13-4 look very nice. But knowing how the templates work is even better. Here are a few tidbits describing the inner workings of Java's disk access code:

- A PrintStream **is something you can use for writing output.**

  A PrintStream is like a Scanner. The big difference is that a Scanner is for reading input and a PrintStream is for writing output. To see what I mean, look at Listing 13-2. Notice the similarity between the statements that use Scanner and the statements that use PrintStream.

  The word PrintStream is defined in the Java API.

- **In Listing 13-2, the expression** new File("rawData.txt") **plays the same role that** System.in **plays in many other programs.**

  Just as System.in stands for the computer's keyboard, the expression new File("rawData.txt") stands for a file on your computer's hard drive. When the computer calls new File("rawData.txt"), the computer creates something like System.in — something you can stuff inside the new Scanner( ) parentheses.

  The word File is defined in the Java API.

- A FileNotFoundException **is something that may go wrong during an attempt to read input from a disk file (or an attempt to write output to a disk file).**

  Disk file access is loaded with pitfalls. Even the best programs run into disk access trouble occasionally. To brace against such pitfalls, Java insists on your adding some extra words to your code.

In Listing 13-2, the added words `throws FileNotFoundException` form a *throws clause*. A throws clause is a kind of disclaimer. Putting a throws clause in your code is like saying, "I realize that this code can run into trouble."

Of course, in the legal realm, you often have no choice about signing disclaimers. "If you don't sign this disclaimer, the surgeon won't operate on you." Okay then, I'll sign it. The same is true with a Java throws clause. If you put things like new `PrintStream("cookedData.txt")` in your code and you don't add something like `throws FileNotFoundException`, the Java compiler refuses to compile your code.

So when do you need this `throws FileNotFoundException` clause, and when should you do without it? Well, having certain things in your code — things like new `PrintStream("cookedData.txt")` — forces you to create a throws clause. You can spend some time learning all about the kinds of things that demand throws clauses. But at this point, it's better to concentrate on other programming issues. Because you're a beginning Java programmer, the safest thing to do is to follow the templates in Listings 13-3 and 13-4.

The word `FileNotFoundException` is — you guessed it — defined in the Java API.

- **To create this chapter's code, I made up the names** `diskScanner` **and** `diskWriter`.

  The words `diskScanner` and `diskWriter` don't come from the Java API. In place of `diskScanner` and `diskWriter`, you can use any names you want. All you have to do is to use the names consistently within each of your Java programs.

- **A call to the** `close` **method ends the connection between your program and the file.**

  In many of this book's examples, you sever the connection between your program and the computer keyboard by calling `keyboard.close()`. The same is true when you call the `close` method for a disk file's scanner or a disk file's `PrintStream` instance. Calling the `close` method reminds Java to finish all pending read or write operations and to break the program's connection to the disk file, the keyboard, or to whatever else holds data for the program.

  This book's examples are pretty simple. If you omit a `close` method call in one of these examples, you might get a warning message from Eclipse, but the world doesn't end. (That is, your program still runs correctly.) However, in a serious, make-it-or-break-it application, the proper placement of `close` calls is important. These `close` calls ensure the proper completion of the program's input and output actions and help free up disk resources for use by other running programs.

Running the sample program

Testing the code in Listing 13-2 is a three-step process. Here's an outline of the three steps:

1. **Create the** rawData.txt **file.**

2. **Run the code in Listing 13-2.**

3. **View the contents of the** cookedData.txt **file.**

The next few sections cover each step in detail.

Creating an input file

You can use any plain old text editor to create an input file for the code in Listing 13-2. In this section, I show you how to use Eclipse's built-in editor.

To create an input file:

1. **Select a project in Eclipse's Package Explorer.**

   In this example, select the 13–02 project (the project containing the code from Listing 13-2).

REMEMBER

   In the Package Explorer, select a branch whose label is the name of a project. (Select the 13–02 branch to run the code in Listing 13-2.) Don't select an item within a project. (For example, don't select the src branch or the (default package) branch.)

2. **On Eclipse's main menu, choose File ➪ New ➪ File.**

   Eclipse's New File dialog box opens.

3. **In the File Name field, type the name of your new data file.**

   You can type any name that your computer considers to be a valid filename. For this section's example, I used the name rawData.txt, but other names, such as rawData.dat, rawData, and raw123.01.dataFile, are fine. I try to avoid troublesome names (including short, uninformative names and names containing blank spaces), but the name you choose is entirely up to you (and your computer's operating system, and your boss's whims, and your customer's specifications).

4. **Click Finish.**

   The file's name appears in Eclipse's Package Explorer. An empty editor (with the new file's name on its tab) appears in Eclipse's editor area.

5. Type text in the editor.

To create this section's example, I typed the text 19.95 5, as shown in Figure 13-4. To create your own example, type whatever text your program needs during its run.

FIGURE 13-4:
Editing an input file.

```
Package Explorer ⊠          ▭ ☐        rawData.txt ⊠
                  🗎 🕱 | 📷 ▽            19.95 5
  🗁 13-02                        ▲
    🗂 src
      ⊞ (default package)
        📄 ReadAndWrite.java
    📚 JRE System Library [JavaS
    📄 rawData.txt
```

WARNING

This section's steps apply when you use Eclipse to create an input file. You can use other programs to create input files, such as Windows Notepad or Macintosh TextEdit. But if you do, you have to be careful about file formats and filename extensions. For example, to create a file named raw123.01.dataFile using Windows Notepad, type "raw123.01.dataFile" (with quotation marks) in the File Name field of the Save As dialog box. If you don't surround the name with quotation marks, then Notepad might add .txt to the file's name (turning raw123.01. dataFile into raw123.01.dataFile.txt). A similar issue applies to the Macintosh's TextEdit program. By default, TextEdit adds the .rtf extension to each new file. To override the .rtf default for a particular file, select Format⇨Make Plain Text before saving the file. Then, when you save the file, TextEdit offers to add the .txt extension to the name of the file. In the Save As dialog box, if you don't want the file's name to end in .txt, uncheck the check box labeled If No Extension is Provided, Use ".txt".

Running the code

To have Eclipse run the code, do the same thing you do with any other Java program. Select the project you want to run (project 13-02, in this example). Then choose Run⇨Run As⇨Java Application.

When you run the program in Listing 13-2, no text appears in Eclipse's Console view. This total lack of any noticeable output gives some people the willies. The truth is, a program like the one in Listing 13-2 does all its work behind the scenes. The program has no statements that read from the keyboard and has no statements that print to the screen. So, if you have a very loud hard drive, you may hear a little chirping sound when you choose Run⇨Run As⇨Java Application, but you won't type any program input, and you won't see any program output.

The program sends all its output to a file on your hard drive. What do you do to see the file's contents?

Viewing the output file

To see the output of the program in Listing 13-2, follow these steps:

1. **In the Project Explorer, select the** 13-02 **project branch.**

2. **On the main menu, choose File ⇨ Refresh.**

3. **In the Project Explorer, expand the** 13-02 **project branch.**

A new file named cookedData.txt appears in the Package Explorer tree (in the 13-02 project).

4. **Double-click the** cookedData.txt **branch in the Package Explorer tree.**

The contents of cookedData.txt appear in an Eclipse editor. (See Figure 13-5.)

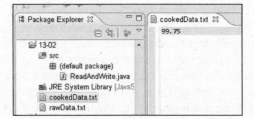

FIGURE 13-5:
Viewing an output file.

Troubleshooting problems with disk files

When you run the code in Listing 13-2, the computer executes new Scanner(new File("rawData.txt")). If the Java virtual machine can't find the rawData.txt file, you see a message like the one shown in Figure 13-6. This error message can be frustrating. In many cases, you know darn well that there's a rawData.txt file on your hard drive. The stupid computer simply can't find it.

FIGURE 13-6:
The computer can't find your file.

```
Problems  @ Javadoc  Declaration  Search  Console 
<terminated> ReadAndWrite [Java Application] C:\Program Files\Java\jre7\bin\javaw.exe (Dec 16, 2011 2:55:36 PM)
Exception in thread "main" java.io.FileNotFoundException: rawData.txt (The system cannot find the file specified)
        at java.io.FileInputStream.open(Native Method)
        at java.io.FileInputStream.<init>(Unknown Source)
        at java.util.Scanner.<init>(Unknown Source)
        at ReadAndWrite.main(ReadAndWrite.java:12)
```

There's no quick, surefire way to fix this problem. But you should always check the following things first:

TIP

» **Check again for a file named** `rawData.txt`.

Open Windows File Explorer or Macintosh Finder and poke around for a file with that name.

The filenames displayed in File Explorer and Finder can be misleading. You may see the name `rawData`, even though the file's real name is `rawData.txt`. To fix this problem once and for all, refer to the "Those pesky filename extensions" sidebar in Chapter 2.

» **Check the spelling of the file's name.**

Make sure that the name in your program is exactly the same as the name of the file on your hard drive. Just one misplaced letter can keep the computer from finding a file.

» **If you use Linux (or a flavor of UNIX other than Mac OS X), check the capitalization of the file's name.**

In Linux, and in many versions of UNIX, the difference between uppercase and lowercase can baffle the computer.

» **Check that the file is in the correct directory.**

Sure, you have a file named `rawData.txt`. But don't expect your Java program to look in every folder on your hard drive to find the file. How do you know which folder should house files like `rawData.txt`?

Here's how it works: Each Eclipse project has its own folder on your computer's hard drive. You see the 13-02 project folder and its `src` subfolder in Figure 13-5. But in Figure 13-7, Windows File Explorer shows the 13-02 folder, its `src` subfolder, and its other subfolders named `.settings` and `bin`. (Mac users can see the same subfolders in a Finder window.)

FIGURE 13-7:
The contents of the 13-02 project folder on your computer's hard drive.

Name	Date modified	Type	Size
.settings	4/9/2017 10:44 PM	File folder	
bin	4/9/2017 10:44 PM	File folder	
src	4/9/2017 10:44 PM	File folder	
.classpath	6/2/2014 3:51 PM	CLASSPATH File	1 KB
.project	6/2/2014 3:51 PM	PROJECT File	1 KB
rawData.txt	6/2/2014 3:51 PM	TXT File	1 KB

The src, bin, and .settings folders contain files of their own. But in Figure 13-7, the rawData.txt and cookedData.txt files are immediately inside the 13-02 project folder. In other words, the rawData.txt and cookedData.txt files live in the root of the 13-02 project folder.

REMEMBER

When you run this section's example, the rawData.txt file should be in the root of the 13-02 project folder on your hard drive. That's why, in Step 1 of the earlier "Creating an input file" section, I remind you to select the 13-02 project folder and not the project's src subfolder.

Figure 13-7 shows input and output files in the root of their Eclipse project. But in general, file locations can be tricky, especially if you switch from Eclipse to an unfamiliar IDE. The general rule (about putting input and output files immediately inside a project directory) may not apply in other programming environments.

Here's a trick you can use: Whatever IDE you use (or even if you create Java programs without an IDE), run this stripped-down version of the code in Listing 13-2:

```java
import java.io.File;
import java.io.FileNotFoundException;
import java.io.PrintStream;

class JustWrite {

    public static void main(String args[]) throws FileNotFoundException {

        PrintStream diskWriter = new PrintStream("cookedData.txt");
        diskWriter.println(99.75);

        diskWriter.close();
    }
}
```

This program has no need for a stinking rawData.txt file. If you run this code and get no error messages, search your hard drive for this program's output (the cookedData.txt file). Note the name of the folder that contains the cookedData.txt file. When you put rawData.txt in this same folder, any problem you had running the Listing 13-2 code should go away.

>> **Check the** rawData.txt **file's content.**

It never hurts to peek inside the rawData.txt file and make sure that the file contains the numbers 19.95 5. If rawData.txt doesn't appear in Eclipse's

REMEMBER

editor area, find the Listing 13-2 project (the project named 13–02) in the Package Explorer. Double-clicking the project's `rawData.txt` branch makes that file appear in Eclipse's editor area.

By default, Java's `Scanner` class looks for blank spaces between input values. So, this example's `rawData.txt` file should contain `19.95 5`, not `19.955` and not `19.95,5`.

TECHNICAL STUFF

The `Scanner` class looks for any kind of *white space* between the values. These white space characters may include blank spaces, tabs, and newlines. For example, the `rawData.txt` file may contain `19.95  5` (with several blank spaces between `19.95` and `5`), or it may have `19.95` and `5` on two separate lines.

Writing a Disk-Oriented Program

Listing 13-2 is much like Listing 13-1. In fact, you can go from Listing 13-1 to Listing 13-2 with some simple editing. Here's how:

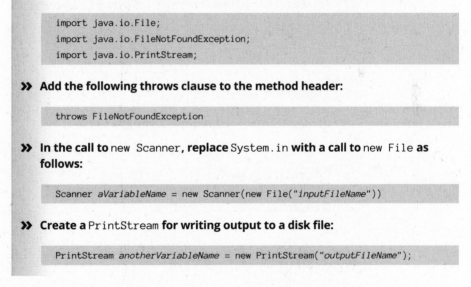

» **Add the following import declarations to the beginning of your code:**

```
import java.io.File;
import java.io.FileNotFoundException;
import java.io.PrintStream;
```

» **Add the following throws clause to the method header:**

```
throws FileNotFoundException
```

» **In the call to** new Scanner, **replace** System.in **with a call to** new File **as follows:**

```
Scanner aVariableName = new Scanner(new File("inputFileName"))
```

» **Create a** PrintStream **for writing output to a disk file:**

```
PrintStream anotherVariableName = new PrintStream("outputFileName");
```

» **Use the** Scanner **variable name in calls to** nextInt, nextLine, **and so on.**

For example, to go from Listing 13-1 to Listing 13-2, I change

```
unitPrice = keyboard.nextDouble();
quantity = keyboard.nextInt();
```

to

```
unitPrice = diskScanner.nextDouble();
quantity = diskScanner.nextInt();
```

» **Use the** PrintStream **variable name in calls to** print **and** println.

For example, to go from Listing 13-1 to Listing 13-2, I change

```
System.out.println(total);
```

to

```
diskWriter.println(total);
```

» **Use the** Scanner **variable name in the call to** close.

For example, to go from Listing 13-1 to Listing 13-2, I change

```
keyboard.close();
```

to

```
diskScanner.close();
```

» **Use the** PrintStream **variable name in a call to** close.

For example, to go from Listing 13-1 to Listing 13-2, I add

```
diskWriter.close();
```

at the end of the main method.

Reading from a file

All the Scanner methods can read from existing disk files. For example, to read a word from a file named mySpeech, use code of the following kind:

```
Scanner diskScanner = new Scanner(new File("mySpeech"));

String oneWord = diskScanner.next();
```

To read a character from a file named letters.dat and then display the character on the screen, you can do something like this:

```
Scanner diskScanner = new Scanner(new File("letters.dat"));

System.out.println(diskScanner.findWithinHorizon(".", 0).charAt(0));
```

TECHNICAL STUFF

Notice how I read from a file named mySpeech, not mySpeech.txt or mySpeech.doc. Anything that you put after the dot is called a *filename extension,* and for a file full of numbers and other data, the filename extension is optional. Sure, a Java program must be called *something*.java, but a data file can be named mySpeech.txt, mySpeech.reallymine.allmine, or just mySpeech. As long as the name in your new File call is the same as the filename on your computer's hard drive, everything is okay.

Writing to a file

The print and println methods can write to disk files. Here are some examples:

>> During a run of the code in Listing 13-2, the variable total stores the number 99.75. To deposit 99.75 into the cookedData.txt file, you execute

```
diskWriter.println(total);
```

This println call writes to a disk file because of the following line in Listing 13-2:

```
PrintStream diskWriter = new PrintStream("cookedData.txt");
```

>> In another version of the program, you may decide not to use a total variable. To write 99.75 to the cookedData.txt file, you can call

```
diskWriter.println(unitPrice * quantity);
```

>> To display OK on the screen, you can make the following method call:

```
System.out.print("OK");
```

To write OK to a file named approval.txt, you can use the following code:

```
PrintStream diskWriter = new PrintStream("approval.txt");

diskWriter.print("OK");
```

>> You may decide to write OK as two separate characters. To write to the screen, you can make the following calls:

```
System.out.print('O');
System.out.print('K');
```

And to write OK to the approval.txt file, you can use the following code:

```
PrintStream diskWriter = new PrintStream("approval.txt");

diskWriter.print('O');
diskWriter.print('K');
```

>> Like their counterparts for System.out, the disk writing print and println methods differ in their end-of-line behaviors. For example, you want to display the following text on the screen:

```
Hankees  Socks
7        3
```

To do this, you can make the following method calls:

```
System.out.print("Hankees  ");
System.out.println("Socks");
System.out.print(7);
System.out.print("        ");
System.out.println(3);
```

To plant the same text into a file named scores.dat, you can use the following code:

```
PrintStream diskWriter = new PrintStream("scores.dat");

diskWriter.print("Hankees  ");
diskWriter.println("Socks");
diskWriter.print(7);
diskWriter.print("        ");
diskWriter.println(3);
```

NAME THAT FILE

What if a file that contains data isn't in your program's project folder? If that's the case, when you call new `File`, the file's name must include folder names. For example, in Windows, your `TallyBudget.java` program might be in your `c:\Users\MyUserName\workspace\13-09` folder, and a file named `totals` might be in a folder named `c:\advertisements`. (See the following figure.)

Then, to refer to the `totals` file, you include the folder name, the filename, and (to be on the safe side) the drive letter:

```
Scanner diskScanner = new Scanner(new File("c:\\advertisements\\totals"));
```

Notice that I use double backslashes to separate the drive letter, the folder name, and the filename. To find out why, look at the "Escapism" sidebar in Chapter 12. The string `"\totals"` with a single backslash stands for a tab, followed by `otals`. But in this example, the file's name is `totals`, not `otals`. With a single backslash, the name `...advertisements\totals"` would not work correctly.

Inside quotation marks, you use the double backslash to indicate what would usually be a single backslash. So the string `"c:\\advertisements\\totals"` stands for `c:\advertisements\totals`. That's good because `c:\advertisements\totals` is the way you normally refer to a file in Windows.

If you want to sidestep all this backslash confusion, you can use forward slashes to specify each file's location. Windows responds exactly the same way to new `File("c:\\advertisements\\totals")` and to new `File("c:/advertisements/totals")`. And if you use UNIX, Linux, or a Macintosh, the double backslash nonsense doesn't apply to you. Just write

```
Scanner diskScanner = new Scanner (new File("/Users/me/advertisements/totals"));
```

or something similar that reflects your system's directory structure.

Writing, Rewriting, and Rerewriting

Given my mischievous ways, I tried a little experiment. I asked myself what would happen if I ran the same file writing program more than once. So I created a tiny program (the program in Listing 13-5), and I ran the program twice. Then I examined the program's output file. The output file (shown in Figure 13-8) contains only two letters.

LISTING 13-5: **A Little Experiment**

```java
import java.io.File;
import java.io.FileNotFoundException;
import java.io.PrintStream;

class WriteOK {

    public static void main(String args[])throws FileNotFoundException {

        PrintStream diskWriter = new PrintStream(new File("approval.txt"));

        diskWriter.print  ('O');
        diskWriter.println('K');

        diskWriter.close();
    }
}
```

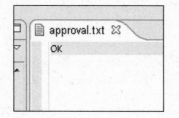

FIGURE 13-8:
Testing the
waters.

Here's the sequence of events, from the start to the end of the experiment:

1. **Before I run the code in Listing 13-5, my computer's hard drive has no** approval.txt **file.**

That's okay. Every experiment has to start somewhere.

2. **I run the code in Listing 13-5.**

The call to new PrintStream in Listing 13-5 creates a file named approval. txt. Initially, the new approval.txt file contains no characters. Later in Listing 13-5, calls to print and println put characters in the file. So, after running the code, the approval.txt file contains two letters: the letters OK.

3. **I run the code from Listing 13-5 a second time.**

At this point, I could imagine seeing OKOK in the approval.txt file. But that's not what I see in Figure 13-8. After running the code twice, the approval.txt file contains just one OK. Here's why:

- The call to new PrintStream in Listing 13-5 deletes my existing approval. txt file. The call creates a new, empty approval.txt file.

- After a new approval.txt file is created, the print method call drops the letter O into the new file.

- The println method call adds the letter K to the same approval.txt file.

That's the story. Each time you run the program, it trashes whatever approval. txt file is already on the hard drive. Then the program adds data to a newly created approval.txt file.

TRY IT OUT

File handling can be tricky. If you run into trouble early on, it's easy to become frustrated. Fortunately, these experiments will get you started on the right track.

RUN BARRY'S PROJECT

Test the waters by downloading the code from this book's website (www.allmycode. com/BeginProg). Follow the instructions in Chapter 2 for importing the code into Eclipse. Run the code in Project 13-02. The 13-02 project comes with its own rawData.txt file. After running the project in Eclipse, check Eclipse's Package Explorer to make sure that the run has created a cookedData.txt file.

WHERE'S MY FILE?

Create an Eclipse project containing the following code:

```java
import java.util.Scanner;
import java.io.File;
import java.io.FileNotFoundException;
import java.io.PrintStream;

class ReadAndWrite {
```

```
public static void main(String args[]) throws FileNotFoundException {
    Scanner diskScanner = new Scanner(new File("data.txt"));
    PrintStream diskWriter = new PrintStream("data.txt");

    diskWriter.println("Hello");

    System.out.println(diskScanner.next());

    diskScanner.close();
    diskWriter.close();
}
}
```

When you run the code, you see an error message in Eclipse's Console view. Why?

WRITE AND THEN READ

Modify the code from the where's-my-file experiment so that the PrintStream diskWriter declaration comes before the Scanner diskScanner declaration.

When you run the code, the word Hello should appear in Eclipse's Console view. After running the code, check to make sure that your Eclipse project contains a file named data.txt.

RANDOM NUMBERS IN A FILE

Create a program that writes ten randomly generated numbers in a disk file. After writing the numbers, the program reads the numbers from the file and displays them in Eclipse's Console view.

Chapter **14**

Creating Loops within Loops

I f you're an editor at John Wiley & Sons, Inc., please don't read the next few paragraphs. In the next few paragraphs, I give away an important trade secret (something you really don't want me to do).

I'm about to describe a surefire process for writing a best-selling *For Dummies* book. Here's the process:

Write several words to create a sentence. Do this several times to create a paragraph.

```
Repeat the following to form a paragraph:
   Repeat the following to form a sentence:
      Write a word.
```

Repeat the previous instructions several times to make a section. Make several sections and then make several chapters.

```
Repeat the following to form a best-selling book in the For Dummies series:
   Repeat the following to form a chapter:
      Repeat the following to form a section:
         Repeat the following to form a paragraph:
```

```
Repeat the following to form a sentence:
    Write a word.
```

This process involves a loop within a loop within a loop within a loop within a loop. It's like a verbal M.C. Escher print. Is it useful, or is it frivolous?

Well, in the world of computer programming, this kind of thing happens all the time. Most five-layered loops are hidden behind method calls, but two-layered loops within loops are everyday occurrences. So this chapter tells you how to compose a loop within a loop. It's very useful stuff.

By the way, if you're a Wiley editor, you can start reading again from this point onward.

Paying Your Old Code a Little Visit

The program in Listing 12-5 (over in Chapter 12) extracts a username from an email address. For example, the program reads

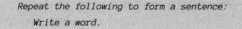

from the keyboard, and writes

```
John
```

to the screen. Let me tell you, in this book I have some pretty lame excuses for writing programs, but this simple email example tops the list! Why would you want to type something on the keyboard, only to have the computer display part of what you typed? There must be a better use for code of this kind.

Sure enough, there is. The BurdBrain.com network administrator has a list of 10,000 employees' email addresses. More precisely, the administrator's hard drive has a file named `email.txt`. This file contains 10,000 email addresses, with one address on each line, as shown in Figure 14-1.

FIGURE 14-1:
A list of email
addresses.

```
email.txt
    John@BurdBrain.com
    Susan@BurdBrain.com
    Horace@BurdBrain.com
    Tom@BurdBrain.com
    Margaret@BurdBrain.com
    Darlene@BurdBrain.com
    Dan@BurdBrain.com
    James@BurdBrain.com
```

The company's email software has an interesting feature. To send email within the company, you don't need to type an entire email address. For example, to send email to John, you can type the username John instead of John@BurdBrain.com. (This @BurdBrain.com part is called the *host name*.)

The company's network administrator wants to distill the content of the email.txt file. She wants a new file, usernames.txt, that contains usernames with no host names, as shown in Figure 14-2.

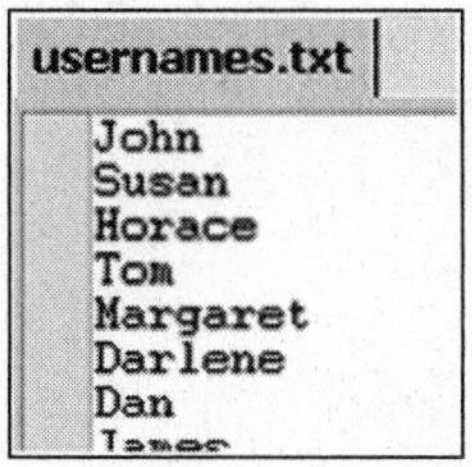

FIGURE 14-2: Usernames extracted from the list of email addresses.

Reworking some existing code

To solve the administrator's problem, you need to modify the code in Listing 12-5. The new version gets an email address from a disk file and writes a username to another disk file. The new version is in Listing 14-1.

LISTING 14-1: **From One File to Another**

```java
import java.util.Scanner;
import java.io.File;
import java.io.FileNotFoundException;
import java.io.PrintStream;

class ListOneUsername {

    public static void main(String args[]) throws FileNotFoundException {

        Scanner diskScanner = new Scanner(new File("email.txt"));
        PrintStream diskWriter = new PrintStream("usernames.txt");
        char symbol;

        symbol = diskScanner.findWithinHorizon(".",0).charAt(0);

        while (symbol != '@') {
            diskWriter.print(symbol);
            symbol = diskScanner.findWithinHorizon(".",0).charAt(0);
        }
```

(continued)

LISTING 14-1: *(continued)*

```
        diskWriter.println();

        diskScanner.close();
        diskWriter.close();
    }
}
```

Listing 14-1 does almost the same thing as its forerunner in Listing 12-5. The only difference is that the code in Listing 14-1 doesn't interact with the user. Instead, the code in Listing 14-1 interacts with disk files.

Running your code

Here's how you run the code in Listing 14-1:

1. **Create a file named** email.txt **in your Eclipse project directory.**

In the email.txt file, put just one email address. Any address will do, as long as the address contains an @ sign.

2. **Put the** ListOneUsername.java **file (the code from Listing 14-1) in your project's** src/(default package) **directory.**

3. **Run the code in Listing 14-1.**

When you run the code, you see nothing interesting in the Console view. What a pity!

4. **View the contents of the** usernames.txt **file.**

If your email.txt file contains John@BurdBrain.com, the usernames.txt file contains John.

For more details on any of these steps, see the discussion accompanying Listings 13-2, 13-3, and 13-4, over in Chapter 13. (The discussion is especially useful if you don't know how to view the usernames.txt file's contents.)

Creating Useful Code

The previous section describes a network administrator's problem — creating a file filled with usernames from a file filled with email addresses. The code in Listing 14-1 solves part of the problem — it extracts just one email address. That's a good start, but to get just one username, you don't need a computer program. A pencil and paper do the trick.

Don't keep the network administrator waiting any longer. In this section, you develop a program that processes dozens, hundreds, and even thousands of email addresses from a file on your hard drive.

First, you need a strategy to create the program. Take the statements in Listing 14-1 and run them over and over again. Better yet, have the statements run themselves over and over again. Fortunately, you already know how to do something over and over again: You use a loop. (See Chapter 12 for the basics on loops.)

Here's the strategy: Take the statements in Listing 14-1 and enclose them in a larger loop:

```
while (not at the end of the email.txt file) {
    Execute the statements in Listing 14-1
}
```

Looking back at the code in Listing 14-1, you see that the statements in that code have a while loop of their own. So this strategy involves putting one loop inside another loop:

```
while (not at the end of the email.txt file) {
    //Blah-blah

    while (symbol != '@') {
        //Blah-blah-blah
    }

    //Blah-blah-blah-blah
}
```

Because one loop is inside the other, they're called *nested loops.* The old loop (the symbol != '@' loop) is the *inner loop.* The new loop (the end-of-file loop) is called the *outer loop.*

Checking for the end of a file

Now all you need is a way to test the loop's condition. How do you know when you're at the end of the email.txt file?

The answer comes from Java's Scanner class. This class's hasNext method answers true or false to the following question:

> Does the email.txt file have anything to read in it (beyond what you've already read)?

If the program's findWithinHorizon calls haven't gobbled up all the characters in the email.txt file, the value of diskScanner.hasNext() is true. So, to keep looping while you're not at the end of the email.txt file, you do the following:

```
while (diskScanner.hasNext()) {
    Execute the statements in Listing 14-1
}
```

The first realization of this strategy is in Listing 14-2.

LISTING 14-2: **The Mechanical Combining of Two Loops**

```java
/*
 * This code does NOT work (but you learn from your mistakes).
 */

import java.util.Scanner;
import java.io.File;
import java.io.FileNotFoundException;
import java.io.PrintStream;

class ListAllUsernames {

    public static void main(String args[]) throws FileNotFoundException {

        Scanner diskScanner = new Scanner(new File("email.txt"));
        PrintStream diskWriter = new PrintStream("usernames.txt");
        char symbol;

        while (diskScanner.hasNext()) {
            symbol = diskScanner.findWithinHorizon(".",0).charAt(0);

            while (symbol != '@') {
                diskWriter.print(symbol);
                symbol = diskScanner.findWithinHorizon(".",0).charAt(0);
            }
```

```
        diskWriter.println();
    }

    diskScanner.close();
    diskWriter.close();
  }
}
```

When you run the code in Listing 14-2, you get the disappointing response shown
in Figure 14-3.

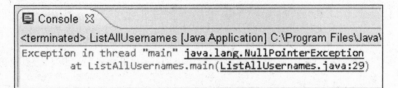

FIGURE 14-3:
You goofed.

How it feels to be a computer

What's wrong with the code in Listing 14-2? To find out, I role-play the computer.
"If I were a computer, what would I do when I execute the code in Listing 14-2?"

The first several things that I'd do are pictured in Figure 14-4. I would read the
J in John, and then write the J in John, and then read the letter o (also in John).

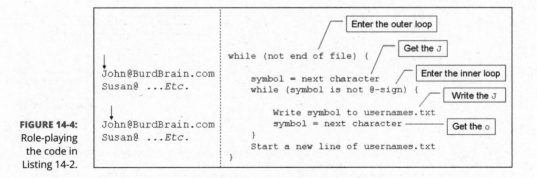

FIGURE 14-4:
Role-playing
the code in
Listing 14-2.

After a few trips through the inner loop, I'd get the @ sign in John@BurdBrain.
com, as shown in Figure 14-5.

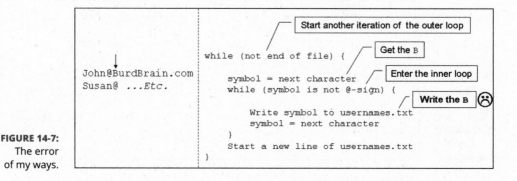

```
                                                      ┌─────────────────────┐
                                                      │ Start another iteration │
                                                      │ of the inner loop       │
                                                      └─────────────────────┘
                           while (not end of file) {

John@BurdBrain.com             symbol = next character
Susan@ ...Etc.                 while (symbol is not @-sign) {     ┌──────────┐
                                                                  │ Write the n │
                                                                  └──────────┘
John@BurdBrain.com                 Write symbol to usernames.txt
Susan@ ...Etc.                     symbol = next character ───────┌──────────┐
                               }                                  │ Get the @  │
                               Start a new line of usernames.txt  └──────────┘

                           }
```

FIGURE 14-5:
Reaching the end
of the username.

Finding this @ sign would jump me out of the inner loop and back to the top of the outer loop, as shown in Figure 14-6.

```
                           while (not end of file) {

                               symbol = next character    ┌──────────────────┐
                               while (symbol is not @-sign) { │ Leave the inner loop │
John@BurdBrain.com                                         └──────────────────┘
Susan@ ...Etc.                     Write symbol to usernames.txt
                                   symbol = next character
                               }
                               Start a new line of usernames.txt
                           }
                             ┌──────────────────────────────┐
                             │ Go back to the top of the outer loop │
                             └──────────────────────────────┘
```

FIGURE 14-6:
Leaving the
inner loop.

I'd get the B in BurdBrain and sail back into the inner loop. But then (horror of horrors!) I'd write that B to the usernames.txt file. (See Figure 14-7.)

```
                                          ┌──────────────────────────────────┐
                                          │ Start another iteration of the outer loop │
                                          └──────────────────────────────────┘
                                                        ┌──────────┐
                           while (not end of file) {    │ Get the B  │
                                                        └──────────┘
John@BurdBrain.com             symbol = next character    ┌──────────────────┐
Susan@ ...Etc.                 while (symbol is not @-sign) { │ Enter the inner loop │
                                                              └──────────────────┘
                                                              ┌──────────┐
                                   Write symbol to usernames.txt │ Write the B │ ☹
                                   symbol = next character    └──────────┘
                               }
                               Start a new line of usernames.txt
                           }
```

FIGURE 14-7:
The error
of my ways.

There's the error! You don't want to write host names to the usernames.txt file. When the computer found the @ sign, it should have skipped past the rest of John's email address.

At this point, you have a choice. You can jump straight to the corrected code in Listing 14-3 (a couple of sections from here), or you can read on to find out about the error message in Figure 14-3.

Why the computer accidentally pushes past the end of the file

Ah! You're wondering why Figure 14-3 has that nasty error message.

I role-play the computer to help me figure out what's going wrong. Imagine that I've already role-played the steps in Figure 14-7. I shouldn't process the first letter B (let alone the entire BurdBrain.com host name) with the inner loop. But unfortunately, I do.

I keep running and processing more email addresses. When I get to the end of the last email address, I grab the m in BurdBrain.com and go back to test for an @ sign, as shown in Figure 14-8.

Now I'm in trouble. This last m certainly isn't an @ sign. So I jump into the inner loop and try to get yet another character. (See Figure 14-9.) The email.txt file has no more characters, so Java sends an error message to the computer screen. (Refer to the NullPointerException error message in Figure 14-3.)

```
... @BurdBrain.com          while (not end of file) {
James@BurdBrain.com
                                symbol = next character
                                while (symbol is not @-sign) {

                                    Write symbol to usernames.txt
                                    symbol = next character ——— Get the m
                                }
                                Start a new line of usernames.txt

                            }
                                    Go back to the top of the inner loop
```

FIGURE 14-8:
The journey's last leg.

TECHNICAL STUFF

Here's why I get a NullPointerException: The email.txt file has no more characters, so the call to findWithinHorizon(".",0) comes up empty. (There's nothing to find.) In Java, a more precise way of describing that emptiness is with the word null. The call findWithinHorizon(".",0) is null, so pointing to a character that was found (charAt(0)) is a fruitless endeavor. Thus, Java displays a NullPointerException message.

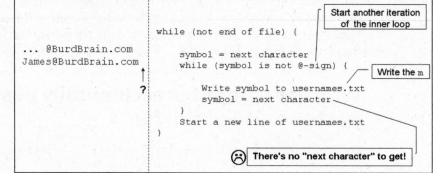

FIGURE 14-9:
Trying to read past the end of the file.

Solving the problem

Listing 14-3 has the solution to the problem described with Figures 14-1 and 14-2. The code in this listing is almost identical to the code in Listing 14-2. The only difference is the added call to nextLine. When the computer reaches an @ sign, this nextLine call swallows the rest of the input line without actually tasting it. (The nextLine call gets the rest of the email address, but doesn't output that part of the email address. The idea works because each email address is on its own separate line.) After gulping down @BurdBrain.com, the computer moves gracefully to the next line of input.

LISTING 14-3: **That's Much Better!**

```
/*
 * This code is correct!!
 */

import java.util.Scanner;
import java.io.File;
import java.io.FileNotFoundException;
import java.io.PrintStream;

class ListAllUsernames {

    public static void main(String args[]) throws FileNotFoundException {

        Scanner diskScanner = new Scanner(new File("email.txt"));
        PrintStream diskWriter = new PrintStream("usernames.txt");
        char symbol;

        while (diskScanner.hasNext()) {
            symbol = diskScanner.findWithinHorizon(".",0).charAt(0);
```

```
        while (symbol != '@') {
            diskWriter.print(symbol);
            symbol = diskScanner.findWithinHorizon(".",0).charAt(0);
        }

        diskScanner.nextLine();
        diskWriter.println();
    }

    diskScanner.close();
    diskWriter.close();
    }
}
```

To run the code in Listing 14-3, you need an email.txt file — a file like the one shown earlier, in Figure 14-1. In the email.txt file, type several email addresses. Any addresses will do, as long as each address contains an @ sign and each address is on its own separate line. Save the email.txt file in your project directory along with the ListAllUsernames.java file (the code from Listing 14-3). For more details, see the discussion accompanying Listings 13-2, 13-3, and 13-4 in Chapter 13.

With Listing 14-3, you've reached an important milestone. You've analyzed a delicate programming problem and found a complete, working solution. The tools you used included thinking about strategies and role-playing the computer. As time goes on, you can use these tools to solve bigger and better problems.

TRY IT OUT

Nothing is more challenging for novice programmers than creating nested loops. That's why I cover looping techniques in this chapter, and in the next two chapters. You might say that I loop through my coverage of programming loops.

Try writing the code that I suggest in the next few paragraphs. Don't be afraid to make lots of mistakes. If you get stuck, slow down, take a step back, and think about what the computer will do when it follows instructions to the letter.

The solutions are on my web page at www.allmycode.com/BeginProg. But don't jump to the solutions until you've experimented with lots of different ideas. Follow this tried-and-true formula:

```
Write some code;
Run your code;
while (your program doesn't work correctly) {
    Step through your code, one statement after another, keeping track
        of the values of the variables and the computer's output as
        Java follows your instructions exactly as they're written;
```

```
    In the step by step execution of statements, notice the place where
        Java does something that you don't want it to do;
    Ask yourself how you'd change the statements so that Java would do
        what you want it to do;
    Change the statements in your code;
    Run your code again;
}
```

END OF THE ROAD

A file named input.txt contains only four characters:

```
Java
```

What's the output when you run the following code?

```java
import java.io.File;
import java.io.FileNotFoundException;
import java.util.Scanner;

public class Main {

    public static void main(String[] args) throws FileNotFoundException {
        Scanner diskScanner = new Scanner(new File("input.txt"));

        while (diskScanner.hasNext()) {
            char symbol = diskScanner.findWithinHorizon(".", 0).charAt(0);
            System.out.print(Character.toUpperCase(symbol));
        }

        diskScanner.close();
    }

}
```

SEEING STARS

In this chapter's "How it feels to be a computer" section, I examine each line of a program's code and ask myself what the computer does when it executes that line. Do the same thing with the following program:

```java
import java.io.File;
import java.io.FileNotFoundException;
import java.util.Scanner;
```

```
class ReadStars {

    public static void main(String args[]) throws FileNotFoundException {

        Scanner diskScanner = new Scanner(new File("input.txt"));
        char symbol;

        while (diskScanner.hasNext()) {
            symbol = diskScanner.findWithinHorizon(".",0).charAt(0);

            while (symbol == '*') {
                System.out.print(symbol);
                symbol = diskScanner.findWithinHorizon(".",0).charAt(0);
            }

            System.out.println();
        }

        diskScanner.close();
    }
}
```

What happens when the input.txt file contains the following characters?

```
*****X***Y*****Z
```

LOOP SOUP

Make a chart to keep track of the changes to the values of i and j as Java executes the following code.

```
int i = 5;
int j;
while (i > 0) {
    System.out.println(i);
    i--;
    j = 3;
    while (j > 0) {
        System.out.print(j);
        j--;
    }
    System.out.println();
}
```

Based on the values in your chart, what will be the output of the code? Run the code in Eclipse to find out whether your prediction is correct.

MAKE SOME CHANGES AROUND HERE

Modify the code from the previous experiment ("Loop soup") so that the output has no lines containing the 321 digit sequence. In place of the 321 lines, the output has lines containing the 123 digit sequence.

SEEING STARS

This experiment comes in two parts. The first part requires only one loop. The second part requires nested loops.

» Write a program that asks the user how many stars to display. When the user enters a number, the program displays that many stars. Here's a sample run:

```
How many stars? 5
*****
```

» Write a program that repeatedly asks whether the user wants to see a row of stars. As long as the user replies with the letter y, the program does what it did in the previous bullet. That is, the program asks the user how many stars to display and then displays that many stars. As soon as the user replies with the letter n, the program stops running.

Here's a sample run of the program:

```
Do you want a row of stars? (y/n) y
How many stars? 5
*****
Do you want a row of stars? (y/n) y
How many stars? 2
**
Do you want a row of stars? (y/n) y
How many stars? 8
********
Do you want a row of stars? (y/n) n
```

To create this program, take the code that you wrote in the previous bullet (Part 1 of "Seeing stars") and surround some of that code inside a second loop.

APROPOS OF NOTHING

In Figure 14-3, the run of a Java program throws a NullPointerException. These NullPointerException messages are never fun, but the more of these messages you encounter, the less frightening they are.

To help desensitize you to NullPointerException messages, generate one of them intentionally. Type the following two lines, one after another, in the JShell window:

```
String name = null;
System.out.println(name.length());
```

» **Improving your nesting techniques**

» **Insisting on a valid response from the user**

» **Looping through enumerated values**

Chapter **15**

The Old Runaround

I remember it distinctly — the sense of dread I would feel on the way to Aunt Edna's house. She was a kind old woman, and her intentions were good. But visits to her house were always agonizing.

First, we'd sit in the living room and talk about other relatives. That was okay, as long as I understood what people were talking about. Sometimes, the gossip would be about adult topics, and I'd become bored.

After all the family chatter, my father would help Aunt Edna with her bills. That was fun to watch because Aunt Edna had a genetically inherited family ailment: Like me and many of my ancestors, Aunt Edna couldn't keep track of paperwork to save her life. It was as if the paper had allergens that made Aunt Edna's skin crawl. After ten minutes of useful bill paying, my father would find a mistake, an improper tally, or something else in the ledger that needed attention. He'd ask Aunt Edna about it, and she'd shrug her shoulders. He'd become agitated trying to track down the problem, while Aunt Edna rolled her eyes and smiled with ignorant satisfaction. It was great entertainment.

Then, when the bill paying was done, we'd sit down to eat dinner. That's when I would remember why I dreaded these visits. Dinner was unbearable. Aunt Edna believed in Fletcherism — a health movement whose followers chewed each mouthful of food 100 times. The more devoted followers used a chart, with a different number for the mastication of each kind of food. The minimal number of chews for any food was 32 — one chomp for each tooth in your mouth. People who did this said they were "Fletcherizing."

Mom and Dad thought the whole Fletcher business was silly, but they respected Aunt Edna and felt that people her age should be humored, not defied. As for me, I thought I'd explode from the monotony. Each meal lasted forever. Each mouthful was an ordeal. I can still remember my mantra — the words I'd say to myself without meaning to do so:

```
I've chewed 0 times so far.
Have I chewed 100 times yet? If not, then
    Chew!
    Add 1 to the number of times that I've chewed.
    Go back to "Have I chewed" to find out if I'm done yet.
```

Repeating Statements a Certain Number of Times (Java for Statements)

Life is filled with examples of counting loops. And computer programming mirrors life (. . . or is it the other way around?). When you tell a computer what to do, you're often telling the computer to print three lines, process ten accounts, dial a million phone numbers, or whatever. Because counting loops are common in programming, the people who create programming languages have developed statements just for loops of this kind. In Java, the statement that repeats something a certain number of times is called a *for* statement. An example of a for statement is in Listing 15-1.

LISTING 15-1: **Horace Fletcher's Revenge**

```java
import static java.lang.System.out;

class AuntEdnaSettlesForTen {

    public static void main(String args[]) {

        for (int count = 0; count < 10; count++) {
            out.print("I've chewed ");
            out.print(count);
            out.println(" time(s).");
        }

        out.println("10 times! Hooray!");
        out.println("I can swallow!");
    }
}
```

Figure 15-1 shows you what you get when you run the program in Listing 15-1:

>> The for statement in Listing 15-1 starts by setting the count variable equal to 0.

>> Then the for statement tests to make sure that count is less than 10 (which it certainly is).

>> Then the for statement dives ahead and executes the printing statements between the curly braces. At this early stage of the game, the computer prints I've chewed 0 time(s).

>> Then the for statement executes count++ — that last thing inside the for statement's parentheses. This last action adds 1 to the value of count.

```
Console 23        Probler
<terminated> AuntEdnaSettle
I've chewed 2 time(s).
I've chewed 3 time(s).
I've chewed 4 time(s).
I've chewed 5 time(s).
I've chewed 6 time(s).
I've chewed 7 time(s).
I've chewed 8 time(s).
I've chewed 9 time(s).
10 times! Hooray!
I can swallow!
```

FIGURE 15-1: Chewing ten times.

This ends the first iteration of the for statement in Listing 15-1. Of course, this loop has more to it than just one iteration:

>> With count now equal to 1, the for statement checks again to make sure that count is less than 10. (Yes, 1 is smaller than 10.)

>> Because the test turns out okay, the for statement marches back into the curly-braced statements and prints I've chewed 1 time(s) on the screen.

>> Then the for statement executes that last count++ inside its parentheses. The statement adds 1 to the value of count, increasing the value of count to 2.

And so on. This whole thing keeps repeating over and over again until, after ten iterations, the value of count finally reaches 10. When this happens, the check for count being less than 10 fails, and the loop's execution ends. The computer jumps to whatever statement comes immediately after the for statement. In Listing 15-1, the computer prints 10 times! Hooray! I can swallow! The whole process is illustrated in Figure 15-2.

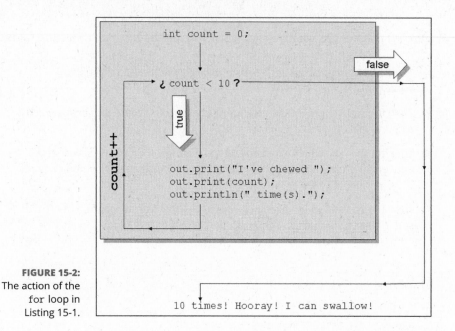

FIGURE 15-2:
The action of the for loop in Listing 15-1.

The anatomy of a for statement

A typical for statement looks like this:

```
for (Initialization; Condition; Update) {
    Statements
}
```

After the word for, you put three things in parentheses: an *initialization*, a *condition*, and an *update*.

Each of the three items in parentheses plays its own, distinct role:

>> **Initialization:** The initialization is executed once, when the run of your program first reaches the for statement.

>> **Condition:** The condition is tested several times (at the start of each iteration).

>> **Update:** The update is also evaluated several times (at the end of each iteration).

If it helps, think of the loop as though its text is shifted all around:

```
//This is NOT real code
int count = 0
for count < 0 {
```

```
    out.print("I've chewed ");
    out.print(count);
    out.println(" time(s).");
    count++;
}
```

You can't write a real for statement this way. (The compiler would throw code like this right into the garbage can.) Even so, this is the order in which the parts of the for statement are executed.

WARNING

The first line of a for statement (the word for followed by stuff in parentheses) isn't a complete statement. So you almost never put a semicolon after the stuff in parentheses. If you make a mistake and type a semicolon, like this:

```
// DON'T DO THIS:
for (int count = 0; count < 10; count++); {
```

you usually put the computer into a do-nothing loop. The computer counts to itself from 0 to 9. After counting, the computer executes whatever statements come immediately after the open curly brace. (The loop ends at the semicolon, so the statements after the open curly brace aren't inside the loop.)

Initializing a for loop

Look at the first line of the for loop in Listing 15-1 and notice the declaration int count = 0. That's something new. When you create a for loop, you can declare a variable (like count) as part of the loop initialization.

If you declare a variable in the initialization of a for loop, you can't use that variable outside the loop. For example, in Listing 15-1, try putting out.println(count) after the end of the loop:

```
//This code does not compile.
for (int count = 0; count < 10; count++) {
    out.print("I've chewed ");
    out.print(count);
    out.println(" time(s).");
}

out.print(count);    //The count variable doesn't exist here.
```

With this extra reference to the count variable, the compiler gives you an error message. You can see the message in Figure 15-3. If you're not experienced with for statements, the message may surprise you — "Whadaya mean 'count cannot be resolved to a variable'? There's a count variable declaration just four lines above that statement." Ah, yes. But the count variable is declared in the for loop's initialization. Outside the for loop, that count variable doesn't exist.

```
  public static void main(String[] args) {
    // This code does not compile.
    for (int count = 0; count < 10; count++) {
      out.print("I've chewed ");
      out.print(count);
      out.println(" time(s).");
    }

    out.print(count); // The count variable doesn't
                      [ count cannot be resolved to a variable ]
  }                   4 quick fixes available:
}                        Create local variable 'count'
                         Create field 'count'
                         Create parameter 'count'
                         Create constant 'count'
```

To use a variable outside of a for statement, you have to declare that variable outside the for statement. You can even do this with the for statement's counting variable. Listing 15-2 has an example.

LISTING 15-2: **Using a Variable Declared Outside of a for Loop**

```java
import static java.lang.System.out;

class AuntEdnaDoesItAgain {

    public static void main(String args[]) {
        int count;

        for (count = 0; count < 10; count++) {
            out.print("I've chewed ");
            out.print(count);
            out.println(" time(s).");
        }

        out.print(count);
        out.println(" times! Hooray!");
        out.println("I can swallow!");
    }
}
```

A run of the code in Listing 15-2 looks exactly like the run for Listing 15-1. The run is pictured in Figure 15-1. Unlike its predecessor, Listing 15-2 enjoys the luxury of using the count variable to display the number 10. It can do this because in Listing 15-2, the count variable belongs to the entire main method and not to the for loop alone.

VERSATILE LOOPING STATEMENTS

If you were stuck on a desert island with only one kind of loop, what kind would you want to have? The answer is, you can get along with any kind of loop. The choice between a while loop and a for loop is about the code's style and efficiency. It's not about necessity.

Anything that you can do with a for loop, you can do with a while loop as well. Consider, for example, the for loop in Listing 15-1. Here's how you can achieve the same effect with a while loop:

```
int count = 0;
while (count < 10) {
  out.print("I've chewed ");
  out.print(count);
  out.println(" time(s).");
  count++;
}
```

In the while loop, you have explicit statements to declare, initialize, and increment the count variable.

The same kind of trick works in reverse. Anything that you can do with a while loop, you can do with a for loop as well. But turning certain while loops into for loops seems strained and unnatural. Consider a while loop from Listing 12-2 in Chapter 12:

```
while (total < 21) {
  card = myRandom.nextInt(10) + 1;
  total += card;
  System.out.print(card);
  System.out.print("     ");
  System.out.println(total);
}
```

Turning this loop into a for loop means wasting most of the stuff inside the for loop's parentheses:

```
for ( ; total < 21 ; ) {
  card = myRandom.nextInt(10) + 1;
  total += card;
  System.out.print(card);
  System.out.print("     ");
  System.out.println(total);
}
```

(continued)

(continued)

The preceding `for` loop has a condition, but it has no initialization and no update. That's okay. Without an initialization, nothing special happens when the computer first enters the `for` loop. And without an update, nothing special happens at the end of each iteration. It's strange, but it works.

Usually, when you write a `for` statement, you're counting how many times to repeat something. But, in truth, you can do just about any kind of repetition with a `for` statement.

Notice the words `for (count = 0` in Listing 15-2. Because `count` is declared before the `for` statement, you don't declare `count` again in the `for` statement's initialization. I tried declaring `count` twice, as in the following code:

```
//This does NOT work:
int count;


for (int count = 0; count < 10; count++) {
    ... etc.
```

And Eclipse told me to clean up my act:

```
Duplicate local variable count                        ^
```

Using Nested for Loops

Because you're reading *Beginning Programming with Java For Dummies*, 5th Edition, I assume that you manage a big hotel. Chapter 16 tells you everything you need to know about hotel management. But before you begin reading that chapter, you can get a little preview in this section.

I happen to know that your hotel has 9 floors, and that each floor of your hotel has 20 rooms. On this sunny afternoon, someone hands you a flash drive containing a file full of numbers. You copy this `hotelData` file to your hard drive and then display the file in Eclipse's editor. You see the stuff shown in Figure 15-4.

This file gives the number of guests in each room. For example, at the start of the file, you see 2 1 2. This means that, on the first floor, Room 1 has 2 guests, Room 2 has 1 guest, and Room 3 has 2 guests. After reading 20 of these numbers, you see 0 2 2. So, on the second floor, Room 1 has 0 guests, Room 2 has 2 guests, and Room 3 has 2 guests. The story continues until the last number in the file. According to that number, Room 20 on the ninth floor has 4 guests.

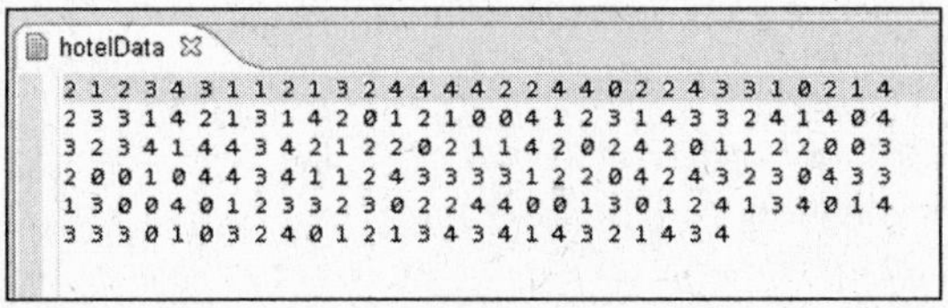

FIGURE 15-4:
A file containing
hotel occupancy
data.

```
hotelData
2 1 2 3 4 3 1 1 2 1 3 2 4 4 4 2 2 4 4 0 2 2 4 3 3 1 0 2 1 4
2 3 3 1 4 2 1 3 1 4 2 0 1 2 1 0 0 4 1 2 3 1 4 3 3 2 4 1 4 0 4
3 2 3 4 1 4 4 3 4 2 1 2 2 0 2 1 1 4 2 0 2 4 2 0 1 1 2 2 0 0 3
2 0 0 1 0 4 4 3 4 1 1 2 4 3 3 3 3 1 2 2 0 4 2 4 3 2 3 0 4 3 3
1 3 0 0 4 0 1 2 3 3 2 3 0 2 2 4 4 0 0 1 3 0 1 2 4 1 3 4 0 1 4
3 3 3 0 1 0 3 2 4 0 1 2 1 3 4 3 4 1 4 3 2 1 4 3 4
```

You'd like a more orderly display of these numbers — a display of the kind in Figure 15-5. So you whip out your keyboard to write a quick Java program.

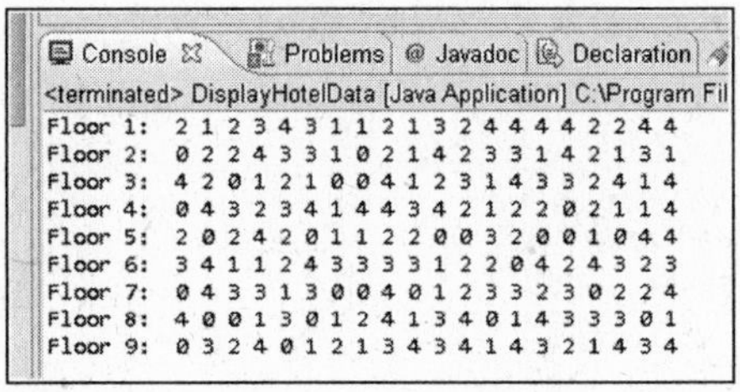

FIGURE 15-5:
A readable
display of
the data in
Figure 15-4.

```
Console   Problems   @ Javadoc   Declaration
<terminated> DisplayHotelData [Java Application] C:\Program Fil
Floor 1:   2 1 2 3 4 3 1 1 2 1 3 2 4 4 4 4 2 2 4 4
Floor 2:   0 2 2 4 3 3 1 0 2 1 4 2 3 3 1 4 2 1 3 1
Floor 3:   4 2 0 1 2 1 0 0 4 1 2 3 1 4 3 3 2 4 1 4
Floor 4:   0 4 3 2 3 4 1 4 4 3 4 2 1 2 2 0 2 1 1 4
Floor 5:   2 0 2 4 2 0 1 1 2 2 0 0 3 2 0 0 1 0 4 4
Floor 6:   3 4 1 1 2 4 3 3 3 3 1 2 2 0 4 2 4 3 2 3
Floor 7:   0 4 3 3 1 3 0 0 4 0 1 2 3 3 2 3 0 2 2 4
Floor 8:   4 0 0 1 3 0 1 2 4 1 3 4 0 1 4 3 3 3 0 1
Floor 9:   0 3 2 4 0 1 2 1 3 4 3 4 1 4 3 2 1 4 3 4
```

As in some other examples, you decide which statements go where by asking yourself how many times each statement should be executed. For starters, the display in Figure 15-5 has 9 lines, and each line has 20 numbers:

```
for (each of 9 floors)
    for (each of 20 rooms on a floor)
        get a number from the file and display the number on the screen.
```

So your program has a for loop within a for loop — a pair of *nested* for loops.

Next, you notice how each line begins in Figure 15-5. Each line contains the word Floor, followed by the floor number. Because this Floor display occurs only 9 times in Figure 15-5, the statements to print this display belong in the for-each-of-9-floors loop (and not in the for-each-of-20-rooms loop). The statements should be before the for-each-of-20-rooms loop because this Floor display comes once before each line's 20-number display:

```
for (each of 9 floors)
    display "Floor" and the floor number,
    for (each of 20 rooms on a floor)
        get a number from the file and display the number on the screen.
```

You're almost ready to write the code. But there's one detail that's easy to forget. (Well, it's a detail that I always forget.) After displaying 20 numbers, the program advances to a new line. This new-line action happens only 9 times during the run of the program, and it always happens *after* the program displays 20 numbers:

```
for (each of 9 floors)
    display "Floor" and the floor number,
    for (each of 20 rooms on a floor)
        get a number from the file and display the number on the screen,
    Go to the next line.
```

That does it. That's all you need. The code to create the display of Figure 15-5 is in Listing 15-3.

LISTING 15-3: ## Hey! Is This a For-by-For?

```java
import java.util.Scanner;
import java.io.File;
import java.io.FileNotFoundException;
import static java.lang.System.out;

class DisplayHotelData {

    public static void main(String args[]) throws FileNotFoundException {

        Scanner diskScanner = new Scanner(new File("hotelData"));

        for (int floor = 1; floor <= 9; floor++) {
            out.print("Floor ");
            out.print(floor);
            out.print(":  ");

            for (int roomNum = 1; roomNum <= 20; roomNum++) {
                out.print(diskScanner.nextInt());
                out.print(' ');
            }

            out.println();
        }

        diskScanner.close();
    }
}
```

The code in Listing 15-3 has the variable `floor` going from 1 to 9 and has the variable `roomNum` going from 1 to 20. Because the `roomNum` loop is inside the `floor` loop, the writing of 20 numbers happens 9 times. That's good. It's exactly what I want.

TRY IT OUT

When it comes to writing code with loops, there's no such thing as having too much practice. Try these problems. Work slowly and don't get discouraged. Remember that solutions are available at www.allmycode.com/BeginProg.

NARCISSIST'S CODE

Write a program that reads the user's name and a number (`howMany`) from the keyboard. The program uses a `for` loop to display the user's name `howMany` times on the screen.

BRITISH POUNDS TO US DOLLARS

In April 2017, one British pound is worth 1.25 US dollars. Write a program to create a simple currency conversion table. In your program, use a `for` loop to display the following table:

Pounds	Dollars
1	1.25
2	2.5
3	3.75
4	5.0
5	6.25
6	7.5
7	8.75
8	10.0
9	11.25

MYSTERY CODE

This experiment comes in two parts:

» Without running the following code, try to predict what the code's output will be:

```
for (int row = 0; row < 5; row++) {
  for (int column = 0; column < 5; column++) {
    System.out.print("*");
  }
  System.out.println();
}
```

After making your prediction, run the code to find out whether your prediction is correct.

» The code in this bullet is a slight variation on the code in the previous bullet. First, try to predict what the code will output. Then run the code to find out whether your prediction is correct:

```java
for (int row = 0; row < 5; row++) {
    for (int column = 0; column <= row; column++) {
        System.out.print("*");
    }
    System.out.println();
}
```

DRAW A PATTERN

This experiment comes in four parts:

» Write a program that reads a number from the keyboard. The program uses a `for` loop to display that number of dashes.

For example, if the user types the number 5, the program displays

```
-----
```

» Modify the program that you wrote in the previous bullet. The modified program uses two `for` loops to display two lines of characters. The second line is one character shorter than the first line. For example, if the user types the number 7, the program displays

```
-------
------
```

» Modify the program that you wrote in the previous bullet. The modified program uses nested `for` loops to display several lines of characters, each shorter than the line that comes before it. For example, if the user types the number 5, the program displays

```
-----
----
---
--
-
```

Hint: The code in this program is much like one of the earlier "Mystery code" snippets.

>> For an extra challenge, modify the code you wrote in the previous bullet so that it displays a slash (/) at the end of each line. For example, if the user types the number 5, the program displays

```
-----/
----/
---/
--/
-/
/
```

TIMES TABLE

This experiment comes in four parts:

>> Write a program that reads a number from the keyboard. The program uses a for loop to display all numbers up to and including that number. For example, if the user types 9, the program displays

```
1    2    3    4    5    6    7    8    9
```

TIP

To put space between the numbers, refer to the "Escapism" sidebar in Chapter 12.

>> Write a program that reads a number from the keyboard. The program uses a for loop to display two times 1, two times 2, and so on up to and including two times the user's number. For example, if the user types 9, the program displays

```
2    4    6    8    10    12    14    16    18
```

>> Write a program that uses nested for loops to display a multiplication table.

```
1    2    3    4    5    6    7    8    9
2    4    6    8    10   12   14   16   18
3    6    9    12   15   18   21   24   27
4    8    12   16   20   24   28   32   36
5    10   15   20   25   30   35   40   45
6    12   18   24   30   36   42   48   54
7    14   21   28   35   42   49   56   63
8    16   24   32   40   48   56   64   72
9    18   27   36   45   54   63   72   81
```

>> For an extra challenge, add a header row and header column to your multiplication table. The resulting display looks like this:

	1	2	3	4	5	6	7	8	9
1	|1	2	3	4	5	6	7	8	9
2	|2	4	6	8	10	12	14	16	18
3	|3	6	9	12	15	18	21	24	27
4	|4	8	12	16	20	24	28	32	36
5	|5	10	15	20	25	30	35	40	45
6	|6	12	18	24	30	36	42	48	54
7	|7	14	21	28	35	42	49	56	63
8	|8	16	24	32	40	48	56	64	72
9	|9	18	27	36	45	54	63	72	81

Repeating Until You Get What You Need (Java do Statements)

I introduce Java's while loop in Chapter 12. When you create a while loop, you write the loop's condition first. After the condition, you write the code that gets repeatedly executed.

```
while (Condition) {
    Code that gets repeatedly executed
}
```

This way of writing a while statement is no accident. The look of the statement emphasizes an important point — that the computer always checks the condition before executing any of the repeated code.

If the loop's condition is never true, the stuff inside the loop is never executed — not even once. In fact, you can easily cook up a while loop whose statements are never executed (although I can't think of a reason why you would ever want to do it):

```
//This code doesn't print anything:
int twoPlusTwo = 2 + 2;
while (twoPlusTwo == 5) {
    System.out.println("Are you kidding?");
    System.out.println("2+2 doesn't equal 5.");
```

```
    System.out.print ("Everyone knows that");
    System.out.println(" 2+2 equals 3.");
}
```

In spite of this silly twoPlusTwo example, the while statement turns out to be the most useful of Java's looping constructs. In particular, the while loop is good for situations in which you must look before you leap. For example: "While money is in my account, write a mortgage check every month." When you first encounter this statement, if your account has a zero balance, you don't want to write a mortgage check — not even one check.

But at times (not many), you want to leap before you look. In a situation when you're asking the user for a response, maybe the user's response makes sense, but maybe it doesn't. Maybe the user's finger slipped, or perhaps the user didn't understand the question. In many situations, it's important to correctly interpret the user's response. If the user's response doesn't make sense, you must ask again.

Getting a trustworthy response

Consider a program that deletes a file. Before deleting the file, the program asks for confirmation from the user. If the user types Y, delete; if the user types N, don't delete. Of course, deleting a file is serious stuff. Mistaking a bad keystroke for a "yes" answer can delete the company's records. (And mistaking a bad keystroke for a "no" answer can preserve the company's incriminating evidence.) If there's any doubt about the user's response, the program should ask the user to respond again.

Pause a moment to think about the flow of actions — what should and shouldn't happen when the computer executes the loop. A loop of this kind doesn't need to check anything before getting the user's first response. Indeed, before the user gives the first response, the loop has nothing to check. The loop shouldn't start with "as long as the user's response is invalid, get another response from the user." Instead, the loop should just leap ahead, get a response from the user, and then check the response to see whether it made sense. The code to do all of this is in Listing 15-4.

LISTING 15-4: **Repeat Before You Delete**

```
/*
 * DISCLAIMER: Neither the author nor John Wiley & Sons,
 * Inc., nor anyone else even remotely connected with the
 * creation of this book, assumes any responsibility
 * for any damage of any kind due to the use of this code,
 * or the use of any work derived from this code,
```

(continued)

LISTING 15-4: *(continued)*

```
* including any work created partially or in full by
* the reader.
*
* Sign here:_____
*/

import java.io.File;
import java.util.Scanner;

class IHopeYouKnowWhatYoureDoing {

  public static void main(String args[]) {

    Scanner keyboard = new Scanner(System.in);
    char reply;

    do {

      System.out.print("Reply with Y or N...");
      System.out.print("  Delete the importantData file? ");
      reply = keyboard.findWithinHorizon(".", 0).charAt(0);

    } while (reply != 'Y' && reply != 'N');

    if (reply == 'Y') {
      new File("importantData.txt").delete();
      System.out.println("Deleted!");
    } else {
      System.out.println("No harm in asking!");
    }

    keyboard.close();
  }
}
```

Deleting a file

A run of the Listing 15-4 program is shown in Figure 15-6. Before deleting a file, the program asks the user whether it's okay to do the deletion. If the user gives one of the two expected answers (Y or N), the program proceeds according to the user's wishes. But if the user enters any other letter (or any digit, punctuation symbol, or whatever), the program asks the user for another response.

```
Console 🖵     Problems  @ Javadoc  Declaration
<terminated> IHopeYouKnowWhatYoureDoing (1) [Java Application] C:\Progran
Reply with Y or N...  Delete the importantData file? U
Reply with Y or N...  Delete the importantData file? 8
Reply with Y or N...  Delete the importantData file? y
Reply with Y or N...  Delete the importantData file? n
Reply with Y or N...  Delete the importantData file? Y
Deleted!
```

FIGURE 15-6:
No! Don't do it!

In Figure 15-6, the user hems and haws for a while, first with the letter U, and then with the digit 8, and then with lowercase letters. Finally, the user enters Y, and the program deletes the importantData.txt file. If you compare the files on your hard drive (before and after the run of the program), you'll see that the program trashes the file named importantData.txt.

If you use Eclipse, here's how you can tell that a file is being deleted:

1. **Create a Java project containing the code in Listing 15-4.**

If you followed the steps in Chapter 2 for importing this book's examples, you can skip this create-a-project step and use the existing 15–04 project.

2. **In the Package Explorer, select the project.**

REMEMBER

Don't select any of the project's subfolders. (For example, don't select the project's src folder.) Instead, select the project's root. For more info about a project's root, see Chapter 13.

3. **In Eclipse's main menu, choose File ⇨ New ⇨ File.**

Eclipse's New File dialog box appears.

TIP

In the New File dialog box, make sure that the name of your project's root folder is in the box's Enter or Select the Parent Folder field. For example, if you followed the steps in Chapter 2 for importing this book's examples, make sure that 15–04 (and no other text) appears in the Enter or Select the Parent Folder field.

4. **In the dialog box's File Name field, type the name of your new file.**

Type **importantData.txt**.

5. **Click Finish.**

6. **Observe that the file's name appears in Eclipse's Package Explorer.**

The name is in the 15–04 project's root directory. You put it in the root directory because, in Listing 15-4, the name importantData.txt (with no slashes or backslashes) refers only to a name in the project's root directory. The program's run has no effect on any files outside of the root directory, even if any of those files has the name importantData.txt.

CROSS REFERENCE

To find out how to refer to files outside of the project's root directory, refer to Chapter 13.

For this experiment, you don't have to add any text to the file. The file exists only to be deleted.

7. **Run the program.**

When the program runs, type **Y** to delete the importantData.txt file.

After running the program, you want to check to make sure that the program deleted the importantData.txt file.

8. **In the Package Explorer, select the project's root (again, for good measure).**

9. **On Eclipse's main menu, choose File ⇨ Refresh.**

Eclipse takes another look at the project directory and lists the directory's files in the Package Explorer's tree. Assuming that the program did its job correctly, the file named importandData.txt no longer appears in the tree.

In Listing 15-4, the statement

```
new File("importantData.txt").delete();
```

is tricky. At first glance, you seem to be creating a new file, only to delete that file in the same line of code! But in reality, the words new File create only a representation of a file inside your program. To be more precise, the words new File create, inside your program, a representation of a disk file that may or may not already exist on your computer's hard drive. Here's what the new File statement really means:

"Let new File("importantData.txt") *refer to a file named* importantData.txt. *If such a file exists, then delete it."*

Yes, the devil is in the details. But smiles are in the subtleties and nobility is in the nuance.

Using Java's do statement

To write the program in Listing 15-4, you need a loop — a loop that repeatedly asks the user whether the importantData.txt file should be deleted. (The action of the loop in Listing 15-4 is illustrated in Figure 15-7.) The loop continues to ask until the user gives a meaningful response. The loop tests its condition at the end of each iteration, after each of the user's responses.

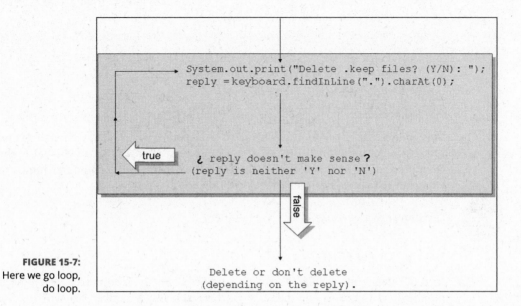

```
System.out.print("Delete .keep files? (Y/N): ");
reply = keyboard.findInLine(".").charAt(0);
```

true

```
¿ reply doesn't make sense ?
(reply is neither 'Y' nor 'N')
```

false

```
Delete or don't delete
(depending on the reply).
```

FIGURE 15-7:
Here we go loop,
do loop.

That's why the program in Listing 15-4 has a *do* loop (also known as a do ... while loop). With a do loop, the program jumps right in, executes some statements, and then checks a condition. If the condition is true, the program goes back to the top of the loop for another go-around. If the condition is false, the computer leaves the loop (and jumps to whatever code comes immediately after the loop).

A closer look at the do statement

The format of a do loop is

```
do {
    Statements
} while (Condition)
```

Writing the *Condition* at the end of the loop reminds me that the computer executes the *Statements* inside the loop first. After the computer executes the *Statements*, the computer goes on to check the *Condition*. If the *Condition* is true, the computer goes back for another iteration of the *Statements*.

With a do loop, the computer always executes the statements inside the loop at least once:

```
//This code prints something:
int twoPlusTwo = 2 + 2;
do {
```

```
    System.out.println("Are you kidding?");
    System.out.println("2+2 doesn't equal 5.");
    System.out.print  ("Everyone knows that");
    System.out.println(" 2+2 equals 3.");
} while (twoPlusTwo == 5);
```

This code displays Are you kidding? 2+2 doesn't equal 5 ... *and so on* and
then tests the condition twoPlusTwo == 5. Because twoPlusTwo == 5 is false, the
computer doesn't go back for another iteration. Instead, the computer jumps to
whatever code comes immediately after the loop.

Get some practice using Java's do statement.

DO I HEAR AN ECHO?

In a do statement, repeatedly read numbers from the keyboard. Display each
number back to the user on the screen. After displaying a number, ask whether the
user wants to continue entering numbers. When the user replies with the letter n,
stop.

Here's a sample run of the program:

```
Enter a number: 5
5
Continue? (y/n) y

Enter a number: 81
81
Continue? (y/n) y

Enter a number: 29
29
Continue? (y/n) n

Done!
```

TALLY HO!

In a do statement, repeatedly read int values from the keyboard and keep track of
the running total. The user says, "I want to stop entering values" by typing one
final int value — the value 0. At that point, the program displays the total of all
values that the user entered.

Repeating with Predetermined Values (Java's Enhanced for Statement)

Most people say that they "never win anything." Other people win raffles, drawings, and contests, but they don't win things. Well, I have news for these people: Other people don't win things, either. Nobody wins things. That's how the laws of probability work. Your chance of winning one of the popular U.S. lottery jackpots is roughly 1 in 135 million. If you sell your quarter-million-dollar house and use all the money to buy lottery tickets, your chance of winning is still only 1 in 540. If you play every day of the month (selling a house each day), your chance of winning the jackpot is still less than 1 in 15.

Of course, nothing in the previous paragraph applies to me. I don't buy lottery tickets, but I often win things. My winning streak started a few years ago. I won some expensive Java software at the end of an online seminar. Later that month, I won a microchip-enabled pinky ring (a memento from a 1998 Java conference). The following year, I won a wireless PDA. Just last week, I won a fancy business-class printer.

I never spend money to enter any contests. All these winnings are freebies. When the national computer science educators' conference met in Reno, Nevada, my colleagues convinced me to try the slot machines. I lost $23, and then I won back $18. At that point, I stopped playing. I wanted to quit while I was only $5 behind.

That's why my writing a Java program about slot machines is such a strange occurrence. A typical slot machine has three reels, with each reel having about 20 symbols. But to illustrate this section's ideas, I don't need 20 symbols. Instead, I use 4 symbols — a cherry, a lemon, a kumquat, and a rutabaga.

Creating an enhanced for loop

When you play my simplified slot machine, you can spin any one of over 60 combinations — cherry+cherry+kumquat, rutabaga+rutabaga+rutabaga, or whatever. This chapter's goal is to list all possible combinations. But first, I show you another kind of loop. Listing 15-5 defines an enum type for a slot machine's symbols and displays a list of the symbols. (For an introduction to enum types, see Chapter 10.)

LISTING 15-5: **Slot Machine Symbols**

```
import static java.lang.System.out;

class ListSymbols {

  enum Symbol {
    cherry, lemon, kumquat, rutabaga
  }

  public static void main(String args[]) {
    for (Symbol leftReel : Symbol.values()) {
      out.println(leftReel);
    }
  }
}
```

Listing 15-5 uses Java's *enhanced for loop*. The word *enhanced* means "enhanced compared with the loops in earlier versions of Java." The enhanced for loop was introduced in Java version 5.0. If you run Java version 1.4.2 (or something like that), you can't use an enhanced for loop.

Here's the format of the enhanced for loop:

```
for (TypeName variableName : RangeOfValues) {
    Statements
}
```

Here's how the loop in Listing 15-5 follows the format:

>> **In Listing 15-5, the word** Symbol **is the name of a type.**

The int type describes values like –1, 0, 1, and 2. The boolean type describes the values true and false. And (because of the code in Listing 15-5) the Symbol type describes the values cherry, lemon, kumquat, and rutabaga. For more information on enum types like Symbol, see Chapter 10.

>> **In Listing 15-5, the word** leftReel **is the name of a variable.**

The loop in Listing 15-1 defines count to be an int variable. Similarly, the loop in Listing 15-5 defines leftReel to be a Symbol variable. So, in theory, the variable leftReel can take on any of the four Symbol values.

By the way, I call this variable leftReel because the code lists all symbols that can appear on the leftmost of the slot machine's three reels. Because all three of the slot machine's reels have the same symbols, I may also have named this variable `middleReel` or `rightReel`. But on second thought, I'll save the names `middleReel` and `rightReel` for a later example.

» **In Listing 15-5, the expression** `Symbol.values()` **stands for the four values in Listing 15-5.**

To quote myself from the previous bullet, "in theory, the variable `leftReel` can take on any of the four `Symbol` values." Well, the *RangeOfValues* part of the `for` statement turns theory into practice. This third item inside the parentheses says, "Have as many loop iterations as there are `Symbol` values, and have the `leftReel` variable take on a different `Symbol` value during each of the loop's iterations."

So the loop in Listing 15-5 undergoes four iterations: an iteration in which `leftReel` has value `cherry`, another iteration in which `leftReel` has value `lemon`, a third iteration in which `leftReel` has value `kumquat`, and a fourth iteration in which `leftReel` has value `rutabaga`. During each iteration, the program prints the `leftReel` variable's value. The result is in Figure 15-8.

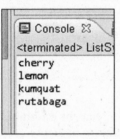

FIGURE 15-8:
The output of
the code in
Listing 15-5.

In general, a *someEnumTypeName.values()* expression stands for the set of values that a particular `enum` type's variable can have. For example, back in Listing 10-7 in Chapter 10, you can use the expression `WhoWins.values()` to refer to the `home`, `visitor`, and `neither` values.

TIP

The difference between a type's name (like `Symbol`) and the type's values (as in `Symbol.values()`) is really subtle. Fortunately, you don't have to worry about the difference. As a beginning programmer, you can just use the `.values()` suffix in an enhanced loop's *RangeOfValues* part.

Nesting the enhanced for loops

Listing 15-5 solves a simple problem in an elegant way. After reading about Listing 15-5, you may ask about more complicated problems: "Can I list all possible 3-reel combinations of the slot machine's four symbols?" Yes, you can. Listing 15-6 shows you how to do it.

LISTING 15-6: **Listing the Combinations**

```java
import static java.lang.System.out;

class ListCombinations {

    enum Symbol {
        cherry, lemon, kumquat, rutabaga
    }

    public static void main(String args[]) {

        for (Symbol leftReel : Symbol.values()) {
            for (Symbol middleReel : Symbol.values()) {
                for (Symbol rightReel : Symbol.values()) {
                    out.print(leftReel);
                    out.print(" ");
                    out.print(middleReel);
                    out.print(" ");
                    out.println(rightReel);
                }
            }
        }
    }
}
```

When you run the program in Listing 15-6, you get 64 lines of output. Some of those lines (from the middle of a run) are shown in Figure 15-9.

Like the code in Listing 15-3, the program in Listing 15-6 contains a loop within a loop. In fact, Listing 15-6 has a loop within a loop within a loop. Here's the strategy in Listing 15-6:

```
for (each of the 4 symbols that can appear on the left reel),
    for (each of the 4 symbols that can appear on the middle reel),
        for (each of the 4 symbols that can appear on the right reel),
            display the three reels' symbols.
```

You start the outer loop with the cherry symbol. Then you march on to the middle loop and begin that loop with the cherry symbol. Then you proceed to the inner loop and pick the cherry (pun intended). At last, with each loop tuned to the cherry setting, you display the cherry cherry cherry combination. (See Figure 15-10.)

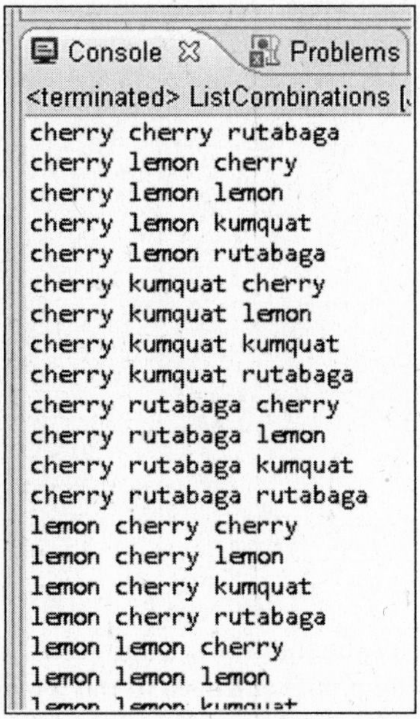

FIGURE 15-9:
Some lines of output from the code in Listing 15-6.

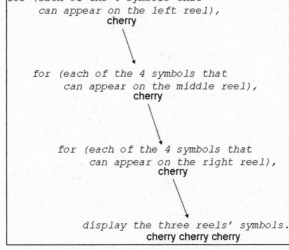

FIGURE 15-10:
Entering loops for the first time in the program of Listing 15-6.

After displaying cherry cherry cherry, you continue with other values of the innermost loop. That is, you change the right reel's value from cherry to lemon. (See Figure 15-11.) Now the three reels' values are cherry cherry lemon, so you display these values on the screen.

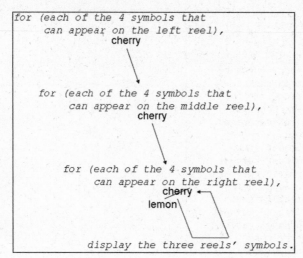

FIGURE 15-11:
Changing from
cherry to lemon
in the innermost
loop.

After exhausting the four values of the innermost (right reel) loop, you jump out of that innermost loop. But the jump puts you back to the top of the middle loop, where you change the value of middleReel from cherry to lemon. Now the values of leftReel and middleReel are cherry and lemon, respectively. (See Figure 15-12.)

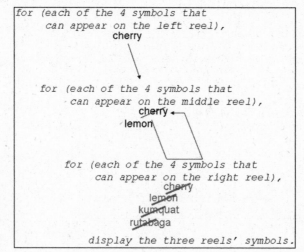

FIGURE 15-12:
Changing from
cherry to lemon
in the middle
loop.

Having changed to lemon on the middle loop, you go barreling again into the innermost loop. As if you'd never seen this inner loop, you set the loop's variable to cherry. (See Figure 15-13.)

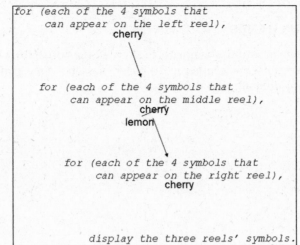

FIGURE 15-13:
Restarting the
inner loop.

After displaying the tasty cherry lemon cherry combination, you start changing the values of the innermost loop. (See Figure 15-14.)

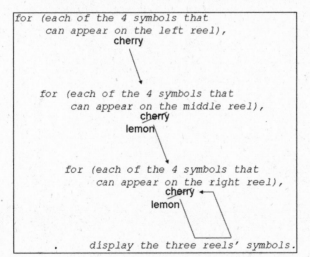

FIGURE 15-14:
Traveling a
second time
through the
innermost loop.

The loop keeps going until it displays all 64 combinations. Whew!

To finish off this chapter, you write code for the paper-scissors-stone game.

TRY IT OUT

ENUMERATE THE POSSIBILITIES

Create an enum type containing the three values in the paper-scissors-stone game. Write a program that uses an enhanced for loop to display the three values.

SHOW YOUR HANDS

Use nested enhanced `for` statements to show all the possibilities when two players compete against one another in the paper-scissors-stone game. The output of your program will look something like this:

```
paper paper
paper scissors
paper stone
scissors paper
... and so on
```

Chapter 16

Using Loops and Arrays

This chapter has ten illustrations. For these illustrations, the people at John Wiley & Sons, Inc. insist on the following numbering: Figure 16-1, Figure 16-2, Figure 16-3, Figure 16-4, Figure 16-5, Figure 16-6, Figure 16-7, Figure 16-8, Figure 16-9, and Figure 16-10. But I like a different kind of numbering. I'd like to number the illustrations `figure[0]`, `figure[1]`, `figure[2]`, `figure[3]`, `figure[4]`, `figure[5]`, `figure[6]`, `figure[7]`, `figure[8]`, and `figure[9]`. In this chapter, you find out why.

Some Loops in Action

The Java Motel, with its ten comfortable rooms, sits in a quiet place off the main highway. Aside from a small, separate office, the motel is just one long row of ground-floor rooms. Each room is easily accessible from the spacious front parking lot.

Oddly enough, the motel's rooms are numbered 0 through 9. I could say that the numbering is a fluke — something to do with the builder's original design plan. But the truth is, starting with 0 makes the examples in this chapter easier to write.

You, as the Java Motel's manager, store occupancy data in a file on your computer's hard drive. The file has one entry for each room in the motel. For example, in Figure 16-1, Room 0 has one guest, Room 1 has four guests, Room 2 is empty, and so on.

FIGURE 16-1:
Occupancy data
for the Java
Motel.

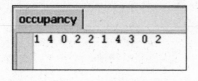

occupancy

1 4 0 2 2 1 4 3 0 2

You want a report showing the number of guests in each room. Because you know how many rooms you have, this problem begs for a `for` loop. The code to solve this problem is in Listing 16-1, and a run of the code is shown in Figure 16-2.

LISTING 16-1: **A Program to Generate an Occupancy Report**

```java
import java.util.Scanner;
import java.io.File;
import java.io.FileNotFoundException;
import static java.lang.System.out;

class ShowOccupancy {

    public static void main(String args[]) throws FileNotFoundException {
        Scanner diskScanner = new Scanner(new File("occupancy"));

        out.println("Room\tGuests");

        for (int roomNum = 0; roomNum < 10; roomNum++) {
            out.print(roomNum);
            out.print("\t");
            out.println(diskScanner.nextInt());
        }

        diskScanner.close();
    }
}
```

Listing 16-1 uses a `for` loop — a loop of the kind described in Chapter 15. As the `roomNum` variable's value marches from 0 to 9, the program displays one number after another from the `occupancy` file. To read more about getting numbers from a disk file like my `occupancy` file, see Chapter 13.

REMEMBER

This example's input file is named `occupancy` — not `occupancy.txt`. If you use Windows Notepad to make an `occupancy` file, you must use quotation marks in the Save As dialog box's File Name field. That is, you must type **"occupancy"** (with quotation marks) in the File Name field. If you don't surround the name with quotation marks, Notepad adds a default extension to the file's name (turning `occupancy` into `occupancy.txt`). A similar issue applies to the Macintosh's TextEdit program. By default, TextEdit adds the `.rtf` extension to each new file.

To override the `.rtf` default for a particular file, select Format⇨Make Plain Text. Then, in the Save As dialog box, remove the check mark from the check box labeled If No Extension Is Provided, Use ".txt". (To override the default for all newly created files, choose TextEdit⇨Preferences. Then, in the Format part of the Preferences dialog's New Document tab, select Plain Text.)

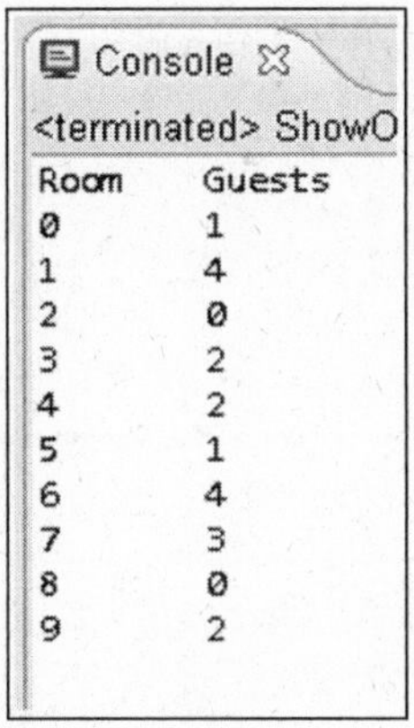

```
Console ⊠
<terminated> ShowO
Room    Guests
0       1
1       4
2       0
3       2
4       2
5       1
6       4
7       3
8       0
9       2
```

FIGURE 16-2:
Running the code
in Listing 16-1.

Deciding on a loop's limit at runtime

On occasion, you may want a more succinct report than the one in Figure 16-2. "Don't give me a long list of rooms," you say. "Just give me the number of guests in Room 3." To get such a report, you need a slightly smarter program. The program is in Listing 16-2, with runs of the program shown in Figure 16-3.

LISTING 16-2: **Report on One Room Only, Please**

```java
import java.util.Scanner;
import java.io.File;
import java.io.FileNotFoundException;
import static java.lang.System.out;

public class ShowOneRoomOccupancy {

    public static void main(String args[]) throws FileNotFoundException {
        Scanner keyboard = new Scanner(System.in);
        Scanner diskScanner = new Scanner(new File("occupancy"));
        int whichRoom;

        out.print("Which room? ");
        whichRoom = keyboard.nextInt();
```

(continued)

LISTING 16-2: *(continued)*

```
        for (int roomNum = 0; roomNum < whichRoom; roomNum++) {
            diskScanner.nextInt();
        }

        out.print("Room ");
        out.print(whichRoom);
        out.print(" has ");
        out.print(diskScanner.nextInt());
        out.println(" guest(s).");

        keyboard.close();
        diskScanner.close();
    }
}
```

```
Which room? 3
Room 3 has 2 guest(s).


Which room? 5
Room 5 has 1 guest(s).


Which room? 8
Room 8 has 0 guest(s).


Which room? 10
Room 10 has Exception in thread "main" java.util.NoSuchElementException
        at java.util.Scanner.throwFor(Scanner.java:817)
        at java.util.Scanner.next(Scanner.java:1431)
        at java.util.Scanner.nextInt(Scanner.java:2040)
        at java.util.Scanner.nextInt(Scanner.java:2000)
        at ShowOneRoomOccupancy.main(ShowOneRoomOccupancy.java:26)
```

FIGURE 16-3:
A few 1-room
reports.

If Listing 16-2 has a moral, it's that the number of `for` loop iterations can vary from one run to another. The loop in Listing 16-2 runs on and on as long as the counting variable `roomNum` is less than a room number specified by the user. When the `roomNum` is the same as the number specified by the user (that is, when `roomNum` is the same as `whichRoom`), the computer jumps out of the loop. Then the computer grabs one more `int` value from the `occupancy` file and displays that value on the screen.

As you stare at the runs in Figure 16-3, it's important to remember the unusual numbering of rooms. Room 3 has two guests because Room 3 is the *fourth* room in the `occupancy` file of Figure 16-1. That's because the motel's rooms are numbered 0 through 9.

GRABBING INPUT HERE AND THERE

Listing 16-2 illustrates some pithy issues surrounding the input of data. For one thing, the program gets input from both the keyboard and a disk file. (The program gets a room number from the keyboard. Then the program gets the number of guests in that room from the occupancy file.) To make this happen, Listing 16-2 sports two Scanner declarations: one to declare keyboard and a second to declare diskScanner.

Later in the program, the call keyboard.nextInt reads from the keyboard, and diskScanner.nextInt reads from the file. Within the program, you can read from the keyboard or the disk as many times as you want. You can even intermingle the calls — reading once from the keyboard, and then three times from the disk, and then twice from the keyboard, and so on. All you have to do is remember to use keyboard whenever you read from the keyboard and use diskScanner whenever you read from the disk.

Another interesting tidbit in Listing 16-2 concerns the occupancy file. Many of this chapter's examples read from an occupancy file, and I use the same data in each of the examples. (I use the data shown in Figure 16-1.) To run an example, I copy the occupancy file from one Eclipse project to another. (Before running the code in Listing 16-2, I go to my old 16–01 project in Eclipse's Package Explorer. I right-click the occupancy file in the 16–01 project and select Copy from the context menu. Then I right-click the new 16–02 project branch and select Paste from the context menu. As usual, Mac users should Control-click instead of right-click.)

In real life, having several copies of a data file can be dangerous. You can modify one copy and then accidentally read out-of-date data from a different copy. Sure, you should have backup copies, but you should have only one "master" copy — the copy from which all programs get the same input.

In a real-life program, you don't copy the occupancy file from one project to another. What do you do instead? You put an occupancy file in one place on your hard drive and then have each program refer to the file using the names of the file's directories. For example, if your occupancy file is in the c:\Oct\22 directory, you write

```
Scanner diskScanner = new Scanner(new File("c:\\oct\\22\\occupancy"));
```

The "Name that file" sidebar in Chapter 13 has more details about filenames and double backslashes.

Using all kinds of conditions in a for loop

Look at the run in Figure 16-3 and notice the program's awful behavior when the user mistakenly asks about a nonexistent room: The motel has no Room 10. If you ask for the number of guests in Room 10, the program tries to read more numbers than the occupancy file contains. This unfortunate attempt causes a NoSuchElementException.

Listing 16-3 fixes the end-of-file problem.

LISTING 16-3: **A More Refined Version of the One-Room Code**

```java
import java.util.Scanner;
import java.io.File;
import java.io.FileNotFoundException;
import static java.lang.System.out;

public class BetterShowOneRoom {

  public static void main(String args[]) throws FileNotFoundException {
    Scanner keyboard = new Scanner(System.in);
    Scanner diskScanner = new Scanner(new File("occupancy"));
    int whichRoom;

    out.print("Which room? ");
    whichRoom = keyboard.nextInt();

    for (int roomNum=0; roomNum < whichRoom && diskScanner.hasNext(); roomNum++) {
      diskScanner.nextInt();
    }

    if (diskScanner.hasNext()) {
      out.print("Room ");
      out.print(whichRoom);
      out.print(" has ");
      out.print(diskScanner.nextInt());
      out.println(" guest(s).");
    }

    keyboard.close();
    diskScanner.close();
  }
}
```

The code in Listing 16-3 isn't earth-shattering. To get this code, you take the code in Listing 16-2 and add a few tests for the end of the occupancy file. You perform the diskScanner.hasNext test before each call to nextInt. That way, if the call to nextInt is doomed to failure, you catch the potential failure before it happens. A few test runs of the code in Listing 16-3 are shown in Figure 16-4.

```
Which room? 0
Room 0 has 1 guest(s).


Which room? 6
Room 6 has 4 guest(s).


Which room? 2
Room 2 has 0 guest(s).


Which room? 10
```

FIGURE 16-4: The bad room number 10 gets no response.

TECHNICAL STUFF

In Listing 16-3, I want to know whether the occupancy file contains any more data (any data that I haven't read yet). So I call the Scanner class's hasNext method. The hasNext method looks ahead to see whether I can read any kind of data — an int value, a double value, a word, a boolean, or whatever. That's okay for this section's example, but in some situations, you need to be pickier about your input data. For example, you may want to know whether you can call nextInt (as opposed to nextDouble or nextLine). Fortunately, Java has methods for your pickiest input needs. A method like if (diskScanner.hasNextInt()) tests to see whether you can read an int value from the disk file. Java also has methods like hasNextLine, hasNextDouble, and so on. For more information on the plain old hasNext method, see Chapter 14.

Listing 16-3 has a big, fat condition to keep the for loop going:

```
for (int roomNum=0; roomNum < whichRoom && diskScanner.hasNext(); roomNum++) {
```

Many for loop conditions are simple "less-than" tests, but there's no rule saying that all for loop conditions have to be so simple. In fact, any expression can be a for loop's condition, as long as the expression has value true or false. The condition in Listing 16-3 combines a "less than" with a call to the Scanner class's hasNext method.

Reader, Meet Arrays; Arrays, Meet the Reader

A weary traveler steps up to the Java Motel's front desk. "I'd like a room," says the traveler. So the desk clerk runs a report like the one in Figure 16-2. Noticing the first vacant room in the list, the clerk suggests Room 2. "I'll take it," says the traveler.

It's so hard to get good help these days. How many times have you told the clerk to fill the higher-numbered rooms first? The lower-numbered rooms are older, and they are badly in need of repair. For example, Room 3 has an indoor pool. (The pipes leak, so the carpet is soaking wet.) Room 2 has no heat (not in wintertime, anyway). Room 1 has serious electrical problems (for that room, you always get payment in advance). Besides, Room 8 is vacant, and you charge more for the higher-numbered rooms.

Here's where a subtle change in presentation can make a big difference. You need a program that lists vacant rooms in reverse order. That way, Room 8 catches the clerk's eye before Room 2 does.

Think about strategies for a program that displays data in reverse. With the input from Figure 16-1, the program's output should look like the display shown in Figure 16-5.

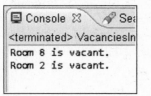

FIGURE 16-5: A list of vacant rooms, with higher-numbered rooms shown first.

Here's the first (bad) idea for a programming strategy:

```
Get the last value in the occupancy file.
If the value is 0, print the room number.


Get the next-to-last value in the occupancy file.
If the value is 0, print the room number.


... And so on.
```

With some fancy input/output programs, this strategy may be workable. But no matter what input/output program you use, jumping directly to the end or to the middle of a file is a big pain in the boot. It's especially bad if you plan to jump repeatedly. So go back to the drawing board and think of something better.

Here's an idea! Read all values in the occupancy file and store each value in a variable of its own. Then step through the variables in reverse order, displaying a room number when it's appropriate to do so.

This idea works, but the code is so ugly that I refuse to dignify it by calling it a listing. No, this is just a "see the following code" kind of thing. So please, see the following ugly code:

```java
/*
 * Ugh! I can't stand this ugly code!
 */
guestsIn0 = diskScanner.nextInt();
guestsIn1 = diskScanner.nextInt();
guestsIn2 = diskScanner.nextInt();
guestsIn3 = diskScanner.nextInt();
guestsIn4 = diskScanner.nextInt();
guestsIn5 = diskScanner.nextInt();
guestsIn6 = diskScanner.nextInt();
guestsIn7 = diskScanner.nextInt();
guestsIn8 = diskScanner.nextInt();
guestsIn9 = diskScanner.nextInt();

if (guestsIn9 == 0) {
    System.out.println(9);
}
if (guestsIn8 == 0) {
    System.out.println(8);
}
if (guestsIn7 == 0) {
    System.out.println(7);
}
if (guestsIn6 == 0) {

// ... And so on.
```

What you're lacking is a uniform way of naming ten variables. That is, it would be nice to write

```
/*
 * Nice idea, but this is not real Java code:
 */


//Read forwards
for (int roomNum = 0; roomNum < 10; roomNum++) {
    guestsInroomNum = diskScanner.nextInt();
}


//Write backwards
for (int roomNum = 9; roomNum >= 0; roomNum--) {
    if (guestsInroomNum == 0) {
        System.out.println(roomNum);
    }
}
```

Well, you can write loops of this kind. All you need are some square brackets. When you add square brackets to the idea shown in the preceding code, you get what's called an array. An *array* is a row of values, like the row of rooms in a one-floor motel. To picture the array, just picture the Java Motel:

>> First, picture the rooms, lined up next to one another.

>> Next, picture the same rooms with their front walls missing. Inside each room, you can see a certain number of guests.

>> If you can, forget that the two guests in Room 9 are putting piles of bills into a big briefcase. Ignore the fact that the guest in Room 5 hasn't moved away from the TV set in a day-and-a-half. Instead of all these details, just see numbers. In each room, see a number representing the count of guests in that room. (If freeform visualization isn't your strong point, take a look at Figure 16-6.)

In the lingo of Java programming, the entire row of rooms is called an *array*. Each room in the array is called a *component* of the array (also known as an array *element*). Each component has two numbers associated with it:

>> **Index:** In the case of the Java Motel array, the index is the room number (a number from 0 to 9).

>> **Value:** In the Java Motel array, the value is the number of guests in a given room (a number stored in a component of the array).

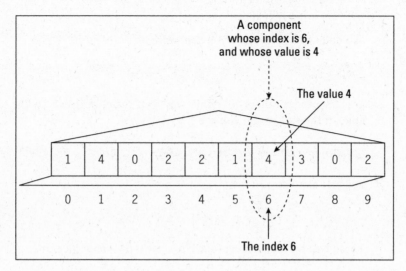

FIGURE 16-6:
An abstract
snapshot of
rooms in the
Java Motel.

Using an array saves you from having to declare ten separate variables: guestsIn0, guestsIn1, guestsIn2, and so on. To declare an array with ten values in it, you can write two fairly short lines of code:

```
int guestsIn[];
guestsIn = new int[10];
```

You can even squish these two lines into one longer line:

```
int guestsIn[] = new int[10];
```

In either of these code snippets, notice the use of the number 10. This number tells the computer to make the guestsIn array have ten components. Each component of the array has a name of its own. The starting component is named guestsIn[0], the next is named guestsIn[1], and so on. The last of the ten components is named guestsIn[9].

REMEMBER

In creating an array, you always specify the number of components. The array's indices always start with 0 and end with the number that's one fewer than the total number of components. For example, if your array has ten components (and you declare the array with new int[10]), the array's indices go from 0 to 9.

TIP

When you create an array variable, you can put square brackets after either the type name or the variable name. In other words, you can write

```
int guestsIn[];
```

as I do in this section, or you can write

```
int[] guestsIn;
```

as some programmers do. Either way, you're defining exactly the same array variable. In the same way, you see

```
public static void main(String args[])
```

and you also see

```
public static void main(String[] args)
```

These two method headers have precisely the same meaning.

Storing values in an array

After you've created an array, you can put values into the array's components. For example, the guests in Room 6 are fed up with all those mint candies that you put on people's beds. So they check out, and Room 6 becomes vacant. You should put the value 0 into the 6 component. You can do it with this assignment statement:

```
guestsIn[6] = 0;
```

On one weekday, business is awful. No one's staying at the motel. But then you get a lucky break: A big bus pulls up to the motel. The side of the bus sports a Loners' Convention sign. Out of the bus come 25 people, each walking to the motel's small office, none paying attention to the others who were on the bus. Each person wants a private room. Only 10 of them can stay at the Java Motel, but that's okay, because you can send the other 15 loners down the road to the old C-Side Resort and Motor Lodge.

Anyway, to register ten of the loners at the Java Motel, you put one guest in each of your ten rooms. Having created an array, you can take advantage of the array's indexing and write a for loop, like this:

```
for (int roomNum = 0; roomNum < 10; roomNum++) {
    guestsIn[roomNum] = 1;
}
```

This loop takes the place of ten assignment statements because the computer executes the statement guestsIn[roomNum] = 1 ten times. The first time around, the value of roomNum is 0, so in effect, the computer executes

```
guestsIn[0] = 1;
```

In the next loop iteration, the value of roomNum is 1, so the computer executes the equivalent of the following statement:

```
guestsIn[1] = 1;
```

During the next iteration, the computer behaves as though it's executing

```
guestsIn[2] = 1;
```

And so on. When roomNum gets to be 9, the computer executes the equivalent of the following statement:

```
guestsIn[9] = 1;
```

Notice that the loop's counter goes from 0 to 9. Compare this with Figure 16-6 and remember that the indices of an array go from 0 to one fewer than the number of components in the array. Looping with room numbers from 0 to 9 covers all rooms in the Java Motel.

REMEMBER

When you work with an array, and you step through the array's components using a for loop, you normally start the loop's counter variable at 0. To form the condition that tests for another iteration, you often write an expression like roomNum < *arraySize*, where *arraySize* is the number of components in the array.

Creating a report

The code to create the report in Figure 16-5 is shown in Listing 16-4. This new program uses the idea in the world's ugliest code (the code from several pages back, with variables guestsIn0, guestsIn1, and so on). But instead of having ten separate variables, Listing 16-4 uses an array.

LISTING 16-4: **Traveling through Data Both Forward and Backward**

```
import java.util.Scanner;
import java.io.File;
import java.io.FileNotFoundException;

class VacanciesInReverse {

    public static void main(String args[]) throws FileNotFoundException {
        Scanner diskScanner = new Scanner(new File("occupancy"));
        int guestsIn[];
        guestsIn = new int[10];
```

(continued)

LISTING 16-4: *(continued)*

```
        for (int roomNum = 0; roomNum < 10; roomNum++) {
            guestsIn[roomNum] = diskScanner.nextInt();
        }

        for (int roomNum = 9; roomNum >= 0; roomNum--) {
            if (guestsIn[roomNum] == 0) {
                System.out.print("Room ");
                System.out.print(roomNum);
                System.out.println(" is vacant.");
            }
        }

        diskScanner.close();
    }
}
```

Notice the stuff in parentheses in the VacanciesInReverse program's second for loop. It's easy to get these things wrong. You're aiming for a loop that checks Room 9, and then Room 8, and so on.

```
if (guestsIn[9] == 0) {
    System.out.print(roomNum);
}
if (guestsIn[8] == 0) {
    System.out.print(roomNum);
}
if (guestsIn[7] == 0) {
    System.out.print(roomNum);
}

... And so on, until you get to ...

if (guestsIn[0] == 0) {
    System.out.print(roomNum);
}
```

Some observations about the code:

>> The loop's counter must start at 9:

```
for (int roomNum = 9; roomNum >= 0; roomNum--)
```

>> Each time through the loop, the counter goes *down* by one:

```
for (int roomNum = 9; roomNum >= 0; roomNum--)
```

>> The loop keeps going as long as the counter is *greater than or equal to* 0:

```
for (int roomNum = 9; roomNum >= 0; roomNum--)
```

Think through each of these three items, and you'll write a perfect `for` loop.

Initializing an array

In Listing 16-4, you put values into the `guestsIn` array by repeatedly reading numbers from a disk file and storing the numbers, element by element, in the array. There's an easier way to put values into an array. When you declare the array, you provide an *array initialization*. Here's how you do it:

```java
class VacanciesInReverse {

    public static void main(String args[]) {

        int guestsIn[] = {1, 4, 0, 2, 2, 1, 4, 3, 0, 2};

        for (int roomNum = 9; roomNum >= 0; roomNum--) {
            if (guestsIn[roomNum] == 0) {
                System.out.print("Room ");
                System.out.print(roomNum);
                System.out.println(" is vacant.");
            }
        }
    }
}
```

In this code, the bold initialization line tells Java to put 1 into `guestsIn[0]`, 4 into `guests[1]`, 0 into `guestsIn[2]`, and so on. This alternative to the code in Listing 16-4 uses no disk files and only one loop.

I don't use array initialization in this chapter's hotel room examples because storing values in a file is a bit more realistic. But you can use array initialization in your programs.

WARNING

The feature that I describe in this section is called an *initialization* because you can't use it as part of an assignment. In other words, you can write

```
int guestsIn[] = {1, 4, 0, 2, 2, 1, 4, 3, 0, 2};
```

but you can't write

```
// Don't do this:
int guestsIn[];
guestsIn = {1, 4, 0, 2, 2, 1, 4, 3, 0, 2};
```

After the end of an array's declaration, you can no longer use curly braces to put values into the array.

Working with Arrays

Earlier in this chapter, a busload of loners showed up at your motel. When they finally left, you were glad to get rid them, even if it meant having all your rooms empty for a while. But now another bus pulls into the parking lot. This bus has a Gregarian Club sign. Out of the bus come 50 people, each more gregarious than the next. Now everybody in your parking lot is clamoring to meet everyone else. While they meet and greet, they're all frolicking toward the front desk, singing the club's theme song. (Oh no! It's the Gregarian chant!)

The first five Gregarians all want Room 7. It's a tight squeeze, but you were never big on fire codes, anyway. Next comes a group of three with a yen for Room 0. (They're computer programmers, and they think the room number is cute.) Then there's a pack of four Gregarians who want Room 3. (The in-room pool sounds attractive to them.)

With all this traffic, you had better switch on your computer. You start a program that enables you to enter new occupancy data. The program has five parts:

>> **Create an array and then put 0 in each of the array's components.**

When the Loners' Club members left, the motel was suddenly empty. (Heck, even before the Loners' Club members left, the motel seemed empty.) To declare an array and fill the array with zeros, you execute code of the following kind:

```
int guestsIn[];
guestsIn = new int[10];

for (int roomNum = 0; roomNum < 10; roomNum++) {
    guestsIn[roomNum] = 0;
}
```

» **Get a room number and then get the number of guests who will be staying in that room.**

Reading numbers typed by the user is pretty humdrum stuff. Do a little prompting and a little `nextInt` calling, and you're all set:

```
out.print("Room number: ");
whichRoom = keyboard.nextInt();
out.print("How many guests? ");
numGuests = keyboard.nextInt();
```

» **Use the room number and the number of guests to change a value in the array.**

Earlier in this chapter, to put one guest in Room 2, you executed

```
guestsIn[2] = 1;
```

So now you have two variables: `numGuests` and `whichRoom`. Maybe `numGuests` is 5 and `whichRoom` is 7. To put `numGuests` in `whichRoom` (that is, to put five guests in Room 7), you can execute

```
guestsIn[whichRoom] = numGuests;
```

That's the crucial step in the design of your new program.

» **Ask the user whether the program should continue.**

Are there more guests to put in rooms? To find out, execute this code:

```
    out.print("Do another? ");
} while (keyboard.findWithinHorizon(".",0).charAt(0) == 'Y');
```

» **Display the number of guests in each room.**

No problem! You already did this. You can steal the code (almost verbatim) from Listing 16-1:

```
out.println("Room\tGuests");
for (int roomNum = 0; roomNum < 10; roomNum++) {
    out.print(roomNum);
    out.print("\t");
    out.println(guestsIn[roomNum]);
}
```

The only difference between this latest code snippet and the stuff in Listing 16-1 is that this new code uses the guestsIn array. The first time through this loop, the code does

```
out.println(guestsIn[0]);
```

displaying the number of guests in Room 0. The next time through the loop, the code does

```
out.println(guestsIn[1]);
```

displaying the number of guests in Room 1. The last time through the loop, the code does

```
out.println(guestsIn[9]);
```

That's perfect.

The complete program (with these five pieces put together) is in Listing 16-5. A run of the program is shown in Figure 16-7.

LISTING 16-5: **Storing Occupancy Data in an Array**

```java
import java.util.Scanner;
import static java.lang.System.out;

class AddGuests {

    public static void main(String args[]) {
        Scanner keyboard = new Scanner(System.in);
        int whichRoom, numGuests;
        int guestsIn[];
        guestsIn = new int[10];

        for (int roomNum = 0; roomNum < 10; roomNum++) {
            guestsIn[roomNum] = 0;
        }

        do {
            out.print("Room number: ");
            whichRoom = keyboard.nextInt();
            out.print("How many guests? ");
            numGuests = keyboard.nextInt();
            guestsIn[whichRoom] = numGuests;
```

```
            out.println();
            out.print("Do another? ");
        } while (keyboard.findWithinHorizon(".",0).charAt(0) == 'Y');
        out.println();

        out.println("Room\tGuests");
        for (int roomNum = 0; roomNum < 10; roomNum++) {
            out.print(roomNum);
            out.print("\t");
            out.println(guestsIn[roomNum]);
        }

        keyboard.close();
    }
}
```

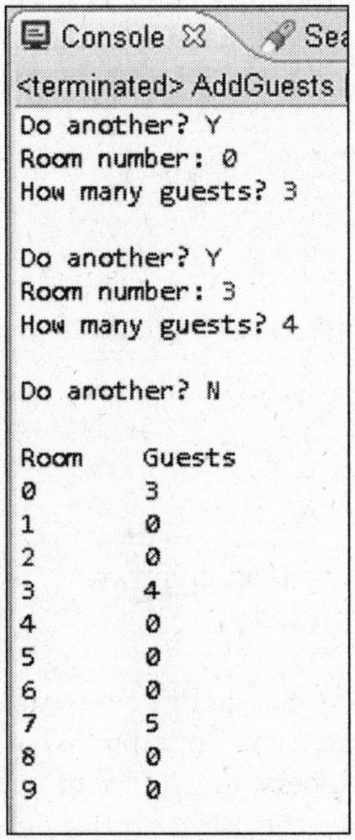

Console ⊠   Sea
<terminated> AddGuests
Do another? Y
Room number: 0
How many guests? 3

Do another? Y
Room number: 3
How many guests? 4

Do another? N

Room   Guests
0   3
1   0
2   0
3   4
4   0
5   0
6   0
7   5
8   0
9   0

FIGURE 16-7:
Running the code
in Listing 16-5.

Hey! The program in Listing 16-5 is pretty big! It may be the biggest program so far in this book. But *big* doesn't necessarily mean *difficult.* If each piece of the program makes sense, you can create each piece on its own and then put all the pieces together. Voilà! The code is manageable.

Looping in Style

Chapter 15's Listing 15-6 uses an enhanced `for` loop to step through a bunch of values. In that program, the values belong to an `enum` type. Well, this chapter also deals with a bunch of values — namely, the values in an array. So you're probably not surprised if I show you an enhanced `for` loop that steps through an array's values.

To see such a loop, start with the code in Listing 16-5. The last loop in that program looks something like this:

```
for (int roomNum = 0; roomNum < 10; roomNum++) {
    out.println(guestsIn[roomNum]);
}
```

To turn this into an enhanced `for` loop, you make up a new variable name. (What about the name `howMany`? I like that name.) Whatever name you choose, the new variable ranges over the values in the `guestsIn` array.

```
for (int howMany : guestsIn) {
    out.println(howMany);
}
```

This enhanced loop uses the same format as the loop in Chapter 15.

```
for (TypeName variableName : RangeOfValues) {
    Statements
}
```

In Chapter 15, the *RangeOfValues* belongs to an enum type. But in this chapter's example, the *RangeOfValues* belongs to an array.

Enhanced `for` loops are nice and concise. But don't be too eager to use enhanced loops with arrays. This feature has some nasty limitations. For example, my new `howMany` loop doesn't display room numbers. I avoid room numbers because the room numbers in my `guestsIn` array are the indices 0 through 9. Unfortunately, an enhanced loop doesn't provide easy access to an array's indices.

And here's another unpleasant surprise. Start with the following loop from Listing 16-4:

```
for (int roomNum = 0; roomNum < 10; roomNum++) {
    guestsIn[roomNum] = diskScanner.nextInt();
}
```

Turn this traditional `for` loop into an enhanced `for` loop, and you get the following misleading code:

```
for (int howMany : guestsIn) {
    howMany = diskScanner.nextInt();   //Don't do this
}
```

The new enhanced `for` loop doesn't do what you want it to do. This loop reads values from an input file and then dumps these values into the garbage can. In the end, the array's values remain unchanged.

It's sad but true. To make full use of an array, you have to fall back on Java's plain old `for` loop.

Deleting Several Files

A program in Chapter 15 deletes a file named `importantData.txt`. The code to delete the file looks like this:

```
new File("importantData.txt").delete();
```

In that code, the `new File` call refers to a single file. It's very nice code, but it doesn't tell you how to delete a bunch of files. How can you write code to deal with several files at once?

Fortunately, Java provides ways to deal with bunches of files. One way uses an array of `File` objects. Listing 16-6 contains a program that illustrates this idea.

LISTING 16-6: **Deleting All** `.txt` **Files**

```
import java.io.File;

class IHateTxtFiles {

    public static void main(String args[]) {

        File folder = new File(".");
        for (File file : folder.listFiles()) {
            if (file.getName().endsWith(".txt")) {
                file.delete();
            }
        }
    }
}
```

In many operating systems (including Windows, Mac OS, and Linux), a single dot stands for the current working directory: the place where a program starts looking for files. For a Java program running in Eclipse, this working directory is the project's root directory. For example, imagine that the code in Listing 16-6 lives in an Eclipse project named 16-06. Then your hard drive contains a folder named 16-06, which in turn contains a folder named src; which in turn contains the IHateTxtFiles.java file. (See Figure 16-8.) The program's working directory is the 16-06 directory. So, in Listing 16-6, the code

```
folder = new File(".")
```

makes folder refer to the directory named 16-06.

FIGURE 16-8:
Your project is in a folder named 16-06.

If you finished reading the previous paragraph, I know what you're thinking. "The project's root directory, 16-06, is a folder, not a file. But the code in Listing 16-6 says folder = new File("."). Why doesn't the code say folder = new Folder(".")? Well, I'm glad you asked. It turns out that most operating systems blur the differences between folders and files. For Java's purposes, the document IHateTxtFiles.java is a file, the folder named src is also a kind of a file, and the folder named 16-06 is also a kind of a file.

In Java, every File object has a listFiles method, and when you call folder.listFiles(), you get an array. Each "value" stored in the array is one of the files in the folder. In Listing 16-6, the enhanced for loop has the same format as the loop in the previous section.

```
for (TypeName variableName : RangeOfValues) {
    Statements
}
```

In Listing 16-6, the *RangeOfValues* is an array. The array contains all the files inside the 16-06 project directory. So the enhanced for loop takes each file inside the 16-06 directory and asks, "Does this file's name end with .txt?"

```
if (file.getName().endsWith(".txt"))
```

If a particular file's name ends with `.txt`, delete that file:

```
file.delete();
```

Figures 16-9 and 16-10 show some "before" and "after" pictures in Eclipse's Package Explorer. Before running this section's example, the 16-06 directory contains things named src, aFile.txt, save.me, and xFile.txt. After running this section's example, the 16-06 directory still contains src and save.me but no longer contains aFile.txt or xFile.txt.

FIGURE 16-9:
Your ugly project, before using our .txt file deletion product.

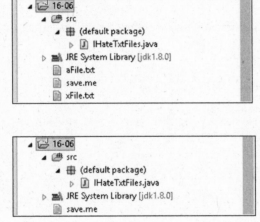

FIGURE 16-10:
Your lovely project, after using our .txt file deletion product.

REMEMBER

After running this section's program, you might not see any changes in Eclipse's Package Explorer. To verify that the project directory no longer contains .txt files, select the 16-06 branch in the Package Explorer. Then, on Eclipse's main menu, choose File ⇨ Refresh.

TECHNICAL STUFF

Eclipse's Package Explorer looks like it's displaying all the files and folders on a part of your hard drive. But looks can be deceiving. Some of the Package Explorer's branches represent neither files nor folders. (For example, in Figures 16-9 and 16-10, the JRE System Library branch represents a bunch of related files — files that may or may not all be in the same directory.) And some of your hard drive's files and folders don't appear in Eclipse's Package Explorer. (In addition to things like src, which appears in Eclipse's Package Explorer, a project's folder typically contains files named .classpath and .project and folders named .settings and bin. These additional files and folders aren't normally displayed in Eclipse's Package Explorer.)

TECHNICAL STUFF

When you call `folder.listFiles()`, the resulting array doesn't include any of the things in subdirectories of the `folder` directory. Just to make sure, I created `dFile.txt` inside the 16-06 project's `src` directory, and then I ran this section's example. After running the program, `dFile.txt` had not been deleted.

TRY IT OUT

Would you like to flex some array muscles? If so, here are some things for you to try.

INITIALIZING AN ARRAY

This experiment comes in three parts:

>> Run the following program to find out how array initialization works:

```
public class Main {

    public static void main(String[] args) {
        int[] myArray = { 9, 21, 35, 16, 21, 7 };
        System.out.println(myArray[0]);
        System.out.println(myArray[1]);
        System.out.println(myArray[5]);
        // System.out.println(myArray[6]);
    }

}
```

>> What happens when you uncomment the last `System.out.println` call in the previous bullet's program and then run the program? Why does this happen?

>> What happens when you try to replace one line of code with two lines in the first bullet's program?

```
int[] myArray;
myArray = { 9, 21, 35, 16, 21, 7 };
```

Does this explain why an array initialization isn't called an array assignment?

PICK AN ELEMENT

Create a program containing the following array initialization:

```
int amounts[] = {19, 21, 16, 14, 99, 86, 31, 19, 0, 101};
```

In your program, ask the user to input a position number — a number from 0 to 9. Have your program respond by displaying the value in that position of the amounts array. For example, if the user inputs 0, the program displays 19. If the user inputs 1, the program displays 21. And so on.

DISPLAY THE ELEMENTS

Create a program containing the following array initialization:

```
int amounts[] = {19, 21, 16, 14, 99, 86, 31, 19, 0, 101};
```

Add code to display all indices and values in the array. The first three lines of output should look like this:

```
The 0 element's value is 19.
The 1 element's value is 21.
The 2 element's value is 16.
```

DISPLAY SOME OF THE ELEMENTS

Create a program containing the following array initialization:

```
int amounts[] = {19, 21, 16, 14, 99, 86, 31, 19, 0, 101};
```

Add a loop that displays the values in even-numbered positions of the array. The program's output is 19 16 99 31 0.

GENERATING SQUARES

I've created a program that uses a loop to generate an array of the first 50 perfect squares. Here's my program, with some code missing:

```
public class Main {

    public static void main(String[] args) {
        int squares[] = _____;

        for (_____) {
            squares[i] = ____;
        }

        System.out.println(squares[0]);
        System.out.println(squares[1]);
        System.out.println(squares[2]);
        System.out.println(squares[49]);
    }
}
```

Fill in the missing code. When you run the program, the output looks like this:

```
0
1
4
2401
```

FIND ONE VACANCY

Someone shows up at the front desk asking for a room. The hotel clerk doesn't need a list of all vacant rooms. All the clerk needs is the number of one vacant room. Any vacant room will do. Modify the code in Listing 16-4 so that it shows only one room number (the number of a room that's currently vacant).

SELECT A ROOM

Modify the code in Listing 16-5 so that it doesn't ask the user which room number to put guests in. The code automatically selects a room from the rooms that are currently vacant.

HOW MANY GUESTS?

Modify the code in Listing 16-4 or Listing 16-5 so that the program displays the total number of guests in the motel. (To do this, the code adds up the numbers of guests in each room.)

PARALLEL ARRAYS

Create a new Eclipse project and put the following code in the project's main method:

```
char[] cipher = { 's', 'f', 'k', 'l', 'd', 'o', 'h', 'z', 'm', 'b',
        't', 'a', 'n', 'g', 'u', 'v', 'i', 'q', 'x', 'w', 'y', 'c',
        'j', 'r', 'p', 'e' };
char[] plain = { 'e', 'q', 's', 'f', 'i', 'n', 'h', 'u', 'r', 'k',
        'g', 'z', 'c', 'y', 'x', 'l', 'm', 'd', 'w', 'a', 'b', 't',
        'p', 'j', 'v', 'o' };
```

This code creates two arrays. In the first array, cipher[0] is 's', cipher[1] is 'f', cipher[2] is 'k', and so on. In the second array, plain[0] is 'e', plain[1] is 'q', plain[2] is 's', and so on.

Finish writing the main method so that when the user types a lowercase letter, the program looks for that letter in the cipher array and responds by displaying the corresponding letter in the plain array.

For example, if the user types the letter s, the program answers back with the letter e. (The program discovers that s is in the 0 position of the cipher array, so the program displays the letter in the 0 position of the plain array. And the letter in the 0 position of the plain array is e.)

Similarly, if the user types f, the program displays q because f is in the 1 position of the cipher array and q is in the 1 position of the plain array.

DECIPHERING CIPHERTEXT

Here's a challenging task for all you ciphertext enthusiasts! Enclose in a loop the code that you wrote for the earlier "Parallel arrays" experiment. Have the user type a word, followed immediately by a blank space. When the user presses Enter, the program repeatedly does what the code in the parallel-arrays experiment did. The program looks up all the user's letters in the cipher array and displays the corresponding plain array letters. For example, if the user types rwpw, the program responds by displaying the word java.

4

Using Program Units

Chapter **17**

Programming with Objects and Classes

C hapters 6, 7, and 8 introduce Java's primitive types — things like `int`, `double`, `char`, and `boolean`. That's great, but how often does a real-world problem deal exclusively with such simple values? Consider an exchange between a merchant and a customer. The customer makes a purchase, which can involve item names, model numbers, credit card info, sales tax rates, and lots of other stuff. A purchase is more complicated than an `int` value. It's more complicated than a `double` value. How do you represent an entire purchase in a Java program?

In older computer programming languages, you treat an entire purchase like a big pile of unbundled laundry. Imagine a mound of socks, shirts, and other pieces of clothing. You have no basket, so you grab as much as you can handle. As you walk to the washer, you drop a few things — a sock here and a washcloth there. This is like the older way of storing the values in a purchase. In older languages, there's no purchase. There are only `double` values, `char` values, and other loose items. You put the purchase amount in one variable, the customer's name in another, and the sales tax data somewhere else. But that's awful. You tend to drop things on your way to the compiler. With small errors in a program, you can easily drop an amount here and a customer's name there.

With laundry and computer programming, you're better off if you have a basket. The newer programming languages, like Java, allow you to combine values and make new, more useful kinds of values. For example, in Java, you can combine a double value, an int value, a boolean value, and maybe other kinds of values to create something that you call a Purchase. Because your purchase info is all in one big bundle, keeping track of the purchase's pieces is easier. That's the start of an important computer programming concept: the notion of *object-oriented programming.*

Creating a Class

I start with a "traditional" example. The program in Listing 17-1 processes simple purchase data. A run of the program is shown in Figure 17-1.

LISTING 17-1: Doing It the Old-Fashioned Way

```java
import java.util.Scanner;

class ProcessData {

    public static void main(String args[]) {
        Scanner keyboard = new Scanner(System.in);
        double unitPrice;
        int quantity;
        boolean taxable;

        System.out.print("Unit price: ");
        unitPrice = keyboard.nextDouble();
        System.out.print("Quantity: ");
        quantity = keyboard.nextInt();
        System.out.print("Taxable? (true/false) ");
        taxable = keyboard.nextBoolean();

        double total = unitPrice * quantity;
        if (taxable) {
            total = total * 1.05;
        }

        System.out.print("Total: ");
        System.out.println(total);

        keyboard.close();
    }
}
```

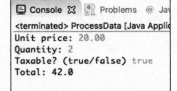

FIGURE 17-1:
Processing a
customer's
purchase.

If the output in Figure 17-1 looks funny, it's because I do nothing in the code to control the number of digits beyond the decimal point. So in the output, the value $42.00 looks like 42.0. That's okay. I show you how to fix the problem in Chapter 18.

Reference types and Java classes

The code in Listing 17-1 involves a few simple values: `unitPrice`, `quantity`, and `taxable`. So here's the main point of this chapter: By combining several simple values, you can get a single, more useful value. That's the way it works. You take some of Java's primitive types, whip them together to make a primitive type stew, and what do you get? You get a more useful type called a *reference type*. Listing 17-2 has an example.

LISTING 17-2: **What It Means to Be a Purchase**

```java
class Purchase {
    double unitPrice;
    int quantity;
    boolean taxable;
}
```

The code in Listing 17-2 has no `main` method, so Eclipse can compile the code, but you can't run it. When you choose Run⇨Run As on Eclipse's main menu, the resulting context menu has no Java Application entry. You can click the tiny Run As button in Eclipse's toolbar and then select Java Application. But then you get the message box shown in Figure 17-2. Because Listing 17-2 has no `main` method, there's no place to start the executing. (In fact, the code in Listing 17-2 has no statements at all. There's nothing to execute.)

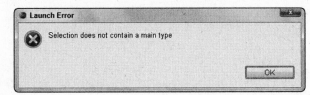

FIGURE 17-2:
The code in
Listing 17-2 has
no `main` method.

Using a newly defined class

To do something useful with the code in Listing 17-2, you need a `main` method. You can put the `main` method in a separate file. Listing 17-3 shows you such a file.

LISTING 17-3: Using Your Purchase Class

```
import java.util.Scanner;

class ProcessPurchase {

    public static void main(String[] args) {
        Scanner keyboard = new Scanner(System.in);
        Purchase onePurchase = new Purchase();

        System.out.print("Unit price: ");
        onePurchase.unitPrice = keyboard.nextDouble();
        System.out.print("Quantity: ");
        onePurchase.quantity = keyboard.nextInt();
        System.out.print("Taxable? (true/false) ");
        onePurchase.taxable = keyboard.nextBoolean();

        double total = onePurchase.unitPrice * onePurchase.quantity;
        if (onePurchase.taxable) {
            total = total * 1.05;
        }

        System.out.print("Total: ");
        System.out.println(total);

        keyboard.close();
    }
}
```

The best way to understand the code in Listing 17-3 is to compare it, line by line, with the code in Listing 17-1. In fact, there's a mechanical formula for turning the code in Listing 17-1 into the code in Listing 17-3. Table 17-1 describes the formula.

TABLE 17-1

Converting Your Code to Use a Class

In Listing 17-1	In Listing 17-3
double unitPrice; int quantity boolean taxable;	Purchase onePurchase = new Purchase();
unitPrice	onePurchase.unitPrice
quantity	onePurchase.quantity
taxable	onePurchase.taxable

The two programs (in Listings 17-1 and 17-3) do essentially the same thing, but one uses primitive variables, and the other leans on the Purchase code from Listing 17-2. Both programs have runs like the one shown back in Figure 17-1.

Running code that straddles two separate files

From Eclipse's point of view, a project that contains two Java source files is no big deal. You create two classes in the same project, and then you choose Run ⇨ Run As ⇨ Java Application. Everything works the way you expect it to work.

The only time things become tricky is when you have two main methods in the one project. This section's example (refer to Listings 17-2 and 17-3) doesn't suffer from that malady. But as you experiment with your code, you can easily add classes with additional main methods. You may also create a large application with several starting points.

When a project has more than one main method, Eclipse may prompt you and ask which class's main method you want to run. But sometimes Eclipse doesn't prompt you. Instead, Eclipse arbitrarily picks one main method and ignores all the others. This can be very confusing. You add a println call to the wrong main method, and nothing appears in the Console view. Hey, what gives?

You can fix the problem by following these steps:

1. **Expand the project's branch in the Package Explorer.**

2. **Expand the** src **folder within the project's branch.**

3. **Expand the** (default package) **branch within the** src **branch.**

   The (default package) branch contains .java files.

4. **(In Windows) Right-click the** .java **file whose** main **method you want to run. (On a Mac) Control-click the** .java **file whose** main **method you want to run.**

5. **On the resulting context menu, choose Run As ⇨ Java Application.**

REMEMBER

You cannot run a project that has no main method. If you try, you get a message box like the one shown earlier, in Figure 17-2.

AN APOLOGY OF SORTS (ALONG WITH AN EXCUSE!)

As far as most professional programmers are concerned, the code in Listings 17-2 and 17-3 is quite simple. In fact, it's too simple. Java programmers don't like expressions such as onePurchase.unitPrice, and they hate declarations such as double unitPrice. Instead, they prefer private double unitPrice along with expressions such as onePurchase.getUnitPrice(). These programmers will tell you that "the code in Burd's examples isn't safe," "Burd's examples promote bad programming practices," and "In the summertime, Burd wears colors that don't match." In fact, these programmers are absolutely correct.

But in my opinion, you learn to walk before you learn to run. Classes and objects are difficult concepts, so I present them in as simple a form as I possibly can. Object-oriented programming is an art as well as a science. It's a way of thinking — a way whose mastery requires time and patience. I have students at the university (some very good students) who spend months wrestling with the fundamentals of classes and objects.

In this book, I don't present the most time-honored, expert-approved way of dealing with classes and objects. Instead, I follow the simplest path to help you get classes and objects into your consciousness. You can learn the better way of doing things after you've become comfortable dividing problems into their object-oriented parts.

And besides, for all the nasty things someone might say about this chapter's simple examples, the examples aren't fake. They run, they produce output, and they illustrate the separating of a class from the main program's code. At the core, that's what object-oriented programming is all about.

So there!

Why bother?

On the surface, the code in Listing 17-3 is longer, more complicated, and harder to read. But think about a big pile of laundry: It may take time to find a basket and to shovel socks into the basket, but when you have clothes in the basket, the clothes are much easier to carry. It's the same way with the code in Listing 17-3. When you have your data in a Purchase basket, it's much easier to do complicated things with purchases.

From Classes Come Objects

The code in Listing 17-2 defines a class. A *class* is a design plan; it describes the way in which you intend to combine and use pieces of data. For example, the code in Listing 17-2 announces your intention to combine double, int, and boolean values to make new Purchase values.

Classes are central to all Java programming. But Java is called an *object-oriented* language. Java isn't called a class-oriented language. In fact, no one uses the term *class-oriented language.* Why not?

Well, you can't put your arms around a class. A class isn't real. A class without an object is like a day without chocolate. If you're sitting in a room right now, glance at all the chairs in the room. How many chairs are in the room? Two? Five? Twenty? In a room with five chairs, you have five chair objects. Each chair (each object) is something real, something you can use, something you can sit on.

A language like Java has classes and objects. What's the difference between a class and an object?

>> An object is a thing.

>> A class is a design plan for things of that kind.

For example, how would you describe what a chair is? Well, a chair has a seat, a back, and legs. In Java, you may write the stuff in Listing 17-4.

LISTING 17-4: **What It Means to Be a Chair**

```
/*
 * This is real Java code, but this code
 *  cannot be compiled on its own:
 */
```

(continued)

LISTING 17-4: *(continued)*

```
class Chair {
    FlatHorizonalPanel seat;
    FlatVerticalPanel back;
    LongSkinnyVerticalRods legs;
}
```

The code in Listing 17-4 is a design plan for chairs. The code tells you that each chair has three things. The code names the things (seat, back, and legs) and tells you a little bit about each thing. (For example, a seat is a FlatHorizontalPanel.) In the same way, the code in Listing 17-2 tells you that each purchase has three things. The code names the things (unitPrice, quantity, and taxable) and tells you the primitive type of each thing.

Imagine some grand factory at the edge of the universe. While you sleep each night, this factory stamps out tangible objects — objects that you'll encounter during the next waking day. Tomorrow you'll go for an interview at the Sloshy Shoes Company. So tonight the factory builds chairs for the company's offices. The factory builds chair objects, as shown in Figure 17-3, from the almost-real code in Listing 17-4.

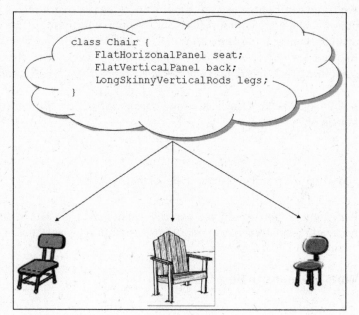

FIGURE 17-3: Chair objects from the Chair class.

In Listing 17-3, the line

```
Purchase onePurchase = new Purchase();
```

behaves like that grand factory at the edge of the universe. Rather than create chair objects, that line in Listing 17-3 creates a Purchase object, as shown in Figure 17-4. That particular line in Listing 17-3 is a declaration with an initialization. Just as the line

```
int count = 0;
```

declares the count variable and sets count to 0, the line in Listing 17-3 declares the onePurchase variable and makes onePurchase point to a brand-new object. That new object contains three parts: an unitPrice part, a quantity part, and a taxable part.

TECHNICAL STUFF

If you want to be picky, there's a difference between the stuff in Figure 17-4 and the action of the statement Purchase onePurchase = new Purchase() from Listing 17-3. Figure 17-4 shows an object with the values 20.00, 2, and true stored in it. The statement Purchase onePurchase = new Purchase() creates a new object, but it doesn't fill the object with useful values. Getting values comes later in Listing 17-3.

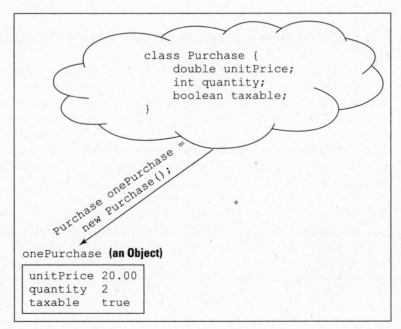

FIGURE 17-4:
An object created from the Purchase class.

Understanding (or ignoring) the subtleties

Sometimes, when you refer to a particular object, you want to emphasize which class the object came from. Well, subtle differences in emphasis call for big differences in terminology. So here's how Java programmers use the terminology:

>> In Listing 17-3, the statement `Purchase onePurchase = new Purchase()` creates a new *object*.

>> In Listing 17-3, the statement `Purchase onePurchase = new Purchase()` creates a new *instance* of the `Purchase` class.

The words *object* and *instance* are almost synonymous, but Java programmers never say "object of the `Purchase` class" (or if they do, they feel funny).

By the way, if you mess up this terminology and say something like "object of the `Purchase` class," no one jumps down your throat. Everyone understands what you mean, and life goes on as usual. In fact, I often use a phrase like "`Purchase` object" to describe an instance of the `Purchase` class. The difference between object and instance isn't terribly important. But it's important to remember that the words *object* and *instance* have the same meaning. (Okay! They have *nearly* the same meaning.)

Making reference to an object's parts

In the `Purchase` code of Listing 17-2, I declare three variables: a `unitPrice` variable, a `quantity` variable, and a `taxable` variable. In real-life, you might say that each purchase has three parts: the unitPrice of an item being purchased, the quantity of items purchased, and the fact that the purchase is or isn't taxable.

When you create a Java class, each of these variables is called a *field*. The `Purchase` class has three fields — namely, the `unitPrice` field, the `quantity` field, and the `taxable` field.

After you've created an object, you use dots to refer to the object's fields. For example, in Listing 17-3, I put a value into the `onePurchase` object's `unitPrice` field with the following code:

```
onePurchase.unitPrice = keyboard.nextDouble();
```

Later in Listing 17-3, I get the `unitPrice` field's value with the following code:

```
double total = onePurchase.unitPrice * onePurchase.quantity;
```

This dot business may look cumbersome, but it really helps programmers when they're trying to organize the code. In Listing 17-1, each variable is a separate entity. But in Listing 17-3, each use of the word `unitPrice` is inextricably linked to the notion of a purchase. That's good.

TECHNICAL STUFF

Every field is a variable, but not every variable is a field. For example, in the following code, the `amount` variable isn't a field because it's declared inside of the `main` method.

```
public static void main(String args[]) {
    double amount;
    amount = 5.95;
    // ... Etc.
```

One way or another, I don't want you to get bogged down thinking about the words *field* and *variable*. A *field* is simply a variable that has a special role inside of a class. When I want to emphasize that special role, I use the word *field*. When I don't want to emphasize that special role, I use the word *variable*. I may even switch back and forth between *field* and *variable* in the same sentence. Who knows? I might call something a *fariable* or a *vield*.

If you care about which word I use and when I use it, good for you. If you don't care, don't worry about it.

Creating several objects

After you've created a `Purchase` class, you can create as many purchase objects as you want. For example, in Listing 17-5, I create two purchase objects.

LISTING 17-5: **Processing Purchases**

```
class ProcessPurchases {

    public static void main(String[] args) {
        Purchase purchase1 = new Purchase();
        purchase1.unitPrice = 20.00;
        purchase1.quantity = 3;
        purchase1.taxable = true;
```

(continued)

LISTING 17-5: *(continued)*

```java
        Purchase purchase2 = new Purchase();
        purchase2.unitPrice = 20.00;
        purchase2.quantity = 3;
        purchase2.taxable = false;

        double purchase1Total = purchase1.unitPrice * purchase1.quantity;
        if (purchase1.taxable) {
            purchase1Total *= 1.05;
        }

        double purchase2Total = purchase2.unitPrice * purchase2.quantity;
        if (purchase2.taxable) {
            purchase2Total *= 1.05;
        }

        if (purchase1Total == purchase2Total) {
            System.out.println("No difference");
        } else {
            System.out.println("These purchases have different totals.");
        }
    }
}
```

Figure 17-5 has a run of the code in Listing 17-5, and Figure 17-6 illustrates the concept.

FIGURE 17-5:
Running the code
in Listing 17-5.

```
Console 🔲    Problems   @ Javadoc   De
<terminated> ProcessPurchases [Java Application] /L
These purchases have different totals.
```

REMEMBER

To compile the code in Listing 17-5, you must have a copy of the Purchase class in the same project. (The Purchase class is in Listing 17-2.) To copy a class's code from one project to another, see Chapter 16. (That chapter's sidebar, "Grabbing input here and there," describes the copy-and-paste routine.)

Listing 17-5 has two purchase objects because the code

```java
new Purchase();
```

is executed two times.

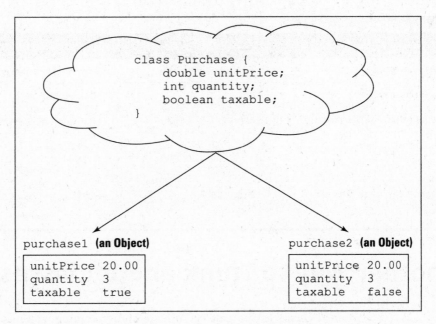

FIGURE 17-6:
From one class come two objects.

TIP

Just as you can separate an int variable's assignment from the variable's declaration

```
int count;
count = 0;
```

you can also separate a Purchase variable's assignment from the variable's declaration:

```
Purchase purchase1;
purchase1 = new Purchase();
```

After you've created the code in Listing 17-2, the word Purchase stands for a brand-new type — a reference type. Java has eight built-in primitive types and has as many reference types as people can define during your lifetime. In Listing 17-2, I define the Purchase reference type, and you can define reference types, too.

Table 17-2 has a brief comparison of primitive types and reference types.

TABLE 17-2   Java Types

	Primitive Type	Reference Type
How it's created	Built into the language	Defined as a Java class
How many are there	Eight	Indefinitely many
Sample variable declaration	`int count;`	`Purchase aPurchase;`
Sample assignment	`count = 0;`	`aPurchase =` `        new Purchase();`
Assigning a value to one of its parts	(Not applicable)	`aPurchase.unitPrice =` `        20.00;`

Another Way to Think about Classes

When you start learning object-oriented programming, you may think that this class idea is a big hoax. Some geeks in Silicon Valley had nothing better to do, so they went to a bar and made up some confusing gibberish about classes. They don't know what it means, but they have fun watching people struggle to understand it.

Well, that's not what classes are all about. Classes are serious stuff. What's more, classes are useful. Many reputable studies have shown that classes and object-oriented programming save time and money.

Even so, the notion of a class can be elusive. Even experienced programmers — the ones who are new to object-oriented programming — have trouble understanding how an object differs from a class.

Classes, objects, and tables

Because classes can be mysterious, I'll expand your understanding with another analogy. Figure 17-7 has a table of three purchases. The table's title consists of one word (the word Purchase), and the table has three column headings: the words *unitPrice*, *quantity*, and *taxable*. Well, the code in Listing 17-2 has the same stuff — Purchase, unitPrice, quantity, and taxable. So in Figure 17-7, think of the top part of the table (the title and column headings) as a class. Like the code in Listing 17-2, this top part of the table tells you what it means to be a Purchase. (It means having an unitPrice value, a quantity value, and a taxable value.)

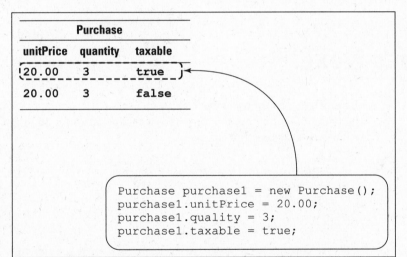

```
class Purchase {
    double unitPrice;
    int quantity;
    boolean taxable;
}
```

Purchase		
unitPrice	quantity	taxable
20.00	3	true
20.00	3	false

FIGURE 17-7: A table of purchases.

A class is like the top part of a table. And what about an object? Well, an object is like a row of a table. For example, with the code in Listing 17-5, I create two objects (two instances of the Purchase class). The first object has unitPrice value 20.00, quantity value 3, and taxable value true. In the corresponding table, the first row has these three values — 20.00, 3, and true, as shown in Figure 17-8.

Purchase		
unitPrice	quantity	taxable
20.00	3	true
20.00	3	false

```
Purchase purchase1 = new Purchase();
purchase1.unitPrice = 20.00;
purchase1.quality = 3;
purchase1.taxable = true;
```

FIGURE 17-8: A purchase corresponds to a row of the table.

Some questions and answers

Here's the world's briefest object-oriented programming FAQ:

>> **Can I have an object without having a class?**

No, you can't. In Java, every object is an instance of a class.

>> **Can I have a class without having an object?**

Yes, you can. In fact, almost every program in this book creates a class without an object. Take Listing 17-5, for example. The code in Listing 17-5 defines a class named ProcessPurchases. And nowhere in Listing 17-5 (or anywhere else) do I create an instance of the ProcessPurchases class. I have a class with no objects. That's just fine. It's business as usual.

》 After I've created a class and its instances, can I add more instances to the class?

Yes, you can. In Listing 17-5, I create one instance and then another. In a for loop, I could create a dozen instances and I'd have a dozen rows in the table of Figure 17-8. With no objects, three objects, four objects, or more objects, I still have the same old Purchase class.

》 Can an object come from more than one class?

Bite your tongue! Maybe other object-oriented languages allow this nasty class cross-breeding, but in Java, it's strictly forbidden. That's one thing that distinguishes Java from some of the languages that preceded it: Java is cleaner, more uniform, and easier to understand.

What's Next?

Listing 17-5 contains some code that makes me nervous. In Listing 17-5, the statements that compute a purchase total appear once, and then appear a second time with only one tiny change:

```
double purchase1Total = purchase1.unitPrice * purchase1.quantity;
if (purchase1.taxable) {
    purchase1Total *= 1.05;
}


double purchase2Total = purchase2.unitPrice * purchase2.quantity;
if (purchase2.taxable) {
    purchase2Total *= 1.05;
}
```

To me, this repetition seems silly. Aren't computers supposed to save us from mundane burdens such as repetitive typing? What if I type these statements correctly the first time, but make a mistake the second time? Maybe I'll copy the bad version a third and fourth time and end up with code that's all messed up!

Repetitive code is error-prone. It's inconvenient and unnecessary. Instead of repeating code, you should be able to summarize your code and then refer to that summarized code repeatedly. With Java's methods, you have precisely that capability. You've used other peoples' methods in many examples throughout this book, and in Chapter 19, you create methods of your own.

This is your chance to write some very classy code.

WHAT'S YOUR BMI?

A person's body mass index (BMI) is the person's weight (in kilograms) divided by the square of the person's height (in meters). For example, a 65 kg person who's 1.65 meters tall has a BMI of 23.875.

>> Create a Person class. Each Person has a weight and a height. In other words, the Person class has two fields: a weight field (a double value) and a height field (another double value).

>> Create another class containing a main method. In the main method, create a Person object. Assign values to the Person object's weight and height fields by reading input from the keyboard. Use the Person object's weight and height fields to calculate the person's BMI. Then output the person's BMI.

>> Modify the main method that you wrote for the previous bullet so that it creates three Person objects and calculates each object's BMI.

A BIT OF MACROECONOMICS

A country's debt-to-GDP ratio is the amount of the government's debt divided by the country's gross domestic product (GDP). For example, a country with 14.3 trillion dollars of debt and 18.5 trillion dollars GDP has a debt-to-GDP ratio of approximately 77 percent. A low debt-to-GDP ratio means that a country can pay off its debts without having to incur even more debt.

Try writing the following code:

>> Create a Country class. Each Country has a debt and a gdp. In other words, the Country class has two fields: a debt field (a double value) and a gdp field (another double value).

>> Create another class containing a main method. In the main method, create a Country object. Assign values to the Country object's debt and gdp fields by reading input from the keyboard.

Also in the main method, ask the user for an acceptable debt-to-GDP ratio. If your Country object's debt-to-GDP ratio is lower than the acceptable value, output the words That's acceptable. Otherwise, output That's not acceptable.

» Modify the main method that you wrote for the previous bullet so that it creates three Country objects and displays That's acceptable or That's not acceptable for each object.

NOTHING IN PARTICULAR

This program isn't about a Purchase class, a Person class, a Country class, or about a class with any obvious real-world relevance:

» Create a Thing class. The Thing class has two fields: a value1 field (an int value) and a value2 field (another int value).

» Create another class containing a main method. In the main method, create a Thing object. Assign values to the Thing object's value1 and value2 fields by reading input from the keyboard. Use the Thing object's value1 and value2 fields to display a sentence about the object. A typical sentence might be

```
This thing has values 42 and 91.
```

» Modify the main method that you wrote for the previous bullet so that it creates three Thing objects and displays a sentence about each of them.

Chapter **18**

Using Methods and Fields from a Java Class

I hope you didn't read Chapter 17, because I tell a big lie at the beginning of that chapter. Actually, it's not a lie. It's an exaggeration.

Actually, it's not an exaggeration. It's a careful choice of wording. In Chapter 17, I write that the gathering of data into a class is the start of object-oriented programming. Well, that's true. Except that many programming languages had data-gathering features before object-oriented programming became popular. Pascal had *records*. C had *structs*.

To be painfully precise, the grouping of data into usable chunks is only a prerequisite to object-oriented programming. You're not really doing object-oriented programming until you combine both data and methods in your classes.

This chapter starts the data-and-methods ball rolling, and Chapter 19 rounds out the picture.

The String Class

The String class is declared in the Java API. This means that somewhere in the stuff you download from Oracle's website (at www.oracle.com/technetwork/java/javase/downloads/index.html) is a file named String.java. If you hunt down this String.java file and peek at the file's code, you find some very familiar-looking stuff:

```
class String {
    ... And so on.
```

In your own code, you can use this String class without ever seeing what's inside the String.java file. That's one of the great things about object-oriented programming.

A simple example

A String is a bunch of characters. It's like having several char values in a row. You can declare a variable to be of type String and store several letters in the variable. Listing 18-1 has a tiny example.

LISTING 18-1: **I'm Repeating Myself Again (Again)**

```
import java.util.Scanner;

class JazzyEchoLine {

    public static void main(String args[]) {
        Scanner keyboard = new Scanner(System.in);
        String lineIn;

        lineIn = keyboard.nextLine();
        System.out.println(lineIn);

        keyboard.close();
    }
}
```

A run of Listing 18-1 is shown in Figure 18-1. This run bears an uncanny resemblance to runs in Listing 5-1 (in Chapter 5). That's because Listing 18-1 is a reprise of the effort in Listing 5-1.

```
Console ☒    Search  Pr
<terminated> JazzyEchoLine [Java A
Do as I write, not as I do.
Do as I write, not as I do.
```

The new idea in Listing 18-1 is the use of a String. In Listing 5-1, I have no variable to store the user's input. But in Listing 18-1, I create the lineIn variable. This variable stores a bunch of letters, like the letters Do as I write, not as I do.

Putting String variables to good use

The program in Listing 18-1 takes the user's input and echoes it back on the screen. This is a wonderful program, but (like many college administrators that I know) it doesn't seem to be particularly useful.

Take a look at a more useful application of Java's String type. A nice one is in Listing 18-2.

LISTING 18-2: **Putting a Name in a String Variable**

```java
import java.util.Scanner;
import static java.lang.System.out;

class ProcessMoreData {

    public static void main(String args[]) {
        Scanner keyboard = new Scanner(System.in);
        String fullName;
        double amount;
        boolean taxable;
        double total;

        out.print("Customer's full name: ");
        fullName = keyboard.nextLine();
        out.print("Amount: ");
        amount = keyboard.nextDouble();
        out.print("Taxable? (true/false) ");
        taxable = keyboard.nextBoolean();
```

(continued)

LISTING 18-2: *(continued)*

```
        if (taxable) {
            total = amount * 1.05;
        } else {
            total = amount;
        }

        out.println();
        out.print("The total for ");
        out.print(fullName);
        out.print(" is ");
        out.print(total);
        out.println(".");

        keyboard.close();
    }
}
```

A run of the code in Listing 18-2 is shown in Figure 18-2. The code stores Barry A. Burd in a variable called fullName and displays the fullName variable's content as part of the output. To make this program work, you have to store Barry A. Burd somewhere. After all, the program follows a certain outline:

> *Get a name.*
> Get some other stuff.
> Compute the total.
> *Display the name* (along with some other stuff).

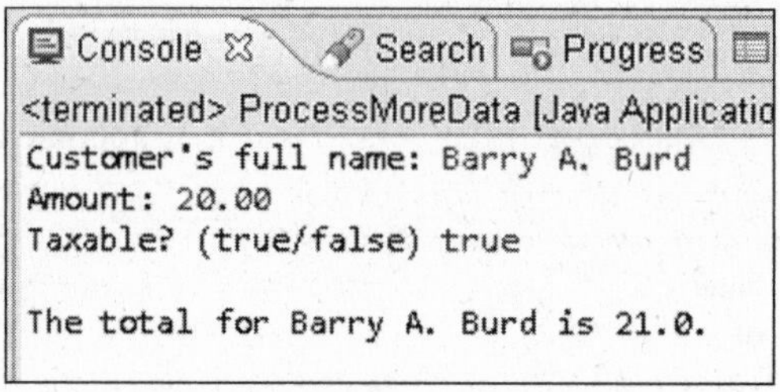

FIGURE 18-2:
Making a purchase.

```
Console ⅩⅩ      Search   Progress
<terminated> ProcessMoreData [Java Applicatio
Customer's full name: Barry A. Burd
Amount: 20.00
Taxable? (true/false) true

The total for Barry A. Burd is 21.0.
```

If you don't have the program store the name somewhere, by the time it's done getting other stuff and computing the total, it forgets the name (so the program can't display the name).

Reading and writing strings

To read a `String` value from the keyboard, you can call either `next` or `nextLine`:

» **The method** `next` **reads up to the next blank space.**

For example, with the input `Barry A. Burd`, the statements

```
String firstName = keyboard.next();
String middleInit = keyboard.next();
String lastName = keyboard.next();
```

assign `Barry` to `firstName`, `A.` to `middleInit`, and `Burd` to `lastName`.

» **The method** `nextLine` **reads up to the end of the current line.**

For example, with input `Barry A. Burd`, the statement

```
String fullName = keyboard.nextLine();
```

assigns `Barry A. Burd` to the variable `fullName`. (Hey, being an author has some hidden perks.)

To display a `String` value, you can call one of your old friends, `System.out.print` or `System.out.println`. In fact, most of the programs in this book display `String` values. In Listing 18-2, a statement like

```
out.print("Customer's full name: ");
```

displays the `String` value `"Customer's full name: "`.

TIP

You can use `print` and `println` to write `String` values to a disk file. For details, see Chapter 13.

Chapter 4 introduces a bunch of characters, enclosed in double quote marks:

```
"Chocolate, royalties, sleep"
```

In Chapter 4, I call this a *literal* of some kind. (It's a literal because, unlike a variable, it looks just like the stuff that it represents.) Well, in this chapter, I can continue the story about Java's literals:

» In Listing 18-2, `amount` and `total` are `double` variables, and `1.05` is a `double` literal.

» In Listing 18-2, `fullName` is a `String` variable, and things like `"Customer's full name: "` are `String` literals.

In a Java program, you surround the letters in a `String` literal with double quote marks.

With enough practice using Java `String` values, you'll never get tied up in knots.

ADDING STRINGS TO THINGS

In Java, you can put a plus sign between a `String` value and a numeric value. When you do, Java turns everything into one big `String` value. To see how this works, replace the last several lines in Listing 18-2 with the following single line:

```
out.println("The total for " + fullName + " is " + total + ".");
```

FUN WITH WORD ORDER

Write a program that inputs six words from the keyboard. The program outputs six sentences, each with the first word in a different position. For example, the output of one run might look like this:

```
only I have eyes for you.
I only have eyes for you.
I have only eyes for you.
I have eyes only for you.
I have eyes for only you.
I have eyes for you only.
```

Using an Object's Methods

If you're not too concerned about classes and reference types, the use of the type `String` in Listing 18-2 is no big deal. Almost everything you can do with a primitive type seems to work with the `String` type as well. But there's danger around the next curve. Take a look at the code in Listing 18-3 and the run of the code shown in Figure 18-3.

LISTING 18-3: **A Faulty Password Checker**

```
/*
 * This code does not work:
 */
import java.util.Scanner;
import static java.lang.System.out;
```

```
class TryToCheckPassword {

    public static void main(String args[]) {
        Scanner keyboard = new Scanner(System.in);
        String password = "swordfish";
        String userInput;

        out.print("What's the password? ");
        userInput = keyboard.next();

        if (password == userInput) {
            out.println("You're okay!");
        } else {
            out.println("You're a menace.");
        }

        keyboard.close();
    }
}
```

```
Console ☒    Search    Progress
<terminated> TryToCheckPassword [Java App
What's the password? swordfish
You're a menace.
```

Here are the facts as they appear in this example:

» According to the code in Listing 18-3, the value of password is "swordfish".

» In Figure 18-3, in response to the program's prompt, the user types swordfish. So in the code, the value of userInput is "swordfish".

» The if statement checks the condition password == userInput. Because both variables have the value "swordfish", the condition *should* be true, but . . .

» . . . the condition is *not* true because the program's output is You're a menace.

What's going on here? I try beefing up the code to see whether I can find any clues. An enhanced version of the password-checking program is in Listing 18-4, with a run of the new version shown in Figure 18-4.

LISTING 18-4: **An Attempt to Debug the Code in Listing 18-3**

```java
import java.util.Scanner;
import static java.lang.System.out;

class DebugCheckPassword {

    public static void main(String args[]) {
        Scanner keyboard = new Scanner(System.in);
        String password = "swordfish";
        String userInput;

        out.print("What's the password? ");
        userInput = keyboard.next();

        out.println();
        out.print("You typed            ");
        out.println(userInput);
        out.print("But the password is ");
        out.println(password);
        out.println();

        if (password == userInput) {
            out.println("You're okay!");
        } else {
            out.println("You're a menace.");
        }

        keyboard.close();
    }
}
```

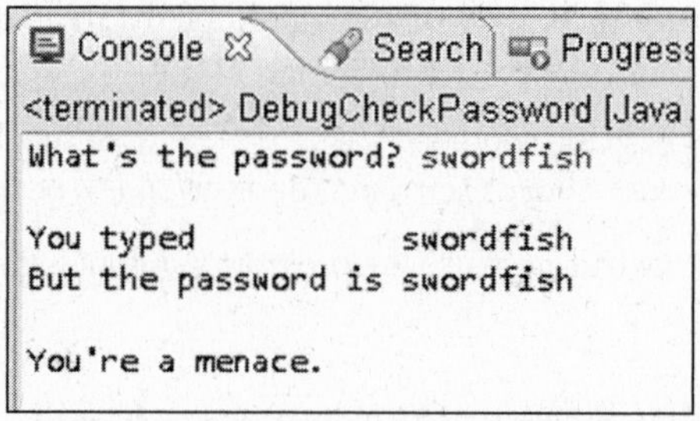

FIGURE 18-4:
This looks even
worse.

```
Console Ⅹ      Search   Progress
<terminated> DebugCheckPassword [Java
What's the password? swordfish

You typed            swordfish
But the password is swordfish

You're a menace.
```

Ouch! I'm stumped this time. The run in Figure 18-4 shows that both the userInput and password variables have value swordfish. So why doesn't the program accept the user's input?

When you compare two things with a double equal sign, reference types and primitive types don't behave the same way. Consider, for example, int versus String:

» You can compare two int values with a double equal sign. When you do, things work exactly as you would expect. For example, the condition in the following code is true:

```
int apples = 7;
int oranges = 7;

if (apples == oranges) {
    System.out.println("They're equal.");
}
```

» When you compare two String values with the double equal sign, things don't work the way you expect. The computer doesn't check to see if the two String values contain the same letters. Instead, the computer checks some esoteric property of the way variables are stored in memory.

REMEMBER

For your purposes, the term *reference type* is just a fancy name for a class. Because String is defined to be a class in the Java API, I call String a reference type. This terminology highlights the parallel between primitive types (such as int) and classes (that is, reference types, such as String).

Comparing strings

In the preceding bullets, the difference between int and String is mighty interesting. But if the double equal sign doesn't work for String values, how do you check to see if Joe User enters the correct password? You do it with the code in Listing 18-5.

LISTING 18-5: **Calling an Object's Method**

```
/*
 * This program works!
 */
import java.util.Scanner;
import static java.lang.System.out;

class CheckPassword {

    public static void main(String args[]) {
        Scanner keyboard = new Scanner(System.in);
```

(continued)

LISTING 18-5:   *(continued)*

```java
        String password = "swordfish";
        String userInput;

        out.print("What's the password? ");
        userInput = keyboard.next();

        if (password.equals(userInput)) {
            out.println("You're okay!");
        } else {
            out.println("You're a menace.");
        }

        keyboard.close();
    }
}
```

A run of the new password-checking code is shown in Figure 18-5, and let me tell you, it's a big relief! The code in Listing 18-5 actually works! When the user types swordfish, the if statement's condition is true.

FIGURE 18-5:
At last, Joe User
can log in.

```
Console ☒      Search  Progr
<terminated> CheckPassword [Java App
What's the password? swordfish
You're okay!
```

The truth about classes and methods

The magic in Listing 18-5 is the use of a method named equals. I have two ways to explain the equals method: a simple way and a more detailed way. First, here's the simple way: The equals method compares the characters in one string with the characters in another. If the characters are the same, the condition inside the if statement is true. That's all there is to it.

REMEMBER

Don't use a double equal sign to compare two String objects. Instead, use one of the object's equals methods.

For a more detailed understanding of the equals method, flip to Chapter 17 and take a look at Figures 17-7 and 17-8. Those figures illustrate the similarities between classes, objects, and the parts of a table. In the figures, each row represents a purchase, and each column represents a feature that purchases possess.

You can observe the same similarities for any class, including Java's String class. In fact, what Figure 17-7 does for purchases, Figure 18-6 does for strings.

String		
value	**count**	**equals**
swordfish	9	**(A method to compare** swordfish **with any string)**
catfish	7	**(A method to compare** catfish **with any string)**

FIGURE 18-6: Viewing the String class and String objects as parts of a table.

The stuff shown in Figure 18-6 is much simpler than the real String class story. But Figure 18-6 makes a good point. Like the purchases in Figure 17-7, each string has its own features. For example, each string has a value (the actual characters stored in the string), and each string has a count (the number of characters stored in the string). You can't really write the following line of code because the stuff in Figure 18-6 omits a few subtle details:

```
//This code does NOT work:
System.out.println(password.count);
```

Anyway, each row in Figure 18-6 has three items: a value, a count, and an equals method. So each row of the table contains more than just data. Each row contains an equals method, a way of doing something useful with the data. It's as though each object (each instance of the String class) has three things:

>> A bunch of characters (the object's value)

>> A number (the object's count)

>> A way of being compared with other strings (the object's equals method)

That's the essence of object-oriented programming. Each string has its own, personal copy of the equals method. For example, in Listing 18-5, the password string has its own equals method. When you call the password string's equals method and put the userInput string in the method's parentheses, the method compares the two strings to see if those strings contain the same characters.

The userInput string in Listing 18-5 has an equals method, too. I could use the userInput string's equals method to compare this string with the password string. But I don't. In fact, in Listing 18-5, I don't use the userInput string's equals method at all. (To compare the userInput with the password, I had to use either the `password` string's `equals` method or the `userInput` string's `equals` method. So I made an arbitrary choice: I chose the `password` string's method.)

Calling an object's methods

In Chapter 17, I create a `Purchase` class:

```
class Purchase {
    double unitPrice;
    int quantity;
    boolean taxable;
}
```

I refer to the `unitPrice` variable, the `quantity` variable, and the `taxable` variable as the `Purchase` class's *fields.*

Calling a string's `equals` method is like getting a purchase's `unitPrice`. With both `equals` and `unitPrice`, you use your old friend, the dot. For example, in Listing 17-3 (in Chapter 17), you write

```
onePurchase.unitPrice = keyboard.nextDouble();
```

and in Listing 18-5, you write

```
if (password.equals(userInput))
```

A dot works the same way for an object's fields and its methods. In either case, a dot takes the object and picks out one of the object's parts. It works whether that part is a field (as in `onePurchase.unitPrice`) or a method (as in `password.equals`).

In fact, fields and methods are similar in so many ways that it's handy to have one word to describe both fields and methods. The word is *members.* In Chapter 17, the `Purchase` class has three members: `unitPrice`, `quantity`, and `taxable`. And in the Java API, the `String` class has about 60 members, one of which is `equals`.

Combining and using data

At this point in the chapter, I can finally say, "I told you so." Here's a quotation from Chapter 17:

> A class is a design plan; it describes the way in which you intend to *combine* and *use* pieces of data.

A class can define the way you *use* data. How do you use a password and a user's input? You check to see whether they're the same. That's why Java's String class defines an equals method.

REMEMBER

An object can be more than just a bunch of data. With object-oriented programming, each object possesses copies of methods for using that object.

Java's String class is impressive, with nearly 60 methods. But that's nothing compared with Java's JFrame class. The JFrame class has hundreds of methods.

TRY IT OUT

SHOW A FRAME

Identify the method calls in the following code:

```java
import javax.swing.JFrame;

public class Main {

    public static void main(String[] args) {
        JFrame frame = new JFrame();
        frame.setSize(300, 300);
        frame.setTitle("This is frame");
        frame.setVisible(true);
    }
}
```

Run the code to find out what it does. (End the run of the code by clicking the square, red Terminate icon near Eclipse's Console view. For details, refer to Chapter 3.)

CHECK THE DOCUMENTATION

Visit https://docs.oracle.com/javase/8/docs/api/javax/swing/JFrame.html to read about the methods belonging to Java's JFrame class. In particular, read about methods named setSize, setTitle, and setVisible.

Static Methods

You have a fistful of checks. Each check has a number, an amount, and a payee. You print checks like these with your very own printer. To print the checks, you use a Java class. Each object made from the Check class has three fields (number, amount, and payee). And each object has one method (a print method). You can see all of this in Figure 18-7.

Check			
number	amount	payee	print
1705	$25.09	The Butcher	(method to cut the check)
1699	$31.27	The Baker	(method to cut the check)
1702	$12.35	The Candlestick Maker	(method to cut the check)

sort

FIGURE 18-7:
The Check class
and some check
objects.

You'd like to print the checks in numerical order. So you need a method to *sort* the checks. If the checks in Figure 18-7 were sorted, the check with number 1699 would come first, and the check with number 1705 would come last.

The big question is, should each check have its own sort method? Does the check with number 1699 need to sort itself? And the answer is no. Some methods just shouldn't belong to the objects in a class.

So where do such methods belong? How can you have a sort method without creating a separate sort for each check?

Here's the answer: You make the sort method be *static.* Anything that's static belongs to a whole class, not to any particular instance of the class. If the sort method is static, the entire Check class has just one copy of the sort method. This copy stays with the entire Check class. No matter how many instances of the Check class you create — three, ten, or none — you have just one sort method.

For an illustration of this concept, refer to Figure 18-7. The whole class has just one sort method. So the sort method is static. No matter how you call the sort method, that method uses the same values to do its work.

Of course, each individual check (each object, each row of the table in Figure 18-7) still has its own number, its own amount, its own payee, and its own print method. When you print the first check, you get one amount, and when you print the second check, you get another. Because there's a number, an amount, a payee, and a print method for each object, I call these things *non-static.* I call them non-static because . . . well . . . because they're not static.

Calling static and non-static methods

In this book, my first use of the word `static` is in Listing 3-1. I use `static` as part of every `main` method (and this book's listings have lots of `main` methods). In Java, your `main` method has to be static. That's just the way it goes.

To call a static method, you use a class's name along with a dot. This is just slightly different from the way you call a non-static method:

>> **To call an ordinary (non-static) method, you follow an object with a dot.**

For example, a program to process the checks in Figure 18-7 may contain code of the following kind:

```
Check firstCheck;
firstCheck.number = 1705;
firstCheck.amount = 25.09;
firstCheck.payee = "The Butcher";
firstCheck.print();
```

>> **To call a class's static method, you follow the class name with a dot.**

For example, to sort the checks in Figure 18-7, you may call

```
Check.sort();
```

Turning strings into numbers

The code in Listing 18-5 introduces a non-static method named `equals`. To compare the `password` string with the `userInput` string, you preface `.equals` with either of the two string objects. In Listing 18-5, I preface `.equals` with the `password` object:

```
if (password.equals(userInput))
```

Each string object has an `equals` method of its own, so I can achieve the same effect by writing

```
if (userInput.equals(password))
```

But Java has another class named `Integer`, and the whole `Integer` class has a static method named `parseInt`. If someone hands you a string of characters and you want to turn that string into an `int` value, you can call the `Integer` class's `parseInt` method. Listing 18-6 has a small example.

LISTING 18-6: **More Chips, Please**

```java
import java.util.Scanner;
import static java.lang.System.out;

class AddChips {

    public static void main(String args[]) {
        Scanner keyboard = new Scanner(System.in);
        String reply;
        int numberOfChips;

        out.print("How many chips do you have?");
        out.print(" (Type a number,");
        out.print(" or type 'Not playing') ");
        reply = keyboard.nextLine();

        if (!reply.equals("Not playing")) {
            numberOfChips = Integer.parseInt(reply);
            numberOfChips += 10;

            out.print("You now have ");
            out.print(numberOfChips);
            out.println(" chips.");
        }

        keyboard.close();
    }
}
```

Some runs of the code in Listing 18-6 are shown in Figure 18-8. You want to give each player ten chips. But some party poopers in the room aren't playing. So two people, each with no chips, may not get the same treatment. An empty-handed player gets ten chips, but an empty-handed party pooper gets none.

In Listing 18-6, you call the Scanner class's nextLine method, allowing a user to enter any characters at all — not just digits. If the user types Not playing, you don't give the killjoy any chips.

If the user types some digits, you're stuck holding these digits in the string variable named reply. You can't add ten to a string like reply. So you call the Integer class's parseInt method, which takes your string and hands you back a nice int value. From there, you can add ten to the int value.

```
Console ⊠                                          ■ ✖ ⁂
<terminated> AddChips [Java Application] C:\Program Files\Java\jre7\bin\javaw.exe (N
How many chips do you have? (Type a number, or type 'Not playing') 30
You now have 40 chips.
```

```
Console ⊠                                          ■ ✖ ⁂
<terminated> AddChips [Java Application] C:\Program Files\Java\jre7\bin\javaw.exe (Nov
How many chips do you have? (Type a number, or type 'Not playing') 0
You now have 10 chips.
```

```
Console ⊠                              ■ ✖ ⁂ ▤ ⛶
<terminated> AddChips [Java Application] C:\Program Files\Java\jre7\bin\javaw.exe (Nov 9, 2011 1
How many chips do you have? (Type a number, or type 'Not playing') Not playing
```

FIGURE 18-8:
Running the code
in Listing 18-6.

TECHNICAL
STUFF

Java has a loophole that allows you to add a number to a string. The problem is, you don't get real addition. Adding the number 10 to the string "30" gives you "3010", not 40.

WARNING

Don't confuse Integer with int. In Java, int is the name of a primitive type (a type that I use throughout this book). But Integer is the name of a class. Java's Integer class contains handy methods for dealing with int values. For example, in Listing 18-6, the Integer class's parseInt method makes an int value from a string.

Turning numbers into strings

In Chapter 17, Listing 17-1 adds tax to the purchase of two items. But a run of the code in Listing 17-1 has an anomaly. (Refer to Figure 17-1.) With 5 percent tax on 40 dollars, the program displays a total of 42.0. That's peculiar — where I come from, currency amounts aren't normally displayed with just one digit beyond the decimal point.

If you don't choose your purchase amount carefully, the situation is even worse. For example, in Figure 18-9, I run the same program (the code in Listing 17-1) with purchase amount 19.37. The resulting display looks nasty.

With its internal zeros and ones, the computer doesn't do arithmetic quite the way you and I are used to doing it. So how do you fix this problem?

FIGURE 18-9:
Do you have
change for
20.3385000
00000003?

```
Console ⊠  Problems  @ Java
<terminated> ProcessPurchase (1) [Java
Unit price: 19.37
Quantity: 1
Taxable? (true/false) true
Total: 20.338500000000003
|
```

The Java API has a class named NumberFormat, and the NumberFormat class has a static method named getCurrencyInstance. When you call NumberFormat.getCurrencyInstance() with nothing inside the parentheses, you get an object that can mold numbers into U.S. currency amounts. Listing 18-7 has an example.

LISTING 18-7: **The Right Way to Display a Dollar Amount**

```java
import java.text.NumberFormat;
import java.util.Scanner;

class BetterProcessData {

    public static void main(String args[]) {
        Scanner keyboard = new Scanner(System.in);
        double unitPrice;
        int quantity;
        boolean taxable;

        NumberFormat currency = NumberFormat.getCurrencyInstance();

        System.out.print("Unit price: ");
        unitPrice = keyboard.nextDouble();
        System.out.print("Quantity: ");
        quantity = keyboard.nextInt();
        System.out.print("Taxable? (true/false) ");
        taxable = keyboard.nextBoolean();

        double total = unitPrice * quantity;
        if (taxable) {
            total = total * 1.05;
        }

        String niceTotal = currency.format(total);
        System.out.print("Total: ");
        System.out.println(niceTotal);

        keyboard.close();
    }
}
```

For some beautiful runs of the code in Listing 18-7, see Figure 18-10. Now at last, you see a total like $20.34, not 20.338500000000003. Ah! That's much better.

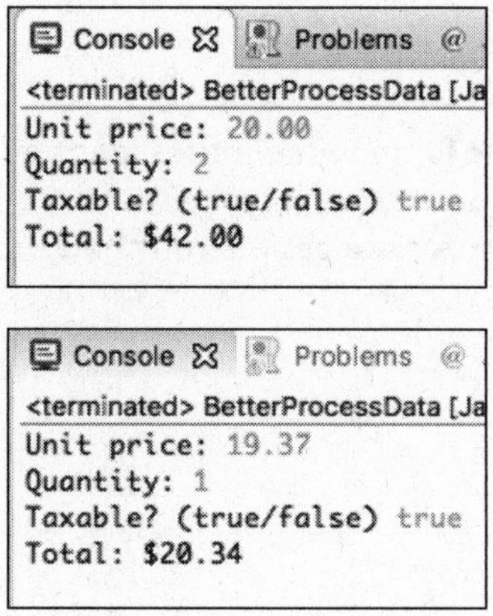

FIGURE 18-10: See the pretty numbers.

How the NumberFormat works

For my current purposes, the code in Listing 18-7 contains three interesting variables:

» The variable total stores a number, such as 42.0.

» The variable currency stores an object that can mold numbers into U.S. currency amounts.

» The variable niceTotal is set up to store a bunch of characters.

The currency object has a format method. To get the appropriate bunch of characters into the niceTotal variable, you call the currency object's format method. You apply this format method to the variable total.

Your country; your currency

The code in Listing 18-7 works well in the United States. But in another country, the currency symbol might not be the dollar sign ($), and you might represent *twenty* with characters other than 20.00.

Java shapes its input and output to match your computer's locale. Imagine, for example, that your computer runs the version of Windows sold in France. Then, as far as Java is concerned, your computer's locale is Locale.FRANCE, and a run of the code in Listing 18-7 looks like the run shown in Figure 18-11.

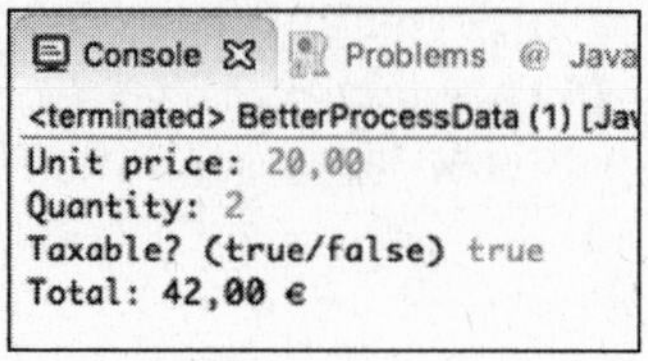

FIGURE 18-11:
A run of
Listing 18-7 on a
computer in
France.

```
Console 🗙    Problems  @  Java
<terminated> BetterProcessData (1) [Jav
Unit price: 20,00
Quantity: 2
Taxable? (true/false) true
Total: 42,00 €
```

In fact, you can customize your code for many countries, and you don't have to buy airplane tickets to do it! My computer is configured to run in the United States. But in Listing 18-8, I use Java's Locale class to get the run shown in Figure 18-11.

LISTING 18-8: **Using a Java Locale**

```java
import java.text.NumberFormat;
import java.util.Locale;
import java.util.Scanner;

class BetterProcessData {

  public static void main(String args[]) {
    Scanner keyboard = new Scanner(System.in);
    keyboard.useLocale(Locale.FRANCE);

    double unitPrice;
    int quantity;
    boolean taxable;

    NumberFormat currency = NumberFormat.getCurrencyInstance(Locale.FRANCE);

    System.out.print("Unit price: ");
    unitPrice = keyboard.nextDouble();
    System.out.print("Quantity: ");
    quantity = keyboard.nextInt();
    System.out.print("Taxable? (true/false) ");
    taxable = keyboard.nextBoolean();

    double total = unitPrice * quantity;
    if (taxable) {
      total = total * 1.05;
    }

    String niceTotal = currency.format(total);
    System.out.print("Total: ");
    System.out.println(niceTotal);

    keyboard.close();
  }
}
```

Understanding the Big Picture

In this section, I answer some of the burning questions that I raise throughout this book: "What does `java.util` stand for?" "Why do I need the word `static` at certain points in the code?" "How can a degree in Horticultural Studies help you sort canceled checks?"

I also explain "static" in some unique and interesting ways. After all, static fields and methods aren't easy to understand. It helps to read about Java's static feature from several points of view.

Packages and import declarations

In Java, you can group a bunch of classes into something called a *package.* In fact, the classes in Java's standard API are divided into about 200 packages. This book's examples make heavy use of three packages: the packages named `java.util`, `java.lang`, and `java.io`.

The class java.util.Scanner

The package `java.util` contains about 75 classes, including the very useful Scanner class. Like most other classes, this Scanner class has two names: a *fully qualified name* and an abbreviated *simple name.* The class's fully qualified name is `java.util.Scanner`, and the class's simple name is Scanner. You get the fully qualified name by adding the package name to the class's simple name. (That is, you add the package name `java.util` to the simple name Scanner. You get `java.util.Scanner`.)

An import declaration lets you abbreviate a class's name. With the declaration

```
import java.util.Scanner;
```

the Java compiler figures out where to look for the Scanner class. So instead of writing `java.util.Scanner` throughout your code, you can just write Scanner.

The class java.lang.System

The package `java.lang` contains about 35 classes, including the ever-popular System class. (The class's fully qualified name is `java.lang.System`, and the class's simple name is System.) Instead of writing `java.lang.System` throughout your code, you can just write System. You don't even need an `import` declaration.

TECHNICAL STUFF

Among all of Java's packages, the `java.lang` package is special. With or without an import declaration, the compiler imports everything in the `java.lang` package. You can start your program with `import java.lang.System`. But if you don't, the compiler adds this declaration automatically.

The static System.out variable

What kind of importing must you do in order to abbreviate `System.out.println`? How can you shorten it to `out.println`? An import declaration lets you abbreviate a *class's* name. But in the expression `System.out`, the word `out` isn't a class. The word `out` is a static variable. (The `out` variable refers to the place where a Java program sends text output.) So you can't write

```
//This code is bogus. Don't use it:
import java.lang.System.out;
```

What do you do instead? You write

```
import static java.lang.System.out;
```

To find out more about the `out` variable's being a static variable, read the next section.

TECHNICAL STUFF

In this chapter, I refer to `out` as a static variable. That's okay. But a more descriptive way to refer to `out` is to call it a static field of Java's `System` class.

ALL YE NEED TO KNOW

I can summarize much of Java's complexity in only a few sentences:

- The Java API contains many packages.

- A package contains classes.

- From a class, you can create objects. Each such object is an *instance* of the class.

- An object has its own copy of each of the class's fields and methods (each of the class's members).

- A class has the one and only copy of each of the class's static fields and static methods (the class's static members).

Shedding light on the static darkness

I love to quote myself. When I quote my own words, I don't need written permission. I don't have to think about copyright infringement, and I never hear from lawyers. Best of all, I can change and distort anything I say. When I paraphrase my own ideas, I can't be misquoted.

With that in mind, here's a quote from an earlier section:

Anything that's static belongs to a whole class, not to any particular instance of the class . . . To call a static method, you use a class's name along with a dot.

How profound! In Listing 18-6, I introduce a static method named `parseInt`. Here's the same quotation applied to the static `parseInt` method:

The static `parseInt` *method belongs to the whole* `Integer` *class, not to any particular instance of the* `Integer` *class. . . . To call the static* `parseInt` *method, you use the* `Integer` *class's name along with a dot. You write something like* `Integer.parseInt(reply)`.

That's very nice! How about the `System.out` business that I introduce in Chapter 3? I can apply my quotation to that, too.

The static `out` *variable belongs to the whole* `System` *class, not to any particular instance of the* `System` *class. . . . To refer to the static out variable, you use the* `System` *class's name along with a dot. You write something like* `System.out.println()`.

If you think about what `System.out` means, this static business makes sense. After all, the name `System.out` refers to the place where a Java program sends text output. (When you use Eclipse, the name `System.out` refers to Eclipse's Console view.) A typical program has only one place to send its text output. So a Java program has only one `out` variable. No matter how many objects you create — three, ten, or none — you have just one `out` variable. And when you make something static, you ensure that the program has only one of those things.

All right, then! The `out` variable is static.

To abbreviate the name of a static variable (or a static method), you don't use an ordinary import declaration. Instead, you use a static import declaration. That's why, in Chapter 9 and beyond, I use the word `static` to import the `out` variable:

```
import static java.lang.System.out;
```

Barry makes good on an age-old promise

In Chapter 6, I pull a variable declaration outside of a `main` method. I go from code of the kind in Listing 18-9 to code of the kind that's in Listing 18-10.

LISTING 18-9: **Declaring a Variable inside the main Method**

```
class SnitSoft {

    public static void main(String args[]) {
        double amount = 5.95;

        amount = amount + 25.00;
        System.out.println(amount);
    }
}
```

LISTING 18-10: **Pulling a Variable outside of the main Method**

```
class SnitSoft {
    static double amount = 5.95;

    public static void main(String args[]) {
        amount = amount + 25.00;
        System.out.println(amount);
    }
}
```

In Listing 18-9, `amount` is a variable belonging to the `main` method. But in Listing 18-10, `amount` is a static field belonging to the `SnitSoft` class.

In Chapter 6, I promise to explain why Listing 18-10 needs the extra word `static` (in `static double amount = 5.95`). Well, with all the fuss about static methods in this chapter, I can finally explain everything.

Refer to Figure 18-7. In that figure, you have checks, and you have a `sort` method. Each individual check has its own `number`, its own `amount`, and its own `payee`. But the entire `Check` class has just one `sort` method.

I don't know about you, but to sort my canceled checks, I hang them on my exotic Yucca Elephantipes tree. I fasten the higher-numbered checks to the upper leaves and put the lower-numbered checks on the lower leaves. When I find a check whose number comes between two other checks, I select a free leaf (one that's between the upper and lower leaves).

A program to mimic my sorting method looks something like this:

```
class Check {
    int number;
    double amount;
    String payee;

    static void sort() {
        Yucca tree;

        if (myCheck.number > 1700) {
            tree.attachHigh(myCheck);
        }
        // ... etc.
    }
}
```

Because of the word `static`, the `Check` class has only one `sort` method. And because I declare the `tree` variable inside the static `sort` method, this program has only one `tree` variable. (Indeed, I hang all my canceled checks on just one yucca tree.) I can move the `tree` variable's declaration outside of the `sort` method. But if I do, I may have too many yucca trees:

```
class Check {
    int number;
    double amount;
    String payee;
    Yucca tree;    //This is bad!
                   //Each check has its own tree.

    static void sort() {
        if (myCheck.number > 5000) {
            tree.attachHigh(myCheck);
        }
        // ... etc.
    }
}
```

In this nasty code, each check has its own number, its own amount, its own payee, and its own tree. But that's ridiculous! I don't want to fasten each check to its own yucca tree. Everybody knows you're supposed to sort checks with just one yucca tree. (That's the way the big banks do it.)

When I move the tree variable's declaration outside of the sort method, I want to preserve the fact that I have only one tree. (To be more precise, I have only one tree for the entire Check class.) To make sure that I have only one tree, I declare the tree variable to be static:

```
class Check {
    int number;
    double amount;
    String payee;
    static Yucca tree;    //That's better!


    static void sort() {
        if (myCheck.number > 5000) {
            tree.attachHigh(myCheck);
        }
        // ... etc.
    }
}
```

For exactly the same reason, I write **static** double amount when I move from Listing 18-9 to 18-10.

To find out more about sorting, read *UNIX For Dummies,* 5th Edition, by John Levine and Margaret Levine Young. To learn more about bank checks, read *Managing Your Money Online For Dummies,* by Kathleen Sindell. To learn more about trees, read *Landscaping For Dummies,* by Phillip Giroux, Bob Beckstrom, and Lance Walheim (all published by Wiley).

TIP

These experiments will help you understand static methods and static fields.

TRY IT OUT

MORE MONEY

Run the following code and identify the static methods that are called in the code:

```
import java.text.NumberFormat;


import javax.swing.JOptionPane;


public class Main {

    public static void main(String[] args) {
```

```
    NumberFormat currency = NumberFormat.getCurrencyInstance();
    String inputString = JOptionPane.showInputDialog("Enter an amount");
    double inputAmount = Double.parseDouble(inputString);
    double oneMore = inputAmount + 1;
    String oneMoreMoney = currency.format(oneMore);
    String message = "One more than that amount is " + oneMoreMoney + ".";
    JOptionPane.showMessageDialog(null, message);
  }
}
```

Hint: Most Java programmers begin the names of classes with capital letters. Any name that starts with a capital letter is probably the name of a class. If you're not sure about a particular name, you can look up that name in Java's API documentation. The documentation is online at https://docs.oracle.com/javase/8/docs/api/index.html?overview-summary.html.

BOOKS FOR DUMMIES

Have a gander at the following code. How many copies of the author field exist during a run of this code? How many copies of the publisher field exist during a run of the code? Why?

```
class Book {
    String title;
    String author;
    static String publisher = "Wiley";
}


public class Main {

    public static void main(String[] args) {
        Book javaForDummies = new Book();
        javaForDummies.title = "Java For Dummies";
        javaForDummies.author = "Barry Burd";


        Book dosForDummies = new Book();
        dosForDummies.title = "DOS For Dummies";
        dosForDummies.author = "Dan Gookin";
    }


}
```

Would the number of copies of the `publisher` field change if you added these two statements to the `main` method?

```
Book.publisher = "John Wiley & Sons, Inc.";
Book.publisher = "A publisher in the United States";
```

If so, why? If not, why not?

USE STATIC AND NON-STATIC FIELDS

Run the following code. Then examine the code to determine why it produces the output that you see in the Console view:

```
class IntegerHolder {
  int value;
  static int howMany = 0;
}

public class Main {

  public static void main(String[] args) {
    IntegerHolder holder1 = new IntegerHolder();
    holder1.value = 79;
    IntegerHolder.howMany++;

    IntegerHolder holder2 = new IntegerHolder();
    holder2.value = 443;
    IntegerHolder.howMany++;

    System.out.println(holder1.value);
    System.out.println(holder2.value);

    System.out.println(IntegerHolder.howMany);

    //System.out.println(IntegerHolder.value); Why is this statement illegal?

    System.out.println(holder1.howMany);       // This statement is legal
                                               // but the statement is
                                               // misleading. Why?

  }
}
```

SOMETHING'S WRONG HERE

What's wrong with the following code? How does the meaning of the word static make a difference? Would adding another static keyword fix the problem? Why?

```
import java.util.Scanner;

public class Main {
    Scanner keyboard = new Scanner(System.in);

    public static void main(String[] args) {
        int numberOfCats = keyboard.nextInt();
        System.out.println(numberOfCats);
    }
```

}JUST THE FACTS

In the following code, why are the fields static?

```
class Facts {
    static int numberOfPlanets = 8;
    static int numberOfMoons = 1;
    static int numberOfContinents = 7;
    static int numberOfOceans = 5;
}
```

You can make the Facts class even better by adding Java's final keyword to each field declaration:

```
class Facts {
    static final int numberOfPlanets = 8;
    static final int numberOfMoons = 1;
    static final int numberOfContinents = 7;
    static final int numberOfOceans = 5;
}
```

A *final* variable's value can't be changed. So, in a main method, the code

```
System.out.println(BetterFacts.numberOfPlanets);
```

is legal, but the code

```
BetterFacts.numberOfPlanets = 9;    // Bad code
```

is not legal.

Chapter **19**

Creating New Java Methods

I n Chapters 3 and 4, I introduce Java methods. I show you how to create a `main` method and how to call the `System.out.println` method. Between that chapter and this one, I make very little noise about methods. In Chapter 18, I introduce a bunch of new methods for you to call, but that's only half of the story.

This chapter completes the circle. In this chapter, you create your own Java methods — not the tired old `main` method that you've been using all along, but rather some new, powerful Java methods.

Defining a Method within a Class

In Chapter 18, Figure 18-6 introduces an interesting notion — a notion that's at the core of object-oriented programming. Each Java string has its own `equals` method. That is, each string has, built within it, the functionality to compare itself to other strings. That's an important point. When you do object-oriented programming, you bundle data and functionality into a lump called a class. Just remember Barry's immortal words from Chapter 17:

> A class . . . describes the way in which you intend to combine *and use* pieces of data.

And why are these words so important? They're important because, in object-oriented programming, chunks of data take responsibility for themselves. With object-oriented programming, everything you have to know about a string is located in the file String.java. So, if people have problems with the strings, they know just where to look for all the code. That's great!

This is the deal: Objects contain methods. Chapter 18 shows you how to use an object's methods, and this chapter shows you how to *create* an object's methods.

Making a method

Imagine a table containing the information about three accounts. (If you have trouble imagining such a thing, just look at Figure 19-1.) In the figure, each account has a last name, an identification number, and a balance. In addition (and here's the important part), each account knows how to display itself on the screen. Each row of the table has its own copy of a display method.

FIGURE 19-1:
A table of
accounts.

Account			
lastName	id	balance	display
Aju	9936	$8,734.00	(method to display account info)
Iap	3492	$6,718.00	(method to display account info)
Ngp	2151	$1,008.00	(method to display account info)

The last names in Figure 19-1 may seem strange to you. That's because I generated the table's data randomly. Each last name is a haphazard combination of three letters: one uppercase letter followed by two lowercase letters.

TECHNICAL STUFF

Though it may seem strange, generating account values at random is common practice. When you write new code, you want to test the code to find out whether it runs correctly. You can make up your own data (with values like "Smith", 0000, and 1000.00). But to give your code a challenging workout, you should use some unexpected values. If you have values from some real-life case studies, you should use them. But if you don't have real data, randomly generated values are easy to create.

To find out how I randomly generate three-letter names, see this chapter's "Generating words randomly" sidebar.

I need some code to implement the ideas in Figure 19-1. Fortunately, I have some code in Listing 19-1.

LISTING 19-1: **An Account Class**

```java
import java.text.NumberFormat;
import static java.lang.System.out;

class Account {
    String lastName;
    int id;
    double balance;

    void display() {
        NumberFormat currency = NumberFormat.getCurrencyInstance();

        out.print("The account with last name ");
        out.print(lastName);
        out.print(" and ID number ");
        out.print(id);
        out.print(" has balance ");
        out.println(currency.format(balance));
    }
}
```

The Account class in Listing 19-1 defines four members: a lastName field, an id field, a balance field, and a display method. So each instance of Account class has its own lastName, its own id, its own balance, and its own way of doing display. These things match up with the four columns in Figure 19-1.

Examining the method's header

Listing 19-1 contains the display method's declaration. Like a main method's declaration, the display declaration has a header and a body. (See Chapter 4.) The header has two words and some parentheses:

» **The word** void **tells the computer that, when the** display **method is called, the** display **method doesn't return anything to the place that called it.**

Later in this chapter, a method does return something. For now, the display method returns nothing.

» **The word display is the method's name.**

Every method must have a name. Otherwise, you don't have a way to call the method.

>> **The parentheses contain all the things you're going to pass to the method when you call it.**

When you call a method, you can pass information to that method on the fly. This display example, with its empty parentheses, looks strange. That's because no information is passed to the display method when you call it. That's okay. I give a meatier example later in this chapter.

Examining the method's body

The display method's body contains some print and println calls. The interesting thing here is that the body makes reference to the lastName, id, and balance fields. A method's body can do that. But with each object having its own lastName, id, and balance variables, what does a variable in the display method's body mean?

Well, when I use the Account class, I create little account objects. Maybe I create an object for each row of the table in Figure 19-1. Each object has its own values for the lastName, id, and balance variables, and each object has its own copy of the display method.

Take the first display method in Figure 19-1 — the method for Aju's account. The display method for that object behaves as though it had the code in Listing 19-2.

LISTING 19-2: **How the display Method Behaves When No One's Looking**

```
/*
 * This is not real code:
 */
void display() {
    NumberFormat currency = NumberFormat.getCurrencyInstance();

    out.print("The account with last name ");
    out.print("Aju");
    out.print(" and ID number ");
    out.print(9936);
    out.print(" has balance ");
    out.println(currency.format(8734.00));
}
```

In fact, each of the three `display` methods behaves as though its body has a slightly different code. Figure 19-2 illustrates this idea for two instances of the Account class.

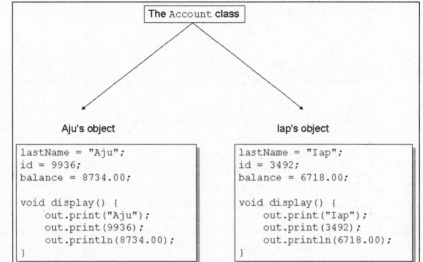

FIGURE 19-2:
Two objects, each with its own display method.

Calling the method

To put the previous section's ideas into action, you need more code. So the next listing (see Listing 19-3) creates instances of the Account class.

LISTING 19-3: **Making Use of the Code in Listing 19-1**

```java
import java.util.Random;

class ProcessAccounts {

    public static void main(String args[]) {

        Random myRandom = new Random();
        Account anAccount;

        for (int i = 0; i < 3; i++) {
            anAccount = new Account();

            anAccount.lastName = "" +
                (char) (myRandom.nextInt(26) + 'A') +
```

(continued)

LISTING 19-3: *(continued)*

```
              (char) (myRandom.nextInt(26) + 'a') +
              (char) (myRandom.nextInt(26) + 'a');

          anAccount.id = myRandom.nextInt(10000);
          anAccount.balance = myRandom.nextInt(10000);
          anAccount.display();
      }
   }
}
```

Here's a summary of the action in Listing 19-3:

```
Do the following three times:
    Create a new object (an instance of the Account class).
    Randomly generate values for the object's lastName, id and balance.
    Call the object's display method.
```

The first of the three `display` calls prints the first object's `lastName`, `id`, and `balance` values. The second `display` call prints the second object's `lastName`, `id`, and `balance` values. And so on.

A run of the code from Listing 19-3 is shown in Figure 19-3.

FIGURE 19-3:
Running the code
in Listing 19-3.

```
🖳 Console ☒   🔍 Search  🔧 Progress  🗔 Properties           ■ ✖ 🌠
<terminated> ProcessAccounts [Java Application] C:\Program Files\Java\jre7\bin\javaw.e
The account with last name Aju and ID number 9936 has balance $8,734.00
The account with last name Iap and ID number 3492 has balance $6,718.00
The account with last name Ngp and ID number 2151 has balance $1,008.00
```

WARNING

Concerning the code in Listing 19-3, your mileage may vary. You don't see the same values as the ones in Figure 19-3. In fact, if you run Listing 19-3 more than once, you (almost certainly) get different three-letter names, different ID numbers, and different account balances each time. That's what happens when a program generates values randomly.

The flow of control

Suppose that you're running the code in Listing 19-3. The computer reaches the `display` method call:

```
anAccount.display();
```

At that point, the computer starts running the code inside the display method. In other words, the computer jumps to the middle of the Account class's code (the code in Listing 19-1).

After executing the display method's code (that forest of print and println calls), the computer returns to the point where it departed from in Listing 19-3. That is, the computer goes back to the display method call and continues on from there.

When you run the code in Listing 19-3, the flow of action in each loop iteration isn't exactly from the top to the bottom. Instead, the action goes from the for loop to the display method and then back to the for loop. The whole business is pictured in Figure 19-4.

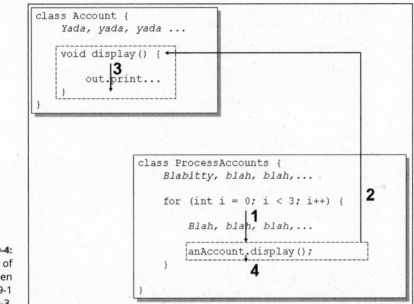

FIGURE 19-4: The flow of control between Listings 19-1 and 19-3.

Using punctuation

In Listing 19-3, notice the use of dots. To refer to the lastName stored in the anAccount object, you write

```
anAccount.lastName
```

To get the anAccount object to display itself, you write

```
anAccount.display();
```

That's great! When you refer to an object's field or call an object's method, the only difference is parentheses:

>> To refer to an object's field, you don't use parentheses.

>> To call an object's method, you use parentheses.

REMEMBER

When you call a method, you put parentheses after the method's name. You do this even if you have nothing to put inside the parentheses.

The versatile plus sign

The program in Listing 19-3 uses some cute tricks. In Java, you can do two different things with a plus sign:

>> **You can add numbers with a plus sign.**

For example, you can write

```
numberOfSheep = 2 + 5;
```

>> **You can *concatenate* strings with a plus sign.**

When you concatenate strings, you scrunch them together, one right after another. For example, the expression

```
"Barry" + " " + "Burd"
```

scrunches together Barry, a blank space, and Burd. The new scrunched-up string is (you guessed it) Barry Burd.

In Listing 19-3, the statement

```
anAccount.lastName = "" +
    (char) (myRandom.nextInt(26) + 'A') +
    (char) (myRandom.nextInt(26) + 'a') +
    (char) (myRandom.nextInt(26) + 'a');
```

has many plus signs, and some of the plus signs concatenate things together. The first thing is a mysterious empty string (""). This empty string is invisible, so it never gets in the way of your seeing the second, third, and fourth things.

Onto the empty string, the program concatenates a second thing. This second thing is the value of the expression (char) (myRandom.nextInt(26) + 'A'). The expression may look complicated, but it's really no big deal. This expression represents an uppercase letter (any uppercase letter, generated randomly).

GENERATING WORDS RANDOMLY

Most programs don't work correctly the first time you run them, and some programs don't work without extensive trial-and-error. This section's code is a case in point.

To write this section's code, I needed a way to generate three-letter words randomly. After about a dozen attempts, I got the code to work. But I didn't stop there. I kept working for a few hours looking for a *simple* way to generate three-letter words randomly. In the end, I settled on the following code (in Listing 19-3):

```
anAccount.lastName = "" +
    (char) (myRandom.nextInt(26) + 'A') +
    (char) (myRandom.nextInt(26) + 'a') +
    (char) (myRandom.nextInt(26) + 'a');
```

This code isn't simple, but it's not nearly as bad as my original working version. Anyway, here's how the code works:

- **Each call to** my Random.nextInt(26) **generates a number from 0 to 25.**

- **Adding** 'A' **gives you a number from 65 to 90.**

  To store a letter 'A', the computer puts the number 65 in its memory. That's why adding 'A' to 0 gives you 65 and why adding 'A' to 25 gives you 90. (For more information on letters being stored as numbers, see the discussion of Unicode characters at the end of Chapter 8.)

- **Applying** (char) **to a number turns the number into a** char **value.**

  To store the letters 'A' through 'Z', the computer puts the numbers 65 through 90 in its memory. So, applying (char) to a number from 65 to 90 turns the number into an uppercase letter. For more information about applying things like (char), see the discussion of casting in Chapter 7.

Pause for a brief summary. The expression (char) (myRandom.nextInt(26) + 'A') represents a randomly generated uppercase letter. In a similar way, (char) (myRandom.nextInt(26) + 'a') represents a randomly generated lowercase letter.

Watch out! The next couple of steps can be tricky:

- **Java doesn't allow you to assign a** char **value to a string variable.**

  In Listing 19-3, the following statement would lead to a compiler error:

```
//Bad statement:
anAccount.lastName = (char) (myRandom.nextInt(26) + 'A');
```

(continued)

(continued)

- **In Java, you can use a plus sign to add a** `char` **value to a string. When you do, the result is a string:**

  So, `"" + (char) (myRandom.nextInt(26) + 'A')` is a string containing one randomly generated uppercase character. And when you add `(char)` `(myRandom.nextInt(26) + 'a')` to the end of that string, you get another string — a string containing two randomly generated characters. Finally, when you add another `(char) (myRandom.nextInt(26) + 'a')` to the end of that string, you get a string containing three randomly generated characters. So you can assign that big string to `anAccount.lastName`. That's how the statement in Listing 19-3 works.

  When you write a program like the one in Listing 19-3, you have to be careful with numbers, `char` values, and strings. I don't do this kind of programming every day of the week — before I got this section's example to work, I had many false starts. That's okay. I'm very persistent.

Onto the empty string and the uppercase letter, the program concatenates a third thing. This third thing is the value of the expression `(char)` `(myRandom. nextInt(26) + 'a')`. This expression represents a lowercase letter (any lowercase letter, generated randomly.)

Onto all this stuff, the program concatenates another lowercase letter. So altogether, you have a randomly generated three-letter name. For more details, see the upcoming sidebar.

TECHNICAL STUFF

In Listing 19-3, the statement `anAccount.balance = myRandom.nextInt(10000)` assigns an `int` value to `balance`. But `balance` is a `double` variable, not an `int` variable. That's okay. In a rare case of permissiveness, Java allows you to assign an `int` value to a `double` variable. The result of the assignment is no big surprise. If you assign the `int` value 8734 to the `double` variable `balance`, the value of `balance` becomes 8734.00. The result is shown on the first line of Figure 19-3.

REMEMBER

Using the `double` type to store an amount of money is generally a bad idea. In this book, I use `double` to keep the examples as simple as possible. But the `int` type is better for money values, and the `BigDecimal` type is even better. For more details, see Chapter 7.

Let the Objects Do the Work

When I was a young object, I wasn't as smart as the objects you have nowadays. Consider, for example, the object in Listing 19-4. This object not only displays itself, but it can also fill itself with values.

LISTING 19-4: **A Class with Two Methods**

```java
import java.util.Random;
import java.text.NumberFormat;
import static java.lang.System.out;

class BetterAccount {
    String lastName;
    int id;
    double balance;

    void fillWithData() {
        Random myRandom = new Random();

        lastName = "" +
            (char) (myRandom.nextInt(26) + 'A') +
            (char) (myRandom.nextInt(26) + 'a') +
            (char) (myRandom.nextInt(26) + 'a');

        id = myRandom.nextInt(10000);
        balance = myRandom.nextInt(10000);
    }

    void display() {
        NumberFormat currency = NumberFormat.getCurrencyInstance();

        out.print("The account with last name ");
        out.print(lastName);
        out.print(" and ID number ");
        out.print(id);
        out.print(" has balance ");
        out.println(currency.format(balance));
    }
}
```

I wrote some code to use the class in Listing 19-4. This new code is in Listing 19-5.

LISTING 19-5: **This Is So Cool!**

```
class ProcessBetterAccounts {

    public static void main(String args[]) {

        BetterAccount anAccount;

        for (int i = 0; i < 3; i++) {
            anAccount = new BetterAccount();
            anAccount.fillWithData();
            anAccount.display();
        }
    }
}
```

Listing 19-5 is pretty slick. Because the code in Listing 19-4 is so darn smart, the new code in Listing 19-5 has very little work to do. This new code just creates a BetterAccount object and then calls the methods in Listing 19-4. When you run all this stuff, you get results like the ones in Figure 19-3.

Passing Values to Methods

Think about sending someone to the supermarket to buy bread. When you do this, you say, "Go to the supermarket and buy some bread." (Try it at home. You'll have a fresh loaf of bread in no time at all!) Of course, some other time, you send that same person to the supermarket to buy bananas. You say, "Go to the supermarket and buy some bananas." And what's the point of all of this? Well, you have a method, and you have some on-the-fly information that you pass to the method when you call it. The method is named "Go to the supermarket and buy some . . ." The on-the-fly information is either "bread" or "bananas," depending on your culinary needs. In Java, the method calls would look like this:

```
goToTheSupermarketAndBuySome(bread);
goToTheSupermarketAndBuySome(bananas);
```

The things in parentheses are called *parameters* or *parameter lists*. With parameters, your methods become much more versatile. Rather than get the same thing each time, you can send somebody to the supermarket to buy bread one time, bananas another time, and birdseed the third time. When you call your goToTheSupermarketAndBuySome method, you decide right there and then what you're going to ask your pal to buy.

These concepts are made more concrete in Listings 19-6 and 19-7.

LISTING 19-6: **Adding Interest**

```java
import java.text.NumberFormat;
import static java.lang.System.out;

class NiceAccount {
    String lastName;
    int id;
    double balance;

    void addInterest(double rate) {
        out.print("Adding ");
        out.print(rate);
        out.println(" percent...");

        balance += balance * (rate / 100.0);
    }

    void display() {
        NumberFormat currency = NumberFormat.getCurrencyInstance();

        out.print("The account with last name ");
        out.print(lastName);
        out.print(" and ID number ");
        out.print(id);
        out.print(" has balance ");
        out.println(currency.format(balance));
    }
}
```

LISTING 19-7: **Calling the addInterest Method**

```java
import java.util.Random;

class ProcessNiceAccounts {

    public static void main(String args[]) {
        Random myRandom = new Random();
        NiceAccount anAccount;
        double interestRate;
```

(continued)

LISTING 19-7: *(continued)*

```
    for (int i = 0; i < 3; i++) {
        anAccount = new NiceAccount();

        anAccount.lastName = "" +
            (char) (myRandom.nextInt(26) + 'A') +
            (char) (myRandom.nextInt(26) + 'a') +
            (char) (myRandom.nextInt(26) + 'a');
        anAccount.id = myRandom.nextInt(10000);
        anAccount.balance = myRandom.nextInt(10000);

        anAccount.display();

        interestRate = myRandom.nextInt(5);
        anAccount.addInterest(interestRate);

        anAccount.display();
        System.out.println();
    }
  }
}
```

In Listing 19-7, the line

```
anAccount.addInterest(interestRate);
```

plays the same role as the line goToTheSupermarketAndBuySome(bread) in my little supermarket example. The word addInterest is a method name, and the word interestRate in parentheses is a parameter. Taken as a whole, this statement tells the code in Listing 19-6 to execute its addInterest method. This statement also tells Listing 19-6 to use a certain number (whatever value is stored in the interestRate variable) in the method's calculations. The value of interestRate can be 1.0, 2.0, or whatever other value you get by calling myRandom. nextInt(5). In the same way, the goToTheSupermarketAndBuySome method works for bread, bananas, or whatever else you need from the market.

The next section has a detailed description of addInterest and its action. In the meantime, a run of the code in Listings 19-6 and 19-7 is shown in Figure 19-5.

REMEMBER

Java has strict rules about the use of types. For example, you can't assign a double value (like 3.14) to an int variable. (The compiler simply refuses to chop off the .14 part. You get an error message. So what else is new?) But Java isn't completely unreasonable about the use of types. Java allows you to assign an int value (like myRandom.nextInt(5)) to a double variable (like interestRate). If you assign the int value 2 to the double variable interestRate, then the value of interestRate becomes 2.0. The result is shown on the second line of Figure 19-5.

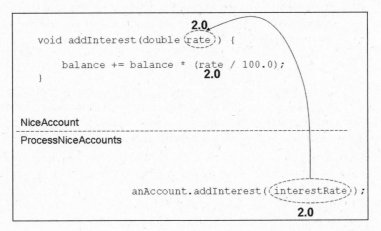

FIGURE 19-5:
Running the code
in Listing 19-7.

```
Console ☒    Search  Progress  Properties              ✖ ✖  
<terminated> ProcessNiceAccounts [Java Application] C:\Program Files\Java\jre7\bin\javaw.exe (
The account with last name Cbj and ID number 6151 has balance $8,983.00
Adding 2.0 percent...
The account with last name Cbj and ID number 6151 has balance $9,162.66

The account with last name Bry and ID number 529 has balance $3,756.00
Adding 0.0 percent...
The account with last name Bry and ID number 529 has balance $3,756.00

The account with last name Dco and ID number 2162 has balance $8,474.00
Adding 3.0 percent...
The account with last name Dco and ID number 2162 has balance $8,728.22
```

Handing off a value

When you call a method, you can pass information to that method on the fly. This information is in the method's parameter list. Listing 19-7 has a call to the addInterest method:

```
anAccount.addInterest(interestRate);
```

The first time through the loop, the value of interestRate is 2.0. (Remember, I'm using the data in Figure 19-5.) At that point in the program's run, the method call behaves as though it's the following statement:

```
anAccount.addInterest(2.0);
```

The computer is about to run the code inside the addInterest method (a method in Listing 19-6). But first, the computer *passes* the value 2.0 to the parameter in the addInterest method's header. Inside the addInterest method, the value of rate becomes 2.0. For an illustration of this idea, see Figure 19-6.

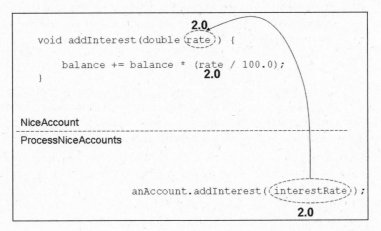

FIGURE 19-6:
Passing a value to
a method's
parameter.

```
                              2.0
    void addInterest(double (rate)) {

         balance += balance * (rate / 100.0);
    }                          2.0

NiceAccount
- - - - - - - - - - - - - - - - - - - - - - - - - - -
ProcessNiceAccounts



            anAccount.addInterest((interestRate));
                                   2.0
```

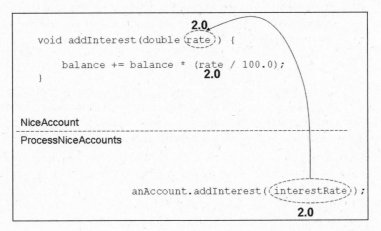

CHAPTER 19 **Creating New Java Methods** 445

Here's something interesting. The parameter in the addInterest method's header is rate. But, inside the ProcessNiceAccounts class, the parameter in the method call is interestRate. That's okay. In fact, it's standard practice.

In Listings 19-6 and 19-7, the names of the parameters don't have to be the same. The only thing that matters is that both parameters (rate and interestRate) have the same type. In Listings 19-6 and 19-7, both of these parameters are of type double. So everything is fine.

Inside the addInterest method, the += assignment operator adds balance * (rate / 100.0) to the existing balance value. For some info about the += assignment operator, see Chapter 7.

Working with a method header

In the next few bullets, I make some observations about the addInterest method header (in Listing 19-6):

>> **The word** void **tells the computer that when the** addInterest **method is called, the** addInterest **method doesn't send a value back to the place that called it.**

   The next section has an example in which a method sends a value back.

>> **The word** addInterest **is the method's name.**

   That's the name you use to call the method when you're writing the code for the ProcessNiceAccounts class. (See Listing 19-7.)

>> **The parentheses in the header contain placeholders for all the things you're going to pass to the method when you call it.**

   When you call a method, you can pass information to that method on the fly. This information is the method's parameter list. The addInterest method's header says that the addInterest method takes one piece of information, and that piece of information must be of type double:

   ```
   void addInterest(double rate)
   ```

   Sure enough, if you look at the call to addInterest (down in the ProcessNiceAccounts class's main method), that call has the variable interestRate in it. And interestRate is of type double. When I call addInterest, I'm giving the method a value of type double.

How the method uses the object's values

The addInterest method in Listing 19-6 is called three times from the main method in Listing 19-7. The actual account balances and interest rates are different each time:

> ≫ **In the first call of Figure 19-5, the balance is 8983.00, and the interest rate is 2.0.**
>
> When this call is made, the expression balance * (rate / 100.0) stands for 8983.00 * (2.0 / 100.00). See Figure 19-7.

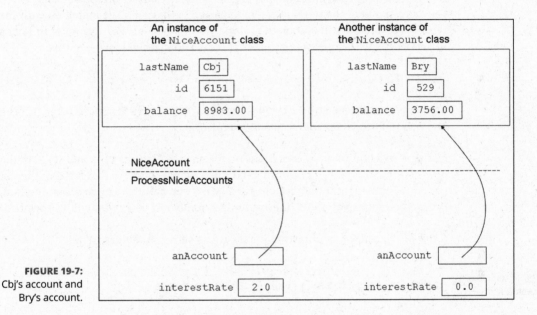

FIGURE 19-7:
Cbj's account and
Bry's account.

> ≫ **In the second call of Figure 19-5, the balance is 3756.00, and the interest rate is 0.0.**
>
> When the call is made, the expression balance * (rate / 100.0) stands for 3756.00 * (0.0 / 100.00). Again, see Figure 19-7.
>
> ≫ **In the third call of Figure 19-5, the balance is 8474.00, and the interest rate is 3.0.**
>
> When the addInterest call is made, the expression balance * (rate / 100.0) stands for 8474.00 * (3.0 / 100.00).

Passing more than one parameter

Take a look at Listings 19-6 and 19-7. In those listings, the `display` method has no parameters and the `addInterest` method has one parameter. Now consider the following code from Chapter 11:

```
char letterGrade;
letterGrade = keyboard.findWithinHorizon(".",0).charAt(0);
```

In that code, the `findWithinHorizon` method call has two parameters: the `String` parameter `"."` and the `int` parameter `0`. That's not unusual. You can create methods with as many parameters as you like. The only restriction is this: When you call a method, the types of the parameters in the call must match up with the types of parameters in the method declaration's header. For example, in Java's API code, the first line of the `findWithinHorizon` method looks like this:

```
public String findWithinHorizon(String pattern, int horizon) {
```

And, in the method call `findWithinHorizon(".",0)`, the first parameter `"."` is a `String`, and the second parameter `0` is an `int`.

Listings 19-8 and 19-9 are variations on the code in Listings 19-6 and 19-7. In the new listings, the `addInterest` method has two parameters: one for the interest rate and another for a number of years. When you call the `addInterest` method, the method repeatedly adds interest for the number of years that you've specified.

A run of the code in Listings 19-8 and 19-9 is shown in Figure 19-8.

LISTING 19-8: **Adding Interest for a Certain Number of Years**

```
import java.text.NumberFormat;
import static java.lang.System.out;

class NiceAccount {
    String lastName;
    int id;
    double balance;

    void addInterest(double rate, int howManyYears) {
        for (int i = 1; i <= howManyYears; i++) {
            out.print("Adding ");
            out.print(rate);
            out.println(" percent...");

            balance += balance * (rate / 100.0);
        }
    }
```

```
        void display() {
            NumberFormat currency = NumberFormat.getCurrencyInstance();

            out.print("The account with last name ");
            out.print(lastName);
            out.print(" and ID number ");
            out.print(id);
            out.print(" has balance ");
            out.println(currency.format(balance));
        }
    }
```

LISTING 19-9: **Calling the Beefed-Up addInterest Method**

```
import java.util.Random;

class ProcessNiceAccounts {

    public static void main(String args[]) {
        Random myRandom = new Random();
        NiceAccount anAccount;
        double interestRate;

        for (int i = 0; i < 3; i++) {
            anAccount = new NiceAccount();

            anAccount.lastName = "" +
                (char) (myRandom.nextInt(26) + 'A') +
                (char) (myRandom.nextInt(26) + 'a') +
                (char) (myRandom.nextInt(26) + 'a');
            anAccount.id = myRandom.nextInt(10000);
            anAccount.balance = myRandom.nextInt(10000);

            anAccount.display();

            interestRate = myRandom.nextInt(5);
            anAccount.addInterest(interestRate, 3);

            anAccount.display();
            System.out.println();
        }
    }
}
```

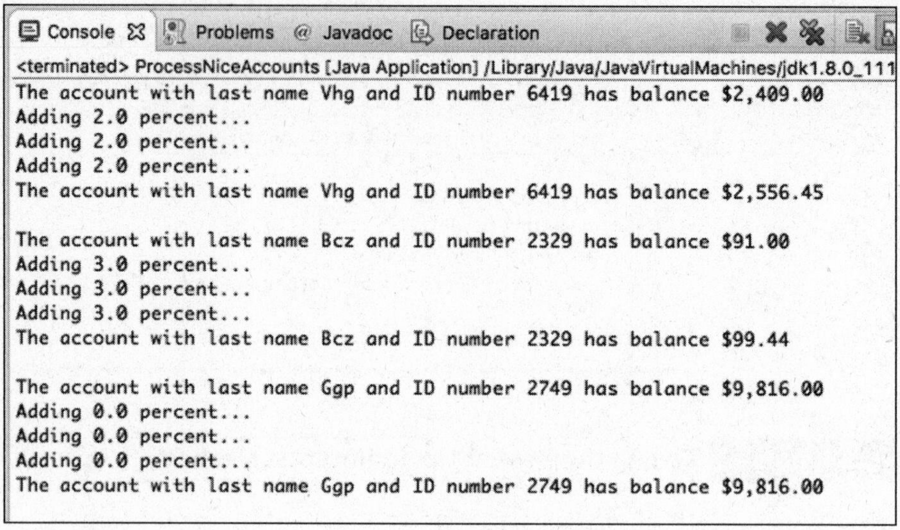

FIGURE 19-8:
Running the code
in Listing 19-9.

The console output shows:

```
Console ⊠  Problems  @ Javadoc  Declaration                    ✖ ✖ ▣ ▣
<terminated> ProcessNiceAccounts [Java Application] /Library/Java/JavaVirtualMachines/jdk1.8.0_111
The account with last name Vhg and ID number 6419 has balance $2,409.00
Adding 2.0 percent...
Adding 2.0 percent...
Adding 2.0 percent...
The account with last name Vhg and ID number 6419 has balance $2,556.45

The account with last name Bcz and ID number 2329 has balance $91.00
Adding 3.0 percent...
Adding 3.0 percent...
Adding 3.0 percent...
The account with last name Bcz and ID number 2329 has balance $99.44

The account with last name Ggp and ID number 2749 has balance $9,816.00
Adding 0.0 percent...
Adding 0.0 percent...
Adding 0.0 percent...
The account with last name Ggp and ID number 2749 has balance $9,816.00
```

Getting a Value from a Method

Say that you're sending a friend to buy groceries. You make requests for groceries in the form of method calls. You issue calls such as

```
goToTheSupermarketAndBuySome(bread);
goToTheSupermarketAndBuySome(bananas);
```

The things in parentheses are parameters. Each time you call your goToThe SupermarketAndBuySome method, you put a different value in the method's parameter list.

Now what happens when your friend returns from the supermarket? "Here's the bread you asked me to buy," says your friend. As a result of carrying out your wishes, your friend returns something to you. You made a method call, and the method returns information (or better yet, the method returns some food).

The thing returned to you is called the method's *return value,* and the type of thing returned to you is called the method's *return type.*

An example

To see how return values and a return types work in a real Java program, check out the code in Listings 19-10 and 19-11.

LISTING 19-10: **A Method That Returns a Value**

```
import java.text.NumberFormat;
import static java.lang.System.out;

class GoodAccount {
    String lastName;
    int id;
    double balance;

    double getInterest(double rate) {
        double interest;

        out.print("Adding ");
        out.print(rate);
        out.println(" percent...");

        interest = balance * (rate / 100.0);
        return interest;
    }

    void display() {
        NumberFormat currency = NumberFormat.getCurrencyInstance();

        out.print("The account with last name ");
        out.print(lastName);
        out.print(" and ID number ");
        out.print(id);
        out.print(" has balance ");
        out.println(currency.format(balance));
    }
}
```

LISTING 19-11: **Calling the Method in Listing 19-10**

```
import java.util.Random;
import java.text.NumberFormat;

class ProcessGoodAccounts {

    public static void main(String args[]) {
        Random myRandom = new Random();
        NumberFormat currency = NumberFormat.getCurrencyInstance();
        GoodAccount anAccount;
        double interestRate;
        double yearlyInterest;
```

(continued)

LISTING 19-11: *(continued)*

```
        for (int i = 0; i < 3; i++) {
            anAccount = new GoodAccount();

            anAccount.lastName = "" +
                (char) (myRandom.nextInt(26) + 'A') +
                (char) (myRandom.nextInt(26) + 'a') +
                (char) (myRandom.nextInt(26) + 'a');
            anAccount.id = myRandom.nextInt(10000);
            anAccount.balance = myRandom.nextInt(10000);

            anAccount.display();

            interestRate = myRandom.nextInt(5);
            yearlyInterest = anAccount.getInterest(interestRate);

            System.out.print("This year's interest is ");
            System.out.println(currency.format(yearlyInterest));
            System.out.println();
        }
    }
}
```

To see a run of code from Listings 19-10 and 19-11, take a look at Figure 19-9.

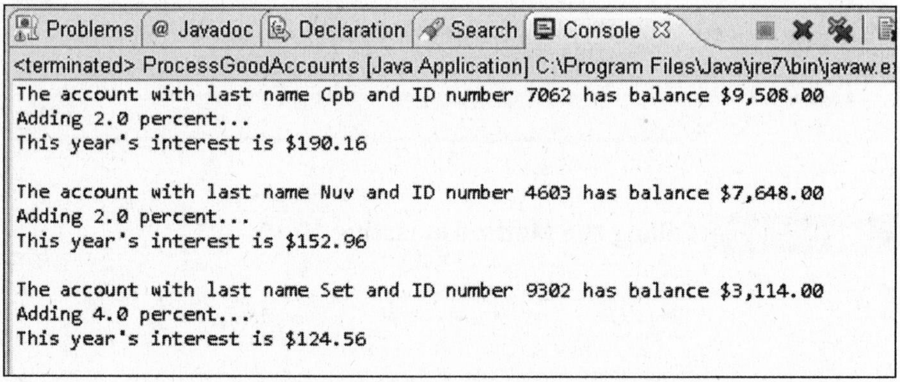

FIGURE 19-9:
Running the code
in Listing 19-11.

```
Problems  @ Javadoc  Declaration  Search  Console ☒        ■ ✖ ✖ 
<terminated> ProcessGoodAccounts [Java Application] C:\Program Files\Java\jre7\bin\javaw.e
The account with last name Cpb and ID number 7062 has balance $9,508.00
Adding 2.0 percent...
This year's interest is $190.16

The account with last name Nuv and ID number 4603 has balance $7,648.00
Adding 2.0 percent...
This year's interest is $152.96

The account with last name Set and ID number 9302 has balance $3,114.00
Adding 4.0 percent...
This year's interest is $124.56
```

How return types and return values work

I want to trace a piece of the action in Listings 19-10 and 19-11. For input data, I use the first set of values in Figure 19-9.

Here's what happens when `getInterest` is called (you can follow along in Figure 19-10):

≫ The value of `balance` is `9508.00`, and the value of `rate` is `2.0`. So the value of `balance * (rate / 100.0)` is `190.16` — one hundred ninety dollars and sixteen cents.

≫ The value `190.16` gets assigned to the `interest` variable, so the statement

```
return interest;
```

has the same effect as

```
return 190.16;
```

≫ The `return` statement sends this value `190.16` back to the code that called the method. *At that point in the process, the entire method call in Listing 19-11 —* `anAccount.getInterest(interestRate)` *— takes on the value* `190.16`.

≫ Finally, the value `190.16` gets assigned to the variable `yearlyInterest`.

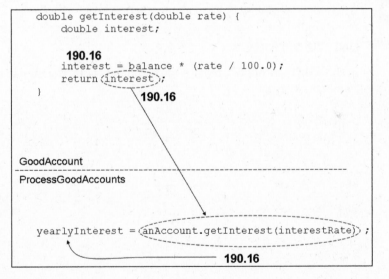

FIGURE 19-10:
A method call is
an expression
with a value.

REMEMBER

If a method returns anything, a call to the method is an expression with a value. That value can be printed, assigned to a variable, added to something else, or whatever. Anything you can do with any other kind of value, you can do with a method call.

Working with the method header (again)

When you create a method or a method call, you have to be careful to use Java's types consistently. Make sure that you check for the following:

>> In Listing 19-10, the getInterest method's header starts with the word double. When the method is executed, it should send a double value back to the place that called it.

>> Again in Listing 19-10, the last statement in the getInterest method is return interest. The method returns whatever value is stored in the interest variable, and the interest variable has type double. So far, so good.

>> In Listing 19-11, the value returned by the call to getInterest is assigned to a variable named yearlyInterest. Sure enough, yearlyInterest is of type double.

That settles it! The use of types in the handling of method getInterest is consistent in Listings 19-10 and 19-11. I'm thrilled!

Write a few programs to learn about creating Java methods.

TRY IT OUT

ONE, TWO, THREE

In the code that follows, replace the comments with statements that do what the comments suggest:

```java
class Counter {
    int count = 0;

    void increment() {
        // Add 1 to the value of count
    }
}


public class Main {

    public static void main(String[] args) {
        Counter counter = new Counter();

        // Call the counter object's increment method

        System.out.println(counter.count);
    }
}
```

TWO, SEVEN, NINETEEN

Modify the code in the previous "One, two, three" paragraph so that

» The increment method has a parameter, and

» The main method calls increment several times, each time with a different parameter value.

The increment method uses its parameter to decide how much to increase the count value.

PROCESS PURCHASES

At the end of Chapter 17, I complain about the repetitive code in Listing 17-5. When you see repetitive code, you can think about creating a method. You replace each repetition with a call to that method. The code's logic lives in one place (the method declaration), and the method calls repeatedly refer to that place. Et voilà! The repetition problem is solved!

Modify the code in Chapter 17 as follows:

» Add a getTotal method to the Purchase class code in Listing 17-2. The getTotal method takes no parameters and returns a double value.

» Replace the repetitive code in Listing 17-5 with two getTotal method calls.

More specifically,

» The getTotal method declares its own total variable.

» The getTotal method multiplies the Purchase object's unitPrice by the object's quantity and assigns the result to the total variable.

» Depending on the object's taxable value, the getTotal method either increases or doesn't increase the total variable's value.

» The getTotal method returns the value of the total variable.

HAS YOUR BMI CHANGED SINCE CHAPTER 17?

In the "What's your BMI?" experiment at the end of Chapter 17, you create a Person class, and your main method calculates a Person object's body mass index (BMI). Improve on that code so that the Person class contains its own getBmi method. The getBmi method calculates the Person object's body mass index from the values of the object's own weight and height fields.

In a separate class, the main method creates three Person objects, assigns values to each Person object's weight and height fields, and calls each Person object's getBmi method.

TWO TIMES NOTHING IS STILL NOTHING

In the "Nothing in particular" experiment at the end of Chapter 17, you create a Thing class, and your main method displays a sentence about a Thing object. Improve on that code so that the Thing class contains its own display method. The display method prints a Thing object's sentence based on the values of object's own value1 and value2 fields.

In a separate class, the main method creates three Thing objects, assigns values to each Thing object's value1 and value2 fields, and calls each Thing object's display method.

MORE MACROECONOMICS

In the "Bit of macroeconomics" experiment at the end of Chapter 17, you create a Country class. Your main method asks the user for an acceptable debt-to-GDP ratio and reports That's acceptable or That's not acceptable after comparing a country's ratio to the acceptable ratio.

Improve on that code so that the Country class contains its own hasAcceptable Ratio method. The hasAcceptableRatio method has one double parameter. That parameter represents the debt-to-GDP ratio that the user has signified is acceptable. The hasAcceptableRatio method calculates the Country object's debt-to-GDP ratio from the values of object's own debt and gdp fields. The hasAcceptableRatio method returns a boolean value: true if the Country object's ratio is acceptable and false otherwise.

In a separate class, the main method creates three Country objects, assigns values to each Country object's debt and gdp fields, and calls each Country object's hasAcceptableRatio method.

Chapter **20**

Oooey GUI Was a Worm

There's a wonderful old joke about a circus acrobat jumping over mice. Unfortunately, I'd get sued for copyright infringement if I included the joke in this book.

Anyway, the joke is about starting small and working your way up to bigger things. That's what you do when you read *Beginning Programming with Java For Dummies*, 5th Edition.

Most of the programs in this book are text-based. A *text-based* program has no windows, no dialog boxes — nothing of that kind. With a text-based program, the user types characters in the Console view, and the program displays output in the same Console view.

These days, very few publicly available programs are text-based. Almost all programs use a *GUI* — a *g*raphical *u*ser *i*nterface. So if you've read every word of this book so far, you're probably saying to yourself, "When am I going to find out how to create a GUI?"

Well, now's the time! This chapter introduces you to the world of GUI programming in Java.

 You can see GUI versions of many examples from this book by visiting the book's website (http://allmycode.com/BeginProg).

The Java Swing Classes

Java's *Swing* classes create graphical objects on a computer screen. The objects can include buttons, icons, text fields, check boxes, and other good things that make windows so useful.

The name Swing isn't an acronym. When the stewards of the Java programming language were first creating the code for these classes, one of the developers named it Swing because swing music was enjoying a nostalgic revival. And yes, in addition to `String` and `Swing`, the standard Java API has a `Spring` class and a Spring Framework. But that's another story.

Actually, Java's API has several sets of windowing components. For details, see the nearby "Java GUIs" sidebar.

JAVA GUIs

Java comes with three sets of classes for creating GUI applications:

- **The Abstract Window Toolkit (AWT):** The original set of classes, dating back to JDK 1.0.

  Classes in this set belong to packages whose names begin with `java.awt`. Components in this set have names like `Button`, `TextField`, `Frame`, and so on.

  Each component in an AWT program has a *peer* — a companion component that belongs to the computer's own operating system. For example, when you create an AWT `Button`, a Mac computer creates its own kind of button to be displayed on the user's screen. When the same program runs on a Windows computer, the Windows computer creates a different kind of button (a Windows button) to display on the computer's screen. The Java code in the AWT interacts with the Mac or Windows button, adding additional functionality where functionality is needed.

  The AWT implements only the kinds of components that were available on all common operating systems in the mid-1990s. So, using AWT, you can add a button to your application, but you can't easily add a table or a tree.

- **Java Swing:** A set of classes created to fix some of the difficulties posed by the use of the AWT. Swing was introduced in J2SE 1.2.

  Classes in this set belong to packages whose names begin with `javax.swing`. Components in this set have names like `JButton`, `JTextField`, `JFrame`, and so on.

  Unlike an old AWT component, a Swing component has no peer. When you create a `JButton` in your Java program, the computer's operating system doesn't create a button of its own. Instead, the JButton that you see is a pure Java object. Java's visual rendering code draws this object on a window. This is both good news and bad news. The good news is, a Swing program looks the same on every operating system. In a Swing program, you can create table components and tree components because Java simply draws them in the computer's window. The bad news is, Swing components aren't pretty. A JButton looks primitive and crude compared to a Mac button or a Windows button.

Java's Swing classes replace some (but not all) of the classes in the older AWT. To use some of the Swing classes, you have to call on some of the old AWT classes.

- **JavaFX:** The newest set of GUI classes in Oracle standard Java. JavaFX comes with new(er) versions of Java 7 and with all later versions of Java.

  Classes in this set belong to packages whose names begin with javafx.

  JavaFX supports over 60 kinds of components. (Sure, you want a Button component. But do you also want an Accordion component? JavaFX has one.) In addition, JavaFX supports multitouch operations and takes advantage of each processor's specialized graphics capabilities.

  For more information about JavaFX, see this chapter's "Code Soup: Mixing XML with Java" section.

Showing an image on the screen

The program in Listing 20-1 displays a window on your computer screen. To see the window, look at Figure 20-1.

The code in Listing 20-1 has very little logic of its own. Instead, this code pulls together a bunch of classes from the Java API.

LISTING 20-1: **Creating a Window with an Image in It**

```java
import javax.swing.JFrame;
import javax.swing.ImageIcon;
import javax.swing.JLabel;

class ShowPicture {

    public static void main(String args[]) {
        JFrame frame = new JFrame();
        ImageIcon icon = new ImageIcon("androidBook.jpg");
        JLabel label = new JLabel(icon);
```

(continued)

LISTING 20-1: *(continued)*

```
        frame.add(label);
        frame.setDefaultCloseOperation(JFrame.EXIT_ON_CLOSE);
        frame.pack();
        frame.setVisible(true);
    }
}
```

Over in Listing 17-3 (in Chapter 17), I created an instance of the `Purchase` class with the line

```
Purchase onePurchase = new Purchase();
```

FIGURE 20-1:
What a nice
window!

In Listing 20-1, I do the same kind of thing — I create instances of the `JFrame`, `ImageIcon`, and `JLabel` classes with the following lines:

```
JFrame frame = new JFrame();
ImageIcon icon = new ImageIcon("androidBook.jpg");
JLabel label = new JLabel(icon);
```

Here's some gossip about each of these lines:

» A JFrame is like a window (except that it's called a JFrame, not a window). In Listing 20-1, the line

```
JFrame frame = new JFrame();
```

creates a JFrame object, but this line doesn't display the JFrame object anywhere. (The displaying comes later in the code.)

» An ImageIcon object is a picture. At the root of the program's project directory, I have a file named androidBook.jpg. That file contains the picture shown in Figure 20-1. So, in Listing 20-1, the line

```
ImageIcon icon = new ImageIcon("androidBook.jpg");
```

creates an ImageIcon object — an icon containing the androidBook.jpg picture.

REMEMBER

For some reason that I'll never understand, you may not want to use my androidBook.jpg image file when you run Listing 20-1. You can use almost any .gif, .jpg, or .png file in place of my (lovely) Android book cover image. To do so, drag your own image file to Eclipse's Package Explorer. (Drag it to the root of this example's project folder.) Then, in Eclipse's editor, change the name androidBook.jpg to your own image file's name. That's it!

» I need a place to put the icon. I can put it on something called a JLabel. So, in Listing 20-1, the line

```
JLabel label = new JLabel(icon);
```

creates a JLabel object and puts the androidBook.jpg icon on the new label's face.

If you read the previous bullets, you may get a false impression. The wording may suggest that the use of each component (JFrame, ImageIcon, JLabel, and so on) is a logical extension of what you already know. "Where do you put an ImageIcon? Well, of course, you put it on a JLabel." When you've worked long and hard with Java's Swing components, all these things become natural to you. But until then, you look everything up in Java's API documentation.

REMEMBER

You never need to memorize the names or features of Java's API classes. Instead, you keep Java's API documentation handy. When you need to know about a class, you look it up in the documentation. If you need a certain class often enough, you'll remember its features. For classes that you don't use often, you always have the docs.

For tips on using Java's API documentation, see my article "Making Sense of Java's API Documentation," at www.dummies.com/programming/java/making-sense-of-javas-api-documentation.

Just another class

What is a JFrame? Like any other class, a JFrame has several parts. For a simplified view of some of these parts, see Figure 20-2.

Like the String in Figure 18-6 (in Chapter 18), the JFrame class has both fields and methods. The fields include the frame's height and width. The methods include add, setDefaultCloseOperation, pack, and setVisible. All told, the JFrame class has about 320 methods.

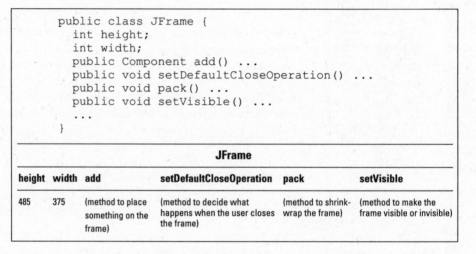

```
public class JFrame {
    int height;
    int width;
    public Component add() ...
    public void setDefaultCloseOperation() ...
    public void pack() ...
    public void setVisible() ...
    ...
}
```

JFrame					
height	width	add	setDefaultCloseOperation	pack	setVisible
485	375	(method to place something on the frame)	(method to decide what happens when the user closes the frame)	(method to shrink-wrap the frame)	(method to make the frame visible or invisible)

FIGURE 20-2: A simplified depiction of the JFrame class.

For technical reasons too burdensome for this book, you can't use dots to refer to a frame's height or width. But you can call many JFrame methods with those infamous dots. In Listing 20-1, I call the frame's methods by writing add(label), frame.setDefaultCloseOperation(JFrame.EXIT_ON_CLOSE), frame.pack(), and frame.setVisible(true).

Here's the scoop on the JFrame methods in Listing 20-1:

>> The call frame.add(label) plops the label onto the frame. The label displays my androidBook.jpg picture, so this call makes the picture appear on the frame.

» A call to frame.setDefaultCloseOperation tells Java what to do when you try to close the frame. (In Windows, you click the X in the upper-right corner, by the title bar. On a Mac, the X is in the frame's upper-left corner.) For a frame that's part of a larger application, you may want the frame to disappear when you click the X, but you probably don't want the application to stop running.

But in Listing 20-1, the frame is the entire application — the whole enchilada. When you click the X, you want the Java Virtual Machine to shut itself down. To make this happen, you call the setDefaultCloseOperation method with parameter JFrame.EXIT_ON_CLOSE. The other alternatives are as follows:

- JFrame.HIDE_ON_CLOSE: The frame disappears, but it still exists in the computer's memory.

- JFrame.DISPOSE_ON_CLOSE: The frame disappears and no longer exists in the computer's memory.

- JFrame.DO_NOTHING_ON_CLOSE: The frame still appears, still exists, and still does everything it did before you clicked the X. Nothing happens when you click X. So, with this DO_NOTHING_ON_CLOSE option, you can become quite confused.

WARNING

If you don't call setDefaultCloseOperation, Java automatically chooses the HIDE_ON_CLOSE option. When you click the X, the frame disappears, but the Java program keeps running. Of course, with no visible frame, the running of Listing 20-1 doesn't do much. The only noticeable effect of the run is your development environment's behavior. With Eclipse, the little square on the Console view's toolbar retains its bright red color. When you hover over the square, you see the Terminate tooltip. To end the Java program's run (and to return the square to its washed-out reddish-gray hue), simply click this little square.

» A frame's pack method shrink-wraps the frame around whatever has been added to the frame. Without calling pack, the frame can be much bigger or much smaller than is necessary.

Unfortunately, the default is to make a frame much smaller than necessary. If, in Listing 20-1, you forget to call frame.pack, you get the tiny frame shown in Figure 20-3. Sure, you can enlarge the frame by dragging the frame's edges with the mouse. But why should you have to do that? Just call frame.pack instead.

FIGURE 20-3:
A frame that hasn't been packed.

>> Calling setVisible(true) makes the frame appear on your screen. If you forget to call setVisible(true) (and I often do), when you run the code in Listing 20-1, you'll see nothing on your screen. It's always disconcerting until you figure out what you did wrong.

Constructor calls

In Listing 17-3 (in Chapter 17), I created an instance of the Purchase class with the line

```
Purchase onePurchase = new Purchase();
```

The code in Listing 20-1 does the same kind of thing. In Listing 20-1, I create an instance of the JFrame class with the following line:

```
JFrame frame = new JFrame();
```

Compare Figure 17-4 (in Chapter 17) with this chapter's Figure 20-4.

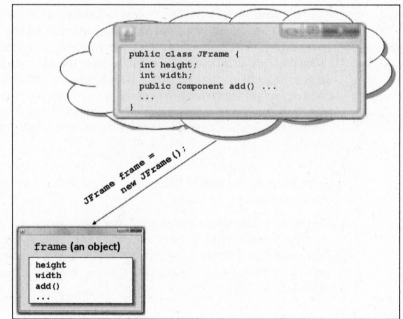

FIGURE 20-4:
An object created from the JFrame class.

In both figures, a new *SomethingOrOther( )* call creates an object from an existing class:

>> **In Chapter 17, I create an instance of my** Purchase **class.**

This object represents an actual purchase (with a purchase amount, a tax, and so on).

>> **In this chapter, I create an instance of the** JFrame **class.**

This object represents a frame on the computer screen (a frame with borders, a Minimize button, and so on). In a more complicated application — an app that displays several frames — the code might create several objects from a class such as JFrame. (See Figure 20-5.)

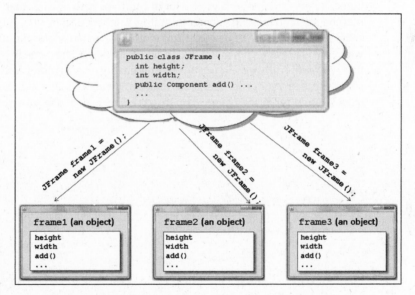

FIGURE 20-5:
Creating three
objects from the
JFrame class.

In Listing 20-1, the lines

```
JFrame frame = new JFrame();
ImageIcon icon = new ImageIcon("androidBook.jpg");
JLabel label = new JLabel(icon);
```

look as though they contain method calls. After all, a method call consists of a name followed by parentheses. You might put some parameters between the open and close parentheses. The expression keyboard.nextLine() is a call to a method named nextLine. So, in Listing 20-1, is JFrame() a call to a method named JFrame? No, it's not.

In the expression new JFrame(), Java's new keyword signals a call to a constructor. A constructor is like a method, except that a constructor's name is the same as the name of a Java class. Java's standard API contains classes named JFrame, ImageIcon, and JLabel, and the code in Listing 20-1 calls the JFrame, ImageIcon, and JLabel constructors.

As the terminology suggests, a *constructor* is a piece of code that constructs an object. So, in Listing 20-1, when you call

```
JFrame frame = new JFrame();
```

you make a frame variable refer to a newly constructed object (an object constructed from the JFrame class).

Constructors and methods have a lot in common with one another. You can't call a method without having a corresponding method declaration somewhere in the code. (In the case of Java's nextLine method, the method declaration lives somewhere inside Java's enormous bunch of API classes.) The same is true of constructors. You can't call new JFrame() without having a constructor for the JFrame class somewhere in your code. And, sure enough, inside the Java API class, you can find a declaration for the JFrame() constructor. The code looks something like this:

```
public class JFrame {
    int height;
    int width;
    public Component add() ...
    public void setDefaultCloseOperation() ...
    public void pack() ...
    public void setVisible() ...
    ...

    /**
     * Constructs a new frame that is initially invisible.
     */
    public JFrame() {
        ...
    }
    ...
}
```

The constructor declaration looks almost like a method declaration. But notice that the constructor declaration doesn't start with public void JFrame() or with public double JFrame() or with public *anything* JFrame(). Aside from the optional word public, a constructor declaration contains only the name of the class whose object is being constructed. More on this in the next section.

The Swing Classes: Round 2

In your Java-related travels, you'll see several variations on the code in Listing 20-1. This section explores one such variation.

This section's example does exactly what the previous section's example does. The only difference is the way the two examples deal with the JFrame class. This section's code is in Listing 20-2.

LISTING 20-2: **Extending Java's JFrame Class**

```java
import javax.swing.ImageIcon;
import javax.swing.JFrame;
import javax.swing.JLabel;

class ShowPicture {

  public static void main(String args[]) {
    new MyFrame();
  }
}

class MyFrame extends JFrame {

  MyFrame() {
    ImageIcon icon = new ImageIcon("androidBook.jpg");
    JLabel label = new JLabel(icon);
    add(label);
    setDefaultCloseOperation(JFrame.EXIT_ON_CLOSE);
    pack();
    setVisible(true);
  }
}
```

TECHNICAL STUFF

When you view Listing 20-2 in the Eclipse editor, you see a little yellow marker. A yellow marker represents a warning rather than an error, so you can ignore the warning and still run your code. If you hover over the marker, you see a tip about something called a serialVersionUID. A *serialVersionUID* is a number that helps Java avoid version conflicts when you send different copies of an object from one place to another. You can get rid of the warning by applying one of Eclipse's quick fixes, but if you're not fussy, don't bother with these quick fixes.

For information about Eclipse's Quick Fix feature, refer to Chapter 5.

**CROSS
REFERENCE**

Extending a class

In Listing 20-2, the words extends JFrame are particularly important. When you see Java's extends keyword, imagine replacing that keyword with the phrase *is a kind of*:

```
public class MyFrame is a kind of JFrame {
```

When you type MyFrame extends JFrame, you declare that your new MyFrame class has the fields and methods that are built into Java's own JFrame class, and possibly more. For example, a JFrame instance has setDefaultCloseOperation, pack, and setVisible methods, so every new MyFrame instance has setDefault-CloseOperation, pack, and setVisible methods (see Figure 20-6).

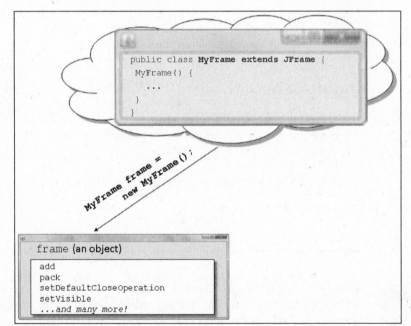

```
public class MyFrame extends JFrame {
  MyFrame() {
    ...
  }
}
```

MyFrame frame =
new MyFrame();

frame (an object)

add
pack
setDefaultCloseOperation
setVisible
...and many more!

FIGURE 20-6:
A MyFrame
instance has
many methods.

When you put the words extends JFrame in your code, you get the JFrame methods for free. The MyFrame class's code doesn't need declarations for methods, such as setDefaultCloseOperation, pack, and setVisible. Those declarations are already in the JFrame class in Java's API. The only declarations in the MyFrame class's code are for brand-new things — things that are specific to your newly declared `MyFrame` class. It's as though Listing 20-2 contained the following information:

```
public class MyFrame is a kind of JFrame {

  And in addition what's in JFrame, MyFrame also has a brand new constructor:
    public MyFrame() {
        // Etc.
    }
}
```

In Listing 20-2, the words `new MyFrame()` get the `MyFrame` constructor to do its work. And the constructor in Listing 20-2 does quite a bit of work! The constructor does the stuff that the `main` method does in Listing 20-1:

» The constructor creates an `ImageIcon` containing the `androidBook.jpg` picture.

» The constructor creates a `JLabel` object and puts the `androidBook.jpg` icon on the new label's face.

» The constructor adds the `JLabel` object.

Time out! What's being added to what? In Listing 20-1, the statement

```
frame.add(label);
```

adds the `JLabel` object to the `frame`. But in Listing 20-2, there's no `frame` variable. In Listing 20-2, all you have is

```
add(label);
```

Well, here's the good news: Inside a constructor declaration, the object that you're constructing is "a given." You don't name that new object in order to refer to that new object. It's as though the constructor's code looked like this:

```
MyFrame() {
    ImageIcon icon = new ImageIcon("androidBook.jpg");
    JLabel label = new JLabel(icon);
    new_frame_that_is_being_constructed.add(label);
    new_frame_that_is_being_constructed.setDefaultCloseOperation
                                        (JFrame.EXIT_ON_CLOSE);
    new_frame_that_is_being_constructed.pack();
    new_frame_that_is_being_constructed.setVisible(true);
}
```

Here's how the constructor in Listing 20-2 finishes its work:

>> The constructor adds the JLabel object to the MyFrame object that's being constructed.

>> The constructor tells the Java Virtual Machine to shut itself down when you close the frame.

>> The constructor shrink-wraps the frame around the image that appears on the frame.

>> The constructor makes the frame appear on your screen.

The extends keyword adds a fundamental idea to Java programming — the notion of *inheritance*. In Listing 20-2, the newly created MyFrame class *inherits* fields and methods that are declared in the existing JFrame class. Inheritance is a pivotal feature of an object-oriented programming language.

TRY IT OUT

Make some changes to this chapter's programs.

Mix it up

Change the order of the statements in the main method of Listing 20-1. Do the same with the statements in the constructor of Listing 20-2. Does the ordering of the statements make a difference? Are there any statements that must come before some other statements in the code?

The permissive ordering of statements in the building of visual objects suggests a different way to think about GUI programming. It's called declarative programming, and I describe it in the next section.

Make it your own

Run the code in Listing 20-1 or 20-2 with your own image file in place of my androidBook.jpg file.

Code Soup: Mixing XML with Java

Go back and feast your eyes one more time on the code in Listing 20-1. Despite Java's object-oriented flavor, the code displays a window using a "do this, then do that" approach:

```
Here's how you show a picture:
    Construct a frame
```

```
Construct an icon containing a certain image
Construct a label containing the icon
Add the icon to the frame
...
Pack the frame
Make the frame be visible
```

This "do this, then do that" approach is called *procedural programming.*

Now imagine you're at the Louvre, looking at the *Mona Lisa.* You don't think, "Da Vinci added a face, then he put a smile on the face, then he added a body, and then a background." The painting doesn't progress from one action to another. Instead, the painting simply *is.*

In the same way, a window in a GUI application doesn't need a procedural progression. Instead, you can describe a window *declaratively.* You write code that says, "Here's how the window looks." The Java Virtual Machine uses your description to decide (on its own) what to display and when.

Consider, for example, the grid in Figure 20-7.

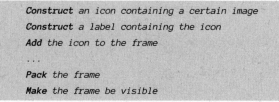

Name	Phone
Alice	555-1234
Bob	555-4321
Carol	555-3000

FIGURE 20-7:
Names and
phone numbers.

The following Swing code creates a grid like the one in Figure 20-7. Don't look at all the details in the code. Instead, notice all the verbs: "set the layout to a new GridLayout, add a label to the frame, set the font, pack the frame, and so on." It's all procedural.

```java
import java.awt.Font;
import java.awt.GridLayout;

import javax.swing.JFrame;
import javax.swing.JLabel;

public class Main {

  public static void main(String[] args) {
    JFrame frame = new JFrame();
```

```
        frame.setLayout(new GridLayout(4, 2));

        JLabel labels[] =
          { new JLabel("Name"), new JLabel("Phone"),
            new JLabel("Alice"), new JLabel("555-1234"),
            new JLabel("Bob"), new JLabel("555-4321"),
            new JLabel("Carol"), new JLabel("555-3000") };

        frame.add(labels[0]);
        frame.add(labels[1]);

        JLabel boldLabel = new JLabel("Name");
        Font boldFont = boldLabel.getFont();
        Font plainFont =
            new Font(boldFont.getName(), Font.PLAIN, boldFont.getSize());

        for (int i = 2; i < 8; i++) {
          labels[i].setFont(plainFont);
          frame.add(labels[i]);
        }

        frame.pack();
        frame.setVisible(true);
    }
}
```

To save the world from its procedural fixation, JavaFX offers a declarative option. Using JavaFX, you can describe a scene as an outline using XML (eXtensible Markup Language) tags. Here's a JavaFX version of the grid from Figure 20-7:

```xml
<GridPane gridLinesVisible="true" layoutX="100.0" layoutY="165.0">
  <children>
    <Label text="Name" GridPane.columnIndex="0" GridPane.rowIndex="0">
      <font>
        <Font name="System Bold" size="12.0" fx:id="x1"/>
      </font>
    </Label>
    <Label font="$x1" text="Phone"
      GridPane.columnIndex="1" GridPane.rowIndex="0"/>
    <Label text="Alice"
      GridPane.columnIndex="0" GridPane.rowIndex="1"/>
    <Label text="555-1234"
      GridPane.columnIndex="1" GridPane.rowIndex="1"/>
    <Label text="Bob"
```

```
       GridPane.columnIndex="0" GridPane.rowIndex="2"/>
    <Label text="555-4321"
       GridPane.columnIndex="1" GridPane.rowIndex="2"/>
    <Label text="Carol"
       GridPane.columnIndex="0" GridPane.rowIndex="3"/>
    <Label text="555-3000"
       GridPane.columnIndex="1" GridPane.rowIndex="3"/>
  </children>
</GridPane>
```

If you're familiar with HTML (the language of web pages), you might recognize some of the tricks in the XML grid code. If not, don't worry. Using a tool named Scene Builder, your computer writes the XML code on your behalf. To see what I mean, keep reading.

Using JavaFX and Scene Builder

GUI programs have two interesting characteristics:

>> **GUI programs typically contain lots of code.**

   Much of this code differs little from one GUI program to another.

>> **GUI programs involve visual elements.**

   The best way to describe visual elements is to "draw" them. Describing them with code can be slow and unintuitive.

To make your GUI life easier, you can use JavaFX and Scene Builder. With Scene Builder, you describe your program visually. Scene Builder automatically turns your visual description into Java source code and XML code.

Installing Scene Builder

Installing Scene Builder is like installing most software. Here's how you do it:

1. Visit http://gluonhq.com/products/scene-builder.

2. Click the Download button.

   When you do, a list of download options appears.

3. Click the button corresponding to your computer's operating system (Windows, Mac, or Linux).

   As a result, the download begins. On a Windows computer, you get an .exe file. Double-click the file to begin the installation.

On a Mac, you get a .dmg file. Depending on your Mac web browser's setting, the browser may or may not expand the .dmg file automatically. If not, double-click the .dmg file to begin the installation.

4. **Follow the installation routine's instructions.**

   On a Windows computer, you accept a bunch of defaults.

   On a Mac, you drag the Scene Builder's icon to the Applications folder.

That's it! You've installed Scene Builder.

Installing e(fx)clipse

Eclipse has its own, elaborate facility for incorporating new functionality. An Eclipse tool is called an Eclipse *plug-in.* When you first install Eclipse, you get many plug-ins by default. Then, to enhance Eclipse's power, you can install many additional plug-ins.

Eclipse's *e(fx)clipse* plug-in facilitates the creation of JavaFX applications. You can add the plug-in to your existing installation of Eclipse, but it's much simpler to download a new copy of Eclipse (a copy with e(fx)clipse already installed). Here's how you get the new copy of Eclipse:

1. **Visit** http://efxclipse.bestsolution.at.

2. **Look for the page containing All-in-One downloads.**

3. **On the All-in One downloads page, look for a way to download a copy of Eclipse for your operating system.**

   Your Eclipse download's word length (32-bit or 64-bit) must match your Java version's word length. For the full lowdown on 32-bit and 64-bit word lengths, see Chapter 2.

4. **Follow the appropriate links or click the appropriate buttons to begin the download.**

5. **Follow the instructions in Chapter 2 to install this new copy of Eclipse on your computer.**

   Place the new copy of Eclipse in a brand-new folder. That way, you don't have to uninstall your old copy of Eclipse. (In fact, it's helpful to have two separate Eclipse installations on your computer.) On my Windows computer, I have a c:\eclipse folder and a c:\eclipseFX folder. Both folders have their own subfolders with names like configuration, features, and plugins. Both folders have their own eclipse.exe file. Similarly, my Mac has both eclipse and e(fx)clipse folders inside the Applications folder.

TIP

When you launch your new copy of Eclipse, the program prompts you for a place on your hard drive for your workspace (the place on your hard drive where this session's Eclipse projects live). At this point, you have a choice:

>> **You can have two different folders for two different workspaces — one workspace for your original copy of Eclipse and a second workspace for your new copy of Eclipse.**

Doing so keeps your original work (for preceding chapters) separate from this chapter's work. Also, with two different workspaces, you can run both copies of Eclipse simultaneously.

>> **Alternatively, you can point both versions of Eclipse to the same folder (and thus, to the same workspace).**

Doing so keeps all your work in one place. You don't have to change workspaces in order to change from your original work to this chapter's work. On the minus side, you can't run two copies of Eclipse using the same workspace simultaneously.

TIP

Don't fret over the decision you make about Eclipse workspaces. In any copy of Eclipse, you can switch from one workspace to another. You can decide on a particular workspace whenever you launch Eclipse. You can also move from one workspace to another by selecting File ⇨ Switch Workspace on Eclipse's main menu.

Creating a bare-bones JavaFX project

There's a wise old saying: "A picture is worth 50 words." And if you count things like `javafx.application.Application` as three separate words, the same picture is worth 70 words. In this section, you create a picture from which Eclipse builds a 70-word Java program. Follow these steps:

1. **Follow the instructions in the previous sections "Installing Scene Builder" and "Installing e(fx)clipse."**

2. **Launch your new copy of Eclipse and click the Welcome screen's Workbench icon.**

3. **From Eclipse's menu bar, choose File ⇨ New ⇨ Project.**

   The New Project dialog box appears.

4. **In the dialog box's list, expand the JavaFX branch. Within that branch, select JavaFX project and then click Next.**

   A New Java Project dialog box appears.

5. **In the New Java Project dialog box, type a name for your project.**

If you're following my instructions to the letter, name the project **MyFirstJavaFXProject**.

6. **Click Finish to close the New Java Project dialog box.**

You see the Eclipse workbench with your newly created project in Eclipse's Package Explorer.

Running your bare-bones JavaFX project

In the previous section, you use e(fx)clipse to create a brand-new JavaFX project. When you run the new project's code, you see the stuff in Figure 20-8. You see a window with nothing inside it.

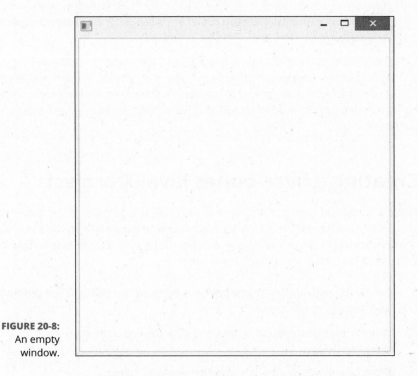

FIGURE 20-8: An empty window.

The fact that this window contains no images, no buttons, no text fields — no *nothing* — comes from the way e(fx)clipse creates your new project. The e(fx) clipse tool populates the project with a minimum amount of code. That way, the new project is a blank slate — an empty shell to which you add buttons, text fields, or other useful components.

Adding Stuff to Your JavaFX Project

I like empty spaces. When I lived on my own right out of college, my apartment had no pictures on the walls. I didn't want to stare at the same works of art day after day. I preferred to fill in the plain white spaces with images from my own imagination. So, for me, the empty window in Figure 20-8 is soothing.

But if Figure 20-8 isn't acquired by New York's Museum of Modern Art, the window is quite useless. (By the way, I'm still waiting to hear back from the museum's curator.) When you create a high-powered GUI program, you start by creating a window with buttons and other widgets. Then you add methods to respond to keystrokes, button clicks, and other such things.

The next section contains some code to respond to a user's button clicks. But in this section, you use an XML file to describe a button and a text field:

1. **Follow the instructions in this chapter's earlier section "Creating a bare-bones JavaFX project."**

   Look in Eclipse's Package Explorer for the new project you create in that section.

2. **Expand the new project's branch in Eclipse's Package Explorer.**

   Look for the application branch, which is inside the src branch.

3. **Right-click (or on a Mac, Control-click) the application branch. On the context menu that appears, choose File ➪ New ➪ Other.**

   The Select a Wizard dialog box appears.

4. **In the Select a Wizard dialog box's tree, expand the JavaFX branch.**

5. **In the JavaFX branch, double-click the New FXML Document item.**

   An FXML File dialog box appears, as shown in Figure 20-9.

6. **In the dialog box's Name field, type a name for your new file and then click Finish.**

   If you're following my instructions faithfully, name the file **Root**.

   TIP

   In Figure 20-9, you type the name Root, but e(fx)clipse creates a file whose full name is Root.fxml.

   This new Root.fxml file describes the layout of the buttons, text fields, and other things in your new JavaFX application. This is the XML document that I make such a fuss about at the start of the earlier section "Code Soup: Mixing XML with Java."

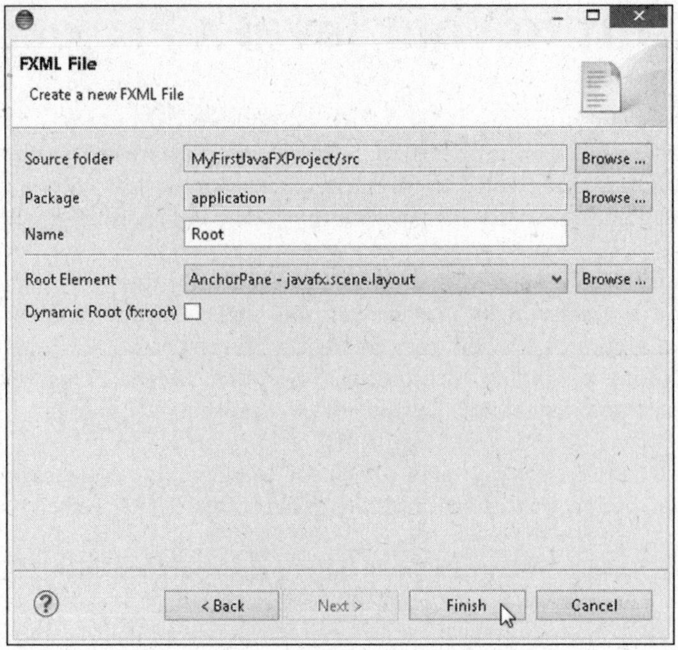

FIGURE 20-9:
The FXML File
dialog box.

7. **Right-click (or, on a Mac, Control-click) the new** Root.fxml **branch in Eclipse's Package Explorer. On the context menu that appears, select Open with SceneBuilder.**

    The Scene Builder application window appears. (See Figure 20-10.)

    The Scene Builder window contains several areas:

    - The middle of the Scene Builder window contains the *Content panel,* where you see a preview your new app. (Currently, there's nothing in your app to see, so the Content panel is a big, empty space.)

    - The upper-left portion of the window contains the *Library panel*, which houses a Containers section, a Controls section, and several other sections.

      In the GUI world, things like buttons, text fields, labels, and check boxes are called *controls*. The Library panel's Controls section forms a palette. To create a GUI window, you drag controls from the palette and drop them onto the Content panel.

    - The lower-left portion of the window contains the *Document panel*, which contains a Hierarchy section and a Controller section. The Hierarchy section contains an AnchorPane item.

      The Hierarchy section contains a tree showing which elements of your window are inside which other elements. The Controller section helps you link the window that you design with the application's Java code.

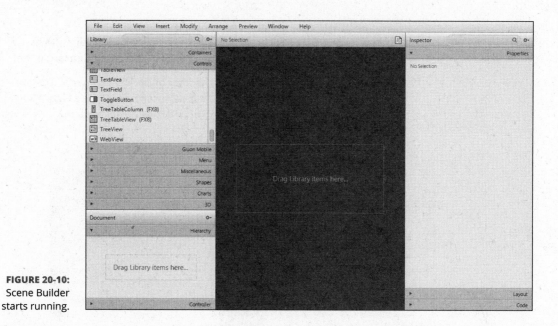

FIGURE 20-10:
Scene Builder
starts running.

- The rightmost portion of the window contains the *Inspector panel*, which contains a Properties section, a Layout section, and a Code section.

  In the Properties section, you describe the features of the elements in your window. In the Code section, you name the Java methods associated with elements in your window.

WARNING

Your mileage may vary! These instructions work on Scene Builder 8.3.0. If you have a different version of Scene Builder, your steps might be a bit different.

8. **Double-click the AnchorPane item in the Hierarchy section.**

   A marker appears in the middle of the Scene Builder's Content panel.

9. **(Optional) Drag the marker in the Content panel to enlarge the AnchorPane. (See Figure 20-11.)**

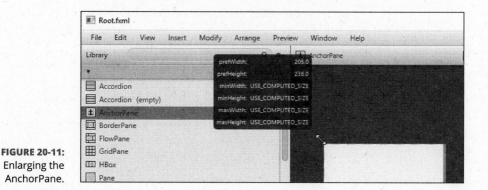

FIGURE 20-11:
Enlarging the
AnchorPane.

10. Find the TextField entry in the Controls section of the Library panel; then drag a TextField control into the AnchorPane in the Content panel.

11. Find the Button entry in the Controls section of the Library panel. Drag a Button control into the AnchorPane in the Content panel. (See Figure 20-12 for a peek at both the TextField control and the Button control.)

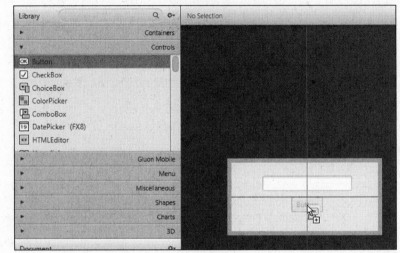

FIGURE 20-12:
A TextField and a Button.

12. On the main menu, select File ⇨ Save.

Doing so saves your new FXML file.

13. Close the Scene Builder application.

When you return to the Eclipse workbench, you can see the new code in your Root.fxml file. (See Figure 20-13.)

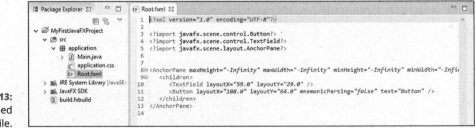

FIGURE 20-13:
The newly coded Root.fxml file.

TIP

Double-click the Root.fxml branch in the Package Explorer to see the file's code. If you don't see the words TextField and Button in the code, click the mouse inside the editor window. (Clicking the mouse updates the editor to reflect the changes made by Scene Builder.) If the code in the editor doesn't seem to be indented properly, click the mouse on a blank area in the editor and press Ctrl+Shift+F (on Windows) or ⌘-Shift-F (on a Mac).

REMEMBER

Any time you want to format the code in Eclipse's editor (making the code easier to read and easier to understand), press Ctrl+Shift+F or ⌘-Shift-F.

14. **Edit the project's** Main.java **file.**

Comment out the BorderPane root statement and add a Parent root statement, as shown in boldface type in Listing 20-3.

The edits in Listing 20-3 connect the application to your newly designed Root.fxml layout.

15. **Run the project.**

When you do, you see the window in Figure 20-14.

FIGURE 20-14:
A run of your project using the Root.fxml file.

LISTING 20-3: **How to Edit the Main.java File**

```
package application;

import javafx.application.Application;
import javafx.fxml.FXMLLoader;
import javafx.scene.Parent;
import javafx.scene.Scene;
import javafx.stage.Stage;
//import javafx.scene.layout.BorderPane;

public class Main extends Application {
  @Override
  public void start(Stage primaryStage) {
    try {
      // BorderPane root = new BorderPane();
      Parent root = FXMLLoader.load(getClass().getResource("Root.fxml"));
      Scene scene = new Scene(root, 400, 400);
```

(continued)

LISTING 20-3: *(continued)*

```
        scene.getStylesheets().
            add(getClass().getResource("application.css").toExternalForm());
        primaryStage.setScene(scene);
        primaryStage.show();
    } catch (Exception e) {
      e.printStackTrace();
    }
  }

  public static void main(String[] args) {
    launch(args);
  }
}
```

As you follow this section's steps, Scene Builder modifies your project's Java code. Having followed this section's steps, you can run the project in the usual way (by choosing Run⇨Run As⇨Java Application). But when the project runs, the application doesn't do anything. When you click the button, nothing happens. When you type in the text field, nothing happens. What a waste!

In the next section, you get the button and the text field to do something.

Taking Action

The program that you create in this chapter is approximately 50 lines long. But until this point in the chapter, you type only one line of code. In this section's instructions, you make a button respond to a mouse click. You do this by typing only a few more lines of code!

1. **Follow the instructions in this chapter's earlier section "Adding Stuff to Your JavaFX Project."**

    As a result, you have code that displays a TextField control and a Button control. It's time to reopen Scene Builder.

2. **Right-click (or on a Mac, Control-click) the** Root.fxml **branch in Eclipse's Package Explorer. On the resulting context menu, select Open with SceneBuilder.**

    The Scene Builder application window appears. (Refer to Figure 20-12.)

3. **In the Scene Builder window, select your app's** Button **control.**

You can do this by clicking the Button control's picture in the Content panel or by clicking the word Button in the Hierarchy section of the Document panel.

When you select the Button control, the Properties section of the Inspector panel displays some information about the Button control. Near the top of the section, you see an item labeled Text. Whatever you type in the field next to the word Text is displayed on the face of the button.

4. **In the field next to the word** Text, **type the word** Capitalize **and then press Enter.**

When you do this, the word Capitalize appears on the face of the Button control in the Content panel. (See Figure 20-15.)

Remember that the Inspector panel contains three sections: the Properties section, the Layout section, and the Code section. At this point, the Properties section is expanded, and the other two sections are collapsed.

FIGURE 20-15:
Working with the
Button control's
properties.

5. **In the Inspector panel, click on the Code section.**

Doing so expands the Code section (at the expense of the Properties section).

6. **In the Code section, look for a field that's labeled On Action. In that field, type** onClick **and then press Enter. (See Figure 20-16.)**

Before typing the word onClick, make sure you see the word Button at the top of the Code section. If you see another word (such as TextField or AnchorPane), you're about to change the wrong component's On Action field.

So much for your Button control! Now, you work with your TextField control.

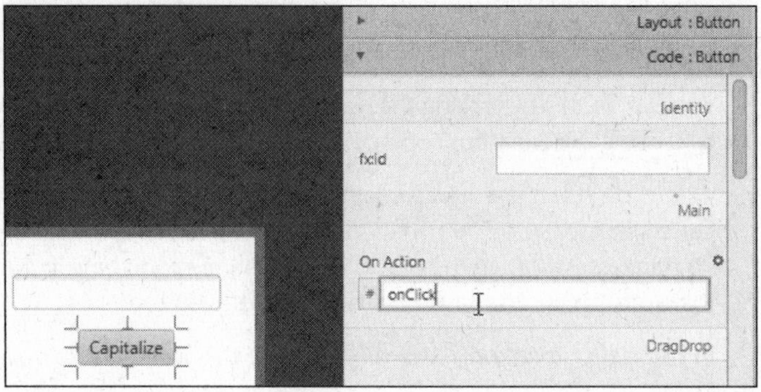

FIGURE 20-16:
When a user
clicks your
Button control,
call the code's
onClick method.

7. **Select your** `TextField` **control (either in the Content panel or in the Hierarchy section of the Document panel).**

8. **In the Code section, look for a field that's labeled** `fx:id`**. In that field, type** `textField` **and then press Enter. (See Figure 20-17.)**

   Before bidding a fond farewell to Scene Builder, you link the Scene Builder's work to the Java code:

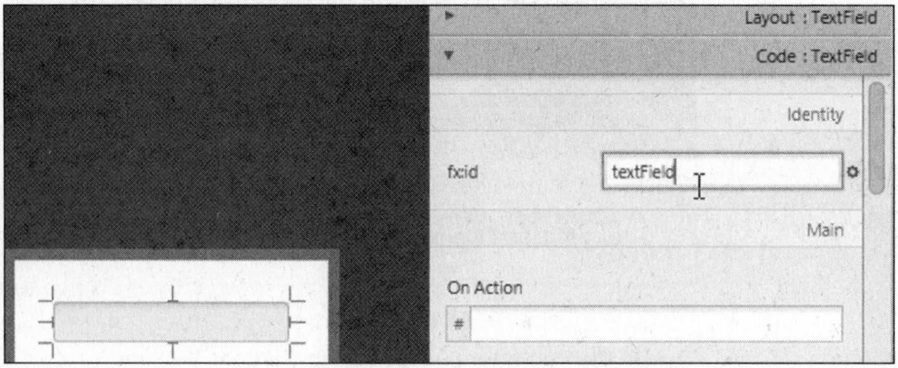

FIGURE 20-17:
Assigning an id to
your `TextField`
control.

9. **Click on the Controller section in the Document panel.**

   Doing so expands the Controller section at the expense of the Hierarchy section.

10. **In the Controller Class field (inside the Controller section), type** application.Main **(with a dot between the two words), and then press Enter. (See Figure 20-18.)**

FIGURE 20-18:
Specifying the FXML file's controller class.

WARNING

You have leeway in carrying out some of the other steps in this section. For example, if you type Click Me! instead of Capitalize in Step 4, the program still runs. But you have very little leeway when you fill in this step's Controller Class field. By default, the e(fx)clipse tool names your program Main.java and puts your program in a package named application. So, in the Controller Class field, you have to point to this application.Main program. If you point somewhere else, you have to rename the program or the package or both. And with more than 40 steps to follow in this chapter so far, you probably don't want to rename things unnecessarily.

At last! Your work with Scene Builder is coming to a close.

11. On the Scene Builder's main menu, select File ➪ Save.

12. Close the Scene Builder application.

Whew! You're back to the Eclipse workbench.

REMEMBER

Eclipse might not update the Root.fxml file's contents automatically when you close Scene Builder. If you don't see the word Capitalize in the code, click the mouse inside the editor window. (Clicking the mouse updates the editor to reflect the changes made by Scene Builder.)

13. In the Main.java file, add the boldface code near the start of Listing 20-4 and near the end of Listing 20-4.

The edits in Listing 20-4 tell Java to change the text that appears in your TextField control when the user clicks your Button control.

And with that step, you have a real GUI application!

14. Run the project.

LISTING 20-4: **How to Edit the Main.java File**

```
package application;

import javafx.event.ActionEvent;
import javafx.scene.control.TextField;
import javafx.application.Application;
```

(continued)

LISTING 20-4: **(continued)**

```java
import javafx.fxml.FXML;
import javafx.fxml.FXMLLoader;
import javafx.scene.Parent;
import javafx.scene.Scene;
import javafx.stage.Stage;
//import javafx.scene.layout.BorderPane;

public class Main extends Application {
  @Override
  public void start(Stage primaryStage) {
    try {
      // BorderPane root = new BorderPane();
      Parent root = FXMLLoader.load(getClass().getResource("Root.fxml"));
      Scene scene = new Scene(root, 400, 400);
      scene.getStylesheets().
          add(getClass().getResource("application.css").toExternalForm());
      primaryStage.setScene(scene);
      primaryStage.show();
    } catch (Exception e) {
      e.printStackTrace();
    }
  }

  public static void main(String[] args) {
    launch(args);
  }

  @FXML
  private TextField textField;

  @FXML
  protected void onClick(ActionEvent event) {
    textField.setText(textField.getText().toUpperCase());
  }
}
```

When you run this section's program, you see something like the screen shots in Figures 20-19, 20-20, and 20-21. *Et voilà!* When you click the button, Java capitalizes your text!

TRY IT OUT

Tweak the program in this section for some exciting results. (Okay. The results may be uninteresting to some people, but they're exciting to me!)

FIGURE 20-19:
A brand-new
frame.

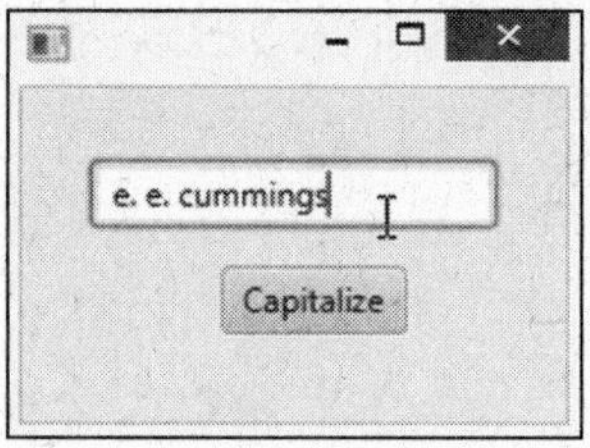

FIGURE 20-20:
The user types in
the text box.

FIGURE 20-21:
Clicking the
button capitalizes
the text in the
text box.

COPY TEXT TO A TEXT FIELD

Use e(fx)clipse and Scene Builder to create a frame with a button and two text fields. When the user clicks the button, Java copies text from the first text field to the second text field.

Hint: You can create both text fields with one declaration:

```
@FXML
private TextField textField, textField2;
```

COPY BETWEEN TEXT FIELDS

Use e(fx)clipse and Scene Builder to create a frame with two buttons and two text fields. When the user clicks the first button, Java copies text from the first text field to the second text field. When the user clicks the second button, Java copies text from the second text field to the first text field.

COPY TEXT TO A LABEL

In JavaFX, a label is similar to a text field. Like a text field, a label may display text. In fact, a `Label` control has a `setText` method, like the `setText` method used in Listing 20-4.

But a label looks different. A label's appearance doesn't invite the user to change the label's text. A label looks like text that's been planted permanently on the frame. Of course, the text isn't permanent, because your code can change a label's text.

Use e(fx)clipse and Scene Builder to create a frame with a button, a text field, and a label. When the user clicks the button, Java copies text from the text field to the label.

Hint: When you declare more than one type of control, each declaration requires its own @FXML annotation.

```
@FXML
private TextField textField;
@FXML
private Label label;
```

CREATE A SMALL CALCULATOR

Use e(fx)clipse and Scene Builder to create a frame with two text fields, a button, and a label. The user types a number in one of the text fields and another number in the other text field. When the user clicks the button, Java displays the sum of the two numbers in the label.

Hint: Whatever Java gets from a text field's `getText` method has `String` type. When you put a plus sign between two `String` values, Java simply pastes the values together — for example, `"42" + "98"` is `"4298"`. Before you can add these values together, you have to convert them to numbers. You do this with Java's `Integer.parseInt` method. (Refer to Chapter 18.)

When you call a label's `setText` method, the call's parameter must have the `String` type. To get a `String` value from an `int` value, use the `Integer.toString` method — for example, `Integer.toString(86)` is `"86"`.

5

The Part of Tens

Chapter **21**

Ten Websites for Java

No wonder the web is so popular. It's both useful and fun. This chapter proves that fact by listing ten useful and fun websites. Each website has resources to help you use Java more effectively. And as far as I know, none of these sites uses adware, pop-ups, or other grotesque things.

This Book's Website

For all matters related to the technical content of this book, visit this outstanding site:

```
www.allmycode.com/BeginProg
```

For business issues — for example, "How can I purchase 100 more copies of *Beginning Programming with Java For Dummies*?" — visit www.dummies.com.

The Horse's Mouth

The official Oracle website for Java is www.oracle.com/technetwork/java.

Consumers of Java technology should visit www.java.com.

Programmers and developers interested in sharing Java technology can go to www.java.net.

Finding News, Reviews, and Sample Code

For articles by the experts, visit InfoQ at www.infoq.com and TheServerSide at www.theserverside.com.

For discussion by everyone (including many very smart people), visit JavaRanch at www.javaranch.com.

Looking for Java Jobs

For job listings, visit Dice at www.dice.com.

Got a Question?

If you're stuck and need help, search for answers and post questions at Stack Overflow (stackoverflow.com).

And don't forget: If you have questions about anything you read in this book, send email to me at BeginProg@allmycode.com, post a question on www.facebook.com/allmycode, or tweet to the Burd with @allmycode.

Chapter **22**

Ten Useful Classes in the Java API

'm proud of myself. I've written around 400 pages about Java using fewer than 30 classes from the Java API. The standard API has thousands of classes, so I think I'm doing very well.

Anyway, to help acquaint you with some of my favorite Java API classes, this chapter contains a brief list. Some of the classes in this list appear in examples throughout this book. Others are so darn useful that I can't finish the book without including them.

For more information on the classes in this chapter, check Java's online API documentation at http://docs.oracle.com/javase/8/docs/api.

ArrayList

Chapter 16 introduces arrays. This is good stuff, but in any programming language, arrays have their limitations. For example, take an array of size 100. If you suddenly need to store a 101st value, you're plain out of luck. You can't change an array's size without rewriting some code. Inserting a value into an array is another problem. To squeeze `"Tim"` alphabetically between `"Thom"` and `"Tom"`, you may have to make room by moving thousands of `"Tyler"`, `"Uriah"`, and `"Victor"` names.

But Java has an `ArrayList` class. An `ArrayList` is like an array, except that `ArrayList` objects grow and shrink as needed. You can also insert new values without pain using the `ArrayList` class's `add` method. `ArrayList` objects are very useful because they do all kinds of nice things that arrays can't do.

File

Talk about your useful Java classes! The `File` class does a bunch of things that aren't included in this book's examples. Method `canRead` tells you whether you can read from a file. Method `canWrite` tells you whether you can write to a file. Calling method `setReadOnly` ensures that you can't accidentally write to a file. Method `deleteOnExit` erases a file, but not until your program stops running. Method `exists` checks to see whether you have a particular file. Methods `isHidden`, `lastModified`, and `length` give you even more information about a file. You can even create a new directory by calling the `mkdir` method. Face it: This `File` class is powerful stuff!

Integer

Chapter 18 describes the `Integer` class and its `parseInt` method. The `Integer` class has lots of other features that come in handy when you work with `int` values. For example, `Integer.MAX_VALUE` stands for the number 2147483647. That's the largest value that an `int` variable can store. (Refer to Chapter 7.) The expression `Integer.MIN_VALUE` stands for the number –2147483648 (the smallest value that an `int` variable can store). A call to `Integer.toBinaryString` takes an `int` and returns its base 2 (binary) representation. And what `Integer.toBinaryString` does for base 2, `Integer.toHexString` does for base 16 (hexadecimal).

JFrame

Chapter 20 has a `JFrame` example. A `JFrame` can be the starting point for an app's appearance on the screen. A `JFrame` is like a window, so you can put buttons, text fields, and other useful widgets on a JFrame. In Chapter 20, I put an image on a JFrame.

A JFrame has one of several different layouts. For example, a *border layout* divides the JFrame into five regions: the NORTH, SOUTH, EAST, WEST, and CENTER regions. An item in the CENTER region is usually the largest. It's the centerpiece of the JFrame. Items in the other border layout regions live on the four edges of the JFrame.

With a *grid layout*, you put items into table cells, and with a *flow layout*, you place items one after another in a row.

JOptionPane

For a quick and easy graphical user interface, use a JOptionPane. Here's some code:

```
String word = JOptionPane.showInputDialog("Enter a word");
JOptionPane.showMessageDialog(null, word);
String string = JOptionPane.showInputDialog("Enter an int value");
int number = Integer.parseInt(string);
number++;
JOptionPane.showMessageDialog(null, "One more is " + number);
```

When you run this code, you see the dialog boxes in Figures 22-1 to 22-4.

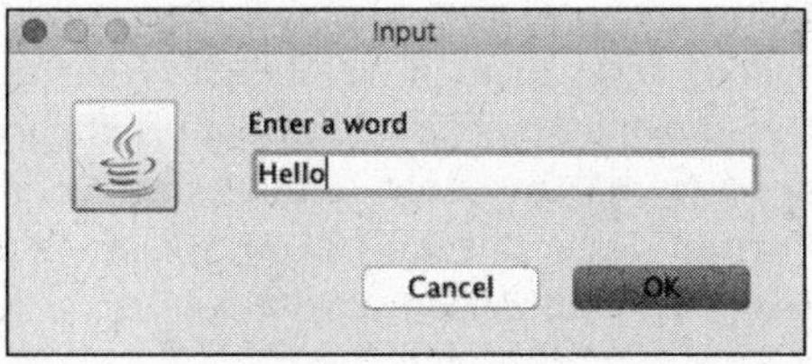

FIGURE 22-1:
Showing an input dialog.

FIGURE 22-2:
Showing a message dialog.

FIGURE 22-3:
Showing another
input dialog.

FIGURE 22-4:
Showing another
message dialog.

Math

Do you have any numbers to crunch? Do you use your computer to do exotic calculations? If so, try Java's Math class. (It's a piece of code, not a place to sit down and listen to lectures about algebra.) The Math class deals with uc, *e*, logarithms, trig functions, square roots, and all those other mathematical things that give most people the creeps.

NumberFormat

Chapter 18 has a section about the NumberFormat.getCurrencyInstance method. With this method, you can turn 20.338500000000003 into $20.34. If the United States isn't your home, or if your company sells products worldwide, you can enhance your currency instance with a Java Locale. For example, with euro = NumberFormat.getCurrencyInstance(Locale.FRANCE), a call to euro.format(3) returns 3,00 € instead of $3.00.

The NumberFormat class also has methods for displaying things that aren't currency amounts. For example, you can display a number with or without commas, with or without leading zeros, and with as many digits beyond the decimal point as you care to include.

Scanner

Java's Scanner class can do more than what it does in this book's examples. Like the NumberFormat class, the Scanner can handle numbers from various locales. For example, to input 3,5 and have it mean "three-and-a-half," you can type myScanner.useLocale(Locale.FRANCE). You can also tell a Scanner to skip certain input strings or use numeric bases other than 10. All in all, the Scanner class is quite versatile.

String

Chapter 18 examines Java's String class. The chapter describes (in gory detail) a method named equals. The String class has many other useful methods. For example, with the length method, you find the number of characters in a string. With replaceAll, you can easily change the phrase "my fault" to "your fault" wherever "my fault" appears inside a string. And with compareTo, you can sort strings alphabetically.

System

You're probably familiar with System.in and System.out. But what about System.getProperty? The getProperty method reveals all kinds of information about your computer. Some of the information you can find includes your operating system's name, your processor's architecture, your Java Virtual Machine version, your classpath, your username, and whether your system uses a backslash or forward slash to separate folder names from one another. Sure, you may already know all this stuff. But does your Java code need to discover it on the fly?

Index

Symbols and Numerics

+= assignment operator, 446

&& (and) operator, 222

* (asterisk), 156

@ sign, 280–281, 314–315, 318

{} (curly braces)

  about, 100

  if statements and, 206

  loops and, 267

  problems with, 121–122

  statements and, 327

$ (dollar sign), 419

\\ (double backslash), 305

== (double equal sign), 409

"" (empty string), 438

// (forward slash), 156, 305

== (is equal to), 189

> (is greater than), 189

>= (is greater than or equal to), 189

< (is less than), 189

<= (is less than or equal to), 189

!= (is not equal to), 189

- (minus sign), 156

! (not) operator, 222

|| (or) operator, 222, 223, 234

+ (plus sign), 156, 438, 440

-- (postdecrement operator), 166

++ (postincrement operator), 164–166, 168–169

-- (predecrement operator), 166

++ (preincrement operator), 163–164, 166, 168–169

"" (quotation marks), 66, 108, 128, 305

% (remainder operator), 156–157

; (semicolons)

  ending statements with, 97–98

  if statements and, 205–206

  in JShell, 146

  method headers and, 118

\ (single backslash), 305

1-statement rule, 217

32-bit systems, 30, 32–34

64-bit systems, 30, 32–34

A

abstract, as a Java keyword, 86

Abstract Window Toolkit (AWT), 458

Account class, 433, 434

action

  Eclipse, 72

  tracing, 268–269

active editor (Eclipse), 74

active view (Eclipse), 74

activities

  arrays, 376–379

  classes, 399–400

  data, 307–308

  decision-making, 218–220

  fields, 406, 413, 426–429

  graphical user interface (GUI), 487–488

  if statements, 245–246

  loops, 285–286, 320–323, 335–338, 344, 351–352, 376–379

  methods, 406, 413, 426–429, 454–456

C

M

About the Author

Dr. Barry Burd received a Master of Science degree in computer science at Rutgers University and a PhD in mathematics at the University of Illinois. As a teaching assistant in Champaign-Urbana, Illinois, he was elected five times to the university-wide List of Teachers Ranked as Excellent by Their Students.

Since 1980, Dr. Burd has been a professor in the department of Mathematics and Computer Science at Drew University in Madison, New Jersey. He has lectured at conferences in the United States, Europe, Australia, and Asia. He hosts podcasts and videos about software and other technology topics. He is the author of many articles and books, including *Java For Dummies, Java Programming for Android Developers For Dummies,* and *Android Application Development All-in-One For Dummies,* all from Wiley.

Dr. Burd lives in Madison, New Jersey, with his wife of n years, where $n > 35$. As an avid indoor enthusiast, Dr. Burd enjoys sleeping, talking, and eating.

Dedication

For Harriet, Sam, and Jennie; Sam and Ruth; Abram and Katie; Benjamin and Jennie. And also for Basheva.

Author's Acknowledgments

Author's To-Do List, May 13, 2017:

Item: Send chocolates to Paul Levesque (the book's project editor) and Becky Whitney (the book's copy editor). As anyone who reads Chapter 4 learns, chocolate is one of the most precious commodities on earth. So when I give chocolate, I give it thoughtfully and intentionally.

Item: Have a plaque erected in honor of Katie Mohr, your acquisitions editor at Wiley. While you worked on other projects, Katie kept insisting that you write this book's fifth edition. (Sure, you wanted a long vacation instead of another book project, but who cares? She was right; you were wrong.)

Item: Send a thank-you note to tech editor Chad Darby, who helped polish your original work and, miraculously, didn't make a lot of extra work for you.

Item: Visit Frank Thornton, Bonnie Averbach, and Herbert Putz at Temple University. Thank them for steering you toward a career as a professor. In any other career, you'd have no time left to write. (And by the way, while you're in Philly, don't forget to stop for a cheesesteak.)

Item: Send email to Gaisi Takeuti at the University of Illinois, and to William Wisdom and Hughes LeBlanc at Temple University. Thank them for teaching you about Symbolic Logic. It has made your life as a computer scientist and mathematician much richer.

Item: Spend more time with your family. (Remind them that you're the guy who wandered around the house before you started writing books.) Renew your pledge to clean up after yourself. Don't be so high-strung, and finish each sentence that you start. Remember that you can never fully return the love they've given you, though you should always keep trying.

Publisher's Acknowledgments

Acquisitions Editor: Katie Mohr
Senior Project Editor: Paul Levesque
Copy Editor: Becky Whitney
Technical Editor: Chad Darby
Editorial Assistant: Serena Novosel
Sr. Editorial Assistant: Cherie Case

Production Editor: Antony Sami
Cover Image: © bestfoto77/Shutterstock

Take dummies with you everywhere you go!

Whether you are excited about e-books, want more from the web, must have your mobile apps, or are swept up in social media, dummies makes everything easier.

Find us online!

dummies.com

Leverage the power

Dummies is the global leader in the reference category and one of the most trusted and highly regarded brands in the world. No longer just focused on books, customers now have access to the dummies content they need in the format they want. Together we'll craft a solution that engages your customers, stands out from the competition, and helps you meet your goals.

Advertising & Sponsorships

Connect with an engaged audience on a powerful multimedia site, and position your message alongside expert how-to content. Dummies.com is a one-stop shop for free, online information and know-how curated by a team of experts.

- Targeted ads
- Video
- Email Marketing
- Microsites
- Sweepstakes sponsorship

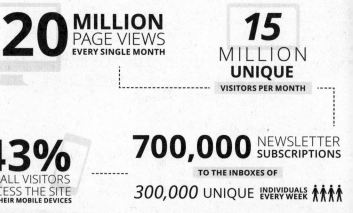

20 MILLION PAGE VIEWS EVERY SINGLE MONTH

15 MILLION UNIQUE VISITORS PER MONTH

43% OF ALL VISITORS ACCESS THE SITE VIA THEIR MOBILE DEVICES

700,000 NEWSLETTER SUBSCRIPTIONS TO THE INBOXES OF
300,000 UNIQUE INDIVIDUALS EVERY WEEK

# of dummies

Custom Publishing

Reach a global audience in any language by creating a solution that will differentiate you from competitors, amplify your message, and encourage customers to make a buying decision.

- Apps
- Books
- eBooks
- Video
- Audio
- Webinars

Brand Licensing & Content

Leverage the strength of the world's most popular reference brand to reach new audiences and channels of distribution.

For more information, visit **dummies.com/biz**

PERSONAL ENRICHMENT

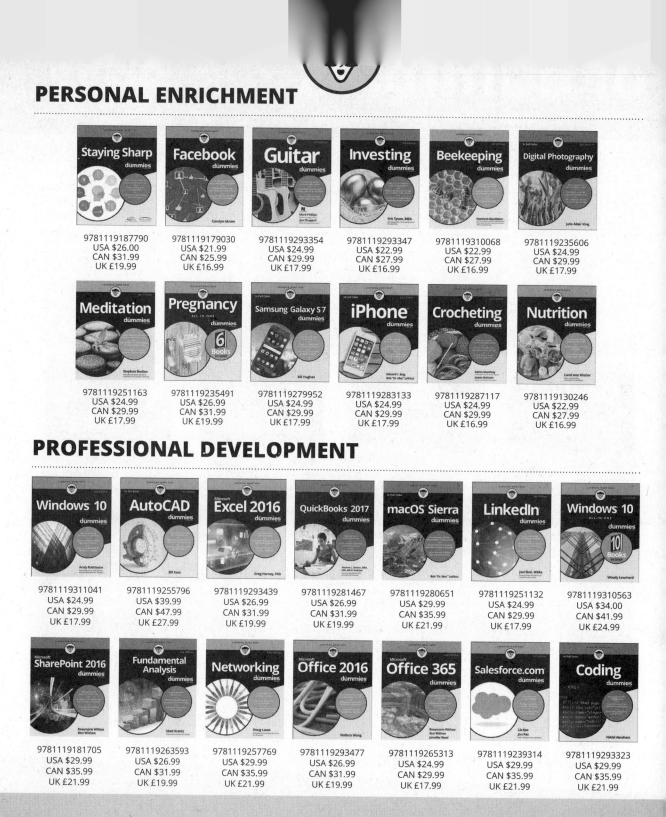

Staying Sharp
9781119187790
USA $26.00
CAN $31.99
UK £19.99

Facebook
9781119179030
USA $21.99
CAN $25.99
UK £16.99

Guitar
9781119293354
USA $24.99
CAN $29.99
UK £17.99

Investing
9781119293347
USA $22.99
CAN $27.99
UK £16.99

Beekeeping
9781119310068
USA $22.99
CAN $27.99
UK £16.99

Digital Photography
9781119235606
USA $24.99
CAN $29.99
UK £17.99

Meditation
9781119251163
USA $24.99
CAN $29.99
UK £17.99

Pregnancy
9781119235491
USA $26.99
CAN $31.99
UK £19.99

Samsung Galaxy S7
9781119279952
USA $24.99
CAN $29.99
UK £17.99

iPhone
9781119283133
USA $24.99
CAN $29.99
UK £17.99

Crocheting
9781119287117
USA $24.99
CAN $29.99
UK £16.99

Nutrition
9781119130246
USA $22.99
CAN $27.99
UK £16.99

PROFESSIONAL DEVELOPMENT

Windows 10
9781119311041
USA $24.99
CAN $29.99
UK £17.99

AutoCAD
9781119255796
USA $39.99
CAN $47.99
UK £27.99

Excel 2016
9781119293439
USA $26.99
CAN $31.99
UK £19.99

QuickBooks 2017
9781119281467
USA $26.99
CAN $31.99
UK £19.99

macOS Sierra
9781119280651
USA $29.99
CAN $35.99
UK £21.99

LinkedIn
9781119251132
USA $24.99
CAN $29.99
UK £17.99

Windows 10
9781119310563
USA $34.00
CAN $41.99
UK £24.99

SharePoint 2016
9781119181705
USA $29.99
CAN $35.99
UK £21.99

Fundamental Analysis
9781119263593
USA $26.99
CAN $31.99
UK £19.99

Networking
9781119257769
USA $29.99
CAN $35.99
UK £21.99

Office 2016
9781119293477
USA $26.99
CAN $31.99
UK £19.99

Office 365
9781119265313
USA $24.99
CAN $29.99
UK £17.99

Salesforce.com
9781119239314
USA $29.99
CAN $35.99
UK £21.99

Coding
9781119293323
USA $29.99
CAN $35.99
UK £21.99

dummies.com

Learning Made Easy

ACADEMIC

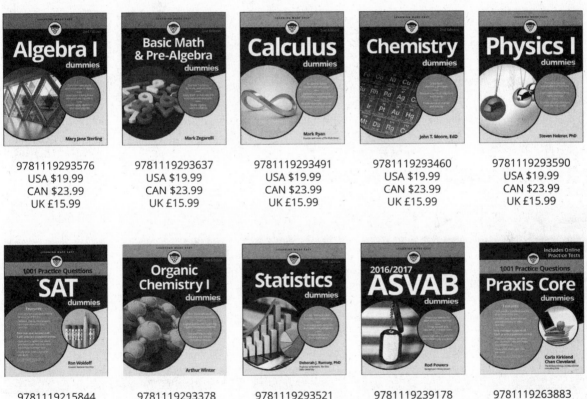

Algebra I dummies
Mary Jane Sterling
9781119293576
USA $19.99
CAN $23.99
UK £15.99

Basic Math & Pre-Algebra dummies
Mark Zegarelli
9781119293637
USA $19.99
CAN $23.99
UK £15.99

Calculus dummies
Mark Ryan
9781119293491
USA $19.99
CAN $23.99
UK £15.99

Chemistry dummies
John T. Moore, EdD
9781119293460
USA $19.99
CAN $23.99
UK £15.99

Physics I dummies
Steven Holzner, PhD
9781119293590
USA $19.99
CAN $23.99
UK £15.99

1,001 Practice Questions **SAT** dummies
Ron Woldoff
9781119215844
USA $26.99
CAN $31.99
UK £19.99

Organic Chemistry I dummies
Arthur Winter
9781119293378
USA $22.99
CAN $27.99
UK £16.99

Statistics dummies
Deborah J. Rumsey, PhD
9781119293521
USA $19.99
CAN $23.99
UK £15.99

2016/2017 **ASVAB** dummies
Rod Powers
9781119239178
USA $18.99
CAN $22.99
UK £14.99

Includes Online Practice Tests
1,001 Practice Questions **Praxis Core** dummies
Carla Kirkland
Chan Cleveland
9781119263883
USA $26.99
CAN $31.99
UK £19.99

Available Everywhere Books Are Sold

ummies.com

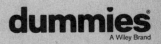

Small books for big imaginations

GETTING STARTED WITH Coding
Get Creative with Code!
Camille McCue, PhD

9781119177173
USA $9.99
CAN $9.99
UK £8.99

MODDING Minecraft
Build Your Own Minecraft Mods!
Sarah Guthals, PhD
Stephen Foster, PhD
Lindsey Handley, PhD

9781119177272
USA $9.99
CAN $9.99
UK £8.99

MAKING YouTube VIDEOS
Star in Your Own Video!
Nick Willoughby

9781119177241
USA $9.99
CAN $9.99
UK £8.99

DESIGNING Digital Games
Create Games with Scratch!
Derek Breen

9781119177210
USA $9.99
CAN $9.99
UK £8.99

GETTING STARTED WITH Raspberry Pi
Program Your Raspberry Pi!
Richard Wentk

9781119262657
USA $9.99
CAN $9.99
UK £6.99

EXPERIMENTING WITH Science
Think, Test, and Learn!
Ruth J. Phillips PhD

9781119291336
USA $9.99
CAN $9.99
UK £6.99

CREATING Digital Animations
Animate Stories with Scratch!
Derek Breen

9781119233527
USA $9.99
CAN $9.99
UK £6.99

GETTING STARTED WITH Engineering
Think Like an Engineer!
Natalie McCue, PhD

9781119291220
USA $9.99
CAN $9.99
UK £6.99

WRITING Computer Code
Learn the Language of Computers!
Chris Minnick and Eva Holland

9781119177302
USA $9.99
CAN $9.99
UK £8.99

Unleash Their Creativity

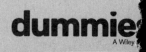